Johan Storm

dhi grétest pràktikal liNgwist in dhi werld

Publications of the Philological Society, 38

Oxford UK & Boston USA

Prof. J. Storm, ov Kristiania, iz probabli dhi grétest pràktikal liNgwist, az ôlso dhi grétest fonetican, in dhi werld. Hî spîks Inglic *kwait* laik a nétiv, Italian, Frenc and Djerman veri nirli az wel, and haz a praktikal noledj ov ôl Romàns and Tiutonik tœNz and ov 200 *Norwîdjan daialekts*!

Paul Passy, writing in *Dhi Fonètik Tîtcer*, 1886

Johan Storm
dhi grétest pràktikal liNgwist in dhi werld
Andrew R. Linn

Johan Storm (1836–1920), Henrik Lund, 1914.
National Library of Norway, Oslo Division, Picture Collection.

Publications of the Philological Society, 38

Oxford UK & Boston USA

Copyright © The Philological Society 2004

ISBN 1-4051-2152-1

First published 2004

Blackwell Publishing
9600 Garsington Road, Oxford, OX4 2DQ, UK

and
350 Main Street,
Malden, MA 02148, USA.

British Library Cataloguing in Publication Data
A catalogue record for this publication is available from the British Library

Library of Congress Cataloging-in-Publication Data
Applied for

Typeset by Joshua Associates Ltd., Oxford
Printed in Great Britain by
the Alden Group, Oxford

CONTENTS

PREFACE

The name Johan Storm will be familiar to many linguists, and not only those interested in the history of linguistics. Internationally he is probably remembered above all for two things. First, he was one of the three "Great S's" in late-nineteenth-century phonetics, when the subject was being established as a serious, independent science. The triumvirate of Johan Storm, Eduard Sievers and Henry Sweet was explicitly named by Otto Jespersen as he reflected on the pioneers without whom his own work 'and that of many others would have been nothing' (Jespersen 1920a: 87). Secondly Storm is remembered, at least in English Studies, for his *Englische Philologie*, that vast and rambling work structured around the study of English philology and particularly phonetics. Few of today's linguists will have opened any of the volumes of this work, whether the original Norwegian version or any of the subsequent German-language volumes; but it stands as one of the monuments of the scientific study of the English language. In his home country of Norway, Storm's name lives on in the field of dialectology, where his phonetic transcription system dominated until very recently. He is also remembered as the strident voice of conservatism in the national language debates of the later nineteenth century, and here he tends to be used as an effigy to burn on the bonfires celebrating the triumph of Nynorsk (see, for example, Skirbekk 2001: 237–238). But he was not simply an irascible reactionary, whom history has gleefully proved wrong. Far from it. And nor was he just a dry English scholar or phonetician. The aim of this book is to correct, or maybe at least provide evidence for reassessing, this fragmented and stereotyped picture.

However, this book is not just about painting a complete picture of a human being. It is also about making Storm *heard*. He was an amazing linguist. As we shall see in Chapter 1, his contemporaries thought so, and history has reinforced this view. So this book is partly about making his views and his ideas, his descriptions and his analyses, accessible. Just because he has been dead for 80 years does not mean that he can't continue to contribute to our ongoing efforts to understand the nature of language and of languages. He wrote a lot, and there is plenty to interest modern students of English, of the Romance languages, and of Norwegian, both its standard forms and its dialects. It must be said – and this is only to be expected – that some of what Storm wrote has rusted and decayed with the passing of time, and I have tried to focus on what continues to be instructive. So this is not an exhaustive account of every last word Storm wrote, or of every last action he carried out; but it does, I hope, capture the essence of what he was about. There is more to say about Storm, and it is to be hoped that my study will generate further investigations of the man and his achievements. I have been better placed to deal with certain aspects of his work than others, and I am aware that I am no expert in the field of Romance Studies. It is perhaps in this area, the most original component of the present book, that most remains to be done.

Because Storm contributed to a variety of subject disciplines, his ideas and his work will be of interest to modern scholars with rather differing backgrounds. For Storm there was just *the living language*. The historical period being studied did not matter and neither did the specific language. Indeed, as we shall see, Storm quite freely used data from one language or period to illuminate linguistic phenomena from another. Twenty-first-century linguists are not, and cannot be, as wide-ranging as Storm, the professor of English and Romance philology who nevertheless contributed more than most to the debate on Norwegian language reform. Consequently I have tried to make the chapters as independent as possible, recognising that readers may come to this book simply as scholars of English, or scholars of French or whatever. There is quite a lot of cross-reference between the chapters – hence the rather overdeveloped system of section numbering – and quotations do recur in different contexts. All the same, I am trying to emphasise the wholeness of Storm and of his 'living language' approach. The book has been conceived as a unity and is best read as such.

I originally envisaged a separate chapter on phonetics, one of the specific areas with which Storm's name is so closely associated. The more I read, however, the more convinced I became that it was impossible, and unjust, to distil Storm's phonetic work out from his work on individual languages. His phonetic insights are so closely wedded to language data that to present them as if they constituted an abstract phonetic theory makes no sense. Indeed, I will argue that Storm cannot properly be described as a phonetician, since his object of study was always language data and never phonetics as an end in itself. He had little time for German contemporaries, who in his view constructed abstract phonetic theories without sufficient immersion in the facts of the living languages. Readers interested first and foremost in Storm as a phonetician will find sections 2.2.4 and 4.3.2 the most relevant.

When in 1998 I began this investigation of the life and work of Johan Storm, I did not know what to expect. What I have discovered has been endlessly fascinating beyond my wildest imaginings. I have not tired of Johan Storm's company for one moment. I have gone through his notebooks and letters and invaded every corner of his life, but I am left with nothing but respect for this brilliant and complicated man. I hope that those who read this book will share my enthusiasm and admiration for him, and will want to blow the dust off his books and get to know him one-to-one. If at any time in the following pages I stand accused of not being completely objective, I do not care. I have gained access to Storm's most intimate writings, I have eavesdropped on his written conversations with friends. I am in his debt.

Writing a book like this takes time, money, help, and support. I can't think when I would have completed this project had I not been fortunate enough to be awarded a Research Fellowship by the Leverhulme Trust, which allowed me time away from university commitments and which enabled me to travel back and forth to Norway and to the south-east of England to where the libraries are. I am most grateful for this, as I am for a Sheffield University research grant, which enabled me to get the project started. I have received help and support from people too numerous to mention by name, but I hope that they will find this book has been improved by their influence. I must, however, thank all those who have given of their time and expertise by reading and advising on draft chapters: the anonymous reader for the Norwegian Research Council, Mike MacMahon, Klaus Johan Myrvoll, Oddvar Nes, Povl Skårup, K. E. Steffens, Kjell Venås, Arne Juul, and Arthur Sandved. These last two gentlemen have gone beyond the call of duty by reading more than one chapter, and their company on the dusty roads of Storm-land has been both a support and a pleasure.

It's hard to say personal thank-yous in the preface to a scholarly tome without sounding corny and sentimental, so I'll do it quickly. When I started this, there were two of us, and now there are four. Thank you, Joanna, for putting up with so many Storm-induced absences, physical and mental, and thank you, Alasdair and Magnus, for being so beautiful. This is for you.

ARL
Sheffield, January 2002

1
JOHAN STORM

1.1. Discovering the Man

1.1.1 When we read Johan Storm's writings today, whether his formal published work or the informal material not intended for publication, we find it difficult to get to know the man who produced those writings. Storm was a husband, the father of nine children, a loyal letter writer, and a generous host to those who visited him, but very rarely does the reader have the opportunity to see the man his family and his friends knew. Pictures of Storm show a formal exterior of correct dress and straight body, of unsmiling austerity. Portrait photographs of the nineteenth and early twentieth centuries often do give the impression of austerity, of the subjects being remote, even hostile. The adjective "Victorian" does more than describe the reign of a British monarch; it describes a personal and moral code which is conventional, reserved, disapproving, unsmiling, and the Norwegian language has borrowed the word from English (*viktoriansk*) with the same meaning. Victorians did smile and enjoy themselves (didn't they?), but the stereotype remains, thanks partly to the impression given by contemporary photographs, not least photographs of Queen Victoria herself. Roland Barthes writes of the 'Victorian nature (what else can one call it)' of those photographs (Barthes 1984: 57). So the unsmiling, remote Storm of the photographs is not necessarily the Storm of reality. However, this is the image which seems to have remained in the minds of those who knew him personally.

One of the more detailed recollections we have of Storm is by Carl Joachim Hambro (1885–1964) in his 1937 book, *Portrœter og profiler*. There is a clear agenda here: to present Storm as a Romantic figure, as someone who suffered for his art. Storm *did* suffer for his art, and it does not take a Freud to suggest reasons from Storm's life, both childhood and adulthood, to explain his "Victorianness". I shall return to Hambro's pen-portrait of Storm in section 1.4, but I want for a moment to consider what Hambro remembered of Storm's physical appearance:

> The thing that captivated one on first seeing Professor Storm, and which forever held one's attention, was his extraordinary, clear, sharp eyes with their strong gaze, eyes which reflected a pure, steadfast and fearless disposition.[1] (Hambro 1937: 59)

---

[1] All translations are my own, except where otherwise stated.

Johan Storm as a young man

Hambro uses the eyes to symbolise the man's character. Discussing his physical appearance elsewhere, Hambro also makes a topos of Storm's 'tight-lipped' (*sammenknepet*) mouth, to symbolise bitterness and disappointment. When Storm failed to get financial support from Parliament for his history of the Norwegian language (see section 4.2.1.2), the outcome was, suggests Hambro, that 'his mouth became a shade more tight-lipped than it had been before' (p. 71). Yet the 'tight-lipped' exterior conceals a 'pure, steadfast and fearless disposition'. This is the colourful, metaphorical, but ultimately rather meaningless, language of romanticising biography, which has not infrequently clouded the historiography of Scandinavian linguistics (see Linn 1997: 62–67), but which nonetheless shows that those who knew Storm were at least aware of the human being behind the professor, so to speak. We find the same thing in Hjalmar Falk's (1859–1928) obituary of Storm, although this time expressed in a more measured way, as befits an obituary: 'The strict and buttoned-up exterior probably concealed a warm heart and a loyal disposition' (Falk 1921: 112). Falk's 'probably' implies that he did not experience the 'warm heart and loyal disposition' himself, but the fact remains that there was more to Storm than the gloomy exterior depicted in the "Victorian" photographs that have come down to us.

His humanity is even harder to discern in his writings than in his physical appearance. We shall discover, as our study of Storm and his work unfolds, that he was a merciless critic, whose technique was systematically to deconstruct the work of those whose views he did not share. In some cases, particularly towards the end of his life, academic abuse descended into personal abuse, most crushingly towards Knud Knudsen (see section 4.1.2.5). Very occasionally however, the strict, unbending critic steps back and allows the human being to step forward, and because this happens so rarely, it is very moving when it does. On 27 June 1898 Storm wrote this simple letter to the editor of the newspaper *Verdens Gang*:

To the editor!

In case you had planned to mention my jubilee on 1 July [25 years as professor], I bid you be so kind as to add that I am unable to receive any visitors on account of a bereavement in the family.

I have today lost a dear son, Gunnar, law student, aged 25.

With thanks for all your previous kindness.

Yours faithfully

Joh. Storm

(NBO Brevsamling 466)

That Storm should have been finding solace in the writing of formal letters the day his son died is in itself moving. I hope that the story of Johan Storm that I am going to tell will be one of a complete human being, one with weaknesses as well as strengths, showing foolishness as well as brilliance, and not just the story of a thinking mind and a writing hand.

1.1.2 There is plenty of documentary evidence available to anyone who wants to study the life and work of Johan Storm. He published compulsively and wrote to the newspapers at the slightest provocation. The surviving *un*published material is also extensive. Many of the letters Storm received, and many of his notebooks, survive in the Norwegian National Library in Oslo and, to a lesser extent, in Bergen University Library. The letters in particular are a fount of information about the personal and professional dynamics of late-nineteenth-century linguistics, since Storm's correspondents rank amongst the foremost linguists of the day: Henry Sweet, Otto Jespersen, Eduard Sievers and A. J. Ellis to name but a few. Sadly, while letters *to* Storm were kept and have survived for posterity in the Norwegian archives, there is very little *from* Storm here, excepting a small number of drafts.[2] On 6 August 1882 he wrote in a draft of an (unsent) letter

[2] I am most grateful to Joan Leopold for informing me of the letters from Storm to Count Angelo de Gubernatis (1840–1913) in the Biblioteca Nazionale Centrale di Firenze.

to Albert Lange, grammar teacher from Elbing in Germany, 'I receive so many letters, that it is impossible for me to answer all of them' (NBO Ms. 4° 1287). However, if we look in the Royal Library in Copenhagen we find what must be one of the most complete and fascinating sets of letters anywhere, let alone in the history of linguistics.

NKS 4291–4° contains 88 letters from Storm to his Danish friend and colleague Vilhelm Thomsen (1842–1927), and if Storm was reserved elsewhere, he certainly made up for it in his frank and sometimes passionate correspondence with Thomsen. It is not clear when Storm and Thomsen first met, but Thomsen certainly joined Storm in Rome for a month in early 1870. The first letter from Storm in the Copenhagen collection was written on 24 April 1873, but in this letter Storm refers to his previous letter (since which he has not heard from Thomsen), so the correspondence was already under way. Storm continued to write to Thomsen, sometimes at the rate of several letters a month, until 1908, by which time his handwriting was pretty much illegible. After this time there is a gap in the archive, but a 1918 Christmas greeting from the Storms to the Thomsens, written by Louise, Johan Storm's wife, indicates that, if nothing else, formal Christmas greetings had kept the relationship alive in the meantime.

1.1.3 Vilhelm Ludvig Peter Thomsen was born in Copenhagen, but he spent most of his childhood in the northern town of Randers, where he attended the Latin School. From there he returned to Copenhagen to attend university, and, as with other characters in our drama, a false start (in Thomsen's case as a student of theology) preceded his linguistic studies. Like Storm, Thomsen had a passion and a tremendous capacity for foreign languages, and he took every opportunity he could to learn new languages. His first publication, a comparative study of Hungarian, appeared in 1867. This, together with his doctoral dissertation of 1869 dealing with Finnish, meant that he was a pioneer in the field of Finno-Ugric philology. In 1869, like his Norwegian friend, he set off on an extended linguistic tour of Europe, to hear the languages and to listen to the great European scholars of language. Thomsen's travels took him further afield than Storm's (see section 3.2.1), but he returned home the following year, and began working as a school teacher. This career was short-lived, and in 1875 he gained a permanent appointment at the university as extraordinary reader in comparative philology. Two years later he was promoted to an ordinary professorship in the same discipline.

The range of languages and linguistic topics on which Thomsen worked is nothing short of stunning (see Sandfeld (1983) for details), but his greatest achievement was probably the successful interpretation of the Old Turkish Orkhon inscriptions in 1893, which until then had confounded scholars. Turkish became Thomsen's dominant interest during the last decades of his life, but he found time for much else besides, including a history of linguistics (Thomsen 1902). Despite the volume of his scholarly output, Thomsen, unlike Storm, was active as an administrator, serving as *rektor* of the university in 1902, and as president of the Danish Academy of Sciences in 1909. In his letters to Thomsen Storm discussed anything and everything, whatever he had on his mind, both personal and professional. Thus topics range from knotty problems in Romance and Slavonic philology and phonetics to Storm's concerns about his health, his accommodation and his family. The sheer detail of the letters makes them a biographer's dream, and I shall return to Storm's letters to Thomsen again and again throughout this book. At the personal level, however, the nature of Storm's relationship with Thomsen deserves comment. A leitmotif of these letters is Storm being upset at Thomsen's failure to reply quickly enough. The surviving letters from Thomsen at NBO Ms. 4° 1287 are full of apologies for his failure to correspond as regularly and fully as he ought. Principal excuses are pressure of work (believable) and laziness (not so believable). A letter of 4 December 1882 thanks Johan and Louise for their hospitality 18 months previously! After a particularly long silence from Thomsen and increasingly desperate letters from Storm, Storm wrote the following to his friend:

> I once had a good friend in Copenhagen, who wrote long and pleasant letters and who supported me in word and deed when I asked him for advice, who used to sign himself 'your faithfully devoted' or 'your always devoted'. What has become of this eternal friendship? Has it been blown away by the wind which passes across the Danish plains? Up here we are not so flighty. Even though we get married and have six children, we still find a moment to devote to old friends. (20 January 1878)

Storm needed Thomsen's friendship. His natural environment was an international one, and he clearly lacked close companionship in the narrow circle of Norway's capital city. Thomsen may not have lived near to hand, and the two men may not actually have met many times during the course of their life, but this was Storm's truest and closest friendship. In fact, his expressions of friendship often read like words more to a lover than to a colleague. Six days after Storm's pathetic and colourful plea just quoted, he heard from Thomsen again, and was ecstatic:

> You probably have many good friends, but I dare say that you have none for whom your well-being is dearer, for whom your friendship is of greater urgency [*mere magtpaaliggende*] and who takes apparent coldness more to heart.

1.2 FACTS AND FIGURES

1.2.1 Johan Frederik Breda Storm was born on 24 November 1836 at Lom in central Norway, where his father, Ole Johan Storm (1806–1850), was acting as parish priest during an interregnum in the living.[3] Ole Johan had married Hanna Jørgine Mathilde Breda (1815–1869) on 26 January 1836, and so Johan was born exactly 10 months into their marriage. He was the first of six children, all boys. They all survived into adulthood, and Gustav (see section 1.2.3), the fifth son, went on to become professor of history in Kristiania (Oslo) and another of the leading Norwegian scholars of the day. The other brothers all took up traditional professions, with the exception of the third brother, William Rudolf (1843–1867), who, like so many other Norwegians at that time, emigrated to America, where he and his fiancée died of yellow fever in Texas (O. Storm 1889). In 1838 Storm senior was appointed parish priest in Rendal, further to the east, towards the Swedish border, and in 1845 he moved south to an equivalent position in Lardal in Vestfold (south-west of the capital), where he was parish priest for Svarstad, Hem and Styrvoll churches. Five years later, aged 44, he died, leaving the 13-year-old Johan as head of the family, the first of a number of events in Storm's life which could easily be cited by the armchair psychoanalyst to account for the 'buttoned-up' exterior remembered by Falk and for the desperate need for a confidant.

Nils Christian Egede Hertzberg (1827–1911) remembered the Storm home in Lardal, where he worked as a private tutor (*Huslærer*) during 1848 and 1849 (Hertzberg 1910: 18–26). He remembered Pastor Ole Storm as a gentle but rather introverted and gloomy man, depressed by financial worries, and not very good company for the 20-year-old tutor. The 12-year-old Johan made a much stronger impression on Hertzberg. Of all the hundreds of pupils who passed in front of Hertzberg over the years, he never encountered another with such a 'voracious hunger for knowledge' (p. 21). Hertzberg writes that, during the period he acted as Johan Storm's tutor – a period of little more than a year – Storm devoured all the knowledge Hertzberg had to offer. Johan was little interested in sport or games, but even at the tender age of 12 demonstrated, according to Hertzberg, an extraordinary ear for languages. When Hertzberg came to leave Lardal in the August of 1849, he had become close to Johan, and he was sorry to bid him farewell, but he had nothing left to teach the boy.

Following her husband's death, Storm's mother moved to Kristiania with her six boys, and, except for some tours overseas, Storm remained in that city for the rest of his life. Kristiania had a formative impact on Storm and his work, and, to understand fully why he developed intellectually the way he did, the nature of that city needs to be considered.

---

[3] Straightforward factual information about Storm's life is taken principally from standard Norwegian biographical reference works, notably Halvorsen (1901) and Seip (1966).

1.2.2 If Norway as a whole has changed dramatically in the past 200 years – from a predominantly rural dependency into a modern nation state – the same is true of its capital city, Christiania, officially renamed Kristiania in 1897 and Oslo in 1925, although during the nineteenth century the names Christiania and Kristiania tended to be used fairly indiscriminately. Nineteenth-century photographs of the city (see, for example, those reproduced in Boye 1967) on the one hand show grand city vistas, much grander than they seem nowadays because the impressive civic buildings of the city centre contrast much more markedly with the often unprepossessing suburbs. On the other hand, the countryside is never far away in these scenes. A picture of Vestre Aker Church, not long after its consecration in 1855, shows it in a completely rural setting (Boye 1967: 82). Now it is just on the edge of the university site at Blindern, and the countryside is physically and psychologically rather further away. The population of the city exploded during the course of the century from around 12,000 as the nineteenth century dawned to nearly 20 times that figure (228,000) by the turn of the twentieth century. A century on and that figure has more than doubled again, but a twentyfold population growth in the course of one century makes quite an impact. It is not just that Kristiania expanded during Storm's lifetime: it made itself into a capital city, gaining a royal palace, a parliament building, a national theatre, the Grand Hotel, noble university buildings and 'other organs of metropolitan life' (Popperwell 1972: 23), all within a small area of the city centre.

The place began to look like a European metropolis, but did it begin to feel like one? Storm described the city disparagingly as a 'big small-town', and Hurum (1984: 391), writing an account of the city's musical life after the 1830s, uses just the same terminology: 'Christiania was no longer a small city [*en liten storby*], but a big small-town [*en stor småby*]'. *Stor småby* is in fact a label often used for Kristiania, but like all clichés it has become a cliché because it is appropriate. Edvard Mørch's *Kristianiaminder* (Recollections of Kristiania) (Mørch 1904) put some meat on the cliché's bones, as he recollects the cultural life of students in the 1840s and 1850s:

> Later we tried, as far as was possible, to sing in four parts, which in my earliest student days was something rather novel. It was only after the students came back after the 1845 meeting in Copenhagen that four-part singing began. Before that we had always sung in unison. (Mørch 1904: 20–21)

Leisure activities change and fashions change, I know, but this really does sound horrendously parochial entertainment!

Merry singing was not all that the city had to offer: there was plenty of entertainment, highbrow and lowbrow, for those who wished to avail themselves of it. Ivar Aasen's diaries (Aasen 1960) (if only Storm had kept diaries like these . . .) give a good record of the variety of cultural activities that could be enjoyed by an intelligent Norwegian linguist in the nineteenth century, and it has to be said that many of them do not really honour a capital city. However, a city's character cannot change overnight, and the provision of grandiose buildings does not immediately engender grandiose sentiment. Aasen lived alone in Kristiania without a formal job to go to.[4] Consequently he did not have the responsibilities of family life or of a workplace to occupy his time and provide him with social interaction. Unsurprisingly, therefore, he went out a lot; Storm by contrast did not. There is little evidence in what I have seen to indicate that Storm made use of what the city had to offer by way of entertainments and socialising. His lifestyle, as we will see in a moment, was the very antithesis of Aasen's: he had a large family and a hugely demanding set of responsibilities in and beyond the university. Leisure activities were presumably not really an option. Nevertheless, Storm, like Mørch, did enjoy the choral opportunities available to him. He mentions in his unpublished lecture notes for the *Short Course in Phonetics for Teachers* (Storm 1890b: 9) that he had for many years been a singer. I do not know which choir, if any, Storm belonged to, but by the later nineteenth century, choirs were a well-established part of the cultural landscape of Kristiania.

One extramural activity in Kristiania in which Storm did take an active interest was Det norske Videnskaps-Akademi (The Norwegian Academy of Sciences), founded in 1857 by academic staff of the university. Storm was proposed for membership by Sophus Bugge (1833–1907) and elected in 1872, just before his appointment as professor. Two years later Johan Storm's brother, Gustav, was elected as a member of the Academy and 'for a generation would be one of the forces which carried the society' (Amundsen 1957: 130). Although Johan was less actively involved in the running of the society than his brother (and here again we can assume that the bachelor Gustav was more inclined to such activity than the father of a large family), Johan did hold office for many years, being chair of the *Historisk-filosofisk Klasse* in the even-numbered years from 1885 to 1902, and vice-chair in the odd-numbered years. He gave six lectures to the Academy and was a regular contributor to discussions (Amundsen 1957: 487–488). The lectures were these:

1874 (6 March): *Om Tonefaldet (Tonelaget) i de skandinaviske Sprog* ('On Intonation (Tone) in the Scandinavian Languages').

1876 (2 June): *Om det oldnorske Sprogs Udvikling og Forandringer* ('On Development and Change in Old Norwegian').

1877 (16 November): *Om det engelske Sprogs Oprindelse og Lydudvikling* ('On the Origin and Phonological Development of the English Language').

---

[4] For more on Aasen and particularly his relationship with Storm, see section 4.1.2.2.

1881 (1 April): *Den videnskabelige Betydning af Studiet af de norske Dialekter* ('The Scientific Significance of the Study of the Norwegian Dialects').

1882 (20 January): *Om Grupperingen af de norske Dialekter* ('On Grouping the Norwegian Dialects').

1886 (5 March): *Om de gammelitaliske Dialekters Indflydelse paa det provincielle Latin og derigjennem paa Italiensk* ('On the Influence of the Old Italic Dialects on Provincial Latin and thereby on Italian').

One each, then, on his "specialities" English and Romance, but four on Scandinavian languages, moving from traditional philology in 1876 to the "new" subject of dialectology in the 1880s.

1.2.3 Gustav Storm (1845–1903) gave numerous lectures in the Academy (see Amundsen 1957: 488–491), and after 1883 was, with just a few short interludes, its General Secretary for twenty years. As a young man Gustav had to take on a series of teaching posts to help the family finances, but he managed to carry out his university studies at the same time. He was appointed a *Universitetsstipendiat* (research fellow) in 1873 and completed his doctorate the following year. He was a highly productive scholar, dedicated to the study of early Norwegian history and to the publication of the source material necessary for its study. He revolutionised the teaching of history at the university, making it a more scholarly and independent academic subject than it had been previously (Koht 1966: 73). In his biography of Gustav, Halvdan Koht sums him up thus:

> He was in many ways a mighty man in Norwegian culture – himself a man with multi-faceted interests, vigorously independent, authoritative, and sharply critical of everything he felt did not live up to the standards of Science. (Koht 1966: 76)

There is some anecdotal evidence to indicate that the brothers Storm did not always see eye to eye. Francis Bull (Bull 1945: 307) recounts a story which was current in his student days during the first decade of the twentieth century:

> In my student days it was said that Johan Storm and his brother Gustav, because of differences of political opinion, did not like to speak to one another, and that one of them would cross the road to avoid meeting the other. The two brothers were certainly extremely different.

Like all such stories, this is not to be treated completely seriously, although it is true that the men were not similar, and Johan with his large family must have spent what free time he had in different ways to the "confirmed bachelor" Gustav, who was said to avoid and ignore women. Nevertheless, Gustav supported Johan when the *Samfundet for norske Maal og Traditioner* (*Society for Norwegian Dialects and Traditions*) was established in 1901.

Twenty years previously the *Foreningen for norske Dialekter og Folketradi-tioner* (*Association for Norwegian Dialects and Folk Traditions*) had been set up by a group of eight scholars, including Johan Storm and Ivar Aasen, but things did not work out well (see section 4.3.2). The society's journal, *Norvegia*, was very much Johan's baby, and he was bitterly disappointed when others failed to support him in this enterprise. However, the society was re-established under the new name, and at the opening meeting in October 1901 Gustav took the chair. One can't help feeling that Gustav took such an active role in the society, of which he was not one of the original founders, out of loyalty to his brother.[5] Sadly Gustav's involvement was short-lived, and it seems as though the aspect of his death which most affected Johan was his inability to continue his work for *Norvegia* – or at least that is what the one-sided notice in the newspaper *Morgenbladet* indicates:

> Professor Johan Storm began today's lecture on the subject of Norwegian Phonetics by reminding the audience of the heavy blow both he and also this science had received through the passing of his brother, Prof. Gustav Storm. By willingly taking on the editorship of *Norvegia*, he had supported this undertaking, which, without state support and with few subscribers, gave good reason for harbouring poor hopes for its future. The professor felt himself too old and weak to take his brother's place. (3 March 1903)

Perhaps they really weren't that close, or – maybe a more plausible explanation – as with Gunnar's death, Johan Storm was not good at expressing proper emotion, at least not publicly.

1.2.4 To return to the story of Johan's life, he was sent to Kristiania Cathedral School, commonly known as the Latin School, 'where stories of his great linguistic ability were long recounted' (Western 1920: 147), and from where he graduated in 1855 with the highest marks. Although he had studied English and Hebrew at school, and although he had explored languages with his private tutor in Lardal, he enrolled at the university to study natural sciences, principally chemistry. This early exposure to scientific method very likely helped dictate the aspects of language in which he would later specialise, as well as the approach he would take to them. Alongside his studies, Storm had to work to support his mother, who naturally lived in difficult circum-stances following the death of her already impecunious husband. Conse-quently, during the period from 1857, when he began his science studies at the university, until 1881, long after his appointment as professor, he, like his brother, worked as a schoolteacher. Hambro (1937: 60) calls this work 'a

---

[5] According to Koht (1966: 75), Gustav Storm had also given a series of popular lectures on Maria Stuart, which he published in book form in 1891, in order to 'secure help for a close relative who was in economic difficulties'.

plague', but there is no doubt that it provided much-needed income, that it gave him teaching experience which would be useful in his university work, and that it aroused an interest in something which would become extremely important to him later on – language-teaching reform.

He continued to develop his interest in modern foreign languages at his own expense, with an extended visit in 1858 to The Netherlands and Belgium, to study Dutch, Flemish and French, and the next year he enrolled as a philology student, graduating from the university in that subject (*klassisk Embedsexamen*) in 1864. Storm's academic "false start" reminds us both of Thomsen and of Otto Jespersen (1860–1943), who started off studying law, but changed to modern languages, partly due to Storm's influence, as Jespersen explains in his autobiography:

My goal was a master's degree in French with Romance languages, but it was too late to start on such a course at the university that semester. So I read on my own what I could envisage would lead to the desired goal, and was lucky enough soon to get hold of Johan Storm's *Engelsk Filologi* [. . .] which had been published a couple of years before, although I had not actually thought of concerning myself with English. But this (the only) volume dealt almost exclusively with phonetics and taught me the necessity of the study of sounds as the basis for any study of language. As Storm was enthusiastic about Sweet, I immediately bought Sweet's *Handbook of Phonetics* and a couple of other books by the English school. (Juul et al. 1995: 33–34)

1.2.5 With this period of formal study behind him, Storm continued to work as a teacher, from now on just at the one institution, Aars's and Voss's School. His passion for languages was undimmed, however, and at the end of January 1869, aged 32, he set off on a one-and-a-half-year journey through France, Italy and Spain to study the languages and people of those countries. He was able to do this via a scholarship from the university's *Hjelmstjerne-Rosencroneske* bequest, and his first book-length publication, *De romanske Sprog og Folk* of 1871, was in essence his travel report. It is a fascinating account (see section 3.2.1), and particularly so in the light of our attempt to find the human being in Storm, in that it does document his fears, mistakes and attitudes as well as simply his findings. When he returns to Norway he does so with his eyes open; and his relationship with his homeland is clearly going to be a difficult one from now on:

And so I returned to my dear fatherland, where I try, in so far as the narrow circumstances allow, to cultivate science [. . .] Under these circumstances I must be all the more grateful that I have been permitted to be able to dedicate myself unhindered to my studies for getting on for a year and a half, and to hear the three most beautiful of Europe's languages being spoken. (Storm 1871: 123)

He repeats his lament over the narrowness of Norwegian research seven years later: 'conditions in Norway result in scientific research only being supported by a few specialists' (Storm 1878b: 1).

Whatever his feelings about the lack of opportunity provided by his 'dear fatherland', contemporary developments in Norway worked out very well for Storm. In 1869, the year he set off on his tour of southern Europe, new legislation (*Lov om offentlige Skoler for den høiere Almendannelse*) introduced a modern syllabus into the schools, embracing sciences, maths and modern languages, on an equal footing with the traditional "Latin line". In response to this, the university established the position of *Universitetsstipendiat i levende Sprog* (Fellow in Modern Languages) to which Storm was appointed in October that year, while still on his travels, and which he took up on his return. From 1 July 1873 the post was made permanent, and Storm became *Professor i romansk og engelsk Filologi*, a position he occupied for 39 years, until his retirement on 1 September 1912 at the age of nearly 76. Such rapid promotion to a professorship will seem surprising to today's readers, but it had been decreed that all official, regius appointments at the university from 1866 onwards were to bear the title of Professor. Although he only ever had the one job, its remit was enormous, and we shall see in due course what Prof. Storm's responsibilities were.

1.2.6 The rest of this book will tell the story of his intellectual and professional achievements, so we shall conclude this biographical introduction simply by providing a sketch of Storm's personal life during his mature adulthood. In Stavanger on 21 July 1865 he married Louise Juliane Christiane Bruun (1840–1927), daughter of Christiane Plesner (1801–1885) and Christian Constantius Henrik Bruun (1812–1877), Dean of Stavanger Cathedral. The Storms had nine children, the eldest, Olaf, being born on 30 April 1866, exactly nine months into the marriage, and the youngest, Aage, on 22 April 1879. The second, Helga, and sixth, Hanna, died in early childhood, and their fifth child, Gunnar, died, as we have already noted, at the age of 25. The remaining children were Aagot, Einar, Ragna and Halvard. With such a large family to support, Storm, like his parents before him, found domestic economy extremely difficult. This is certainly the reason why he continued to work as a schoolteacher alongside his university professorship.

Financial worries can be discerned in unofficial and official writings alike. In evident response to a grumbling letter from Storm, Henry Sweet (1845–1912) wrote:

I am indeed sorry to hear that professors' salaries in Norway are so low; they ought to be sufficient to enable a man to devote all his energies to teaching and study, and I hope, with you, that before long there will be an improvement. (Letter of 14 August 1875. NBO Ms. 8° 2402 J^{iv})

In 1877 Storm applied to Parliament for financial support to allow him to write a history of the Norwegian language, a *Værk over det norske Sprog* (*Work on the Norwegian Language*), as he described it. (We will return to this application and the work proposed in it on several occasions, since the proposed work and the failure of parliament to support it explain some important stages in Storm's intellectual development. See particularly section 4.2.1.2.) Storm takes the opportunity here to detail his financial circumstances. It was one thing to whinge in a private letter to his friend, Henry Sweet, but it was quite another to set out his domestic problems in a public document. We have already established that Storm was a reserved person, so his circumstances must have been really serious to take this drastic step, and the humiliation in rejection must have been all the more painful. He draws attention to his 'straitened circumstances' and is forced to admit that he is 'probably the only Romance professor in the world who has not had the wherewithal to get a copy of *Littrés franske Lexikon* [*Dictionnaire de la langue française*]'. Such an absurdity is, in Storm's words, 'characteristic of Norwegian conditions'. From here on he generalises the argument to suggest that, unless something is done to improve the position of Norwegian professors, the intellectual life of the nation will wither, a possibility which must surely have caused alarm bells to ring in the government of this new and growing nation:

It is well known that not a single married professor in this country lives off his salary, and indeed scarcely any unmarried ones [. . .] One is forced to put up with shoddy lecture preparation; one is unable to advance scholarship and heighten the regard of our country abroad [. . .] If something is not done about this soon, the era of great intellectual achievements in Norway will soon be over, and we will enter a period of intellectual poverty, which will constitute a pitiful contrast with the earlier period.

He returns finally to the specific wretchedness of his own circumstances:

I shall permit myself to state that I am 40 years old, have a wife and five children, and am also on the second-lowest salary of 900 speciedaler + bonus of 150 speciedaler [. . .] It is obvious to everybody, who has lived in Kristiania with a family, that this amount is utterly inadequate.

A letter from Sweet the following year indicates that there was, at least for the academic community in general, a positive outcome to Storm's representations to parliament:

I was very glad to hear of the augmentation of your salaries at Christiania, + also to think that I may have contributed to the happy result. (Letter of 15 July 1878. NBO Ms. 8° 2402 J^v)

1.2.7 The relationship between Storm's "public" and "private" writings is an interesting one. Some of what Storm wrote as private, unpublished work is written in such a way that it is clear he nonetheless conceived it as public. In July 1876 he travelled to Copenhagen for the first meeting of Scandinavian philologists (see section 3.3.2.4), in connection with which he wrote a *Dagbog paa Udenlandsreisen Juli 1876* [*Diary on my Foreign Travels, July 1876*] (NBO Ms. 8° 2402 K). There is no evidence that this was commissioned by a publisher, nor that Storm intended to seek a publisher for it, and it is actually unfinished. The final entry is on 4 August: 'I will now try to continue the diary in so far as that is possible after such a long time-lapse'; but nothing ever came of it. Although this must then have been a private record, he makes the following observation about Danish women:

It is really so generally recognised how lovely and lively Danish ladies are, that I will not delay the reader on the matter. But I personally felt the need to express it.

Storm makes a highly personal observation about his feelings towards women, the sort of personal observation we find so rarely in the writings of this private, reserved person, yet it is addressed to a *reader*. Could it be that this private man was not able to express himself except through the anonymous medium of writing for an unknown reader? On the other hand, could it be that he tended not to reveal his thoughts and feelings fully in his notebooks because he knew that they *would* be read one day, as indeed they have been? It was, until the middle twentieth century, quite common for "great men" to take copies of their private writings, so that those writings could enter the public domain after their death. Storm was typical when he asked Thomsen:

Do you ever take copies of your letters? I have started to do it with letters which have some scientific content. It is good for me with my wretched memory. I go to someone who has a copying press and get it done in just a few minutes. (Letter of 4 January 1874)

Reading someone's personal notebooks is a strange experience for the historian/biographer. Our ethical code forbids us to read the diaries or letters of a living person, but we feel quite free to plunder and publicise the private world of the dead, whose memories are in other ways sacred: 'do not speak ill of the dead', we are told. Reading the private papers of someone who is dead (Storm) gives the researcher (me) the same feelings of excitement at entering a private world and discovering the secrets there, as revelations from the diaries or letters of a *kjendis*, of a living "star". In the linguistic world Johan Storm *was* a star, so shouldn't I have the same scruples about revealing his private details as I would about revealing the contents of a film star's diary? Scruples do not worry us, of course, because the emotionally bankrupt process of scholarship has made exposure of information legitimate if it is in the name of research. While it might be *personally* irresponsible of me to betray Storm's private world, it would be *professionally* irresponsible for me not to reveal information which could have a bearing on our understanding of Storm and his work, and hence of the history of linguistics. On 18 February 1889 Sweet wrote to Storm:

> Your reference to my wife amuses me. Altho the daughter of a learned man, she speaks an excruciating Cockney dialect with (-ɔɪ sɔr im, ʃilin, gitin) = I saw him, shilling, getting +c. (nau) = no, (næu) = now +c. I have got her out of her worst vulgarisms, I am happy to say. (These details are, of course, strictly confidential, + not intended for publication). (NBO Ms. 8° 2402 J^{vi})

This bit of information is relevant to our understanding of the history of linguistics, in that it clearly reveals some of the attitudes of a linguist whose views and writings on phonetics and on English were enormously influential. However, Sweet, for obvious reasons (his wife was one of the few people he did not want to offend), said that this information shouldn't be made public, and I have just made it public.

Moral and ethical considerations may seem out of place in a book like this. We would not know what we do about how the understanding of language has developed, why the assumptions of modern linguistics are what they are, if we denied ourselves access to the notebooks, letters and diaries of those involved. In short, a scholar would be irresponsible not to examine available unpublished materials when they provide such a mine of information about the making of our subject. Nonetheless, a human being is irresponsible who does not respect another human being, and it is my small duty here to remind the community of scholars that we only have the right to enter someone else's private world because our search for understanding, over which Academia stands guardian, suspends our normal social code. Langholm (1999: 44) comments on this issue too, referring to the *Forskningsetiske retningslinjer for samfunnsvitenskap, jus og humaniora* (*Ethical Guidelines for Research in the Social Sciences, Law and Humanities*), where it is advised that:

> Research surrounding deceased persons must be carried out with respect [. . .] Respect for the dead and for surviving relatives dictates that researchers choose their formulations with care.

But back to Storm.

1.2.8 Storm's extensive duties kept him at home a great deal, but he also found the time to travel. In the summers of 1880 to 1886 inclusive he travelled extensively in Norway, principally although not exclusively in the southern parts of the country, collecting dialect data (see section 4.3.1.7). These journeys were funded by grants from the university, and they also included a visit to Copenhagen to record the speech of Icelandic and Faroese speakers there. He recorded his findings in little black octavo notebooks which are now catalogued in the National Library in Oslo under *Sør-østlandske målføre* (*South-eastern dialects*). These notebooks, covering the whole period from 1880 to 1903, deal with more than just the dialects of south-east Norway, and they contain more than just dialect notes. In fact they contain quite a lot of information about Storm the man and about the practices of a nineteenth-century fieldworker.

The notebook he took with him on his July 1880 trip (NBO Ms. 8° 775 A^i) literally enables us to look into his underwear drawer, but the historiography of linguistics really wouldn't benefit from knowing how much underwear Storm took to Telemark. Since however, at this point in the story of Johan Storm we are trying to establish some information about the man, it is worth mentioning that he was clearly quite a heavy smoker, both of cigars and a pipe – not that this was untypical in his day. Aasen too was known to be an active smoker, to the extent that Tiedemanns tobacco company used his image in advertisements for their tobacco, Aasen's favoured brand. Storm's monthly costs between January 1874 and September 1877 indicate that, while most money was spent on books, pipe tobacco was something he bought with striking regularity (NBO Ms. 8° 775 A^i). He was, however, a healthy person. He made regular and lengthy visits to the countryside in search of dialect data, and he lived to a good age. Furthermore he had a daily fitness routine, a routine he recommended to Thomsen.

Of the utmost importance to Storm was going to bed early, at about 2200 or 2230. On 25 March 1878 he told Thomsen that this had been his practice over the past couple of years, that he had become as a new person with twice the capacity for work – and he certainly did have a tremendous capacity for work. If going to bed early really was Storm's secret, then we should all follow his example. At the other end of the day he got up at 0630, worked for an hour, ate breakfast, went for a half-hour walk and then worked until midday. He held lectures at the university or school classes between midday and 1400, when he went for another walk, and ate again at 1500. After his main meal, he rested or slept and then read some 'light literature' while he smoked his pipe. More work then followed between 1730 and 2000 or 2030; he never did any work between that time and going to bed. He might read some French or Italian literature in the evening, but he did not regard that as work. Storm was lucky in a sense, because he lived at a time when all domestic chores were dealt with by others, by his wife and by the servants, so he was able to follow this daily routine uninterrupted. There was no time set aside in this routine for playing with his children, or talking to his wife, or meeting friends. He was a "Victorian" figure of course, but it is clear from his papers that he loved his wife and family very dearly, and, although he frequently holidayed separately from the rest of his family, I think we can assume that he did make time for them, as much as Victorian men ever did.

Johan Storm was a great believer in a healthy lifestyle as well as a structured one, as he explained to Thomsen ten years later in a letter of 7 November 1888:

> I wash in cold water, do physical exercises [for half an hour] and massage or beat myself [to help his rheumatism], and walk for about two hours each day, including my obligatory trip "to town" and to the university each day. I live 25 minutes' walk from the university, and there's no real advantage to be gained by using the tram.

All the same, in a letter to Ludvig Maribo Benjamin Aubert (1838–1896) on 27 June 1883 he asks to be excused his duties as an assessor (*Censor*) for the *Examen Artium* (the school-leaving exam) that year, since he has:

> [. . .] in recent years suffered a great deal from chronic gastric catarrh which causes extreme weakness, and means that I cannot tolerate any form of over-exertion, and it also makes me very sensitive to changes in the weather, such that a slight cooling in the weather causes a relapse. (NBO Brevsamling 14 D5)

Cynics might suggest that he asked to be excused his duties in 1883 since he had already had to interrupt his dialectological travels the previous three years to carry out his duties as *Censor*. In 1883 he had Sweet with him and may well not have wanted to break up the party. In any case there is no mention of stomach complaints in his report for that summer (Storm 1885b), although he had complained of suffering from 'catarrhus gastricus' in letters to Thomsen as early as 1876. He sought to counteract this condition by eating less and by avoiding meat, following the 'vegetarian method', something that had been recommended to him by a Swedish doctor (letter to Thomsen, 26 January 1878). Storm does complain about his health rather regularly in his letters to Thomsen, but it is only the ongoing stomach thing, the rheumatism and occasional lumbago which bother him. On balance, Storm told Thomsen, he enjoyed comparatively good health.

1.2.9 Storm visited Britain on a number of occasions and made the acquaintance of some British scholars. He spent six weeks in England in 1876, where he had dinner with the phonetician Alexander John Ellis (1814–1890), whom he visited again in 1889 when Ellis was an old man. He met Henry Sweet at this time and probably also visited J. A. H. Murray (1837–1915), editor of the *Oxford English Dictionary*, since Murray writes in a letter of 2 June 1893, 'Are you at all likely to pay us a visit here again?' (NBO Ms.

2402 J^{ii}). Whether this visit occurred at the same time as Storm visited Ellis, I don't know.

In 1884 Storm went to Edinburgh as the official delegate from Det kongelige Frederiks Universitet in Kristiania and to collect an honorary doctorate from the University of Edinburgh in its tercentenary year. While he was in Edinburgh he stayed with the Rev'd John S. Black, assistant editor of the ninth edition of *Encyclopædia Britannica*, and it was then that Storm's involvement with *Encyclopædia Britannica* began (see section 3.2.3). Storm was in very exalted company.[6] On 17 April 1884, 122 international luminaries received the degree of Doctor of Laws including Hermann Ludwig Ferdinand von Helmholtz (1821–1894), Dmitri Ivanovich Mendeleyev (1834–1907), Louis Pasteur (1822–1895), Leopold von Ranke (1795–1886) (*in absentia*, presumably because of his advanced age), and Alfred Lord Tennyson (1809–1892). While on the doctorate visit, Storm visited Sweet at his home in Hampstead, London.

Little information about any of these journeys across the North Sea survives, so it is not possible to say what Storm learnt from them. Visits by other scholars to Storm's home in Kristiania are better documented, and we shall return to some of these later when we examine Storm's involvement in the international academic community.

1.2.10 Throughout his adult life Storm lived centrally in Norway's capital city, in the well-to-do area known as Hegdehaugen, immediately to the north-west of the city-centre university site. The census of 1865 shows the newly married Storms and one servant (Karen Erikke Melgaard, aged 22) to have been living at Christian Augusts Gade 3, lodging with two other families at the house of Mrs Cecilie Møller. When he began corresponding with Thomsen in 1873, the family was residing at Pilestrædet 30. In 1874 they moved to Holbergs Gade 33, and a letter to Ivar Aasen written in 1883 shows them to have been at Fearnleys Gade 11 at that time (NBO Brevsamling 174). The rented accommodation in which the family lived was a not infrequent cause for complaint (see letter to Thomsen, 13 February 1875). Fearnleys gate 11 (to use the modern spelling) is now occupied by a modern apartment block, but now, as then, it is located in a quiet and rather opulent part of the city.

The 1900 census shows Storm to have been living at Kirkeveien 39, round the corner from Fearnleys gate, and the *Oslo Adressebok* for 1891 and for 1919 contains the same information. Storm bought this new house in 1884, and moved there with his family in early 1885.[7] The house has long since been demolished, and, like Fearnleys gate 11, the site is now occupied by a

---

[6] My thanks are due to the staff of Edinburgh University Library for their help in locating this information.

[7] My thanks are due to the staff of *Riksarkivet* in Oslo for their help in locating this information.

small apartment block. Nevertheless, the plot is large, and it is easy to form an impression of what the house and its garden must have looked like. Across the road is Frogner Park, where, after the turn of the century, Gustav Vigeland (1869–1943) began his monumental display of sculptures. Storm did not live long enough to see this programme fulfilled, and I suspect he would have disapproved of Vigeland's work. Kirkeveien is now Oslo's inner ring road, busy and noisy; but a short walk away from the main road, behind Kirkeveien 39, quickly gives a sense of what this area must have been like when Storm lived there. Buildings are grand and stuccoed, and quiet opulence pervades the air. Storm's health-imparting walk down to the city centre would have been very pleasant, probably taking him through the Royal Park behind the Palace and on to Karl Johans gate, Oslo's main thoroughfare. The city was small and Storm was well known, so, despite his emphasis on brisk physical exercise, I think we can assume that he stopped frequently to pass the time of day with people, except perhaps with his brother. The Storm residence was quite a large private house, and in addition to his family, there were two young serving girls, Marthe Rasmussen, born in 1878 in Louise Storm's home town of Porsgrunn, and Frida Larsson, a Swedish citizen, born in 1880 in Kil in Värmland. Storm was an unyielding critic, constantly on the warpath against what he perceived as bad language, and his 1900 census return contains this additional comment:

NB General comment: This form is couched in such dark and mysterious expressions that, even after a great deal of pondering, I have not always managed to discover the hidden meaning. J. St.

On the surface Storm lived a relatively unremarkable life: a family man who spent the whole of his adult life living in one place, doing one job. This lifestyle provided a stable basis for his work. He simply could not have achieved the extraordinary amount that he did achieve if he had sought to do so against a background of upheaval. His childhood had been characterised by much physical upheaval coupled with the psychological and emotional disturbance of his father's death, so it is little wonder that Storm chose the quiet lifestyle when he was old enough to decide his way of life for himself. Despite professional disappointments and personal sadnesses, which everybody has to face at some time or another, he lived a full and active life to the very end, publishing the three large volumes of his *Større fransk Syntax* between the ages of 75 and 83. He seems always to have been working, an irrepressible observer and collector of information. His inability to stop observing and collecting resulted in probably the major weakness in his work: a lack of analytical and theoretical distance. He had an encyclopedic knowledge of language and languages, but he was never quite able to stand back and consider all this data at a distance. 'Tight-lipped' was his mouth and so was his approach to his work. If he had opened up and allowed himself the leisure to articulate a general theory, then not only, I

Johan Storm later in life

believe, would he have been Norway's greatest linguist and a pioneer in the fields of phonetics, dialectology and applied linguistics, but he would have been on a level with that other great bourgeois linguist, Ferdinand de Saussure (1857–1913), who famously published very little. While at the end of his life Storm was publishing his vast collection of data, the *Større fransk Syntax*, Saussure, also in the last years of his life, was giving his general lecture series. That is the difference. I do not wish to descend into cheap armchair psychology, but studying the history of linguistics involves finding explanations for why it is the way it is. Why Storm's work is the way it is, and therefore why the linguistics to which he made such a massive contribution is the way it is, can partly at least be explained by the nature of the man. There are those historians, of course, who regard such information as irrelevant to a history of ideas, as though ideas simply "have themselves", as though human beings are not involved in that history, but those are not historians who are genuinely looking for explanations and answers.

1.3 STORM ON HIMSELF

I have already commented that Storm was not a personal writer. Consequently autobiography is not a genre we should expect him to have embraced enthusiastically. There is one surviving autobiographical account, albeit one produced reluctantly: the information given in the 1877 application. Although Storm was interviewed by *Aftenposten* on 1 March 1907, and this interview appeared on the front page of the newspaper, he gave away no personal information.

Storm (1877a) contains autobiographical information relating to his personal position, recounted only because his financial circumstances are so difficult, and evidence is needed to support his bid to improve those circumstances. His description of himself is in terms of pure statistics. He is a certain age, has certain family responsibilities and earns a certain amount of money. He has taught certain subjects and has a certain workload at the university (see section 1.5.3). Although this information is being used for a particular purpose, it is rather typical of Storm that he should describe himself unsentimentally in a list of facts and figures. He even presents his own standing as a scholar by way of a list of publications. Testimonials from other scholars are explicitly shunned:

> With regard to my qualifications it would be easy for me to get glowing references for myself from the leading linguists of western Europe, but I don't attach any particular significance to such references, and find that a list of my writings provides a weightier testimonial [. . .] (Storm 1877a: 4)

Of course testimonials are rarely objective, and many of 'the leading linguists of western Europe' were close colleagues, and even friends, but it is typical of Johan Storm that he should prefer to let the facts speak for themselves. While Henry Sweet was a much more arrogant man, his method of applying for a Chair at Oxford University demonstrates the same disregard for testimonials, as he explained in a letter to Storm:

> I suppose you followed the history of the Merton professorship of English at Oxford. I sent in my name without testimonials, not expecting to have any chance, but I was rather surprised when Napier got it. (NBO Ms. 8° 2402 J[vi])

For both scholars the facts are (or should be) enough. Two years later in 1879, explaining why the English school of phonetics is preferable to the German (see section 2.2.4.2) Storm writes in *Engelsk Filologi* that 'it is obvious that one must start with the facts' (Storm 1879a: 32). In this brief autobiographical account Storm may not provide many insights into his life and nature at the surface level, but the manner in which he presents his life ('the facts') does provide a good insight into his character and his methods.

1.4 OTHERS ON STORM

1.4.1 Obituaries, necrologies and other tributes written after the death of a great person, whether they be a scholar, a politician, an artist or anything else, usually observe normal social customs regarding the dead: they are largely favourable and even glorifying in both tone and content. Thus it is dangerous to assume that what people write after somebody's death is a true reflection of what others really thought of that person during his or her lifetime. Although Falk (1921) and Hambro (1937) cannot praise Storm's academic achievements enough, they cannot find much that is positive to say about the *man*, indeed they cannot find anything to say about the man at all, except to suggest that there was a warmth beneath the formal exterior. In the preface to Storm (1920) Olai Skulerud (1881–1963) appears to have the same problem: it is not difficult to list Storm's considerable achievements, but words expressing his personality do not come easily:

> That highly valued scholar and teacher, that person who was so warmly interested in everything noble and great, is no longer in our midst. Professor Storm's name will go down in history, with an honourable place in our nation's consciousness, among the men who raised our national heritage in the nineteenth century by the significant contribution he made to the investigation of our folk language, and by the love for our people, with which his research was closely interwoven [. . .] Blessed be Johan Storm's memory! (Storm 1920: viii)

'That person who was so warmly interested in everything noble and great' is an unusual way of describing someone, and gives the impression of euphemism, or at least of words that have been formulated unnaturally, which "stick in Skulerud's throat" (or pen). Surely if Skulerud had remembered Storm as a kind or generous man, as a humble or upright man, as possessing any of the great nineteenth-century attributes, then he would have said so. Skulerud had known Storm well. He had been a student of Storm's, and later a fellow academic linguist.[8] His tribute too portrays Storm as a list of achievements, and not as a human being, and Jespersen's obituary of Storm in the Danish newspaper, *Berlingske Tidende* (Jespersen 1920b), is similarly unforthcoming on the man.

August Western knew Storm better than most,[9] and his recollections provide an ever-so-slightly more profound glimpse of the man whom others sensed, but perhaps never experienced. Like his father, Storm was, according to Western 'of a somewhat introverted disposition' (Western 1920: 152), but:

---

[8] Handwritten lists of the names of students attending Storm's English class in 1900 and 1901 include that of Skulerud (inserted in NBO Ms. 8° 2402 C: 'Germaniske Konsonanter især engelske i Forhold til de beslægtede Sprog').

[9] For more on Western, see section 2.2.4.2.3.

Those who got to know him more closely, and particularly those who came into closer contact with him as a private individual and in his home, soon found that a warm, nay even tender heart beat beneath the rather buttoned-up exterior. (Western 1920: 153)

Falk was almost certainly quoting Western when he wrote that Storm's 'buttoned-up exterior probably concealed a warm heart', but nevertheless the repetition of the image strengthens its credibility. There was an outer Storm, a public Storm, a Storm who sat for photographs, who taught and published; and there was another Storm underneath, a vulnerable Storm he was perhaps afraid to let out.

Another tribute which appeared following Storm's death was the *Mindetale* (necrology) by Adam Trampe Bødtker (1866–1944), Storm's successor (from 1914) as professor of English philology. Bødtker speaks very highly of Storm's academic skills and achievements, but again the person is extremely ghostly. We learn, metaphorically, of Storm's "other-worldliness", but at least this fact provides a tiny insight into Storm's private world:

Up to an advanced age he had an astronomical telescope in the garden, and guided young philologists in the celestial paths. (Bødtker 1922: 51)

Otherwise Bødtker's only personal recollection is similar to Hambro's and Falk's recollections, of a stern Victorian:

The authoritative figure of Johan Storm commanded respect. His gaze sliced through imprecisions and approximations, and he compelled young people to learn at the same time as he forged a bond with them.

Storm had a long life, and for Storm life and work were the same thing. (Bødtker 1922: 53)

Is this the answer then? Apart from star-gazing and singing, did Storm simply not allow himself a life outside his work? That would certainly explain how he managed to achieve so much.

Francis Bull's (1887–1974) recollection of Storm was written over 30 years after Storm's death, and Bull had only known Storm when the subject of his recollections was an old man. As a consequence he is able to be more objective, and less constrained by the conventions of his genre, than those writing or speaking immediately following Storm's death. Bull writes of the privilege of being taught by 'five significant representatives of that great generation in our intellectual history – Ibsen's and Bjørnson's fellow students', and elements of the standard Storm hagiography are present in Bull's account. Thus we encounter the leitmotifs of subsequent Storm commentaries, his 'incomparably good ear' and the fact that he was an 'outstanding phonetician' (see section 1.7). Accordingly, 'he could be angry and unpleasant towards those who did not have a good ear for languages' (Bull 1945: 306).

A final tribute to Storm which deserves mention here is the centenary article by the Slavist Olaf Broch (1867–1961) in *Aftenposten*, published on Tuesday 24 November 1936. Broch sounds the same paean to Storm's phonetic skills ('in this pioneering work Johan Storm proved to be a heaven-sent technician of the science'), but again it is his teaching and the legacy of that teaching which is the main focus of the piece, the remote yet powerful influence of 'the strict university teacher'. We shall return to Storm's teaching in section 1.5, but we should note here that, despite the remoteness of the man, commentators have felt compelled to write about him as a teacher who evidently made an impact on at least some of his students.

1.4.2 In the surviving letters to Storm there are some comments on the man's character, but it has to be borne in mind that letters written to a person are not really the place to look for completely neutral points of view. Jespersen's letters to Storm (NBO Ms. 8° 2402 J[1]), which begin in 1884, when Jespersen was still a young man of 24 and Storm a well-established scholar and authority, indicate that Storm initially took a lot of interest in Jespersen and showed him some kindness, not only in responding so fully to Jespersen's enquiries, but also in sending him copies of his work. A letter from the English phonetician Laura Soames (1840–1895) evidences greater kindness still, both actual and implied. She visited Kristiania for a few days in the July of 1891, and twice visited Storm at his home during this stay. In one of Storm's notebooks (at NBO Ms. 4° 1287 (*Fonetiske Samlinger* V)) we find a list of 'problematic words that she was so good as to read out both loudly and clearly'. This took place on 8 July 1891 with Knud Brekke present,[10] presumably as much as a chaperone as an independent phonetic ear! It is evident from the categories of words that Storm gave her that he was interested in data on common rapid-speech processes, such as vowel reduction and deletion, and the quality of the liquids. In a letter written at the end of her visit to Kristiania (10 July 1891), she proclaims herself to be 'as proud as a peacock to find what a good opinion you have of my book'.[11] Unlike Henry Sweet, Storm had a high opinion of Soames's work – in fact Storm and Sweet disagreed rather strongly on the matter – and he was quite happy to give compliments where compliments were due. From what Soames goes on to write in the letter, Storm had a reputation for being generous in his opinion of other people's work:

> Mr Passy says I ought not to be too much elated if you praised my book, because you are so kind as always to take the most favourable view of other people's performances [. . .]

[10] For more on Knud Olai Brekke see section 2.2.4.2.3.
[11] *An Introduction to Phonetics (English, French and German) with Reading Lessons and Exercises* (1891).

So here at last is a positive statement about the man, Storm. There are many reasons why insights into Storm's personality have not survived in the literature, perhaps the most decisive being that articles in academic journals and suchlike do not on the whole contain personal reminiscences or comments on a person. Personal information is perhaps a more common feature of academic obituaries and tributes nowadays, but not 100 years ago. I am just sorry that there are not more images to be had of the man in whose ghostly company I have spent so much time. That is a personal regret (and writing in the year 2001 I have no worries about including personal observations), but I also regret that we do not have better information about who Storm was and thus why he worked and behaved the way he did.

1.5 STORM THE TEACHER

1.5.1 One of the lists Storm uses to characterise himself in the 1877 application to parliament is a list of his teaching responsibilities at the university. He was (to begin with at least) solely responsible for the teaching of English and the Romance languages, and in addition he chose to give public lectures on Norwegian in the absence (until 1899) of a university lecturer in that field. This meant that his teaching load was heavy by any standards. University teachers spend a lot of time complaining about what and how much they have to do. In Storm's case the complaints were well and truly justified.

Det kongelige Frederiks Universitet in Kristiania (Oslo) was founded in 1811, and the first teacher of French at the university was Mathurin René Orry, appointed *lektor* in 1815 and granted the status of professor a year later, remaining in post until 1822. At the end of 1817 Professor Ludvig Stoud Platou (1778–1833), first professor of history and statistics at the university, published an account of the university's position six years after its foundation (cited in Gran 1911: 171). Platou notes that a number of the staff who, according to the university's strategic plan, should have been appointed, are not yet in post. Included amongst these unfilled positions are 'readers in Latin philology, the Icelandic language and Scandinavian archæology, oriental languages [. . .] along with a teacher of the German and English languages'. This implies a lack of commitment by the university to linguistic subjects – subjects which may have been seen as a luxury at this stage of the university's development, since they did not directly relate to training the professionals needed to administer the bodies and souls of the new nation. In any case Orry was succeeded by John Andreas Messell (1789–1850), a resident of Kristiania, appointed lektor in English and Italian in 1822, and from 1834 until his death professor of English, Italian and French (see also section 2.1.2.1). Other language appointments were made prior to Storm's. Carl Richard Unger (1817–1897) replaced Messell in the field of

Romance and Germanic philology, but his publications were exclusively in
the Germanic field, specifically Old Norwegian. The other posts covered
oriental languages (Christopher Andreas Holmboe, 1796–1882), Finno-
Ugric (Jens Andreas Friis, 1821–1896), Semitic (Jens Peter Broch, 1819–
1886), and comparative Indo-European philology ((Elseus) Sophus Bugge,
1833–1907).

I shall let Storm speak for himself on the subject of his teaching
responsibilities:

> As fellow and professor in English and Romance philology, I have held
> lectures from 1871 onwards on various relevant topics such as: Italian
> language and language-history, including working through selected
> passages; English pronunciation and historical phonology; working
> through modern English and French literature; interpretation of Shake-
> speare and Molière; working through Old French texts like the *Chanson de
> Roland*; historical French phonology from Latin onwards; English histor-
> ical grammar (morphology) and Old English; excerpts from Chaucer,
> covering older English pronunciation and its development into modern
> pronunciation, based on the most recent investigations. All these lectures
> have been well attended, especially the lectures on Shakespeare, with up to
> 100 in the audience, gentlemen and ladies, amongst whom were several
> English. I have in addition held popular lectures on our mother tongue,
> also for a group of about 100 listeners. (Storm 1877a: 3)

This refers to his teaching across a number of years, but what is more
impressive than the amount of teaching he did is the breadth of coverage. It
was possible to be truly expert in more than one field 125 years ago, yet
Storm's teaching does reflect his enormous capacity for amassing knowledge. The need to cover English and the Romance languages in their
entirety meant that some aspects of those languages had to be sidelined,
and Storm was simply unable to teach some subjects he would otherwise
have wished to. His notes for a series of lectures on French grammar, which
he started in September 1897, survive amongst his papers (NBO Ms. 8° 2402
F^{iv}). He begins the opening lecture by saying that French (and English)
grammar has always been one of his favourite subjects, but that he has been
prevented from delivering lectures on grammar until now, on account of
having to teach other sides to language, specifically phonetics, history of the
languages and practical skills.

1.5.2 The study of modern languages became increasingly important as the
nineteenth century reached its conclusion, and as time went by further
appointments were made to assist Storm. His interests were first and
foremost linguistic, and his use of literature in teaching was essentially as
a body of linguistic data for studying the history of the languages and for use
in practical classes. Soon after his appointment as professor there was

therefore agitation within the faculty for an additional appointment in the area of literature. Olaf Skavlan (1838–1891) had from 1871 been research fellow in (principally Nordic) literary history, and in 1877 he was promoted to an extraordinary professorship in general European literary history. In 1895 he was succeeded by Christen Christian Dreyer Collin (1857–1926), a very productive writer on English and Norwegian literature and a Shakespeare and Bjørnson scholar. Collin's post had the same job description as Skavlan's, albeit as a readership (*dosentur*) rather than a professorship (*professorat*) in general European literary history. At the same time yet another appointment was made in this field, but with a more specific remit. (Oluf) Eilert Løseth (1858–1945) took up a readership in Romance literature, thus enabling Collin to concentrate on English. In the persons of Storm, Collin and Løseth the teaching of English and Romance language and literature was well covered. (In 1914, after Storm's death, Collin was appointed professor of European literature and Løseth professor of Romance philology – see sections 2.1.2 and 3.1.2 for more information on the teaching and study of English and the Romance languages at the university.)

Another aspect of language teaching required at the university was practical skills. In 1887 the faculty recommended that 1,000 kroner per year be made available 'for practical training in French and English for philological students' (quoted in Sandved 1998: 55). The university supported this recommendation, but nothing further was done about it until the mid-1890s. It was increasingly evident that teachers of modern languages would need to have a high level of attainment in speaking and writing those languages when they went out to work in the schools, but provision for gaining these skills while at the university was inadequate. Storm wasn't able to provide enough bread-and-butter language teaching on top of his other academic commitments, and the only really satisfactory means for students to improve their language skills was an extended stay in the relevant country. Following the failure to appoint practical teachers in 1887, a report in the national newspaper *Morgenbladet* (10 February 1887) took a dim view of this outcome, noting amongst other things that 'at the moment practical education in these languages has to a large degree to be sought by way of residence abroad, for which relatively few can afford the means'. So proper training in modern languages was in danger of becoming something only the wealthy could afford. When the faculty renewed its proposal in the mid-1890s, others came out in full support of the need to appoint teachers who could give language students the practice they required. Professor Sophus Bugge wrote an appendix to the faculty's proposal, entitled 'On language-teachers in the modern languages at the university' ('Om Sproglærere i de levende Sprog ved Universitetet'), where he drew attention to the arguments about the skills required of language teachers, and to the necessity for proper provision of teachers. Storm entered the debate himself, but, interestingly, he was consistently and uncharacter-istically mild in his contributions to it, and did not demonstrate the polemic and spleen which characterise his contributions to the other public debates in which he became involved. In 1895 he published a piece in the journal *Vor Ungdom* where his non-confrontational view is summed up as follows:

> By making use of every opportunity to mix with natives, together with rigorous and continuous study, one can achieve much. But the fact remains that the appointment at the university of native teachers in the modern languages is to a high degree desirable and necessary. (Storm 1895a: 20)

Storm had spelled out his views on the subject in full in the preface to the *Engelsk Filologi* of 1879, so his position was known; it is quite possible that, since nothing had happened for 16 years, he was not very hopeful that anything would happen now, hence his mildness. In 1879 he had written, 'I here put forward this thought for consideration by the relevant authorities, and hope that in the fullness of time it might be realised' (Storm 1879a: viii). As at other times as well, the 'relevant authorities' ignored Storm.

A less relaxed line was taken by those students who made their views known in the national press. In the January of 1895, H. A. Var had taken up the cudgels and penned a fierce critique of the university and the state for not providing adequate support for university-level language teaching. The following month six further philology students wrote to back up the initial correspondent:

> [. . .] The university has just one teacher of English and French, and it must be clear to everyone that five hours per week is far too little for tuition in both the scientific study and the practical acquisition of these important languages. (*Morgenbladet*, 15 February 1895)

The involvement of Bugge and the very public involvement of disaffected students clearly had some impact, and this time the government ministry responsible took the proposal forward to parliament. In the budget for 1897/1898 4,000 kroner was made available for practical language teaching. Sidney Thurgood (b. 1854), a native English speaker resident in Kristiania, was appointed to teach practical English, and Løseth and Herman Rømer (d. 1899) were appointed to cover French and German respectively.

It might seem unnecessary to have spent so many words on the issues surrounding the appointment of practical language teachers at the univer-sity. However, the whole scenario demonstrates that Storm was more than just a pioneer in his scholarship. He was responsible for inventing the study of the modern languages as university subjects in Norway. It was not automatically accepted that native speakers would be needed in the teaching of languages, because there was no model to follow in Norway. This fact both benefited and disadvantaged Storm as a teacher. The benefit was that he was relatively free to teach what he wanted, without any presuppositions about what teaching modern languages at university level entailed. In fact he very rarely repeated a course: he liked to vary what he taught, depending on what was occupying his thoughts at the time. The disadvantage was that he often had to fight to prove the need for certain things he should have been able to take for granted, like a decent salary and the employment of practical teachers. Despite the fact that Storm had been agitating for the appointment of these staff for some time, *Morgenbladet* was able to report the following:

> Two respected schoolmen have grants at the present time to carry out investigations abroad concerning the practical training of would-be school-teachers, and until the outcome of these investigations is available, the ministry is not able to support the recommendation. (10 February 1887)

So Storm was a pioneering teacher who, like all pioneers, had to shoulder great responsibility, and who only gradually saw the fruits of his labours, often in the face of misunderstanding and lack of support. Nevertheless, Sandved (1998: 120) is right to state that, as Storm's personal reputation throughout Europe grew, the university, by association with him, became, at least in the fields of English and Romance studies, 'so far removed from any "provincial university" that it on the other hand comprised a European centre of power within this branch of "the new philology"'.

1.5.3 Scholars employed in universities today find it hard to devote equal attention to research, teaching and administrative responsibilities. How much more of a challenge must this have been to someone like Storm who, through the combination of a vast intellect and sheer hard work, built up a 'European centre of power' from nothing. Surely some aspect of his work must have suffered? Well yes, it seems as though, his lifelong campaign to improve the teaching of modern languages at all levels of education notwithstanding, he was not a terribly interested or inspiring lecturer himself. If Hambro's recollections of his time as a student in Kristiania are as typical as he claims, Storm's uninspiring lectures were merely one aspect of what was a very poor provision by the university and the city from the point of view of students:

> The university did nothing for the students, gave them no guidance, gave out no syllabus, provided no access to food or drink of any sort within the academic portals [. . .] There were two worlds – the professor's and that of the students; and all the students from out of town were strangers in a strange city, a city which opens no gates of hospitality to them. It is unsurprising that hundreds of students, after completing their period of study, departed from the university with a deep grudge against a capital city which spared them no thought, and of whose life they never became a part. (Hambro 1950: 18)

Some of Storm's own lecture notes survive, and it is therefore possible to form an idea of what his lectures must have been like. He preferred to write out what he was going to say in full. He doesn't seem to have followed this practice throughout his lecture courses – one assumes it would simply have become too time-consuming – but his lectures certainly start out following this method. His public lecture on Norwegian from 1875 begins with 'Ladies and Gentlemen!' Nothing is left to chance. Even interjections are written out in full ('Nu vel, saa er det Bondens Modersmaal [. . .]'), and where an extra word is to be inserted, it is written carefully in the margin ('I have the greatest respect [and interest – *in margin*] for the dialects [. . .]') (NBO Ms. 8° 2402 K).

Storm took great pride in the work he did to promote improved teaching methods for modern languages, and in his English lectures from 1896/1897 he is not modest about his reform work:

> The latest *teaching methods* have moved away more and more from the *theory* of languages and placed the main emphasis on their *practice*. I have single-handedly been involved in advancing this movement as a reform or improved method of language teaching. (NBO Ms. 8° 2402 E)

He has every right to boast about his work in this area. He was truly committed to the campaign, and the books he wrote which employed his reformed method met with a very enthusiastic reception. We shall return to this aspect of Storm's work in section 2.3.3 below, but I mention it here because what he campaigned for, and what he did in his language-teaching books, contrast quite strikingly with his lectures. He didn't always find it easy to practise what he preached. Just as he was too set in his ways to use the reformed Norwegian spelling that he put forward (see 4.1.3.6/7), so he was not good at lecturing in the lively way advocated and exemplified in his books. To be fair, there is a difference between formal lectures on the history and structure of a language, on the one hand, and practical instruction in learning that language (where he was able to apply his views on teaching reform much more effectively), on the other, but Storm's accusation that most materials for learning French were 'dull and tedious' (Storm 1892b: vii) could probably have been directed at his own lectures.

Because Storm liked to write out what he was going to say in full, it is unlikely that, when his lecture notes break down into long lists of examples, these simply formed the skeleton for a connected presentation. It is more likely that he presented the examples to the students straight. The lectures on English grammar (although he doesn't appear to have got any further than Old English vowels), from which I have just quoted, rapidly dwindle into strings of examples, and the 1899/1900 lectures on *Engelsk Lydhistorie* (English Historical Phonology), which, although a continuation of the earlier lecture series, have still not got beyond Old English vowels, contain very little commentary alongside the detailed examples. Here then we have a course on Old English vowels lasting five years, covering eight semesters, much of which seems to have consisted of examples of the vowels and their alternants in use in various positions. Sandved (1998: 79) describes this, from a modern pedagogical point of view, as an 'endless journey in the wilderness', and it is hard to imagine that even the students who took the course would have perceived any real direction in these lectures. Nonetheless 29 students took 'History of the English language' in the first semester of 1900, so Storm clearly had a loyal following. His course on French grammar for the year 1897/1898 evidences the same meticulous preparation of the opening sections, and then just lots of examples. What is striking, particularly in the French lecture notes from 1897, is just how few corrections and crossings-out he had to make. He knew exactly what he was going to say and was able to call upon the relevant examples to support his points. Hambro recollects Storm's lectures on French prepositions, and his impression of them is exactly as we would expect:

> During [my] years as a philologist, [Storm's] lectures on French consisted purely and simply of lengthy litanies on the prepositions à and de – with hundreds and hundreds of examples of verbs which took à or de. There was something moving, but almost discomforting, about seeing him trudging in with the numerous books of lecture notes which constituted his precious collections. And if a student wished to give him particular pleasure, he would bring along a rare construction he had come across involving à or de. And with the joyful care of the collector Storm gummed the example into one of his albums. (Hambro 1950: 127)

Western (1920: 152) provides further evidence for the somewhat turgid nature of Storm's lectures, writing that he lacked the ability to provide the bigger picture and to 'electrify' his audience.

Storm was above all a collector of data, and he had detailed knowledge of the languages with which he worked. He was not adept at systematising this data, however, and two observations by Jespersen are relevant in this respect:

> Storm is the rapid observer, who, with his fine musical ear, is able in a flash to grasp a foreign accent with tremendous precision, and, by means of a faithful memory, hold onto it. (Jespersen 1933: 77)

Here Jespersen pays homage to Storm's extraordinary listening and remembering skills, but he later points out that Storm was himself aware of the potential weakness inherent in this talent:

> 'I am not a systematist like you', Storm said to me in one of our first conversations [. . .] His thorough knowledge and great industry would have benefited the world more if from the beginning he had worked – not

necessarily from a finished system, but from a method that might evolve into a system. (Juul et al. 1995: 248)

We will come back to this characteristic of Storm and what it meant for his work and for the linguistics to which he contributed, but we should note that this is not just a personal weakness of Storm's (if indeed it is a weakness); it is at least in part a function of the intellectual climate in which he worked. The new practical (*applied*) linguistic issues which occupied Storm – phonetics, dialectology and the teaching of the modern languages – were not yet sufficiently established to have developed truly general, theoretical frameworks. Storm, like all pioneers, had to contribute to the groundwork, the collection of data, the initial practical considerations, which needed to be in place before these elements of language could be generalised about. It is likely that Storm was attracted to precisely these areas, that he was the right man in the right place at the right time, because his abilities lay in collecting and remembering large amounts of language data – in which case he should not be blamed for failing to systematise, for failing to make a significant contribution to traditional philology. When he transgressed into areas in which some sort of explanation, system or theory was expected, like lectures on English philology, the applied linguist was rather out of his depth. I am not suggesting that Storm did not understand the more theoretical byways of contemporary language study – his critical writings show that he under-stood them very well – but rather that he was temperamentally unsuited to them. The study of English and Romance languages at the university was, as we noted above, very much what Storm made it, since nobody had trodden that ground before, but he was *Professor i engelsk og romansk **Filologi*** and he was obliged to teach this. The recollections of several of his former students do rather support my sense of that teaching not being desperately successful.

1.5.4 Hjalmar Falk remembered Storm as an inspiring schoolteacher, but an uninspiring lecturer:

> The present author can from his own experience testify to the fact that Storm's teaching turned out to be something of a revelation to his pupils. By comparison with this it was rather a disappointment to hear him at the university. Storm was no speaker and did not appear inspiring. (Falk 1921: 112)

A reviewer ('T.D.') of the first volume of *Større fransk Syntax*, by contrast, remembers the effortless insights of Storm's lectures on French, and had clearly been inspired by them:

> Many of our university-educated men and women, even those outside the realms of actual specialists, will with profound thanks remember Storm's lectures, in which he humorously and easily, playfully and without any

apparent show, let drop his insightful observations [. . .] (*Aftenposten* 2 July 1911)

Storm did not in fact regard his lectures as particularly important, and seems to have been more interested in the practical classes he gave, and which he continued to give even after the appointment of Thurgood, Løseth and Rømer. Again this shows that he had a greater (indeed unforgettable) commitment to the practical, the *living* side of language than to the philological, the historical, although, having trained in the middle of the nineteenth century, it would have been unthinkable for him to discard philological study completely. In this way, Storm was no different from Saussure, whose *Cours de linguistique générale* is for the most part a standard textbook on the methods and findings of historical-comparative linguistics. Storm expresses his (unofficial) attitude towards lectures quite unambiguously in some advice he gave to Vilhelm Thomsen:

> Don't work on your lectures too much – it is scarcely worth it. Instead invest your main energies in writing. As a rule I spend an hour a day on lectures, and use the rest of the day for my own work. In the long run I find that this is also more fruitful for the lectures. (Letter of 26 January 1878)

The recollections Storm's students have of his *practical* classes are generally much more positive. Bødtker (1922: 53) euphemistically remembers Storm's drab lectures, but enthusiastically conjures up a colourful picture of Storm in his practical classes:

> At the lectern Storm was less of a lecturer than a reader. He will most of all be remembered as the leading figure in practical language acquisition. Here he was at the heart of his life's work, and here he could abandon himself completely. When he went through the plays of Shakespeare or Molière, he liked to take the leading role himself; we won't forget his King Lear or his Harpagon in a hurry.

Francis Bull (1945: 306–307), remembering the same classes, felt the same impact; and although the features he remembers are slightly different, they also suggest a Storm we have not yet met: a person enthusing and light-hearted. In his practical classes, as Bødtker says, he was 'at the heart of his life's work', in there amongst the 'living language', happier *doing* language rather than *thinking* about it:

> [. . .] he brought us up to feel the tone and the rhythms of the spoken language, and in his treatment of Shakespeare's plays he could serve up amusing theatrical recollections of how this or that speech was or should have been delivered. Nevertheless, I can well appreciate the justification of the only – and then only indirect – spiteful remark Sophus Bugge is to have made. Someone compared Johan Storm with the old Latinist

Professor L. C. M. Aubert, and Bugge's voice rang out: 'Aubert could think.'

1.6 Working Methods

1.6.1 In the summer of 1895 Jespersen visited Storm in Kristiania (see Juul et al. 1995: 99), a visit he recollected in his autobiography, during which he was struck by Storm's working methods:

> During a visit to Kristiania I saw Johan Storm's method of working: he used quarto notebooks, in which each new quotation had to be entered immediately in the right place after it was found. This meant constant leafing back and forth in these notebooks while the entries were being made and at the same time required him to remember where something similar had been encountered before. This, along with Storm's method, which is particularly evident in the second edition of *Englische Philologie* [. . .], where the comments are linked to a single one of a number of works which Storm is critically examining, mean that his many valuable insights do not become so useful and accessible as they might otherwise easily have been. (Juul et al. 1995: 248)

Fortunately many of the notebooks survive, and they bear out Jespersen's observations. Storm used an a priori system for ordering his notes, which meant that, when he came to collect his data, it had to fit into this pre-ordained system. His notebooks on the language of Norwegian writers, for example, begin with pages dedicated to the etymology of words those writers used,[12] so he would have a page or several pages for words of Danish origin, words of German origin, words of Norwegian origin and so on. These pages are followed by pages for each vowel, and then each consonant, and then each grammatical category. Storm's method was then to read the writings of the author in question, starting with Absalon Pedersen (1528–1575) and continuing up to and including contemporary writers in Norwegian Landsmål, and enter words in the notebook on the appropriate page. This obviously led to a rather arbitrary systematisation of the data, and one which it was not easy to cross-reference. It would not have been too problematic in those cases where Storm did not find much interesting data, as with A. E. Erichsen and S. Bretteville Jensen's *Norske Læsebok* of 1901–1904, but some of the notebooks are very full and very battered, implying that Storm referred to them a lot. The notebook containing examples from Asbjørnsen's and Moe's collection of folk tales looks to have been particularly well used. In *De store Forfatteres Sprog og Retskrivning* (The Language and Orthography of the Great Authors), which appeared

---

[12] NBO Ms. 4° 1290 H$^{ix-xlix}$.

in instalments in the national daily newspaper *Aftenposten* between September and November 1900, Asbjørnsen and Moe's *Folke-Eventyr* (Folk Stories) (see section 4.2.3.2.2) receives the ultimate praise:

> The real reformers, who, without catching anyone unawares and without any revolution, at one fell swoop introduced the full Norwegian language form into literature, are *Asbjørnsen* and *Moe* in their immortal *Folk Tales* [. . .] *Asbjørnsen* and *Moe's* work is the *foundation for the whole of the subsequent, continuously growing Norwegianisation* of our written language, which even grew under their hands.

So these notebooks, with their rather eccentric layout, formed the basis for Storm's work. Jespersen thought that they constituted a strange working method, and I must say that I would also have found them very difficult to work with, but the notebooks are like an untidy desk. To the observer an untidy desk looks like the embodiment of disorganisation and confusion, but the owner of the desk often has a clear overview of the desk's contents and can find everything easily. Everyone evolves different working methods, and the little notebooks with their a priori sections suited Storm. They suited his preference for data rather than theory. In his 1811 *Vejledning til det Islandske eller gamle Nordiske Sprog* (Guide to the Icelandic or Old Norse Language) Rasmus Rask (1787–1832) devised a system for presenting the grammatical structure of a language; he used this system rigidly to compare the grammatical systems of a large number of languages, some of which he didn't even know (see Linn 1996; Hovdhaugen et al. 2000: 159–164). Storm is doing something similar in these notebooks. A common system, even if it is not always an ideal system, at least enables comparison, particularly where the data are new. In fact Rask and Storm have several things in common. Both linguists wrote about an extraordinarily large number of language varieties. Both tended to produce work which was the fruit of their own interests, rather than what was expected of them: Rask worked on Danish when others hoped he would produce treatments of the Oriental languages he had studied on his travels, and Storm worked on Norwegian dialects when others were trying to persuade him to make further contributions to general philology. (Sweet wrote to him, for example, in July 1878 urging him to 'come out with a Comparative Tonology of Norse, Danish, Swedish, English + French' (NBO Ms. 8° 2402 Jᵛ).) Both probably in this way damaged their reputations, or at least prevented their work having the influence it might otherwise have had. Both limited their influence in the international linguistic community by publishing much of their work in their native languages. Both were comparativists, principally concerned with data, since they were carrying out pioneering studies of many of the varieties with which they worked. And in terms of method they both adopted a rigid a priori method and are therefore prone to accusations of being unsystematic. Their working methods were not very flexible, it is true, and did not easily lend themselves to the creation of general theories, but that was not what either linguist was trying to do. They were both collectors and comparers. That was their skill, and their greatness lies in the fact that they deployed their skill at stages in the history of linguistics when just such work was needed. It would be the job of subsequent generations to do the theorising. Storm knew Rask's work, and took full and careful notes from a number of his publications.[13] While the work of the two men shows certain striking similarities, I would not wish to suggest any more significant line of influence from Rask to Storm.

Storm's dialect work uses the same a priori system for comparative purposes. We shall return to this when we go on later to look at that work and at his phonetic work in detail, but to shed some more light on his working methods it is useful to consider here the questionnaire he sent out in the early 1880s supporting his comparative dialect study. In 1882 he published the *Norsk Ordliste til Lydlæren*, a list of sample words 'intended for those who propose to study Norwegian dialects' (Storm 1882a: 1). Prior to this he had sent a letter round to parish priests, including a provisional word-list, encouraging them to assist him in his attempt to produce an overview of the dialects. Replies to his request for information came in slowly but surely and are testimony to a general interest in the Norwegian dialects at this time and of goodwill towards this sort of project. Most responses came from the priests themselves, but in some cases the questionnaire had been passed on to another, better-qualified person. Storm wrote in his accompanying letter:

> You would do me a great service by telling me what the following words are called in your village. The aim is to get an overview of the distribution of word-forms across the various villages. It is desired that the words be written exactly according to the pronunciation, leaving out all silent letters, but otherwise using the usual spelling. As this is just a first attempt, I'm not giving any detailed guide to the description of the sounds, which could easily confuse people and put them off [. . .] This information will not be published, but simply used in an overview of the eastern Norwegian dialects, on which I am working. Any other pieces of information will be received with gratitude. (NBO Ms. 4° 1285 B[i])

There then follow 22 lists of common words and phrases. This is of course a rigid system, one which assumes that the same words and the same sounds within those words are going to be equally significant in each dialect. But what other method could Storm employ? He was not an Ivar Aasen (see Section 4.1.22), receiving an income to dedicate his life to recording and comparing dialect data personally. One of the tags often used to describe Aasen is 'the great systematist' (*den store systematiker*). Dagfinn Worren, for

---

[13] NBO Ms. 4° 1287[xii].

example, opens *Ivar Aasen-almanakken* with the words 'Ivar Aasen (1813–1896) var ein systematikar' (Worren 1996: 1)), but the sort of systematising that Aasen did, creating a standard language, demands the time and dedication that Storm, with all his commitments, could not possibly have afforded. The few transcriptional *Vink* ('hints') that Storm gives in his letter, such as the means for indicating schwa (he suggests the symbol which would later be adopted by the International Phonetic Association, namely [ə]) or indicating "thick l", the retroflex tap found in eastern (including northern) Norwegian dialects (he suggests a dot under the *l*), are just sufficient to help the informants indicate sounds for which there is no obvious alphabetical equivalent, but not so many as to confuse the non-specialist with technical detail. Here, then, Storm shows himself to have a clear idea of what is *practically* achievable in a pioneering study. His method could indeed be accused of being unsystematic, but it generated results which could be easily analysed, and thus proved itself to be a wholly appropriate one.

1.6.2 Storm's notebooks indicate a number of interesting things about the modus operandi of this linguist. First he painstakingly cut relevant items out of newspapers and journals and stuck them into his notebooks. As well as his own newspaper and journal contributions, these *Udklip* ('clippings') constitute a mixture of articles and reviews on subjects of interest to Storm, and examples of language use, particularly what Storm regarded as bad language use. One notebook (NBO Ms. 4° 1290 2 A), entitled *Unorsk* (*Un-Norwegian*), is subdivided (according to Storm's characteristic method) into sections like *Vulgarismer* (*Vulgarisms*) and *Barbarismer, Sprogfeil* (*Barbarisms, Linguistic Errors*), and into it Storm pasted clippings accompanied by his comments. Letters he received are all painstakingly gummed into notebooks in the same way, sometimes with his handwritten comments, but more often simply for the record. This collection of letters and printed materials could be seen as obsessive, reflecting Storm's inability to open up, to let go; but whether his motives were morbid or scholarly, it is another example of the working methods of the data collector, organising his material in an inflexible but clear and efficient way.

Second, the notebooks testify to Storm's constant interest in language. He was not a nine-to-five scholar, for whom the study of language was simply a job. Some of his notebooks were evidently precisely what their name implies: books for making notes in, books which he carried with him to note down any interesting things he came across. The notebooks which are now catalogued as NBO Ms. 8° 775 A[xviii] and A[xxi], for example, contain a variety of jottings on a variety of subjects – addresses, costs, lists of books and other things besides – but they also include dialect transcriptions. Storm was a true fieldworker who recorded real language as he found it, not as it came back to him when he was sitting in his study. Once again we witness the collector in action, and once again we witness the concern for the *living language*, rather than for any sort of ideal or abstraction; but in addition we witness the linguist whose ears were always open to linguistic information. Storm's dialectological method contrasts markedly with that of the other great nineteenth-century collector of Norwegian dialect material, Aasen. Aasen's dialectology was programmatic in that he was from the outset using the dialects to serve a particular purpose. He travelled around the country collecting dialect information with the intention of creating a standard Norwegian from it, or, put another way, finding a standard within it. Either way, Aasen adopted what Stephen Walton (1996: 335–342) calls 'the cumulative method', which 'proceeds straight from the material in a union of theory and empiricism' (p. 336). Admittedly Storm aims to produce 'an overview of the eastern Norwegian dialects' through a comparison of them, but he is not driven by any assumption about the relationship between those dialects. He doesn't theorise. For Storm the dialects are a living legacy, a wonderful example of the living language 'with its laws and its freedoms, its different levels and its colourful variety' (Storm 1911a: xiv–xv). Aasen's form of Norwegian was metaphorically for Storm the *murderer* of the living dialects:

> Give us *living dialects* with their genuine popular character, fresh naturalness and affecting innocent character, and spare us from the *dead, stiff, artificial Landsmaal*. (Storm 1903a: 89)

The dialects should, in Storm's view, speak for themselves and not be pushed into different shapes by linguists with their ideas and ideals. Storm uses a (rather muddled) musical image to indicate the difference between his approach on the one hand and Aasen's approach on the other:

> Each dialect is one key of a particular sort of sound. Aasen has selected the harmonious notes and unified them in a choir or a beautiful chord. We on the other hand let every dialect sing its own melody in its own register, and compare the character of the different tone pictures. (Storm 1884a: 7, n. 1)

We have travelled rather a long way from Storm's notebooks, so let us return to them for the third and final clue to Storm's working methods that I wish to mention here. Storm's handwritten papers show that he worked quickly and surely. In most of his drafts (as in his lecture notes) there are surprisingly few corrections or alterations. On 20 December 1875 he began work on a draft of his proposed *Work on the Norwegian Language*. Eleven days later, New Year's Eve, he had completed 12 pages with very few alterations, and this was over the Christmas period (NBO Ms. 8° 2402 K). Storm seems to have found writing easy and natural. Because he published so much, he was very well practised and proficient in the art. His writing is always fluent and persuasive.

1.7 RECEPTION OF HIS WORK

1.7.1 There is no doubt that Storm was held in the highest esteem by the community of scholars. The French phonetician Paul Passy (1859–1940), writing in 1886 in *Dhi Fonètik Tîtcer*,[14] described him like this:

> Prof J. Storm, ov Kristiania, iz probabli dhi grétest pràktikal liNgwist, az ôlso dhi grétest fonetican, in dhi world. Hî spîks Inglic *kwait* laik a nétiv, Italian, Frenc and Djerman veri nirli az wel, and haz a praktikal noledj ov ôl Romàns and Tiutonik tœNz and ov 200 *Norwîdjan daialekts*!

Passy was not the only contemporary linguist to lavish praise on Storm. Henry Sweet wrote in 1879:

> Storm has long been known as the foremost authority on the pronunciation of the Romance languages, and his practical command of sounds is, as far as my experience goes, unrivalled. (Sweet 1879: 270)

Sweet is not as wild in his enthusiasm as Passy had been, but a single warm word is remarkable coming from Sweet, who was otherwise unfailingly rude and cantankerous. Five years later Sweet was still singing the praises of Storm's linguistic ability. It was reported in the *Proceedings of the Philological Society* for 1884 that Sweet had delivered a paper entitled 'The Norwegian dialects' on 21 March that year, and that:

> Mr Sweet said that he could bear the fullest testimony to the thuro accuracy and reliability of Prof. Storm's observations, having had every opportunity of putting them to the fullest test.

Sweet and Passy were close acquaintances, even friends, of Storm's, so perhaps we should look to the views of more neutral commentators. Jespersen knew and visited Storm, it is true, but he did not hesitate to write critically of Storm where criticism was due (see section 2.1.3.1), so it can be assumed that comments by Jespersen constitute a more objective contemporary view of Storm. In 1888 Jespersen reviewed *Franske Taleøvelser* (Storm 1887a), and wrote that:

> Prof. Storm's well-deserved renown as one of the leading language-experts of our time [is] a better recommendation for his new book than all the laudatory adjectives I could put together. (Jespersen 1888: 478)

So across Europe, or at least in Britain, France and Scandinavia, Storm's reputation went before him. He was acknowledged as one of the great linguists of the day, whose name could be taken as a guarantee of quality. He seems to have been less well known in Germany, although his *Engelsk Filologi* did achieve its international reputation by way of its German

---

[14] The predecessor of the *Journal of the International Phonetic Association*.

translation, and his *Franske Taleøvelser* appeared in two German editions. German reviews of his books were fairly uniformly enthusiastic, but as far as I can tell, his personal reputation was not nearly so great in Germany as it was in the other countries. I assume this was because, on the one hand, he did not work on the German language as an object of study and, on the other, because he was not as closely associated with the "German school" of phonetics as he was with the "English school" (see section 2.2.4.2). It is also significant that it was a British university which awarded him an honorary doctorate. His other formal academic affiliations were all in a southerly and westerly direction too. He was chosen to represent his country at congresses in Lisbon (1880) and London (1894). In 1872 he became a member of the *Société de Linguistique de Paris*, and a life member from 1874. He was also a corresponding member of the *Accademia degli Agiati* in Roverto, of the *Modern Language Association* of America, and of the *Kongelige danske Videnskabernes Selskab* in Copenhagen (Halvorsen 1901: 487).

1.7.2 It will become increasingly clear as this book progresses that Storm worked at the interstice of two axes: a vertical axis, so to speak, into Norway, and a horizontal one out into Europe. His Norwegian face and his European face were quite different from each other. While he was held in the highest regard by the international community of scholars, his views on Norwegian, and indeed on Norway, tended to make him unpopular at home. The Landsmål community, the proponents of what would later come to be called Nynorsk (see section 4.1.2), found his views on Landsmål infuriating and mistaken.[15] Their irritation can be felt in an article entitled 'Johan Storm paa Krigstien' ('Johan Storm on the Warpath') which appeared in the publication *Den 17. Mai* in 1902:

> One of the most able performers is little Johan Storm. At least once every equinox he has to come out. And it's always the same notes that 'blast' out of him. He knows that people have short memories, so the task is to grind out the same thing over and over again.

What these 'notes' were we shall see later, but it is sufficient to record for now that his views and the man who voiced those views ('little Johan Storm') were not well received in this community.

His views on the other emerging Norwegian standard, *Dano-Norwegian* (see section 4.1.2.5), were not well received by its principal advocate, Knud Knudsen. As already noted, Knudsen came in for a harsh and personal

---

[15] Storm's own spelling of *Landsmål* was *Landsmaal*, as was usual at the time. Throughout this book I use *Landsmaal* in quotations from Storm and his contemporaries, and *Landsmål* and *Nynorsk* are dictated as far as possible by the chronological context. The same applies to the name of the other variety of Norwegian: *Rigsmaal/Riksmål/Bokmål/Dano-Norwegian*. The fact that the *Rigsmaal* of Storm's day is not the same linguistico-political animal as modern *Riksmål* muddies the waters even more! (See section 4.1.2 on the Norwegian language situation.)

attack by Storm, and unsurprisingly he did not respond warmly to this onslaught. Knudsen's counter-attack reached its zenith in *Morgenbladet* on 9 June 1895:

> Prof. Storm and 'Morgbl.' on the language question in a way make up a long-standing engaged or married couple. Both are of the extreme right [*af højreste højre*] and are therefore in advance set against anything new which is put forward. Amongst other things, as I said, they are against all our attempts to reform the language, both the Landsmaal and the Dano-Norwegian reforms.

Unfortunately these somewhat hysterical words (headed 'K.K.'s Last Words on Language Reform') were printed posthumously, but they again indicate the reception Storm got when he polemicised against those whose views he did not share.

Even someone as outspoken as Storm did have his followers in Norway. Knudsen's charge of a marriage between Storm and the right-wing press is not unfounded, and these newspapers kept the reading public aware of Storm's successes and of his role as the principal institutional language authority of the day. From August 1902 Storm was linguistic adviser to the National Theatre, something which *Aftenposten* (19 March 1902) greeted 'joyfully'. *Morgenbladet*, Storm's media partner, exhibited the sort of irrational pride and adoration of which only a lover is capable:

> Professor *Johan Storm* is now engaged as the Theatre's linguistic consultant. A new element in the many and great services the professor has rendered to our native language would be achieved if he succeeded, in conjunction with the stage management, in cleansing our theatrical language of the errors and lapses of taste, which have all too often diminished the lustre of otherwise brilliant performances. (14 August 1902)

The news of Storm's work is received with rapture. Johan Storm would be the saviour of the theatre, casting his 'lustre' over it. Even the more popular newspaper *Verdens Gang* (The Way of the World) kept the public informed about Storm's work for the Norwegian language, announcing, for example, on 8 January 1903, that he had 'in preparation a proposal for new spelling rules, which are more in keeping with developments than those which currently apply in the schools'.

There were those who objected strongly to Storm, his views and his methods, but there can be no doubt that he was a high-profile figure in contemporary Norway.

1.7.3 We shall consider the reception of his publications, rather than of the person and what he stood for, when we look at contemporary reviews of those various publications. However, it is relevant to mention just two reviews here, in connection with his differing receptions at home and abroad.

In his predictably positive review of *Englische Philologie* (Regel 1882), Ernst Regel observes that:

> Only one person complains about Storm, and that is B. Schmitz (see his posthumous work in the second edition of the third supplement to the *Encyclopedia*). That deserving man is no longer with us, and I'm not going to go into details. I must just say this: his comments seem to be written in bitterness, and yet he had no real reason to be embittered towards Storm. (p. 407)

A less than positive reception is frowned upon by the international academic community, a community which should feel no bitterness, only gratitude, towards Storm for his great contribution to the international world of scholarship, since, in the words of Sweet's German review of *Englische Philologie*:

> Storm's book is nothing short of indispensable for anyone involved in English, in modern philology generally, or in general phonetics. (Sweet 1881: 1408)

The second edition of Bernhard Schmitz's (1819–1881) *Encyclopedia of the Philological Study of the Modern Languages, principally French and English* (1875–1881) is a work not dissimilar to *Engelsk Filologi/Englische Philologie*. It consists of an overview of philological literature, bound up with a commentary on that literature, and is divided into four parts: (1) Linguistics in General; (2) Literature on French–English Philology; (3) Methods for Independent Study of the Modern Languages; (4) Methods for Teaching the Modern Languages. The three parts of the *Encyclopedia* proper appeared in instalments between 1875 and 1877, and so were not able to take Storm's major publication on English into account. However, Schmitz later added three supplements (itself a very Stormian thing to do), and, as Regel noted, it was in the third supplement that Schmitz addressed Storm's contribution to English philology (Schmitz 1881: 125–138). Schmitz does have words of praise for Storm's work. He finds that Storm has performed a valuable service in reminding German scholars that the history of English language and literature did not end in the year 1600, and that older periods should not be overvalued vis-à-vis more recent periods of linguistic and literary history (p. 126). Schmitz also admits that Storm's notes on current English usage are admirable (p. 129). All the same, he is at great pains to find fault with the detail of *Englische Philologie*, and I am less diplomatic than Regel when I reveal that Schmitz picks a fight with Storm because Storm did not praise his work highly enough in *Englische Philologie*. The heart of Schmitz's fault-finding project lies in the statement: 'I mention in passing that he does the second edition of our *Encyclopedia* a great injustice' (p. 128). Storm is honest, certainly, and he does criticise Schmitz for not being completely up-to-date. Storm also corrects some errors, but he is complimentary to Schmitz where compliments are due (Storm 1892a: 11–13). Schmitz, like Knudsen, died trying to claw back his reputation from Storm's clutches, but Knudsen and Schmitz were not the only writers who attacked Storm because Storm had attacked them. It seems that objective reviews of Storm's work were uniformly positive, and negative tones are only to be heard when the reviewer nursed some personal bitterness towards Storm.

Schmitz's bitterness here seems positively friendly compared with the splenetic rantings of one 'Sproglærer J. Dahl' in his review of *Engelsk Filologi* which appeared in the newspaper *Bergens Tidende* in 1879. Now 'language teacher Dahl' was truly bitter. He was very upset by what Storm had written about his *Haandbog i engelsk* (Handbook of English), and Dahl's response, via his lengthy (27-page) review of *Engelsk Filologi*, probably says more about Dahl himself than it does about Storm. Dahl accuses the *Engelsk Filologi* of being 'a true product of our "local conditions"', of exhibiting 'bigotry, which, like all fanaticism, stems from a sublime and blind disdain for all common sense'. He concludes this tirade with the view that *Engelsk Filologi* is a 'one-sided, tendentious work' (p. 2). He criticises Storm's knowledge of English and of Norwegian, as well as the treatment of Knudsen by that loving couple, Storm and *Morgenbladet*. Dahl made a grave error in attacking Storm in this way, since Storm was never more devastating in his written criticism than when he was dissecting the writings of his opponents. Storm's response appeared, naturally enough, in *Morgenbladet* (17 November 1877), under the title 'En ny Art Anmeldelser' ('A new form of review'), and he concluded with some sound advice to Dahl: 'Si tacuisses, philosophus mansisses!'

This sorry little episode shows Storm's methods in full spate, but it also shows that he was not met with the same almost universal respect and enthusiasm by his countrymen as he was by overseas scholars (except Schmitz!).

1.8 POSTERITY

1.8.1 So much for the reception of Storm in his own lifetime, but what has become of his reputation since his death in 1920? We have considered some of the obituaries, some of the immediate reactions to his passing (section 1.4); but time is a great leveller, and glowing obituaries are no guarantors of a place in the history books.

The history of linguistics has a canon. Since the first general histories of linguistics were written there has been a mainstream of schools and scholars whose work, it is implied, forms the core of linguistic studies and teachings throughout the ages. This is not the forum in which to investigate this fact further, but the admission of a linguist to this historical canon, to this gallery of luminaries, is (whatever else it might indicate) evidence of their perceived greatness continuing beyond their lifetime.

Storm inevitably appears in specialist histories of those parts of linguistics in which he was particularly actively involved – thus in the *Index Nominum* to Sandved (1998) there are more references to Storm than to any other individual. (William Shakespeare comes a close second!) Storm is mentioned several times in the 1996 *Studies in the Development of Linguistics in Denmark, Finland, Iceland, Norway and Sweden* (Henriksen et al. 1996), four times in the paper on the study of phonetics in Scandinavia up to 1900 (Elert 1996), four times in the historical overview of Nynorsk language-research (Jahr 1996) and once in 'Dialektforskningen i Danmark med særligt henblik på forholdet til strukturalisme og sociolingvistik' ('Dialect research in Denmark, with particular regard to its relationship to Structuralism and to sociolinguistics') (Pedersen 1996). Counting references is a very coarse guide to the esteem accorded a scholar by history, but it does provide a measure of sorts. Matthews's (1993: 19) count of references to other scholars made in the 1958 *Readings in Linguistics* (Joos 1958) very tellingly points up the isolationism of the "post-Bloomfieldians" (to use Matthews's preferred term). Nine mentions of Storm's name might seem rather paltry if Storm was genuinely one of the greatest linguists of the late nineteenth century, as Passy's and Sweet's comments, as well as scattered comments in reviews and reports, imply that he was.

In another specialist history, however, where we might expect Storm to have a key role – a history of Romance studies in Scandinavia (Spang-Hanssen 1982) – his name is not mentioned once. There is, I think, a reason for this, namely that Storm's work in Romance studies became over-shadowed by the work of the following generation of Danish scholars. Storm's *magnum opus* in this field was his *Større fransk Syntax*, which fits perfectly Spang-Hanssen's description of what characterises Romance lin-guistics in Scandinavia:

> I think that more than anybody else [Kristian Sandfeld] has established the now prevailing Scandinavian tradition for synchronic syntactic studies in an empiricist style, that is to say with a minimal, but relatively solid, theoretical framework, and a mass of documentation. His first purely synchronic study, on subordinate clauses in French, is from 1909. (Spang-Hanssen 1982: 257)

Storm's *Større fransk Syntax* was his final work, the result of a lifetime's study, whereas Sandfeld's publication formed the basis for a *tradition*. We shall look at this question of Storm's position within Romance Studies in more detail in Chapter 3. On the whole, though, it is reasonable to say that Storm's contributions to Scandinavian dialectology and to the study of English and French have been remembered and given due recognition by history.

His contribution to phonetics has tended to receive both greater recognition and at the same time less recognition by history. Konrad Koerner (1995 and elsewhere) lists a number of different types of history writing in linguistics, one of which (type III) 'is intended neither to advocate a particular framework or "paradigm" nor to attempt to provide an argument in favor of a scientific revolution within the discipline' (p. 5). This is the general history of linguistics, the tradition in which the canon of "great men" has emerged. Brief histories in this genre tend not to mention Storm – he has not become canonical to that extent – but more detailed general histories do make mention of his phonetic work. This is what I mean by his phonetics achieving greater recognition by history than other areas of his work. An example of a general history of linguistics in which Storm figures is the volume from which I have just quoted, the *Concise History of the Language Sciences* (Koerner & Asher 1995). Here we encounter a very interesting phenomenon. *Because of* his relative marginality to the canon, Storm's *greatness* has become enshrined, or fossilised, in the history books. In general not much is known about Storm in the academic community, because little of any detail has (thus far) been written about him (see next section). Consequently, references to him and his work tend to be formulaic and predictable, which is what I mean by Storm receiving *less* recognition in this type of history. General historians of linguistics are unable to add to or detract from the received wisdom that Storm was in some way superlative. He is mentioned six times in Koerner & Asher (1995), on four occasions as a name in a list of key phoneticians of that period, and on the other two occasions in the following terms:

1 [Henry Sweet's] *Handbook* [*of Phonetics*] was a response to a request from Johan Storm (1836–1920), the outstanding Norwegian phonetician [. . .] (p. 385)

and:

2 Johan Storm was Professor of Romance and English Philology at the University of Kristiania (now Oslo), Norway from 1873 to 1912. He was a highly gifted phonetician, who exercised a strong influence on his contemporaries Henry Sweet and Eduard Sievers. (p. 398)

So Storm ('outstanding', 'highly gifted') and the importance of his work (as an influence on others) have become standard statements in the historiography of linguistics. One might have expected more detail on Storm and his work if he were truly so gifted and influential but, typically, no more detail is forthcoming. Perhaps a more specialised study of the history of phonetics in Scandinavia (Elert 1996) will provide more detail, beyond the formulas of greatness and influence:

Johan Storm (1836–1920) was professor of Romance and English philology at the University of Kristiania 1873–1912. Based on his own great
interest in the dialects of his homeland, Storm wrote an article in 1877 on
the great interest in dialect transcription in Sweden. He also presented
Lundell's dialect alphabet in Norwegian journals. He worked himself to
create a phonetic alphabet, which was particularly appropriate for the
Norwegian dialects. It was first published in 1884 in the journal *Norvegia*.
(p. 23)

Storm's phonetic work has passed into history as being of international
importance, but it is belittled by never receiving proper discussion on its own
terms. Even in this brief presentation by Elert, Storm's own work comes
second to what he did to publicise Lundell and Swedish work. Storm
remains the phonetician who was brilliant and influential, but nobody has
really shown much interest in asking why. You don't get to be called 'dhi
grétest fonetican in dhi werld' by your colleagues without some justification,
and that justification is one of the things that the present book has been
written to investigate.

   Why has history come to deal with Storm like this? It is partly due to the
comments his more famous contemporaries made about him. We have
already seen Sweet and Passy publicising Storm's skill as a phonetician,
and both Sweet and Eduard Sievers published important works on phonetics
in which they acknowledged Storm's influence on them. Sweet's *Handbook
of Phonetics* was written in response to Storm's request for 'an exposition of
the main results of Bell's investigations, with such additions and alterations
as would be required to bring the book up to the present state of knowledge'
(Sweet 1877: ix), and in this respect Storm has appeared to history as a sort
of catalyst, causing phonetic work to happen, rather than doing it himself. In
fact Sweet attempted in return to take the role of catalyst for Storm. In the
small and close-knit world of phonetics at this time, the principal actors were
frequently in contact with each other, trying to persuade one another to do
some of the large amount of work they perceived as important, but which
they did not have the time to do themselves. In the same year as the
Handbook of Phonetics was published, Sweet was writing to Storm, telling
him that he 'must clear off [his] book for the students as soon as [he] can
[since] it is a sin to keep such philanthropic works back' (NBO Ms. 8° 2401
J[iv]). Six weeks later he was urging Storm to 'bring out some general work of
intonation', and again the following month 'to publish something on tone'.
It was not a one-way street from Storm the encourager to Sweet the doer, as
the history books imply. The Preface to Sweet's *The Sounds of English*
(Sweet 1908) gives a sense of this dynamic milieu:

   In early youth I enjoyed the inestimable privilege of being a pupil of A. M.
   Bell, the author of *Visible Speech*, and of personally discussing phonetic
   questions with such authorities as A. J. Ellis, Prince L. L. Bonaparte,

J. Storm, and afterwards E. Sievers, together with many others – in fact with nearly all the pioneers of modern phonetics. (pp. 3–4)

As to Sievers, he refers to Storm's work and findings throughout his *Grundzüge der Phonetik*, and his debt to Storm is explicitly acknowledged:

> After Sweet's work, Storm's presentation of individual parts of phonetics (in his *Englische Philologie*, hereafter referred to simply as 'Storm'), which is now also readily available to Germans, is strongly to be recommended for study. (Sievers 1881: vii)

But in the *Vorwort* to the third edition (Sievers 1885) he specifically mentions Storm's influence on the nature of the book. The first edition (Sievers 1876) had been entitled *Grundzüge der Lautphysiologie* (Essentials of Sound Physiology) and was very much in the spirit of a science of speech rather than a study of languages. By the second edition of 1881 the title had changed to reflect the new emphasis on the phonetics of actual languages: *Grundzüge der Phonetik zur Einführung in das Studium der Lautlehre der indogermanischen Sprachen* (Essentials of Phonetics as an Introduction to the Study of the Phonology of the Indo-European Languages). As Kohler (1981: 162) tells us:

> Sievers made a deliberate move away from the medical and physical orientation of the research into speech sounds customary at his time, towards a linguistic outlook that was dominated by the diachronic approach from the 1870s onwards.

Sievers spells out Storm's role in this development:

> If in the second edition I have moved away from this point of view by the insertion of rather more numerous examples from foreign languages (which was made particularly necessary in the discussion of Bell's vowel system), this happened principally on the advice of Storm, who believed that the book would thereby be rendered more useful for the particular interests of the professional phonetician. (Sievers 1885: vi)

Storm steps forward in both Sweet's and Sievers's accounts as a sort of spokesperson for contemporary phonetics, advising on the needs of the burgeoning subject. In any case, the received view of Storm stems from these accounts; but the reality of Sweet's and Sievers's comments is a Storm actively engaged in setting the direction of phonetics, not just in his own work but through the work of his contemporaries too. (Hovdhaugen et al. (2000: 302) support the view that Storm's position in the historiography of linguistics is due in no small measure to his 'international networking'.)

1.8.2 A survey of the literature on Storm will not hold us up for long. There are only four book-length studies which concentrate on Storm, as well as one briefer publication.

Storm's phonetic alphabet continued to be used in work on the Norwegian dialects long after his death. Over the years it underwent significant modification but, being designed specifically for the phonetic transcription of dialects, has served its purpose very well, and has indeed, by virtue of being truly phonetic, been a more appropriate resource than the system advocated by the International Phonetic Association, which is at its heart phonemic. Unsurprisingly, then, we find a presentation of Storm's phonetic alphabet and its modifications compared with IPA symbols (Nes 1982 (1975)). By the time of the fourth edition (1982) Nes had collected 233 symbols from Storm's writings and from other dialectological studies which used Storm's symbols as a basis. Nes begins the presentation with an introduction, setting Storm's phonetic work in the context of earlier and contemporary phonetics, explaining the principles for Storm's choice of symbols, and comparing Storm's system with the IPA system. The introduction fills 19 pages and the list of symbols a further 10. This is a brief publication then, but one of great practical value, and, in the spirit of Storm himself, one based on impressive data collection.

In 1986 Helle Holter submitted a thesis to the Institutt for nordisk språk og litteratur, as it was then called, at the University of Oslo, subtitled *Johan Storm som språkpolitiker* (Johan Storm as a Language-Politician).[16] Holter focuses on Storm's contributions to various aspects of the Norwegian language and attempts to analyse his views on the language. This is a substantial study, and one based on close scrutiny of both published and unpublished materials, but it has itself remained unpublished. Arthur O. Sandved's 1998 book, *Fra 'kremmersprog' til verdensspråk: Engelsk som universitetsfag i Norge 1850–1943*, to which I have already made reference, takes a third area of Storm's activity into consideration, namely his teaching of and research into English. Sandved looks at this as part of his more general study of English from its emergence as a university subject in Norway up to the closure of the university during the Second World War. In 1999 Arne Juul published a short study of Storm, focusing on aspects of Storm's work of personal interest to Juul, principally Storm's relationship with Danish scholars and his work on language teaching (Juul 1999). 'In this article', Juul writes, 'I will focus on certain aspects of Storm which are of particular interest in the context of a Danish subject-history, when he is considered as a university-teacher and linguist' (Juul 1999: 51). Juul's personal approach makes this a highly readable and compelling introduction to Storm. An extended version (Juul 2002) has since appeared, and this further indicates Storm's power to inspire and enthuse those who read him.

[16] A big thank-you to Helle Holter for the long-term loan of the dissertation.

Juul's *Den levende fonograf: Nordmændenes Professor Higgins*, in conjunction with Sandved's book, perhaps indicates a small surge of interest in Storm and his work, at least in his university work.

There are good reasons why Storm's work is of continued interest and relevance. Language teaching has, since Storm's day, blossomed into big business, and for many the study of language teaching is coterminous with applied linguistics, that most populous wing of the rambling mansion which is linguistics. I shall suggest later that Storm and the other members of the "Anglo-Scandinavian school" of linguistics were in fact the founders of what we now call applied linguistics. Secondly, Storm and his like-minded contemporaries oversaw a shift in emphasis within the science of language from theory-driven studies under the Neogrammarians to data-driven studies.[17] There are indications that linguistics at the turn of the twenty-first century is undergoing just such a shift in emphasis from theoretical work towards more data-driven work on language variation and historical topics. Thirdly, the engineering of the Norwegian language is an ongoing issue, and I will suggest that, a century later, Storm's prophecies as to the development of written Norwegian have in some respects been fulfilled. Fourthly, that consummate and meticulous collector of data left a mass of material on late-nineteenth-century English, French and Norwegian, a treasure trove for scholars working on the history of those languages. Scholarship is not of value in and for itself, and any researcher who thinks that is simply arrogant. The adulation of Storm's contemporaries and of historiography made me *think* that this book might be worth writing, but the discovery that Storm still has so much to offer us today in our continued attempts to understand the nature of language and of individual languages *convinced* me that it was worth writing.

The present book is the first attempt to provide a unified description and evaluation of the full range of what Storm did. There are probably two reasons why this has not been done before. First, Storm was a conservative at a time when language radicalism was the order of the day in Norway, and he did not encourage disciples, who might have taken the task on. Secondly, in an academic world where the monograph remains the dominant mode of research output, it takes an individual with a somewhat eclectic, even eccentric, range of interests to cover all sides of Storm's life and work. I would not pretend for a moment that I am fully qualified to do this, but perhaps I have the (mis)fortune to be more of a 'Jack of all trades' than other historians of linguistics – or maybe I'm just more foolhardy.

As far as Storm would have been concerned, all his work grew from a common root, the living language. Institutionally his work has been divided up, because it has been important to phoneticians on one level, "Anglists" on another, learners of French on another, and so on. This "dismemberment" of

---

[17] See Robins (1974) for a discussion of the theory–data cycle in the history of linguistics.

Storm is continued in this book: to be both writable and readable, a book needs to be divided up into manageable sections, and it makes sense to dedicate separate chapters to different sides (institutionally speaking) of Storm's activity. However, these chapters are held together by two *røde tråder* (red threads) (to use the Norwegian phrase), two common themes: Johan Frederik Breda Storm, the human being, from whom the work literally flowed; and the notion of 'the playful life of the living language' ('det levende Sprogs spillende Liv') (Storm 1911a: xiv). The living language was what drove the man. He hated anything which "killed" language. He hated stultifying teaching methods, he hated artificial written forms, he hated anything which separated language from the people who use it. We started this part of the book by looking at the austere physical appearance of Storm. What Falk and Hambro sensed beneath the man's surface was a passion for language. This passion sometimes led him astray, and it sometimes made him enemies, but it made him impossible to ignore, and it is a passion which still has plenty to teach linguistics today.

2

ENGLISH

2.1 BACKGROUND

2.1.1 *Storm's Knowledge of English*

2.1.1.1 There is no doubt that Storm's knowledge of English was excellent. We have already heard his contemporaries' comments on the quality of his English, particularly his pronunciation skills. That most harsh of critics, Sweet, who spent plenty of time talking to Storm, praised both his pronunciation of the language and his usage:

> [. . .] his pronunciation of English and command of its idioms is so perfect that an ordinary observer might converse with him for hours without suspecting him to be a foreigner. (Sweet 1879: 270)

Sweet's implication is that *he* was no 'ordinary observer', so we assume that he was aware of certain non-native phonetic or idiomatic features. As we shall see later on in this chapter, Storm combined practical ability in English with a profound knowledge of the language's structure and history. How did he manage to achieve such a high level of competence in the language at a time when it could not be studied adequately at university level and when there was no proper provision for its study in the schools either?

Storm seems to have had the opportunity to learn some English while a pupil at Kristiania Cathedral School. Modern languages did not figure on the school curriculum when Storm was a boy, and it only became possible to study English formally in the grammar schools in 1857, two years after he had left school. Even then, provision for English in the schools appears to have been limited (Sandved 1998: 23). In his 1877 application to parliament for support in writing the *Værk over det norske Sprog*, Storm refers, however, to having learnt some English when at school and to two sources for this:

> Prof. L. K. Daa's brilliant teaching contributed in no small measure to this. Alongside that I took every opportunity to study the pronunciation of native speakers, especially the English, which I managed to reproduce correctly. (Storm 1877a: 2)

Ludvig Kristensen Daa (1809–1877) was a teacher at Kristiania Cathedral School during Storm's time as a pupil there. Daa is an interesting figure in many ways, but in our context he is interesting for his enthusiasm for things British, and for the striking parallels between his and Storm's careers. He appears to have been attracted to Britain via politics:

Especially characteristic of him is something he said in public [. . .] that, 'as soon as he began to think about political matters, he adopted the principles of the Whigs'; English reformist politics of the thirties became his great model, and English history one of his most important studies. He could give the impression of being an absolute "anglomaniac". (Koht 1926: 157)

Since Daa is described here as an 'anglomaniac', it is not surprising that he gave extracurricular teaching in English from which Storm was able to benefit. Daa was also a precursor of Storm's in language curriculum reform. In the year of Storm's birth he wrote to *Morgenbladet*, the newspaper with which Storm would later develop such a close relationship, on behalf of the students of philology, advocating replacing Hebrew with a modern language or Old Norwegian, a proposal he was able to see through in Parliament himself nine years later (Koht 1926: 158). In the same year he provided history teaching at the university ('his very first lecture topic was English history' (Koht 1926: 159)), standing in for Professor Cornelius Enevold Steenbloch (1773–1836) during the latter's illness; but when Steenbloch died, Daa failed to become his successor because, many thought, of his political views. Being sidelined because his face didn't fit in the contemporary political climate was something which Storm would experience too. Although Daa and Storm were of different political hues, it is likely that Daa was a significant influence on the young Storm. His love for English and his willingness to embrace causes he thought important may well have rubbed off on the impressionable, fatherless pupil at Kristiania Cathedral School. One further observation about Daa, made by Koht in his biographical account, could, in its generalities, also have been written about Storm:

He was one of the few Norwegian scholars who at that time maintained active links with foreign scholarship. He took part in conferences, not only in the Scandinavian countries, but also in England and France, the last time at the 1875 conference of Americanists in Nancy. Overseas scholars, who visited Kristiania, seldom failed to visit him in his home. (p. 167)

In addition to Daa's teaching, mixing with native speakers was evidently for Storm a successful means to acquiring a good knowledge of the language. The British colony in Kristiania numbered some 86 adults in 1864 and 94 adults by 1876 (Derry 1975: 15), and these figures do not include native English speakers from other parts of the world. Mixing with native speakers is a practice he would later recommend for his own students, although he was aware of its limitations:

By using every opportunity to mix with natives, together with diligent and sustained study, one can achieve much. But it remains definite that the appointment of native-speaker teachers of modern languages at the university is to a high degree both desirable and necessary. (Storm 1895a: 20)

Storm's recollections of his initial English studies indicate why simply mixing with native speakers is not enough for most language learners. *He* was able to produce the correct pronunciation, but others less gifted in this respect could not be guaranteed the same level of success. There is plenty of evidence that Storm had a remarkable ear for languages, even though this fact has assumed semi-mythical status. He had a great talent for distinguishing phonetic detail, and there is little point trying to guess where he learnt this skill. Without further adding to the purple prose on the subject of Storm's 'fine ear', we must acknowledge that his success as a practical linguist lay partly in his ability to apply a natural talent for this sort of detailed listening, remembering and reproduction of sounds.

In his 1887 'Om en forbedret undervisning i levende Sprog', Storm gives a fuller account of the process by which he learnt English:

As a schoolboy I learnt English at home of my own accord. First of all I read a bit of grammar, as much as was necessary to understand the forms. I pondered long over the pronunciation rules, which I found deeply unclear. I soon began to read a simple reader and from there went over to the novels of Marryat and others. I read book after book with increasing satisfaction and soon gained a satisfactory knowledge of the most important vocabulary. At the same time I took every opportunity to hear the language spoken by natives. Finally, when a student, I received some tutoring from an educated English lady, who spoke English unusually beautifully [. . .] (Storm 1887b: 182–183)

So Storm was one of only a handful of Scandinavian school children who studied English prior to the school reforms of the later nineteenth century. He wasn't able to study for an undergraduate degree in modern languages, but the undergraduate studies he followed were the best that someone with an interest in the modern languages could follow in 1850s Norway. His initial interest in the natural sciences (see 1.2.4 above) was very likely the outcome of a more general interest in the modern syllabus. The "modern subjects" or *Realia* embraced a wide range of disciplines which had in common little more than the fact that they were not the Classics. Although this course of study was the one under which the modern languages were organised institutionally, it was certainly not a course of study focusing on linguistic subjects, Storm's real concern. There does not appear to be any evidence showing why Storm abandoned this course of study and transferred instead to the traditional course in classical philology, but I agree with Sandved, who supposes that:

> Storm presumably came round to the fact that, despite everything, the old philology course constituted a better foundation for further studies in modern languages than the modern course did. (Sandved 1998: 66)

We have already dealt in Chapter 1 with Storm's subsequent travels, his exposure to the modern languages, and his immersion in the blossoming European linguistic milieu, so I won't go into it again here. However, we do have a sort of answer to the question of how Storm became such an outstanding scholar of English when he grew up in a country and at a time where the formal study of the language was not a serious option. He was fortunate as a boy to be at a school where there was – unusually – an opportunity to learn English, and he was fortunate to be living in the capital city, where he could mix with native speakers. He furthered his interests at university as best he could given the limitations on studying modern foreign languages, and finally he was able to put what he had learnt into practice during his period abroad in England and southern Europe. His ability to seize whatever opportunities arose for the study of modern languages (and opportunities weren't much better elsewhere in Europe – see below) built on a remarkable natural talent, and one which doesn't have to be mysticised. Storm was simply very good with foreign languages. They were his *métier*. Once again a comparison with Rasmus Rask is appropriate (see section 1.6.1 for a comparison of the two men's working methods).

2.1.1.2 Rask had attended a forward-looking school in terms of its language curriculum. Although he was not able to study English at Odense Cathedral School, he managed to learn some by working on his own, in addition to the Latin, Greek, Hebrew, Danish, French and German he learnt in school. Complementing this self-study, Rask, like Storm, sought out practical assistance (from 'a good friend' (see Linn 1996: 309)), and as a university student in Copenhagen he attended the lectures given by Thomas Christopher Bruun (1750–1834) (see section 2.1.3.1). Rask, then, like Storm, did what he could to gain a knowledge of the language while at school, found opportunities for conversation, and attended what classes he could at the university. Despite relatively little time spent in English-speaking countries, as is the case with Storm, Rask managed to achieve an impressive command of the language. Bruun is supposed to have said to Rask, 'Now you should see about becoming my colleague in Norway, for there are only few there whose English is so good' (Hjelmslev 1941: i. 156). It is clear from reading Rask's studies of English (see Linn 1996) that his practical command of the language was somewhat lacking in certain respects, so this is a rather sad indictment of the level of English among Norwegians in the early years of the nineteenth century. To be fair, Rask's dedication to English was to its earliest phases (e.g. Rask 1817) rather than to the modern language, and in addition he applied himself to a startlingly wide range of other languages.

However, we have already compared Rask's and Storm's working methods, and it is certainly appropriate to compare their "linguistic minds" too, learning languages to a high level in unpromising circumstances.

2.1.2 *English at the University*

2.1.2.1 The first teacher of English at the new Kongelige Frederiks Universitet in Kristiania was appointed 11 years after the foundation of the university as the successor to an earlier teacher of French, Mathurin René Orry, who had held his post from 1815 until 1822. Orry was the one exception to the new king's practice of non-intervention in university affairs. According to Collett (1999: 40), Carl Johan took the initiative of appointing Orry, initially as lektor and later as professor, without the university knowing anything of Orry's professional qualifications for the post. As had been typical further south in Europe up to this time, the post was anyway not a scientific one. Its holder was required to teach modern languages, rather than teach about those languages or undertake research into them, and consequently the teaching load was broad rather than deep. This first teacher of English, John Andreas Messell, was initially appointed in 1822 as lektor in English and Italian, but responsibility for the teaching of French was subsequently included in his job description. In 1834 Messell was named professor of these languages, although the increase in status did not bring with it any requirements for an increased level of scholarship. He remained in post until his death. In his description of the first 100 years of the university, Gerhard Gran states that 'neither Orry nor Messell was anything more than a practical language teacher' (Gran 1911: 306), but it should be said that Messell taught a wide range of literary and linguistic subjects, including Old French and Old English.

The notion of a university language teacher as a sort of mechanical language-teaching machine rather than an academic specialist lived on in the university, even when a profounder level of scholarship was required of such people. This is why Messell's successor, Carl Richard Unger, and his successor, Storm, had what nowadays seems like an extraordinarily broad remit. It is also true that the serious study of modern languages was a newcomer to the groves of academe, so it had not yet had the chance to be further subdivided in any clear and consistent fashion. There were fewer academic staff employed in universities then than there are today, so those staff were necessarily responsible for more general subject areas. Furthermore, it was still possible in the mid-nineteenth century for scholars to be expert in a number of different spheres. All this is well known, but the fact remains that the early university history of modern languages as the responsibility of 'language masters' (see next chapter for more on these language masters) meant that those involved in the teaching of 'the new philology' maintained an unacceptably burdensome workload for an unacceptably long time, a workload to which they could never do proper justice.

2.1.2.2 On Messell's death the university authorities decided that his replacement should be a scholar rather than purely and simply a language teacher, and that the post should take on a 'scholarly character' (quoted in Sandved 1998: 26). It is only to be expected that a new university in the renewed capital city of a new nation in the modern world should seek to enhance the status of the work being undertaken within its walls. Messell's post had covered English on the one hand and French and Italian on the other, a rather arbitrary collection of languages, dictated in large measure by what that individual was able to teach. A more informed decision was taken about the nature of the post in 1850, a decision which served merely to increase the linguistic requirements of the post's holder, and which shows what a vague idea the university authorities at that time had about the nature of linguistic scholarship. It was agreed that, if the post were to have the required academic status, the new appointee would 'immediately find himself in the area of comparative linguistic study' (quoted in Sandved 1998: 26), and that the post should cover Romance languages as before, but in addition to English it should also embrace Old Norse, an obvious concern for a nation busily establishing its future by reference to its past. Thus the hopelessly demanding post advertised was this:

> a lectureship in Germanic and Romance philology with an obligation to lecture on the comparative grammar and history of the Germanic languages and of the most significant Romance languages. (quoted in Sandved 1998: 27)

For some very obvious reasons there was only one applicant, Unger, appointed in 1851 as a lektor and promoted to a professorship the following year. Unger's appointment was in Romance and Germanic philology, but, as I remarked above, there is no way he could have given equal attention to all aspects of his subject. He managed to cover English and Romance topics in his teaching, but his publications were exclusively in the Germanic sphere, specifically Old Norwegian (Storm described him as 'the Nestor of Germanic language research' (1878b: 1)). This was not just whimsy. In 1845 the university regulations had, at Daa's instigation, admitted Old Norwegian as an optional alternative to Hebrew in the *filologisk Embedsexamen*, the traditional philology course. Although he is remembered in linguistics perhaps first and foremost as the author (with Peter Andreas Munch (1810–1863)) of a pioneering grammar of Old Norse (see Hovdhaugen et al. 2000: 216), it is worth saying a little bit about Unger here, since he was the person (in name if not so much in practice) responsible for English philology prior to Storm taking up his appointment at the university.

Unger studied philology at the University of Kristiania without taking the *filologisk Embedsexamen* since, 'like so many other outstanding linguistic talents [he] had difficulties with mathematics' (!) (Heyerdahl 1975: 392), which was then included in that examination. He was, with P. A. Munch, one of the first students of the ancient Scandinavian languages at the university. After periods of study in Copenhagen, Paris and London he was appointed a research fellow in 1845. This led to the *lektorat* in 1851 and the professorship in 1862. Although he was principally concerned in his own work with Old Norwegian, he did lecture on English, German, Spanish and Italian literature. His knowledge of Shakespeare appears to have been particularly good, and 'it was said that U. possessed a knowledge of the Shakespeare and Calderón literature probably unrivalled by anybody else at that time in Norway' (Heyerdahl 1975: 395) – not that there was much competition!

2.1.2.3 I have already referred on several occasions to Arthur O. Sandved's 1998 book, *Fra 'kremmersprog' til verdensspråk: Engelsk som universitetsfag i Norge 1850–1943* (From 'Shopkeeper's Language' to World Language: English as a University Subject in Norway 1850–1943). I make no apology for this: it is an excellent study and I would be foolish not to make full use of the research carried out by Sandved and presented in that book. In my review of Sandved's book in the journal *English Studies* (Linn 2000), I wrote the following:

> [. . .] the book, one of value to scholars the world over interested in the history of [English Studies], its practitioners and its students, is written in a language most will find inaccessible [. . .] and it is to be hoped that a version of the book for an English-speaking audience will become available. (Linn 2000: 175–176)

For these two reasons – the quality of Sandved's study and the desirability of its contents being accessible to an English-speaking readership – the rest of this section on the development of English Studies at the University of Kristiania during Storm's tenure of the professorship will be based on the account in Sandved (1998).

2.1.2.4 We noted in Chapter 2 that Storm's appointment at the university was the outcome of the new legislation of 1869 giving the modern subjects a new status in the schools. What Storm taught, however, and what his students studied, was the outcome of another legislation of 1871, the Law on Higher Education Courses for Public School Teachers (*Lov om Embedsexamener for Lærere ved de offentlige Skoler for den høiere Almendannelse*). This was promulgated in direct response to the law of 1869 and replaced a previous ruling concerning examinations for teachers of the modern subjects dating from 1851, when Unger had been appointed. Until the time of Storm's appointment, as we have seen, the teaching of English was distinctly ad hoc. With Unger its content had become more scholarly, but its frequency had diminished. There was not anyway much demand for English teaching in the university. Some modern language work was required for the *Examen Artium* (the school-leaving exam for which the university was responsible from 1869 to 1882) and this had to be examined, but English was simply an optional subject for the undergraduate *Examen Philosophicum*, and not a popular one at that. With the 1871 legislation things changed, and the study of modern languages within the new teacher-training course was at last given a clear syllabus:

> Detailed knowledge of French and English language and literature. For both literatures, a special study of one of the more important authors, genres or periods [. . .]

> Knowledge of the fundamentals of the history and development of the English language from Anglo-Saxon and from Romance.

> Practice in the spoken and written use of both languages.
>
> (Quoted in Storm 1879a: 1)

In Chapter 2 we met the personnel responsible for the teaching of the three sides to modern language study – literature, language and practical skills – and noted that Storm himself covered all three to a greater or lesser extent. In fact he found it hard to let go, even after the appointment of new colleagues to take some of the responsibility off his shoulders. The new colleague, who would cover the practical teaching of English, was Sidney Thurgood ('den elskværdige [the amiable] Sidney Thurgood' (Hambro 1950: 129)), a stalwart of the expatriate community and secretary to the committee of St Edmund's Anglican Church from 1901 to 1925. After Thurgood's appointment Storm continued to hold practical classes, partly because the practical side to language was for him the most important – it was where his heart lay – but partly also because he felt that all modern language work at the university was his domain. He was the obsessive collector. He liked to introduce new courses rather than consolidate old ones. He liked to bring in more examples rather than formulate a theory about them. He restlessly planned new projects before he had finished existing ones. His teaching and other scholarly activity did cover a wide range of subjects, but in an unforced observation to his brother Gustav early on in his career (9 May 1875), Johan wrote of his 'best and most original lectures, namely those on Eng. Gramm.' (NBO Brevsamling 86). The focus of Storm's activity would change as his career progressed and he came to devote more and more attention to Norwegian, but, despite the scope of his teaching, and despite his apparent wish to maintain this scope, there was an obvious hierarchy of preference in Storm's mind. He did not find time to lecture on French grammar until 1897, where he described grammar in general as one of his 'favourite objects of study'; so in reality, while he clearly aimed to keep the whole landscape of modern languages at the university under his control, it was no more possible for him than it had been for Unger, Storm's greater efforts notwithstanding.

There was, then, a clear syllabus for trainee modern language teachers from 1871 onwards, and it was a syllabus that covered the full range of *Filologi* as it was understood at that time – literary history, the history and comparison of the languages and the development of practical skills. However, there was no officially prescribed reading, no *pensum*, in support of the requirements for the examinations. This fact was the chief motivation behind *Engelsk Filologi*, which aimed to provide students with a detailed guide to the available reading (see section 2 below). August Western wrote in 1894, a quarter of a century after Storm had taken up a post at the university, that:

> We, who belong to that first cohort of those who have been through the linguistic-historical teachers' exam under the existing regulations, know from our own experience how much time can be wasted, because we didn't know what or how we should read. (Western 1894: 83)

Western was Storm's greatest disciple, and these words were not meant as a criticism of the great man, but rather of the committee responsible for laying down the *pensum* to be followed. Nonetheless Storm did have overall responsibility for the teaching, examination and administration of English, and, knowing him as we do, it should not surprise us to learn of this lack of a formal, neat and tidy list of works.

What was in practice studied by the students during these years was eventually codified in the *Studieplan* of 1898. The English literature to be studied is specified in detail here. Thus specific *Canterbury Tales* are listed, and a choice of Dickens novel is allowed between *The Pickwick Papers* and *David Copperfield*. By contrast the specific requirements for the language side are vague:

> Detailed knowledge of contemporary English and French language, together with practice in the spoken and written use of the same.

> An overview of the historical development of the two languages.

> For Anglo-Saxon H. Sweet is to be read: *Anglo-Saxon Primer* and *First Steps in Anglo-Saxon*.

> (Quoted in Sandved 1998: 90)

Both the lack of detail and what is actually prescribed are in fact very telling, and they show the personality of Storm fully reflected in the empire he had created. This *Studieplan* is a codification of what had in practice developed. It is radically different from the regulations which had been set down in 1871 at the beginning of Storm's career and which, in theory, he should have been following in the intervening period. The first language requirement specified in 1871 had been 'Knowledge of the fundamentals of the history and development of the English language from Anglo-Saxon and from Romance'. In 1898 this has moved into second place and has been significantly reduced to the very general 'overview of the historical development of the two languages'. By contrast, the very general 'practice' in using both languages in written and spoken form, which in 1871 did not lead to any specified level of attainment – it was merely exercise – takes pride of place 25 years later, when a teaching programme had actually developed, and now encapsulates 'detailed knowledge' of the contemporary language. Of course Sweet's *Anglo-Saxon Primer* (first published in 1882 and still in print today) was (and possibly still is) the leading textbook in its field, so its inclusion here should not surprise us, but it is worth noting that the one text specified in this part of the *Studieplan* is written by Storm's old friend, Sweet. The lack of detail here is as interesting as what is prescribed. Because Storm's teaching tended not to stick to any definite pattern and must from time to time have appeared to lack direction, and because Storm was not someone who would commit himself to things, those who had been taught by him must have found it hard to formulate a description of the syllabus. They could state with absolute certainty that detailed knowledge of the contemporary languages lay at the heart of his teaching, and that the teaching also involved some sort of (hard-to-follow) overview of the history of the languages, but they were possibly unable to see any more precise structure than that. We have already considered the views of Storm's students when I attempted in Chapter 2 to paint a picture of the man, so I shall not return to those views here. Instead, and again drawing on Sandved, we shall briefly consider the sort of students who studied English at Det kongelige Frederiks Universitet during Storm's reign.

2.1.2.5 Sandved asks four major questions about the students who studied English in this period and I shall summarise his answers to those same questions in this section, as well as providing further commentary on them from the point of view of Storm. The questions are:

1 How many students chose English?
2 With what subjects did those students combine English?
3 To what end did the graduates use their education in English?
4 Who were those who studied English?

2.1.2.5 (1) In purely numerical terms, 183 students took English in the period 1874–1910. This represents 3.3 per cent of the total student body in that period. At first glance this looks like a tiny proportion of students passing through the university, and in one sense it is indeed a small percentage. But to these students may be added the 134 (2.4 per cent of the total number) students of modern foreign languages who took the course of study laid down by the 1871 regulations, but did not choose English. The 1871 regulations for the linguistic-historical teachers' exam divided the available subjects into four groups from which candidates had to select two. These four groups were: (1) Classical Philology; (2) Norwegian with Old Norwegian and German; (3) History and Geography; (4) French and English. Thus it was possible for students not to take English, but it was not possible to take English without French.

In a letter to Thomsen (17–23 December 1882) Storm gives his views on the teaching of these groups of subjects. He believes that students taking group 2 suffer on account of Unger being too gentle with them ('un ange de bonté') and consequently the best students turn to group 4 instead. As to group 1, Storm states that the linguistic component is more or less as demanding as it has always been, but that the history and philosophy which used to 'round off' the old syllabus are now lacking. He does not know much about group 3 (history and geography), he says, but his attitude is typical of a traditionalist when discussing "new" subjects:

As to the History-Geography group, I have little knowledge of it, but it is evident that such a course of study must be to a large extent one-sided.

Storm would have liked a different arrangement, one which he regards as more 'rounded', less 'one-sided', and which he sets out in this letter to Thomsen:

(a) English, (German?), French, with their respective ancient languages, and Latin, with perhaps associated World History?

(b) German, Norwegian, Old Norwegian, Old German, Gothic, with Latin and World History?

Such groupings reflect Storm's own passions, but the complete concentration on languages old and new, with grudging admission of history and complete rejection of geography, would not, I imagine, have been very popular!

In the nineteenth century Det kongelige Frederiks Universitet was still overwhelmingly a training academy for the traditional professions. Thus in this period 46.1 per cent of students studied law, 24 per cent studied medicine and 17.1 per cent studied theology. Once this combined student body, comprising 87.2 per cent of all students, is taken out of consideration, it will be realised that numbers taking the linguistic-historical teachers' examination were not actually that small when viewed alongside figures for comparable courses of study. The 317 students taking this exam may be compared with the 190 students in the same period who took the mathematical-scientific teachers' exam. Like the linguistic-historical teachers' exam, this was divided into four groups, two of which had to be selected by candidates. The four groups were: (1) mathematics and astronomy; (2) physics and chemistry; (3) natural history and geography; (4) either

(a) Norwegian with Old Norwegian and German or (b) French and English. So group 4 of the scientific exam comprised either group 2 or group 4 of the linguistic-historical exam. It is interesting to note that the modern languages are still seen as part of the *Realfag*, the modern syllabus in general, on the one hand, by contrast with the Classics on the other. It is interesting too that the Germanic language English is nonetheless, from a Norwegian perspective, felt to have more in common with French than with the continental and peninsular Germanic languages.

Total numbers of modern language students peaked around the year 1890 – the largest number of English students was 20 in 1892 – but this figure corresponds with a surge in student numbers across the university at that time. There were in each year of this period typically between three and eight 'linguistic-historical' students with English, according to the figures provided by Sandved, and a similar number without English. A final point to note with regard to student numbers passing through Storm's classrooms is that, of the 183 students taking English, only four were women: one in 1896, one in 1899 and two in 1906 (Sandved 1998: 169) – all therefore towards the end of the period.

2.1.2.5 (2) As we noted above, students were required to study two groups of subjects, so, in addition to English/French, students were required to select a second cluster of subjects. The statistics given in Sandved (1998: 179–180) do not hold any surprises. Students with an interest in English and French tended naturally to turn to the third modern European language available for study, namely German, which came in group 2 along with Norwegian. The statistics also indicate – and again there is no surprise here – that numbers choosing classical philology diminished rapidly during the late nineteenth century, such that 14 students took group 1 between 1884 and 1893 and no student took this group in the period from 1904 to 1910. As a consequence of the demise in classical philology, numbers taking group 3 rose accordingly.

Despite his lifelong and passionate advocacy of the *living* modern languages, Storm was the product of the education he had himself received and deeply regretted the decline in the Classics. On 3 December 1876, five years after the new exam regulations had come in, and drawing on his initial experience of the new system, Storm wrote a long letter to Sophus Bugge, professor of comparative Indo-European philology). Storm had started writing to Bugge in 1869, just before he set off on his study tour. What started as simple factual questions about Old Norse became a much fuller and more wide-ranging correspondence, and one which continued until 1903 (see NBO Brevsamling 2).[1] By 1876 Storm's letters to Bugge were frank and

---

[1] Storm often mentions Bugge in his letters to Thomsen.

full, and this letter of 3 December is worth quoting in some detail, given the rather surprising views contained in it:

> [. . .] The study of the modern languages, far from undergoing any decline, is each day gaining greater and greater significance, and becoming more and more the principal subject in the schools. These languages are already that in the Modern School [Realskolen], particularly in the English stream of the Middle School and in the Modern Sixth Form [. . .] Men who have concentrated all their energies on them are now more than ever needed as teachers of these subjects. The current teachers' exam has shown itself to be insufficient. It gives rise to merely desultory and fragmentary studies, and particularly those who only study modern languages in general demonstrate a regrettable immaturity in their whole outlook and great looseness of detail. I believe therefore that, besides resuming the old philological course, a new teacher's exam must be set up covering *philology of the modern languages in conjunction with Latin* [. . .] I wish for the main emphasis to be placed on the historical development of the modern languages, but believe that the study of Latin is absolutely necessary, both because the study of this language is in itself so stimulating, and because it is impossible to gain any deeper insight into the development of French without further knowledge of Latin. But I wish for the study of Latin to be largely limited to linguistic study, based on wide reading [. . .] (Storm's emphasis)

Storm doubtless rejoiced over the rapid advances made by the modern languages in the wake of the revised school programme from 1869. He is clearly much less enthusiastic about the teaching he is himself engaged in. His complaints about the 'desultory and fragmentary studies' ('spredte og fragmentariske Studier') are the result of the exam system which required students to take a range of different subjects from two of the specified groups. He must have felt that his students did not show the same dedication to English that he showed himself, although seeing what was required of them, such lack of single-mindedness was unavoidable. It should be remembered too that Storm, while not as offensive as Sweet, was by nature very critical of anything other than the highest standards. Given his condemnation of his students' studies as 'spredte og fragmentariske', it is hard to imagine how the introduction of yet another subject, Latin, would improve matters. Despite his professional and personal attachment to the modern languages, he clearly believed in the importance of the Classics, and he stated the same opinion, but much more forcibly, seven years later:

> The modern syllabus [Realdannelsen], especially in its current form, does not provide the general pedagogical and human benefits that a classical education does [. . .] Firstly the modern syllabus has no centre, no principal subject [. . .] If the modern syllabus does have any principal

subject, it must be *mathematics* [. . .] But this subject is of such an abstract and specialised nature that it is probably the least fitting of all the subjects to constitute the heart of education [. . .]

What a different impact the classical syllabus has, in the reading of the immortal masterworks with their classical form and eternally young, truly human and often elevated thoughts! (Storm 1883)

Nobody was forcing Storm to express this view, to the detriment of his own subject and his own students, and in support of the modern subjects' arch-enemy. So why did he?

That he was dissatisfied with the current arrangements for the linguistic-historical teachers' exam is fully understandable. He viewed it as an arbit-rary collection of subjects, which were impossible for students to address in detail, and he felt that the syllabus needed more structure. Why he suggests that mathematics should form the central subject in this structure is unclear. My guess is that he proposes maths precisely to demonstrate how unsuitable it would be in this role. Storm's discursive technique was always to set up a thesis in order to demolish it, and it was therefore desirable to set up the thesis in such a way that demolition was a straightforward job. So maths is shown in typically Stormian detail to be 'the least fitting of all the subjects to constitute the heart of education'. Why does he then go on to praise the Classics? Why not propose French or English as a centre for the *Realfag*? On a later occasion he does sing the praises of French as a fitting replacement for the Classics within education:

The study of the ancient classical languages, Latin and Greek, this previously unsurpassed means of education, is in line to be scrapped in Norway. Now the French language is, in my opinion, the only one that can to any extent replace this loss for general education [. . .] It is a true descendant of Latin, bearer of the classical traditions [. . .] French is the world language which should not be missing from a general education. (Storm 1897a: p. v)

French may be the bearer of the classical traditions, in Storm's words, but it is merely a substitute for the real thing, for the 'previously unsurpassed means of education'. We return therefore to the original question: why did Storm have such a high regard for a classical education when his life was dedicated to the form of education which replaced it, in Norway as elsewhere in Europe?

Storm, as we have already remarked, had received a classical education himself, and one of his first scholarly undertakings was the revision of Curtius's Greek grammar (Curtius 1866). He is not the only person in history to have believed that the education they themselves had received was more demanding, more worthy and more profound than the education received by subsequent generations. Many readers of this book will certainly identify with Storm on this. (I and the rest of my generation firmly believe that the O[rdinary]-level examinations we took when we were 16 were considerably harder than the G[eneral] C[ertificate of] S[econdary] E[ducation] examinations which replaced them!) Storm's own university education in the Classics was specialised and could therefore be seen as deep rather than broad. It had been developed over a long period of European history and so was venerable. And a classical education did not lead to a specific profession. It was a general education, untainted by the vulgarity of practical application.

Storm was caught with one foot in the past and one foot in the future, and this caused him to stumble. Just as his intellectual identity has to be defined by seeing him with one foot in Europe and another foot in Norway (I've now given him four feet), so it needs to be understood as belonging in part to the world of Henry Sweet and in part to the world of Ludvig Cæsar Martin Aubert (1807–1887), professor of Latin at Kristiania from 1840 who held that position for 35 years, 'thus educating a whole generation of Norwegian philologists' (Hovdhaugen et al. 2000: 263). Storm could not be expected simply to throw off what he knew and what was part of his own make-up, especially when the alternative to it, from the educational point of view, was so 'fragmentary' and unsatisfactory. When he wrote in 1883 of classical education and 'the reading of the immortal masterworks with their classical form and eternally young, truly human and often elevated thoughts', Storm was to a large extent suffering from nostalgia and using these feelings in his rhetoric about the state of modern language studies. He would never have abandoned the study of the modern languages – they had been his passion since childhood – but as always he is prepared to use whatever rhetoric it takes to raise awareness of problems and to improve the status quo. He humiliated himself in 1877 in his attempt to get better pay, and he humiliates his subject and his students here to raise awareness of the need for reform in teaching methods. He concludes in 1883 as follows:

> My principle for education in the modern languages, which I have always pointed out, and which has gained a significant following abroad, is that one must begin at the beginning, i.e. start from the simplest basis for language, the living language.

Ah, the living language again! He never really wanted to bring back the Classics, did he?

This section on subject combinations amongst students of English/French students at the university has come a long way from the simple statistical information with which it started. However, Storm's attitude towards the Classics is important. It seems curiously at odds with his better-known views on language teaching and study; but Storm was not a simple person and neither was his situation a simple one. Modern languages had been taught at the university from 1815, it is true, but this doesn't mean that Storm didn't need sometimes to show respect to the Classics. Even in his new, forward-looking university the relationship between the classicists and the modernists cannot have been easy, especially since the Classics were so conspicuously in decline, and this decline was so conspicuously to the advantage of the modern languages.

2.1.2.5 (3) The answer to the question 'To what end did the graduates use their education in English?' is brief and undramatic. Whether full-time or part-time, whether temporarily or permanently, 93 per cent (170 of the 183 English students) became secondary school teachers. This is totally unsurprising: that is what they had trained to do, and given the growth in modern languages in the schools, there was a demand for suitably qualified people. Storm may have insisted on the importance of knowledge for knowledge's sake, but the teaching he provided served the same end as the teaching provided by his colleagues in law, medicine or theology. The university remained the training ground for Norway's professional classes.

Storm's students left the university as fully qualified members of a profession, but their social background, i.e. who they were when they arrived in Storm's lecture hall, was not so uniform or clear-cut.

2.1.2.5 (4) Sandved (1998: 181 ff.) problematises in detail the process of drawing up appropriate categories for the division of the student body by social background, and I shan't go into this here. Suffice it to say that statistics drawn from Sandved conceal a number of difficult questions about how to categorise different forms of parental employment/class/economy/cultural concerns and so on. It is certainly relevant for us to know who Storm taught, for whom he wrote his lectures, on whom he practised his teaching, by whom he was surrounded during his time at the university. However, this is a book about Johan Storm and not about his students, so I shall do no more here than give a few simple figures, with apologies to the detailed statistical presentation given by Sandved – but Sandved was writing a different book.

The fathers of students taking the linguistic-historical exam with English/French in the period 1874–1910 were most often in trade (14.8 per cent), in industry (14.2 per cent) and in the Church (11.5 per cent). Students with mercantile backgrounds of various sorts choosing English is not very surprising, given the perceived, nay actual, importance of English as a language of business. This analysis is supported by the fact that students with family backgrounds in trade who took the linguistic-historical exam *without* English/French do not appear in the top three categories. Of these students 15.7 per cent had family backgrounds in industry, 14.2 per cent in the Church, 12.7 per cent in education at secondary school or university level and only 11.9 per cent in trade. Interesting among those students without English/French is the greater presence of those whose fathers worked in education. Here, of course, the native language and the national heritage language of Old Norse provided a greater attraction.

2.1.2.6 We now have a pretty full picture of the English, and by association the French, that was taught in Det kongelige Frederiks Universitet during Storm's occupancy of the Chair. I have referred above to Storm's 'empire' and to his 'reign'. These were not unmotivated descriptions. Storm was the first proper scholar of the modern languages at the university – for different reasons Messell and Unger can be discounted – and he held office for exactly 43 years. I have described Storm as 'Victorian', which he most definitely was. His reign at the university cannot perhaps be compared with the 64-year-reign of Queen Victoria, and nor can his empire be compared with that presided over by the queen. However, Storm presided over university subjects which he can be credited with establishing in Kristiania and which grew in popularity and stature under him. His influence and fame spread far beyond the university and indeed far beyond Kristiania and Norway, and it is that fame with which we are concerned in this book. But the university was his "seat" (his Chair, his *Cathedra* and his power base), and his emissaries permeated the teaching of modern languages throughout Norway:

> But even when this dwindling band [those who continue in Storm's spirit in the secondary schools], the band in whose consciousness the old professor still exists as a living person, is completely gone, the continued traces of Johan Storm's work will still exert their influence for many a year, and the impact of them will probably never completely disappear [...] So, year after year, and for years to come, without knowing it, hundreds and hundreds of young people leave our schools as 'Johan Storm's pupils'. (Broch 1936)

Well, to an extent this is the hyperbole one expects in this genre of writing – a tribute to Storm on the centenary of his birth. Nonetheless, one can't help wondering whether the justified fame Norwegians have throughout Europe for their skill in foreign languages (especially amongst the British, who are equally famously dreadful at foreign languages) isn't in part due to the influence of Storm through these teachers, and their rational and practical method of language teaching. This is speculation, but Storm's influence from his seat in the university across geographical space and through historical time is undeniable.

2.1.3 *The University Study of English in Europe*

2.1.3.1 Storm and Det kongelige Frederiks Universitet were not the only ones in Europe establishing teaching and research into modern foreign languages in the course of the nineteenth century. In this book we are looking at Storm in two lights: Storm the Norwegian and Storm the European. Part of understanding Storm the European is to see him in the context of colleagues elsewhere trying to do the same things as he was, whether phonetics, dialectology, reforming teaching methods, steering the course of university disciplines or whatever. So in this section we will briefly consider the development of English Studies (and by association French Studies as well) in other northern European countries which were in some way academically linked with Norway.

Prior to the foundation of the university in Kristiania in 1811, and to an extent afterwards as well, Norwegians tended on the whole to travel to Copenhagen for their university studies. This was a logical choice, since Copenhagen was the capital of the Danish kingdom of which Norway was part until 1814. Above I mentioned Thomas Christopher Bruun, whose lectures on English Rask attended from 1809 onwards. Bruun (see section 2.1.1.2) lectured in English and French at the pædagogisk Seminarium in Copenhagen from 1800, and his post clearly indicates that teaching in English and in French were linked together at that stage, and that these languages were first and foremost of interest to would-be teachers. In 1802 Bruun began teaching at the university as well, where he was appointed extraordinary professor of English, and where he held practical classes and lectured on English authors (see Nielsen 1979: 268–269). We can see here a clear antecedent of the teaching model that Storm would inherit.

The situation in Denmark in the first decade of the nineteenth century was much the same as it would be in Norway half a century later. Education in modern foreign languages was introduced into the grammar schools at this time and teaching in the pædagogisk Seminarium responded to that development. To begin with English languished badly in the schools, partly due to the lack of suitably qualified teachers and partly, as had been the case in the eighteenth century too, because English skulked in the shadow of French and German. There were political reasons why English was unpopular in Denmark in the early nineteenth century (see Linn 1996: 312) and we don't have to go far back in time to find an aesthetically negative attitude towards the English language in Denmark. Charles Julius Bertram wrote in 1749 of the popular Danish view of English as the 'Scum, Dregs, and Refuse' of all languages (see Linn 1999: 185).

Bruun was then the first to bear the title of professor of English language and literature at the University of Copenhagen (K. Sørensen 1971: 94). On Bruun's death in 1834 the post in English remained unfilled until 1851 when one George Stephens took up the position (see Linn 1996: 310). He was appointed in the same year as Unger was appointed to his *lektorat* in Norway and, like Unger, he was subsequently awarded a professorship. Like Unger too his main interests lay outside English, in Stephens's case in the realm of runology. Unlike Unger, though, Stephens was a dilettante, an interesting man (see the 1996 study by Kabell) but certainly not a scholar of Unger's standing. As Sørensen (1971: 94–95) relates:

> It was only when Otto Jespersen was appointed professor in 1893 that it became possible to study English on a sound basis.

Jespersen's appointment in Copenhagen can be compared with the appointment of Unger in Kristiania as a conscious attempt by the university authorities to break away from modern-language teaching as a practical, pedestrian undertaking, and move towards placing it on a more scholarly footing. After Stephens's departure, reports Nielsen:

> In a document of 14 March 1893 the Faculty went through the four applicants, and, with regard to the fact that one of them was an Englishman, emphasised that there was here 'no question of a post simply for a language-teacher', the position was 'a strictly academic post, which covered the complete range of English philology'. The document concluded by recommending Otto Jespersen (1860–1943). (Nielsen 1979: 276)

Interestingly, this transformation in the status of English came about much later in Denmark than in Norway; but in both countries developments in the subject of English at university level were linked to individual scholars. With Jespersen, Denmark got its Storm, one might say, a versatile and brilliant scholar in his early 30s who would go on to dedicate his life on the one hand to the university which employed him and on the other to the international development of linguistics. To be fair, Jespersen achieved a greater eminence than Storm, and there are clear reasons for this – reasons of personality, of opportunity, of presentation – but they will take us further away from the course of English Studies in Europe in the nineteenth century, which is the job in hand. Having mentioned Jespersen, however, with regard to the development of the study of English, it is perhaps worth remembering that it was reading Storm's *Engelsk Filologi* which helped to launch Jespersen's linguistic career, and from that point on Jespersen evidently regarded Storm as the master, although the admiration was not always mutual. In 1885, only a few years after coming under the influence of *Engelsk Filologi*, Jespersen was writing to Storm:

> Permit me to send with this letter the two first sheets of a little English grammar *of the spoken and written language*, which I intend to publish as soon as possible. I am most anxious to hear the opinion of an expert on this attempt to provide a slightly more contemporary grammar than those used up to now. (NBO Ms. 8° 2402 J^i, 7 June 1885)

Storm was initially very enthusiastic about Jespersen. He became aware of Jespersen the year before (1884) and wrote to Thomsen (22 November 1884): 'I believe that in him I have found a promising young phonetician.' By 1890 the paternal tone has turned into admiration: 'He will soon become Scandinavia's leading phonetician.' However from this point on Storm starts to grumble more and more about what he perceives as Jespersen's arrogance and lack of respect. Storm's interest in Jespersen finally dissipated on the publication of Jespersen's *Fonetik*. Storm was apoplectic about what Jespersen wrote about him, and his fury rumbles through several letters to Thomsen. In handwriting that is difficult to read, he scrawled on 3 January 1898: 'I have neither the wish nor the time to bother any more with J.'

2.1.3.2 In Sweden the teaching of modern languages at university level probably goes back to the seventeenth century, but it was for a long time the responsibility of the so-called language masters. Since the teaching provided by the language masters focused on French, with other languages very much as add-ons to the principal activity of French teaching, I shall deal with the language master tradition in more detail in the next chapter (section 3.1.3.3) – see also Zettersten (1983). Suffice it to say that there appears to have been some teaching of English at the University of Greifswald (until 1815 in Swedish territory) as far back as 1686 (Zettersten 1983: 44) although no detail of this teaching – provided by Johannes Sebastian Saltzmann according to university records – survives. Teaching by language masters in Greifswald was introduced in 1754, but English was not included in this provision until 1777. English teaching at Åbo University (now in Finnish territory (Turku)) began in 1725 and is the longest established. Uppsala joined Åbo in 1736 and Lund instituted English teaching in 1738 (or there-abouts – see Bratt 1977: 55).[2] Although Lund was the last to bring in English teaching, it clearly had, in the person of Ifvar Kraak (1708–1795), a highly gifted teacher (see Bratt 1977: 55 ff.). After Kraak the English teacher at Lund assumed the status of docent. Bratt (1977: 58) reports that 'a docent-ship did not bring with it any salary', but at least the post-holder was on an equal footing with other academic staff of the university. Christopher Daniel Bunth (1761–1831), who took over the *docentur* in 1786, wrote a number of teaching books in language and literature, and his successor, Håkan Fredrik Sjöbeck (1768–1828), wrote a dissertation in 1794 on the history of the English language. So in Lund there was a real commitment by the university to the teaching and study of English, and by the end of the eighteenth century there was even a nascent research culture.

The situation in Uppsala was rather different. It is possible that English had a higher profile in Lund due to that university's proximity to Gothenburg and thereby to trade with Britain (Bratt 1977: 62). In any case, opportunities for studying English in Uppsala were much fewer in the eighteenth century, until Carl Gustaf Mannercrantz (1721–1794), a

[2] Åbo and Greifswald were both lost to Swedish territory in the early nineteenth century, and I shall make no more mention of them here, since they were not part of the Swedish linguistic milieu known to Storm.

dedicated and productive teacher, sought and was granted permission to teach English in 1772. The patchy provision of English teaching, linked closely to the presence of individuals willing and able to provide it, continued in Uppsala, and Bratt (1977: 154) reports that there is no mention of English teachers at Uppsala University during the first three decades of the nineteenth century. There were a number of able language masters from 1830 onwards, and an *adjunktur* (lectureship) in French and English was established in 1846, replacing the old language master positions, and supplementing a similar post in German and Italian from 1837. Thus, although the tradition of modern-language teaching goes back further in Sweden than in Denmark, in what is nowadays Sweden's oldest university it was very ad hoc. A chair in modern languages was proposed in 1850 but the motion was rejected by the university. Eventually a chair was created in 1858 for Carl Wilhelm Böttiger (1897–1878), the adjunkt in German and Italian. This professorship in 'modern European linguistics and modern literature' was gradually subdivided into specific language families and then specific languages over the following decades (see Bratt 1984: 49), and it was only in 1904, with Axel Erdmann (1843–1926), that a chair in English *language* was specified. Erdmann was one of the leading lights in the Scandinavian teaching reform movement (see section 2.3) and one of those closely involved with discussions about language teaching reform at the 1886 Philologists' Meeting in Stockholm. It is interesting to note how these people, whose careers took similar institutional routes in the three peninsular Scandinavian countries, should have had such common interests and interacted so closely.

To return to Lund for a moment, where the climate for the teaching and study of English had been so much more favourable than at Uppsala in the eighteenth century, a professorship in modern languages was set up here by virtue of a rather eccentric benefaction of 1813. The professor of Greek and Oriental languages, Matthias Norberg (1747–1826), donated the means for such a chair provided that it went to his nephew, Jonas Stecksén (1773–1835). Stecksén proved himself competent, and in 1816 was appointed to a full professorship in English, French and German, although without many of the rights of the other professors. Because of the unusual nature of his appointment and the oddity of a professor in something so vulgar as modern languages, Stecksén was, according to Bratt (1977: 159), 'treated more like a language master than a professor'. The presence of other private language teachers in Lund (as also in Uppsala), coupled with very limited interest amongst the students in studying modern languages (there were five takers in 1825, only one of whom studied English (Bratt 1977: 160)), would indicate that Stecksén's professorship was not a success, and although modern-language teaching had got off to such a promising start in Lund, the early nineteenth century constituted a dip in its development. After Stecksén's death, the *Professor Norbergianus* was reconstituted as a chair in modern languages and aesthetics, but now with all the normal rights of a professor at Lund University. The chair remained unoccupied for some years and was eventually filled in 1840 by Carl August Hagberg (1810–1864), who was until then docent in Greek in Uppsala, and who, like Storm, had recently returned home from a period of travel abroad. Hagberg became a distinguished Shakespeare translator, and Sven Rydberg (1789–1865) (who had occupied the Norberg professorship as a caretaker from 1835 to 1840) looked after the language teaching. After Hagberg's retirement the post was reconstituted again, now as a professorship in 'nyeuropeisk lingvistik och modern litteratur', following the contemporary lead of Uppsala, and new chairs in aesthetics and Nordic languages were set up. As happened in Uppsala, the chair was subsequently subdivided into Germanic languages on the one hand and Romance languages on the other, and eventually Erik Björkman (1872–1919) in 1904 took up a new Germanic chair with responsibility for English language. He had, like his three predecessors, studied in Uppsala, and he left a year after his appointment in Lund to become the first professor of English language at the newly founded Högskolan i Göteborg (Gothenburg College).

Despite the longer history of English teaching in Sweden than in Norway, thanks to the existence in Sweden of longer-established universities, English as a university subject cannot be said to have been on a really firm footing until the later nineteenth century. This is represented by the appointment in 1860 of the historical-comparative linguist Emmanuel Matthias Olde (1802–1885) as professor at Lund (Sven Rydberg, although eminent, had held a post in philosophy and merely helped out by teaching English language) and of Erdmann to the Uppsala Chair in Germanic languages in 1892 (later moving to English language). So Kristiania did not lag behind the more ancient Scandinavian universities in the field of modern language studies, specifically English studies, and Storm was in fact the first scholar of really international importance to occupy a Chair of English philology in a Scandinavian university. This certainly contributed to his international reputation in English language studies. The situation of French was rather different in the Scandinavian universities, as we shall see in the next chapter, and this different situation also had its role to play in Storm's fluctuating fortunes as an international authority on the Romance languages.

2.1.3.3.0 With Germany and Britain we are moving further away from Norway, but the development of English as a university subject in both these countries needs to be considered briefly as we build up the context for Storm's work on English. Germany led the way in university-level teaching and research in English, and it was in Germany that the *Englische Philologie* was published, the work which really established Storm's influence and status. Britain is of course the homeland of the language. (Storm's pioneering concern for American English is something we will come back to a bit later on.) English is evidently not a foreign language in Britain, so its position as a university subject and its mode of study raise different issues altogether – but Storm's relationship with Sweet and other British scholars is significant against this background.

2.1.3.3.1 The growth in the study of English in Germany was directly related to political factors. During the eighteenth century the dominance of France began to diminish and the position of Britain began at the same time to strengthen; thus the desirability of learning French, which had previously been unquestioned, began to diminish too, and knowledge of English came to be viewed as an important skill. This situation was strengthened during the nineteenth century until 'the Industrial Revolution made English the language of the spirit of the times' (Finkenstaedt 1983: 51). There was not such a direct relationship between historical events and the study of English in Scandinavia, where it was probably more a case of following Germany's lead in educational matters.

Language masters dominated the early history of university English studies in Germany too. These teachers and, by association, the subjects they taught were gradually looked down upon with the steady "intellectualisation" of university studies. Finkenstaedt (1983: 90) cites Schröer (1887) when he states that by the late nineteenth century there had been a hard battle to raise up English and Romance philology 'from the shackles of a superior language-master subject [. . .] and into being an autonomous science [. . .]'. With the intellectualisation of English language studies during the nineteenth century, attention came to focus on the earlier varieties of the language, specifically Old English. In the climate of the German university system, the new philology really had to prove itself. Even those involved in the teaching reform movement needed to earn their reputations by turning to historical philology. Storm was fortunate in Norway, in his new university, not to have to carry all this baggage with him:

It is probable that English, as the youngest of the philologies, wanted to be particularly "serious" in its emphasis on Old and Middle English. The fact that even "reformers" like Viëtor and Schröer worked intensively on the earlier periods in their publication and teaching work points to that. In any case this focus clearly characterised English Studies everywhere until the First World War. (Finkenstaedt 1983: 67)

As in Norway the English that was taught in the universities was often the servant of the requirements for student teachers, and the emphasis in the schools in the late nineteenth century was firmly on the written language. Outline syllabuses were published in leading journals of the day: *Anglia* in 1884 (R. P. Wülcker) and *Englische Studien* in 1889 (E. Koelbing). (*Englische Studien* specialised in the review of new language teaching materials and contributions to the teaching reform debate at school and university level:

see section 2.3.) These syllabuses are noteworthy for their concentration on early varieties of English and on literature, even though they were idealised syllabuses proposed by reformers in leading reforming journals. Wülcker's proposed syllabus begins with 'phonetic lectures [*Lautphysiologisches Kolleg*] with special emphasis on the modern languages' and 'Neuenglische grammatik' in the first semester, but thereafter historical and literary study predominate. Koelbing allows even less room for the study of the modern language. Wülcker's stipulation that every semester should contain 'exercises in spoken English, in "parlieren"' (1884: 134) should be noted however, and both proposals allow for a period of study abroad.

As to chairs, which is one of the yardsticks we have employed so far in establishing the status of university English studies in the various countries, German chairs formally committed to English (rather than professorships in some more general subject which could include English) are the product of the second half of the nineteenth century. Ordinary professorships in Romance languages tended to come first, given in part the more academic status and greater social prestige of the Romance languages as opposed to "utilitarian" English (Finkenstaedt 1983: 55). The first ordinary professorship in Romance languages was established in 1867 (Adolf Tobler (1835–1910) in Berlin). Ordinary professorships in English tended to be established after extraordinary professorships had been in place first, so this further delayed the establishment of such chairs. The first proper chairs were established in the early 1870s, and once the ice had been broken, the rest of the German universities followed quickly, such that:

> Within one generation (1872–1904) English philology at all existing German-speaking universities had been provided with its own professor, and by 1900 there were only a few places where there was still no ordinary professor. (Finkenstaedt 1983: 59)

Admittedly Storm's professorship in English and Romance philology from 1873 still combined English with other languages, but, despite its much shorter history, Norway was, in the last quarter of the nineteenth century, very much on a level with the other cognate European countries with regard to the university provision of English. And Norway was in fact well in advance of the language's homeland.

2.1.3.3.2 English arrived late at the medieval universities of Oxford and Cambridge, and the birth pains were considerable. As Aarsleff (1983: 169) notes:

> [. . .] the general state of the English universities between 1750 and 1850 was not such that the new philology could hope to prosper within their walls, or even gain admission.

Such work of a philological nature that was carried out rested by and large in the hands of amateurs, 'people who had more enthusiasm than scholarly acumen' (Aarsleff 1983: 169). Anglo-Saxon studies had long been of interest in Britain, and Oxford had a short-lived lectureship in Anglo-Saxon in the mid-seventeenth century, and a new post (the Rawlinsonian Chair) in this academic area was established in 1795, but the learning exhibited by its holders was, at least until the mid-nineteenth century, not impressive. The situation was not much better in the Scottish universities (Aarsleff 1983: 178). British scholars in the early and mid-nineteenth century who were serious about the study of English found their way to German universities (as Sweet did) and to a lesser extent to Copenhagen (at least in the case of Benjamin Thorpe (1782–1870), English translator of Rask (Rask 1830)).

English philology, more generally and in the richer form understood by Storm, did not penetrate the walls of Oxford until much later in the century and the establishment of the Merton professorship in English language and literature in 1885, 16 years after Storm's appointment to the university in Kristiania. The post was advertised in very general terms. The professor would be required to 'lecture and give instruction on the history and criticism of English language and literature, and on the works of approved English authors' (from Palmer 1965: 79). Given such a broad remit and such a novel post, there was a large field of applicants. Sweet of course did not apply, believing his reputation alone would be sufficient to secure him the job, but, as we have seen, he did not get the post and was intensely bitter about it. Instead the post went to Arthur Sampson Napier (1853–1916), at the time *professor extraordinarius* in Göttingen, who had trained in Germany – where else could he have trained? The position of the subject of English at Oxford, and of modern languages more generally (see next chapter), during the nineteenth century and on into the twentieth was never an easy one, and there were many in the university who did not view them as fit objects of academic study. After heated debate (see Palmer 1965: chs. 6 & 7) a statute was finally approved by the university in 1894. This statute ordained that the Merton professorship should be amalgamated with the Rawlinsonian Chair of Anglo-Saxon and a new chair in English literature established. It also decreed that a syllabus be drawn up. The topics for study decided upon by a 'Board of Studies' (constituted under the terms of the 1894 Statute) were the following (from Palmer 1965: 113):

1. Old English Texts (*Beowulf* and Sweet's *Anglo-Saxon Reader*)
2. Middle English Texts (*King Horn, Havelok, Laurence Minot, Sir Gawain and the Green Knight*)
3. Chaucer (selections) and *Piers Plowman* (selections)
4. Shakespeare (about six plays)
5. History of the English Language

6.   History of English Literature to 1800
7.   Gothic (*St Mark's Gospel*) and translations from Old and Middle English
8.   Critical paper
9./10. Special Subjects

This was a course of study designed for native speakers, and so practical language classes did not have a part to play. Nonetheless, with its total disregard for the modern language and its almost exclusive emphasis on early literature, this syllabus shows Oxford to have been completely out of touch with linguistic developments in Europe, specifically those stemming from Kristiania and the professor of English and Romance philology there. Sweet held a readership in phonetics at Oxford from 1901 – he did eventually get his Oxford post, although it wasn't a professorship – but 'he had little or nothing to do with the making of the English School' (Palmer 1965: 141). On his death in 1912 he was not replaced, thus Oxford managed to avoid the wind of change blowing from Europe for even longer.

Cambridge had admitted English earlier than Oxford had, allowing its study from 1878 as part of the modern and medieval languages tripos (course), but it was not until 1926 that it became possible to study English on its own. From the outset the bias of the course was naturally historical, and changes up to 1926 served only to add more literature components. Writing in 1885, Sweet took a dim view of the new Cambridge tripos:

> [. . .] it is a litl dishartning to find a body of English professors drawing up a scheme of modern languages, and deliberately omitting from it all mention of fonetics, the very backbone of the study – and this three years after Storm's *English Filology* has been made generaly accessibl in the German edition. (Sweet 1885a: 594)

As the nineteenth century progressed, new universities were established, universities without centuries of tradition and which correspondingly had a more modern outlook. Although established in 1832, the University of Durham offered no systematic teaching in English until the twentieth century (Palmer 1965: 63). University College, London, with its Utilitarian outlook (by contrast with Durham's theological one), however, appointed a professor of English language and literature shortly after its foundation. The Revd Thomas Dale, dean of Rochester Cathedral, took up this post in October 1828 (Palmer 1965: 18) and the courses he proposed to teach, as outlined in his inaugural lecture, bore all the hallmarks of an eighteenth- rather than a nineteenth-century approach to English:

> 1.   The History of the Language, comprehending a view of its origin, formation, progress and perfection. – I use the term perfection in a relative sense (for absolute perfection can be predicted of no language whatso-

ever); but we may assume that a language to whose stock of words no material addition has been made for upwards of two centuries, may now be accounted *stationary*, or perfect in its proportion to its capacity.

2. The Philosophy of the Language, under which head I include the classification and analysis of its constituent parts, or sorts of words; their relation to, and dependence on, each other; the principles of pronunciation and orthography; the etymologies of words; the construction of sentences; the force and harmony of periods; in short, all that relates to the genius and structure of the language.

3. The Use and Application of the Language in various kinds of speaking and composition, commencing with the plain and perspicuous, and proceeding upward to the elevated and majestic style. (Palmer 1965: 19–20)

Dale left this post after two years, but in 1835 took up the equivalent post at the newly founded King's College in London, where the chair was instead in English literature and history, reflecting the Evangelical (moralistic) principles underlying the foundation of the college.

Higher education also became available outside the capital during the nineteenth century, and English was a natural subject to be taught in the new university colleges springing up in the industrial cities of the Midlands and the north of England for the education of the working classes. The first such was Owens College in Manchester (1850); this was later joined by Leeds (the Yorkshire College of Science, 1874), Sheffield (Firth College, 1879), Birmingham (Mason College, 1880), Liverpool (University College, 1881) and Nottingham (University College, also 1881). Teaching in these new institutions focused on English literature and more recent English literature at that, perhaps another reason why the ancient universities were unwilling to introduce modern studies. However, George Moore Smith (1858–1940) wrote to Jespersen that 'in his teaching at the University of Sheffield he had been able to use the chapters [of Jespersen's *Progress in Language, with Special Reference to English*] particularly dealing with the history of English, whereas his students did not have so much interest in the rest, which deals with the development of language in general' (Juul et al. 1995: 209). An interesting exception to this apparent lack of interest in general linguistic issues in the new university colleges (subsequently universities) is Liverpool. According to Palmer (1965: 141), Sweet was offered the post of lecturer in English language at Liverpool in 1898, but turned it down. Whether or not Sweet was in fact offered any post at Liverpool, either a lectureship or a professorship, appears to be clouded in mystery (Mike MacMahon, personal correspondence). But the phonetician and language-teaching reformer Wilhelm Viëtor served in the German department there from 1882 to 1884, i.e. when *Der Sprachunterricht muss umkehren!* (Language Teaching

Must Change Its Ways!) was published (see 2.3.1 below), and Richard John Lloyd (1846–1906), with Storm, Sweet, Jespersen, Lundell, Passy and others one of the initial editorial board members of Viëtor's *Phonetische Studien*, was reader in phonetics at Liverpool from 1899. Under different circumstances Liverpool could perhaps have become a centre for the new philology based on phonetics and language teaching reform. These new colleges, built on a mixture of civic pride, industrial wealth and social principles, did not initially give cause for glee from the point of view of academic English in the language's homeland. Palmer (1965: 64) concludes:

> By the 1880's, then, English studies were in a curious state. They were expanding rapidly, but the expansion was only lateral, within the lower levels of the academic hierarchy. And, as is so often the case with hasty developments, the foundations were ramshackle and lacked proper coordination.

When these colleges received their university charters in the years around the turn of the century academic standards began to rise rapidly, but in Storm's lifetime there was nothing in England to challenge the standing of Kristiania as a centre for the study of the English language.

2.2 *ENGELSK FILOLOGI/ENGLISCHE PHILOLOGIE*

2.2.1 *The 1879 Version*

2.2.1.1 Storm's *Engelsk Filologi* appeared in its first (Norwegian) edition in 1879 with the full title:

> *Engelsk Filologi. Anvisning til et videnskabeligt Studium af det engelske Sprog for Studerende, Lærere og Viderekomne* af Johan Storm, Professor i romansk og engelsk Filologi ved Kristiania Universitet. *I: Det levende Sprog* [English Philology. Guide to the Scientific Study of the English Language for Students, Teachers and the Advanced Reader [. . .] I: The Living Language]

Storm first mentions such a work in May 1877 in a letter to Thomsen. He has been badly wounded by the failure of parliament to support his study of Norwegian, and he seems to take on the work which would eventually lead to *Engelsk Filologi* as an escape from the work on Norwegian and the painful associations it now has for him. His original plan was to include French:

> I have in the meantime allowed my great work, which was so demanding, to rest for a while, and am now writing a *Guide to the Study of English and French Philology*, from which I expect a certain degree of satisfaction.

By December 1877 Storm had dropped the idea of a French section, and by the following year the provisional title showed where the emphasis was going to lie:

Anvisning til Studiet af engelsk Filologi, med Indførelse i den fonetiske Literatur [Guide to the Study of English Philology, with an Introduction to the Phonetic Literature]

The final title, although concealing the phonetic bias of the book, at least appealed to a wider audience.

Engelsk Filologi was published in Kristiania and was intended for the home market. Storm specifies that it was written in direct response to the 'new linguistic-historical teachers' examination' (Storm 1879a: 1). However, he already had his eye on the international market, and the second page of the book states that 'eine deutsche Bearbeitung wird vom Verfasser vorbereitet' ('a German edition is being prepared by the author'). That further work in this area could be expected from the author is also indicated by the fact that this is only volume 1. We remember that it was the written language which dominated in school education in Germany and that this was reflected in university education. In marked contrast to this tradition is this first textbook for university-level English to be produced in Norway, dealing as it does with Storm's obsession, the living language. It is true that the Norwegian tradition of basing language learning on the spoken form is due very much to Storm and his proselytisation, and subsequently to the Quousque Tandem movement (see 2.3.2 below), but the living language at the heart of language education in Norway actually pre-dates Storm. English was introduced into the *Folkeskole* in the early 1870s in some places, specifically along the south coast, for practical reasons:

We know that where English was introduced in the 1870s, one of the main reasons was, as we would now say, 'the need for practical language proficiency', which both individuals and society as a whole had. It was a particular desire to provide help in mastering those situations would-be merchants and seafarers would encounter. (Gundem 1979: 27)

The study of 'the living language' in Storm's sense of that phrase on the one hand, and acquiring practical language skills on the other, are not the same thing. In fact Storm condemns purely practical teaching 'which neither has nor needs any science' (Storm 1879a: vi–vii). Nonetheless Storm's dedication to the spoken language was not based on a void in Norway. He could count on the support of the Folkeskole tradition of English teaching which, according to Gundem, gradually seeped up into the higher schools. So the production of a book of this sort, even though it was intended only as a first volume – 'The subsequent sections are intended to encompass grammar and language history' (p. ix) – would not have caused the same surprise in Norway as it might well have done in some German university circles.

2.2.1.2 Forord/Fortale

Storm begins the preface to *Engelsk Filologi* with a definition of what he means by 'the living language' (*det levende Sprog*). Since this notion is so central to what Storm believes linguists should study, and so central to how he believes the Norwegian language should develop, it is worth quoting him at length on the subject. *Det levende Sprog* forms the basis for Storm's view of the study of language, and it correspondingly forms a basis for modern phonetics, dialectology and applied linguistics, as well as a basis for the ethos of the Norwegian Riksmål movement. This is not an exaggeration, and here is Storm's explanation:

> This first part of my *Engelsk Filologi* deals with "the *living* language". The word is here used in its broadest meaning, not just relating to the living spoken language, but relating to the literary language up to and including the Bible and Shakespeare, since up to that point literature and language are the property of the people and live on in tradition. Beyond that time they cease to do so. Spenser no longer belongs to the British public. His language is too remote from the current language to be generally accessible. (Storm 1879a: i)

So the living language is the language in either variety, written or spoken, which is *real* or *alive* to its users. This is in striking contrast to the conventional object of philological study – the ancient literature, and forms of the spoken language which have undergone change.

One can't help feeling that, when Storm is writing about language in general, he is really writing about Norwegian. Thus when discussing the orthographies of European languages (1871: 128) he remarks, 'just as the process by which the language develops goes unnoticed, so should that of the orthography also be.' It is the conventional view that Storm's views on the contemporary development of Norwegian were inspired by his knowledge of the development of other longer-standardised languages such as English and French. The opposite may be true to some extent in that his current, day-to-day concern with the development of his own language exercised an influence on what he wrote about other languages, almost as though he were drawing up his views on Norwegian in safer, less politically motivated arenas. In the 1881 *Englische Philologie* he writes of his wish to 'free the English language as far as possible from all foreign elements':

> I should like to remove from it all baubles, everything artificial, everything puffed-up. I should like, so to speak, to show the *language in its naked beauty*. (Storm 1881a: vii)

Such an aim is a vain hope for an "omnivorous" language like English, but is just the sort of rhetoric to be heard in contemporary debates about Norwegian. In any case we can certainly say that his attitude towards and treatment of individual languages stemmed from a true general linguistic philosophy, that of *det levende Sprog*.

He goes on:

> The spoken language is the source. It is that which decides what is idiomatic and what is not. The written language is obviously the noblest form of the language, constituted by the nation's great authors and built up generation by generation. But many artificial elements, learned Latinisms, fashionable French phrases and grammatical pedantries intrude here and tarnish the purity of the language. (Storm 1879a: ii)

These words are a continuation of Storm's linguistic manifesto. This is his first major academic book, and its opening salvo is not a series of acknowledgements to other scholars or apologies for the book's potential shortcomings, but a linguistic programme. And he continues to demolish previously held linguistic certainties: 'The highest authority in languages is not the grammarians [. . .] Above the grammarians stand the authors, and above these stands usage' (Storm 1879a: ii). He is clearly in the realms of a general philosophy. This is a statement about 'languages'. Such abstractions seem a peculiar opening to what is after all a student textbook in English. But these notions are strongly felt and form the basis for all Storm's work, so he needs to state them here at the beginning – the beginning not only of this book but of the volumes which will follow, as well as the beginning of his serious publishing career.

There are two more "programmatic" paragraphs following on from what we have already presented, and like the ones we've already dealt with, they begin with a bald, controversial statement of fact. The first begins: 'Until now grammar has been either one-sidedly practical or one-sidedly historical' (p. ii). Storm wants to rectify this situation, to exemplify a new approach to grammar which reconciles the (in his view) anti-practical approach of the German School (p. vi) with the unscientific approach of the Norwegian practical tradition. He wants to rectify the faults of existing school grammars with their 'endless parade of arbitrary rules together with their many equally arbitrary exceptions' (p. ii), by showing how 'both rules and exceptions can be explained and become pleasurable and clear instead of a torment' (p. iii). However Storm was emphatically not a card-carrying Neogrammarian. Jankowsky (1972) has explained with great clarity that there was much more to the group of linguists who have been called Neogrammarians than simply an obsession with the exceptionlessness of sound laws. Storm certainly shares a number of their ideas, some of which he seems to have been advocating just as early as the better-known German scholars with whom they are associated. For example Jankowsky writes:

> To those inclined to give full credit for having recognized the importance of everyday speech to modern linguistics only, it may come as a surprise to

read that as early as 1878, Brugmann and Osthoff, in order to develop sound principles for comparative linguistics, based their demand for dealing with contemporary languages on the necessity of avoiding the literary language and of coming to grips with the 'echte, naturwüchsige, reflexionslose alltagssprechen'. (Jankowsky 1972: 133)

Well, here is Storm only a year later with a much stronger formulation of this idea: 'The spoken language is the source.' Storm's interest in dialects was at least in part inspired by the same understanding as led Hermann Paul to dialect studies – 'it would bring him closer to language reality' (Jankowsky 1972: 157). However, in one important respect Storm was independent of the mainstream Neogrammarians. In the words of the final "programmatic" paragraph:

> Language is an expression of the human spirit. It is not a product of unchanging laws like dead, senseless nature [. . .] It is largely regular, but its laws grow and modify with it. (pp. ii–iii)

Here as elsewhere Storm is constantly trying to reconcile the Norwegian and the (broadly) European. He was able to see the best in both and create an original, but better picture as a result, his own special vision of *det levende Sprog* at the heart of linguistics. As he wrote in 1881:

> The intention in the present work is not to oppose the Historical School. Quite the contrary. There is no movement that I wish to support more in the mainly practically inclined North. The intention is simply to *complete* their researches via an attempt to give the modern period its due, as I attempt to penetrate the spirit of the living language. (Storm 1881a: vii)

It would be possible to go on citing line after line of the 1879 *Forord* and, given that it is written in Norwegian and is therefore inaccessible to many readers, I am tempted just to provide an English translation here and have done with it. This is powerful stuff. It is the rhetoric of a man in the white heat of something he passionately believes in, and it represents a view of language we can still benefit from reading today. However, the book you are reading is trying to understand and explain Storm, to deal with the "why" beneath the "what", so I will now, instead of just letting Storm speak for himself (by far the best way – see Linn (2001)), give a summary of and commentary on the rest of this important piece of programmatic writing.

Storm's own position vis-à-vis the international academic community emerges unambiguously from the allegiances he professes in the course of this *Forord*. Gaston Paris's 'fitting' words are quoted (p. iii), and Henry Sweet is praised in extravagant terms. (Mutual adulation between Sweet and Storm in prefaces became something of a habit.) By contrast, Storm takes the opportunity to criticise members of the German School, specifically Mätzner, who 'does not observe the living language sharply enough' (p. iii).

(Interestingly, Storm formulates this criticism rather more carefully and indirectly in the German edition of the book!) Another group he criticises – and it almost goes without saying that Storm criticises somebody or other – is those who are too proud of their own practical linguistic skills. This criticism is a rite of passage for Storm, a symbolic rejection of the young Storm and the adoption of a new role. He is no longer the language "whizz", but the mature scholar, the linguistic sage. He was just into his 40s when he wrote this book, a sort of unofficial *Habilitationsschrift*. In his only other book-length publication to date, he had not been particularly humble about his own practical language skills. However, the mature Storm explicitly denegrates such skills as superficial:

> As soon as one can speak a couple of foreign languages, one immediately thinks one is something out of the ordinary. One fancies so easily that one "speaks like a native". With more scientific study in pursuit of the truth, this disappears. The deeper one penetrates, the less one realises that one can do. But one does not become despondent, since one has much to rejoice over in the fact that one has solved many mysteries, and the unresolved problems spur one on to new discoveries. (p. vi)

This is clearly the mature view. No longer are quickly acquired transitory thrills enough. Instead true 'rejoicing' is to be achieved in the searching. There is something religious in the equivalence between 'scientific' ('videnskabeligt') and 'truth-seeking' ('sandhedssøgende'). The ultimate human endeavour, the scientific endeavour, is by implication the attempt to get beyond the superficially human, to find the truth (or The Truth). I have not uncovered any direct, unambiguous evidence that Storm was an overtly religious person, nor am I likely to do so. Someone so Victorian with respect to his personal life cannot be expected to lay bare his soul in correspondence, and even less so in his publications. But Storm had grown up the son of a pastor and had therefore been exposed to conventional Lutheranism from early childhood. It is sometimes true that the offspring of the clergy explicitly reject rather than accept what has been forced upon them throughout their childhood. Storm was not a rebel, though. He was personally conservative as much as he was politically Conservative, so I think we can assume that he maintained the traditional religious beliefs of his childhood, and that his life and work were underpinned by conventional Lutheran Christian beliefs and values, values which he clung to on the death of Gunnar. There is a comment in his most open and personal publication, written by the young, enthusiastic Storm rather than by the mature "scientific" Storm, *De romanske Sprog og Folk*, which appears to support this assumption:

> The actual people down here [in Italy] have in fact always been heathens, in that they have had a religion which has principally comprised outward ceremonial and rote-learned prayers. (Storm 1871: 54)

The traditional Lutheran is *very* tight-lipped indeed about traditional Catholicism as found in its homeland. For Storm, a Christianity based on public ceremonial rather than on the Lutheran foundations of Scripture and personal belief is not Christianity at all. I shall not pursue Storm's personal religious beliefs any further, as it would soon become little more than speculation, although we will necessarily return to the question of Johan Storm and religion when we discuss his involvement in Bible translation in section 4.2.3.1. Storm's private beliefs died with him. Nonetheless, we must remember that he was a whole person and his linguistic philosophy was part of a whole *Weltanschauung* rooted in a very clear code. This is not the place to do it, and I'm not sure that it could be done rigorously, but it would be very instructive to try to discover to what extent the history of Western linguistics has been shaped by the underlying Christianity of its practitioners. I can't take on the whole of Western linguistics here or anywhere, but the Lutheranism underlying this *Forord* at least is really rather fascinating, as we shall see in a moment.

If Storm presented himself as a new, mature figure in *Engelsk Filologi*, the rest of the academic community came to see him as such too. In September 1876 Henry Nicol, Sweet's cousin, wrote to Storm concerning the benefits of using the *Visible Speech* method of transcription:

> I am pleased to hear that you appreciate Visible Speech; my cousin Sweet was quite surprised at your great practical command of sounds and your excellent ear, so I have no doubt that you will very soon master it thoroughly. (NBO Ms. 8° 2402 J[iv])

Following the reviews of *Engelsk Filologi* nobody would again address Storm in this "my dear boy" fashion, and nor would anyone again be surprised at his 'great practical command of sounds'.

A further pioneering notion expounded in the *Forord* to *Engelsk Filologi* concerns the proposed role of students in their university-level modern-language education. Storm insists that this role should be an active one: that students should not simply passively accept the word of the teacher, but involve themselves actively in the investigation of language:

> Linguistic research here touches on the natural sciences and becomes like them an empirical science. Students should not as a matter of course relinquish this work to the professors [. . .] Nothing is more pressing for the student than to observe living language in his own and in foreign languages himself [. . .] Only then can the student hope to become a good teacher: when he does not treat his studies as bread-and-butter work, but studies for the sake of studying; when he does not only respond passively, but digests and uses the material, such that it becomes alive in him. In this way the subject matter becomes not so much an external act of memory, but a part of his intellectual life [. . .] (1879a: vi)

I promised a few moments ago that I would not pursue the relationship between Storm's probable religious life and his views on language, and I will stick to my word; but the Christian background to *Engelsk Filologi* is inescapable. I don't need to point out the religious connotations of how, for Storm, understanding *det levende Sprog* becomes part of the student's 'inner life' and furthermore an inner life which is more than just an 'external act of memory' like (in Storm's view) Roman Catholicism. Storm is not just passionate about *det levende Sprog*. He preaches it with missionary zeal. This is not so much an academic preface as a sermon.

The essence of a good sermon lies in its beginning and its end, the points where the whole of the congregation is actually listening. This sermon began with the heart of the matter, what in a Norwegian Lutheran church would be the *prekentekst* (the text of the day on which the sermon is based): 'This first part of my *Engelsk Filologi* deals with "the *living* language".' If the sermon is properly constructed, the ultimate message will be in its concluding words:

And I wish herewith to recommend my book to students for diligent use. May it grant them something of the joy with which its preparation has furnished me! Much in it is incomplete and fragmentary. Many problems are still unresolved. We have still only gained a small insight into the truth. But when we remain faithful to the truth, we have cause to hope that continued research will open up new vistas to us and cast light on many dark points. Human understanding has its limits, but within them there is always room for progress. (1879a: x)

If there was ever any doubt that Storm was steeped here in the rhetoric of the sermon, then this final paragraph must dispel that doubt. 'A small insight into the truth.' 'When we remain faithful to the truth.' 'Cast light on many dark points.' 'Human understanding has its limits.' There it is. As Storm undergoes his rite of passage into maturity, the youngster becomes the adult through the son becoming his pastor-father. At the very end of *De romanske Sprog og Folk* Storm apologised to the reader for the incompleteness of the presentation, but there the reasons were fully human:

It was not for any great length of time that I was able to study [the languages and life of the three main Romance countries] on the spot. I have had even less time to recount the impressions made on my travels. This has to be my excuse for the incompleteness of the presentation. (Storm 1871: 129)

Now the reason for incompleteness is the humble one that 'human understanding has its limits'. A fascinating, a really fascinating transition in the life of the scholar and in the life of the man.

2.2.1.3 Indledende Bemærkninger

After a list of abbreviations used in the book, the actual presentation begins. This section, the 'Opening remarks', is not as passionate as the *Forord*, but Storm takes great pains to stress one of his passions, the importance of the study of phonetics in language learning. The book is, Storm explains, a guide for students taking the linguistic-historical teachers' examination in English, and a guide based on some years' experience of this exam in operation. The basis for a study of English or French – and here Storm agrees totally with one of Sweet's catchphrases – is 'scientific fonetics as the indispensabl foundation of all study of language, whether practical or theoretical' (Sweet 1885a: 578):

> The real language is the spoken language, and the spoken language consists of sounds. The first condition for knowing a language is therefore to know its sounds. Without this one can certainly enter into its spirit to an extent, but it just remains like a dead language. (Storm 1879a: 2)

Here language life (or death) and 'spirit' are once again juxtaposed, but I think I've explored this point enough for now.

Storm then goes on to deal with a string of practical problems facing a Norwegian speaker who tries to pronounce French or English correctly but who inevitably suffers from interference from his or her mother tongue. Concentration on specific practical problems facing a language learner is the tradition that Daniel Jones made famous in England (see Jones (1918) and subsequent editions),[3] a tradition inherited directly from Paul Passy and a tradition of which Storm was one of the founders. Many of Storm's recommendations and observations about language learning are based on personal experience. In short, it was fully and internationally recognised that Storm had a remarkably native-sounding pronunciation of English and French. Storm may claim now that this is not something to be proud of in itself, but he *was* proud of it and justly so. Consequently the methods he used must have been effective ones. He writes here, for example, of the importance of mixing with native speakers, which he had himself done, and of attending lectures when abroad, as he had himself done when in France in the period prior to his appointment at the university. Taking Storm's own course, he states (p. 6), is a poor substitute for real practical experience with native speakers, since – and here we return to Storm's oft-repeated and problematic dichotomy – 'the purpose of a university is scientific, not practical'.

Storm never really made a distinction between the 'scientific' and the 'practical' study of languages, either in what he wrote or in how he practised as a university teacher of modern languages. In his own person he embodied

---

[3] See Collins & Mees (1999) for an excellent and fascinating account of Jones and his work.

the practical and scientific approaches to language combined. But, partly because university authorities throughout northern Europe had made such a fuss of consciously replacing an old 'practical' tradition with a new 'scientific' one, and partly because the regulations for the linguistic-historical teachers' exam differentiated between the practical and the scientific approach, the dichotomy remained. It is similar to the modern distinction between phonetics and phonology. Institutionally, through university courses, textbooks etc., a distinction is still made between phonetics and phonology, and for these purposes it can be helpful; but in reality the two feed off each other and are, for most other purposes, closely interrelated aspects of the same thing, namely the study of sounds, both 'practical' and 'scientific'.

Storm gives a number of very sensible, helpful tips in this section, both to students and to self-taught language learners, as to what forms of exercises they might employ. This very modern-style applied linguistics, or more specifically this guide to language-learning methodology, would later be dealt with more fully by Sweet (1885a/1899) and Jespersen (1901/1904).

Practice in pronunciation may be the basis of all language study, but 'practice will soon turn out to be inadequate without theory' (p. 8). Storm makes this categorical statement distinguishing the two approaches to language study, but he again suggests a confluence of the two: that scientific study is more practical than so-called practical study since it brings greater insights which can then be applied to greater effect in the classroom (p. 9). I suspect that Storm's vagueness about what constituted the 'practical' study of languages lies in the ambiguity of the word *praktisk*, which, like 'practical' in English, embraces two things in this context. On the one hand it signifies *exercises* and on the other hand the application of theory. In fact this ambiguity has lain at the heart of the struggles by so-called "applied linguists" to be taken seriously by their so-called "theoretical" colleagues. Storm does not need to make the distinction – a distinction also made by Henry Sweet in the quotation above – since he states that scientific (historical) insights into a language can be applied both in the classroom and in one's own practical use of the language; conversely, the scientific approach to language should also embrace what was conventionally felt to belong to the practical side, the modern language:

We do not wish for an impractical scientificality [*Videnskabelighed*], not leading to any goal, but a study of the science of language, which can ease the understanding and acquisition of the contemporary language's phenomena. It should also be noted here that the scientific study of language does not only consist of language history, but also a systematic and detailed knowledge of the contemporary language. In order to be able to explain the phenomena one has first and foremost to understand the phenomena themselves. (1879a: 10)

As so often we find Storm at a turning point, working with received ideas but in fact thinking in quite a different way himself. He is quite clear in *Engelsk Filologi* about the different aspects of language study being interrelated:

> A combination of scientific and practical studies is thus necessary for the fruitful acquisition of modern languages. It is necessary to know *what, why* and *how*: firstly *what* a Norwegian expression translates as in the foreign language (practical knowledge); next *why* it translates thus (grammar); and finally *how* it got to be what it is (history of the language). (p. viii)

His view gains a more mature and clearer formulation two years later:

> The best approach is therefore: a complete presentation of the living language, seen in the light of the history of the language. The two are mutually dependent. (Storm 1881a: vi)

So studying *det levende Sprog* demanded a blurring of the distinction between "practical" and "scientific", but Storm's "practical" treatment of "scientific" language study (as in *Engelsk Filologi*) was less successful than his "scientific" treatment of "practical" language materials (as in the *Franske Taleøvelser*). To use the modern distinction again, he was an applied linguist and not a theoretical one. This blurring of the boundaries between the practical and the scientific in language study goes some way towards explaining an apparently extraordinary statement made in perhaps his most programmatic writing of all, the *Indledning* to *Norvegia* of 1884:

> [. . .] our goal is scientific profit. Science does not above all seek that which is practical, but that which is instructive. (Storm 1884a: 10)

Before leaving the *Indledning* in which Storm explains the philosophy behind the book, as compared with the philosophy of language we encountered in the *Forord*, we must just look at what he claims to be his 'intention in what follows' (p. 13). Why is this important for us today? We operate at the beginning of the twenty-first century with a very different notion of English Studies from the specific 'Engelsk Filologi' of 100 years ago. "The new philology" as a university subject is briefly and reasonably unambiguously described, although the exact balance between literature, language history and the contemporary language was open to debate, and was indeed debated (see section 2.3). Anyway, the twenty-first-century "richness" of university English across the world has grown out of notions of university English proposed and adopted by its first proponents, men like Storm. And the *Engelsk Filologi* was one of the first, if not the first, major book intended as a university textbook for English. So:

> My intention in what follows is to point out to students the best and the most recent, the most necessary and the most suitable resources for the fruitful philological study of the English language. I have also had to

mention some books to counsel against them. I append critical, explanatory and supplementary observations with regard to whatever most needs explanation [. . .] I have dealt with some points in special excursuses, such as the spoken language and the vulgar language, subjects which have not previously been objects for a complete scholarly presentation. The order in which the various subjects are treated indicates the order of studies I would recommend to be followed in general. One should begin with the practical acquisition of the living language and a full study of the literature, then study the older periods of the language via some of the most significant texts, and only then, in context, study scientific grammar, language history and etymology [. . .] (1879a: 13–14)

The work is a glorified annotated reading list. There is much that is original about it and it is a scholarly tour de force. The learning, or rather the collection of knowledge it evidences, is humbling. However, it remains an annotated bibliography associated with the course taught by Storm at Det kongelige Frederiks Universitet. The reason why the reading lists I prepare for my students are not published to enormous acclaim and are not subsequently translated into German is because the *Engelsk Filologi* is a rather special bibliography and my reading lists are not. Being so closely associated with a particular Norwegian course, though, the *Engelsk Filologi/ Englische Philologie* never had the impact it really deserved. In his review of *Englische Philologie* J. N. Wagner (1881: 515) wrote:

It will lead [whoever wants to undertake the study of English philology] up to the vestibule of the sanctuary, to which others will open the door and make known the interior.

This is attractively put, but the fact remains that the *Engelsk Filologi* is to a large extent derivative, a collection and discussion of other people's work. Yes, this was what Storm did best on the "scientific" side, and a point comes in the development of a discipline when a critical summary of the state of that discipline needs to be made; but, as Bødtker wrote, looking back on Storm's achievement:

The dust of neglect has settled on the majority of the works to which Storm dedicated such detailed discussion. They feel like dross, which one wants to see peeled off in order to arrive unencumbered at Storm himself. (Bødtker 1922: 52)

For this reason, and to spare the reader an interminable procession of information that time has proved unimportant, I do not intend to go through the contents of *Engelsk Filologi* in anything like the same detail our "close reading" of the *Fortale* and *Indledning* has involved. We, like Bødtker, want to 'arrive unencumbered at Storm himself', and an indigestible litany of detail was, for Storm's lectures as for *Engelsk Filologi*, a 'weakness from the formal point of view' (Bødtker 1922: 52), so I heed Bødtker's warning! In any case, we will have the opportunity to come back to some of the more significant detail in its more mature form when we look at the German revisions of *Engelsk Filologi* below.

2.2.1.4 *Contents*

The table of contents is as follows:

The first thing to notice about the make-up of the book is the somewhat haphazard structure. The book opens with a general section heading, 'Pronunciation', as if this is to be the first of several sections so headed, but there is no further subdivision. It strikes the reader as odd when for example, 200 pages later, under the heading of 'Pronunciation', discussion has turned to the merits of different editions of Shakespeare. Similarly, it must surprise any reader who has just started to read a chapter on 'Reading authors and the study of literature' suddenly to be faced with a section on *Talesproget* (Colloquial English). Storm gives a sort of explanation as to why he addresses colloquial English at this point:

What we learn above all from novels, short stories and tales is the normal *spoken language*, which has achieved a more faithful representation in few other literatures beside the English. I want to emphasise here in particular what can be observed of the *movement of the spoken language* through the attentive study of dialogue. (Storm 1879a: 126)

Just as Storm in practice saw no hard and fast lines between the "scientific" and "practical" sides to language study, so for him the study of literature is similarly part of the investigation into *the living language*. The literature of English is a corpus of examples of the language in life. This is why Storm can make the apparently absurd statement that 'what we learn above all from novels [. . .] is the normal *spoken language*'. He is really not interested in literary worth, the moral content or anything else. He admits that poetry contains 'that which is beautiful [*det skjønne*]', but it is not worthy of comment since 'it has preserved archaic words and expressions, notably Germanic (Anglo-Saxon) ones, where French forms are current in the spoken language' (p. 194). Literature is only relevant as language in use.

Storm wrote quickly – we know that – but I also think he wrote without much planning, hence the haphazard structure, and it is far worse in the *Større fransk Syntax* (see section 3.3.1). He was a bottle of linguistic data ready to come bubbling out, and he could not control the flow. This is why, no matter how many volumes of *Englische Philologie* he wrote, he simply could not get beyond the first stages, because the examples just kept on coming. This is why his five-year lecture course on Old English failed to get much beyond the vowels (see section 1.5.3 above). This is why *Engelsk Filologi* had 90 pages of 'Additions and corrections' (one quarter of the book's total length). The *practical* approach to the *scientific* study just couldn't work for Storm, either temperamentally or in terms of the original material he had at his disposal. While he was engaged in the act of writing it may have seemed to him logical to treat 'The spoken language' at the beginning of the chapter on 'Reading authors and the study of literature', but it is confusing for the reader, and in a better-planned book it simply wouldn't have happened. We can say that *Engelsk Filologi* was a written outpouring of what was going round in Storm's head, making perfect sense to him with his vision of the living language, and making sense to us who can reconstruct that vision now with the benefit of hindsight. But his poor students!

The 'Additions and corrections' were the result of further data collection by Storm and of comments made on the manuscript by Sweet:

Since the printing of this book, thanks to unforeseen circumstances, has ended up taking over six months, a not insignificant amount of new material has been added in the meantime, just as on certain points the author has been able to correct earlier opinions. (Storm 1879a: 244)

Six months will not strike the modern reader as very long at all for a book to appear in print, but for Storm the search for philological knowledge went on inexorably. As we saw in Chapter 1, he was observing and collecting all the time, and it did not occur to him to wait and systematise the new data in the revised German edition, which he was preparing anyway. The cork simply wouldn't stay in the bottle and the data had to fizz out. It is possible that Storm had the good of his students at heart and he wanted the material to be as full as it possibly could be. He writes, for example, of a new dictionary of idioms (p. 262), of which book 'I have seen the first instalment, which looks very promising.' However, I would argue that the completely unsystematic list of additions is actually born of a sort of religious fervour, a desire to be as close to "The Truth" as possible, whatever the cost.

We will discuss the phonetic components in section 2.2.4, and we shall deal with Storm's original work on colloquial English and American English later on in this chapter too. We can therefore now make a few general concluding remarks about the *Engelsk Filologi* as part of Storm's output and development as a linguist. It was clearly for him a transitional undertaking. First, in it he reaches maturity as a scholar of international ranking. He takes on the whole of the European academic community in his comments throughout the book. He is sometimes very favourable and he is sometimes highly critical. His comments are made with the absolute assurance of someone secure in his position. Despite his critical treatment of the literature, if the reviews are anything to judge by, *Engelsk Filologi* was embraced with almost unalloyed enthusiasm by the community it took on. It was a success. The Norwegian took on Europe and won. Secondly, it was also a personal transition, a crusade to reach personal maturity, which he achieved through the rhetoric of the *Forord*. Success was in some ways short-lived, however. The book, despite the international acclaim, was never reprinted in Norway. Thirdly, and in the light of the previous points, it is in this book that Storm moved away from being truly and purely Norwegian in identity to being at least in part European, a quite different thing. He had abandoned publication on Norwegian for this English enterprise, so it was also a symbolic transition from Norway to Europe, yet at the same time it was written for the home market. It left Storm stranded at the national border. There is an apparently throwaway observation in *Engelsk Filologi*:

> Exceptionally few manage completely to acquire the "accent" of a foreign language [. . .] without either having learned it from childhood or having lived abroad for many years, with a partial loss of nationality. (1879a: 2)

Storm did not himself spend many years living abroad, so why should he have felt able to write so categorically of partial loss of nationality? Because in *Engelsk Filologi* and in the *Værk over det norske Sprog* debacle (see section 4.2.1.2) preceding it, this is precisely what he had experienced.

2.2.2 *The 1881 Version*

2.2.2.1 In 1879 Storm promised a German version of the *Engelsk Filologi*; it appeared just two years later with the full title, being a direct translation of the Norwegian title: *Englische Philologie. Anleitung zum wissenschaftlichen Studium der englischen Sprache. Vom Verfasser für das deutsche Publikum bearbeitet. I: Die lebende Sprache.* The book is essentially a translation of the 1879 Norwegian version, but, Storm being Storm, the collection of material and the search for a full understanding of the language has continued in the meantime, resulting in revision and expansion: 'almost no page has remained unaltered [. . .] the material has in particular been significantly expanded' (p. viii).

The first question that faces us is why Storm chose to translate the *Engelsk Filologi* into German. It is clear that it needed to be translated into a better known European language if it was to make any impact outside Scandinavia, and it is clear that some of the material oriented towards Norwegian readers or the specific requirements of the Norwegian exams needed to be revised. However, the book deals with the English language, and there is lots of evidence that Storm's command of English was native-like, so would it not have been more logical to prepare an English translation? The anonymous reviewer of the *Engelsk Filologi* in *The Spectator* (Anon. 1882) had called for an English translation and had ventured so far as to suggest that 'the writer of such a translation [. . .] from a pecuniary point of view [. . .] will by no means lose his reward' (p. 803). As is often the case, it seems to have been Sweet's influence which was decisive. He wrote to Storm on 24 October 1878:

> I have just finished looking over the sheets of your Philology. It is uncommonly interesting, + will be quite a revelation to your countrymen, + also to the Germans. Have you made any arrangements about translating it into German? If not, there is not much chance of its getting known here, which it ought to be – to show our educational authorities what studying English really is. (NBO Ms. 8° 2402 J^v)

If Sweet wanted the work to be known 'here', i.e. in Britain, why did he not suggest it be translated into English? First, German was much more the international language of scholarship than English in the late nineteenth century, particularly in the area of linguistics, so a German version could be expected to reach more of the right readers than an English-language version. Secondly, Storm had not previously had much success getting his works published in Britain. Sweet had reported such a failure just three years earlier. Storm's proposal that the Philological Society publish what Sweet calls a 'Treatise on Norwegian Phonetics' had been rejected by the editorial triumvirate of Sweet, Ellis and Furnivall. The British market for Storm's books did not improve. Macmillan refused to produce an English version of

the advanced French dialogues since they did not think there would be
enough of a market, despite the fact that the intermediate level dialogues had
sold well (letter of 6 September 1897 – NBO Ms. 8° 2402 F6ᵛ). Thirdly,
Germany was viewed as the home of the new philology and therefore the
natural home for major new publications in this field. Storm was of course
more at home in French than in German, but a French edition was out of the
question since Storm held French linguistic scholarship in such low regard,
and there would anyway have been, in Storm's view, no call for such a work
in France. In his review of *Englische Philologie* (Joret 1882),[4] Charles Joret
(1839–1914) regretted the fact that there was no French edition of the work.
Storm responded to Joret's comments by writing, 'If I have not produced a
French edition of my book, it is because it seems to me that French readers
are little interested in this sort of research' (Storm 1882b).

There appears to have been the possibility of an American (English-
language) edition. The only evidence that this possibility was ever mooted is
a letter to Storm from Edwin Dodds, an admirer from Newcastle upon Tyne
in England, who wrote to Storm between 1879 and 1881, and whose letters
are catalogued in Bergen University Library at Ms. 743e. On 28 December
1879 Dodds wrote:

> I should advise you to accept the offer of the Norwegian-American
> student, I should let him translate the work and I should sell him copyright
> at the sum you mention, one hundred dollars per edition [. . .] Do you
> think he will be able to translate from the German edition? There seem to
> me to be many difficulties in the way of bringing out the book in England.
> As you remark, it would be difficult to find a satisfactory translator, and
> almost as hard to find a publisher for it seems to me that there is very little
> interest taken in these studies by the British public [. . .]

So a German edition it was. Storm had not spent any considerable time in
a German-speaking country, in fact he had made the conscious decision not
to do so when on his travels in 1869/1870 (Storm 1871: 21). As far as I can
tell he had not spent much time or energy learning German either. How then
did he manage to translate this substantial work in a relatively short space of
time into what was acknowledged by reviewers to be excellent German? I
think that all we can do is to marvel with J. N. Wagner at Storm's
extraordinary ability:

> How [. . .], without committed and continuous work, could he, Norwegian
> as he is, manage to write such a substantial work on English philology in a
> German whose style is completely beyond reproach! (Wagner 1881: 517)

Storm's life and work are of course characterised by just such a striving –
'committed and continuous work' – and this could well be his epitaph. In the

---

[4] All reviews are listed in Breymann (1897: 103).

Vorwort (Preface) to the 1881 *Englische Philologie* Storm gives his credentials for writing about the various languages, and all he can say about his
knowledge of German is: 'German I have spoken and heard a great deal'
(p. ix). Although his skills in written German were not found wanting by
reviewers, Storm is aware that his abilities in German do not measure up to
those in other modern European languages, and he makes a small apology
(p. x) for any 'linguistic unevenness'. While this apology is extremely fleeting
– he states that any unevenness in the German is only at the expense of
greater clarity from which he suggests German readers could learn – it
nevertheless contrasts with the enormous confidence in foreign languages
demonstrated elsewhere in his writings. It is clear that Storm and his
Norwegian publisher did try to find a translator, but getting the book
translated was not going to be financially advantageous. Storm therefore
had to take on the job himself, an undertaking he did not relish:

> I am toying with the idea of revising the book for a German readership, if
> it won't be too demanding. I have had very little practice in writing
> German. (Letter to Thomsen, 7 February 1879)

It is very likely that Storm had some assistance from German speakers, and
Oskar Vistdal, author of the recent book on the polyglot Georg Sauerwein
(Vistdal 2000), believes that Sauerwein was one such assistant (*personal
correspondence*).

2.2.2.2 Vorwort

The preface to the 1881 German edition is noticeably shorter than the 1879
preface, and there are two reasons for this in terms of Storm's development
as a figure of authority. The rite of passage had been achieved in 1879 and
there is no need now for the same sort of testimonial. Neither is there the
same need for humility since, with the successful publication of *Engelsk
Filologi*, Storm's standing had been established. Already in its year of
publication Sweet had described it as a work 'which cannot be neglected
by any English philologist, and its publication is the greatest boon to foreign
students that could well be conceived' (Sweet 1879: 271). So Storm could
launch the German edition into the academic community with his head held
high. As part of his journey to maturity in 1879 he had developed the theme
that mere knowledge of foreign languages was as nothing compared with the
search for understanding. All this has disappeared in 1881; instead Storm
can state with utter confidence: 'I have the advantage of being rather familiar
with several languages' (p. ix).

As we chart Storm's development as a linguist by plotting the development of *Engelsk Filologi* as it moves into its subsequent German editions,
there is only one more observation to make about the new briefer, sharper,
more confident preamble; it concerns the very first paragraph and the

definition of the all-important *levende Sprog*. To remind ourselves, he wrote
in 1879:

> This first part of my *Engelsk Filologi* deals with "the *living* language". The
> word is here used in its broadest meaning, not just relating to the living
> spoken language, but relating to the literary language up to and including
> the Bible and Shakespeare, since up to that point literature and language
> are the property of the people and live on in tradition. Beyond that time
> they cease to do so. Spenser no longer belongs to the British public. His
> language is too remote from the current language to be generally access-
> ible.

The German equivalent of two years later runs as follows:

> This first part of my *Englische Philologie* deals with "the *living* language".
> The word here means firstly the contemporary *educated colloquial
> language* [*die jetzige 'gebildete Umgangssprache'*]. Only this contains the
> idiomatic usage, which also constitutes the basis for the written language.
> On the other hand, by virtue of its numerous variations and artificial
> forms, the written language must be subjugated to the spoken language, if
> we are to find the standard form. Here the language returns to its simplest
> form of expression. (Storm 1881a: v*)*

Only then in the following paragraph does he go on to write: 'secondly I also
use this word in a broader sense, of the written and literary language living in
tradition [. . .]' and to translate the rest of the 1879 opening paragraph. This
is noteworthy because the 1879 and 1881 texts are so nearly the same in
other respects. Any alteration is significant, and an alteration to the
prekentekst is particularly significant. The significance is that Storm's view
of *die lebende Sprache* is now more clearly formulated and at the same time
more radical. Little by little his view of *die lebende Sprache* is breaking away
from the received view of philologists, like a butterfly escaping from its
chrysalis. As he matures, he allows himself to throw off the received wisdom
which has been holding back the full formulation of his linguistic philosophy. To begin with in 1879 he had dutifully held on to the written
language as an equal partner in *det levende Sprog* because it was really too
radical for the only-just-mature Storm to do otherwise. In 1881 however he
feels able to go further, and he will go further still in later editions. *Die
lebende Sprache* can now be hierarchised; it has a *zunächst* and a *zweitens*, a
'first' and a 'secondly'. And above all the object of study for modern
philology is 'contemporary educated colloquial language', a phrase em-
phasized in the text. This phrase is of course highly redolent of contemporary debates about Norwegian and what variety of the language should form
the basis for the development of the written language.

    Once again we get the sense that Storm's general philosophy of language is
based on his philosophy of Norwegian. His convictions as to the way

forward for Norwegian are based on this same view of what philology should be about: 'I have always been in agreement with the principle of the Knudsen line in language reform,' he wrote in 1888, 'basing the written language on the living, educated spoken language' (1888a: 115). And when he writes that he has always been in agreement with Knudsen's language reform principle, he really has. As we have seen before, Storm's general views about language and about the specific languages he worked on remained remarkably unaltered throughout his life. They were real convictions, almost doctrines. The words I have just quoted are from 1888, therefore after he wrote the *Englische Philologie*, but the earliest formulation of them of which I'm aware, is from 1869 and concerns Norwegian:

> By "mother tongue" we here mean the common *spoken language*, used by the *educated classes* around the country, not only in its written form, but also, and especially, as it really sounds, namely in day-to-day speech. (*Udkast til Oldn. Sproghistorie* 1869. NBO Ms. 8° 2402 A^i)

This is one of the earliest things Storm wrote. Although it forms the introduction to what is supposed to be a history of Old Norwegian, he just can't help himself and launches straight into "The Programme". Interestingly, however, it is a less assured version than the 1879 version we have already considered, since back in 1869 he starts with the written language ('not only in its written form'), the acceptable language medium for study and analysis, and only then ('but also') introduces the spoken variety. So the spoken language, and the educated variety of it, is always at the heart of Storm's studies of standard languages, but as his personal stature grows, so his formulation of this view becomes more and more assured and dogmatic.

2.2.2.3 *Contents*

The organization of the 1881 version has been tidied up a little bit, as though Storm has taken some time to consider the overall structure of the work. But there is still a large number of ad hoc features. Once again Storm is unable to organise his thoughts or work in a rounded way, and instead just pours out his current knowledge. The most striking example of this structural weakness lies in the final chapter (7) on *Grammatik*. A nineteenth-century reader, or for that matter a twenty-first-century reader, would probably have expected a book on the English language to contain a substantial treatment of the language's grammar, certainly its morphology and probably its syntax too. The greatest nineteenth-century publication on language was Grimm's *Deutsche Grammatik*, like Storm's publications a vast repository of examples. Not only is Grimm's work highly organised and tightly structured, but it is devoted principally to grammatical information. It is true that, by the time Storm was writing, attention in linguistics had turned more and more to sound systems and indeed phonetics, but six pages out of the 468 pages (1.3 per cent) dedicated to grammar is hardly representative of the importance grammar had for virtually every contemporary linguist – except Sweet and Storm! Even Sweet managed to publish grammatical works (e.g. Sweet 1886), but he kept them separate. Storm admits quite readily in *Englische Philologie* that grammar is an incomplete afterthought:

> I had originally intended to deal with grammar in a separate volume [but] it seems to be most expedient briefly to discuss the most important publications here. Perhaps I will then deal with the grammar more fully at a later stage. (Storm 1881a: 417)

The hope expressed here proved to be vain. In the 1892/1896 revision of *Englische Philologie*, grammar occupies 10 of 1,098 pages (0.9 per cent).

The table of contents evidences greater subdivision of the text, which in turn evidences greater thought about its structure. Here, for example, the subheading *Aussprache* (Pronunciation), which in 1879 appeared to apply to the whole book, is now specified as covering pages 18–129 only, i.e. chapters 1 and 2 (*Allgemeine Phonetik* and *Englische Aussprache*). Where there were five (subdivided) chapters in 1879, there are now seven. The other new chapter (6: *Literaturgeschichte* (Literary history)) is, like *Grammatik*, an afterthought. Its contents might be useful to readers, and particularly to philological students, who would certainly have liked more than just three pages of bibliographical guidelines on the history of English literature, but it does not enhance the scholarly value of the book, especially since Storm once again writes:

> According to the original plan, literary history was to be treated in the second (historical) part of this work. But it seems more practical just briefly to discuss here the most important publications in this field. (Storm 1881a: 414)

(The 1896 version had grown to six pages.) "Work", for Storm, is always "in progress". It is rather churlish to dwell on structural weaknesses in the *Englische Philologie* at the expense of showing what was original and pioneering in Storm's work, and he did admit that he was 'weak' in the area of literary history. However, two of the things we want to know about Storm are: (1) how his mind worked; and (2) what his importance was for contemporary and subsequent linguistics. These "afterthoughts" tell us much about how his mind worked and also about why a work hailed by other professional linguists as a work of genius failed to survive into the twentieth century.

2.2.2.4 Storm makes a number of excurses during the course of *Engelsk Filologi/Englische Philologie*, and it is here that his original contributions to the subject make their most striking appearances. There are lengthy footnotes and a number of these excursuses in the early part of the book – they are signified by the use of a smaller font – but the first really substantial excursus concerns colloquial English. The sections on 'Colloquial language', 'The vulgar language' and 'American English' cover between them 134 pages (29 per cent of the book) and are virtually entirely printed in this smaller font, indicating the extent of Storm's original contributions. These sections constitute a stream of consciousness as Storm's observations flow into each other, one suggesting another. He starts *Die Umgangssprache* (Colloquial Language) by justifying the study of its forms from a "scientific" point-of-view: colloquialisms are a motivating factor in language change (p. 207). The subsequent discussion, although unstructured, is always descriptive and never judgmental in stark contrast to the English grammars of a century before. Storm has little time for grammarians in the prescriptive tradition. Of Lindley Murray (1745–1826), who only gets two brief mentions, Storm writes simply, 'This man was, as is well known, a great pedant' (p. 249). Storm's discussion is also scholarly, treating colloquial usage with the same comparative rigour that a previous generation had heaped upon standard forms. Thus he makes frequent comparison with similar colloquial forms in other European languages. Again, this is not done in any formal way, but rather as those comparisons occur to him. This way of working may lead to a text which is difficult to navigate, but the reader shares in Storm's voyage of discovery. It is as if he is sharing his thoughts with the reader rather than giving a cold account of them, and this is in some ways actually a strength in his writings. *Englische Philologie* 1881 is surprisingly readable, and the wealth of information is rarely boring, except where the lists of examples become stultifying. It is therefore still worth reading today, and it is really indispensable for anyone interested in nineteenth-century English.

A substantial section of *Die Umgangssprache* concerns the argument between Dean Henry Alford, the author of *The Queen's English* (Alford 1864) and G. Washington Moon, who penned a biting criticism of Alford – *The Dean's English* (Moon 1865). Storm goes against popular opinion by siding with Alford against what he calls the 'classical-conservative' stance of Moon. Storm may have thought of Lindley Murray as a pedant, but 'in Moon he met his match' (p. 249). The Alford vs. Moon controversy, although very bitter at the time, is now as good as forgotten, but Storm's observations stemming from the case in many instances remain sound, or at least had wider importance at the time of their writing beyond the narrow confines of the Alford vs. Moon debate. This is why it is regrettable that so much in *Englische Philologie* is wedded to the discussion of particular works on which 'the dust of neglect' has collected. The Alford/Moon case enables Storm to develop a detailed argument about the nature of language change, the relationship between colloquial and standard usage and the relationship between the spoken and the written language. He does this, as is his technique elsewhere, by citing and then attacking specific observations made by Moon and reviewers and critics who had taken Moon's side. If only Storm could have extracted his generalisations from the specifics, he could have formulated the theories about language which constantly lurk beneath the surface detail.

2.2.2.5 Storm's highly anti-prescriptive approach continues into *Die Vulgär-sprache*, where he notes that 'even aberrations of language are philologically interesting' (p. 259). He continues later in this section with a class of vulgarisms 'which cannot be traced back directly to the ancient language'. Of these he writes 'even these often have great philological interest' (p. 275). In holding this point of view Storm was a pioneer, if not the pioneer, taking the notion of the philological centrality of the *living* language beyond simply a study of dialects. He has the very twentieth-century view that the job of linguistics is simply to deal with language as it is found. If speakers use a form, then that form is rightfully an object of linguistic enquiry, regardless of whether it is a standard form or not. His attempt at a phonetic description of non-standard English is most interesting in this respect (pp. 296–298). This is not the description of any particular accent, but rather a general phonology of "vulgar" English, a presentation of some of the rules which seem to characterise non-standard English. Most of his examples are taken from written English, particularly Dickens, but his understanding of the pronunciation of 'vulgar words' used by Dickens and others is based on his own observations in England. The phonology is structured like the rest of the book: observations flow from a particular heading, in this case from a particular letter. The vowels are treated first, and then the consonants, as in Storm's notebooks: no phonological system is constructed, and nor would we expect one. However, careful, informed, non-prescriptive observations about non-standard English pronunciation, by somebody who is acknow-ledged to have been one of the greatest "linguistic ears" and experts on the English language ever to have lived, is a fantastic source of information for anyone interested in English of this period. Again, it is just a shame that this information is hidden in what on the surface appears to be a lengthy annotated bibliography.

2.2.2.6 Norway underwent a process of political and cultural upheaval during the nineteenth century. One manifestation of this was the massive emigration to America. Storm's surprising interest in American English and his dedication of 41 pages (8.8 per cent) of *Engelsk Filologi/Englische Philologie* to this variety of English was a response to these Norwegian circumstances. There were many people of Norwegian birth in America which meant that many Norwegians had family and friends who used American English. Storm recognises the gulf between the practical needs of ordinary people and the scholarly interests of linguists:

While I have to pass over the English dialects in this book, I have found it expedient to go into American English more closely, all the more so as so many Germans and Scandinavians learn this language in America, whilst only language scholars study dialects such as the Scottish and Irish. (Storm 1881a: 301)

Here is a very good example of Storm's conflation of the "practical" and the "scientific". His "scientific" treatment of this variety of English serves a practical purpose, and it is all the more useful to students of American English by providing insights rather than just descriptions. He begins with a very brief overview of American authors who use the most distinctively American English, and then he moves on to discuss specific features of American English under the bibliographical heading of *Americanisms* by M. Schele de Vere. Storm criticises de Vere's knowledge of English usage and accuses him of *Sammlermanie* (collecting mania) (and Storm should know what that particular disease is like!), but he takes de Vere's observations as the starting point for his own observations and scholarly notes.

While Storm's notes on de Vere are mostly lexical, he also attempts a brief grammar and phonology of American English. The grammar (p. 332) is of course highly unsystematic, comprising a list of grammatical forms he has encountered in his reading of American authors. He comments on adverbs being used adjectivally, on various auxiliary verbs and on the use of *any*, *some* and *as*. It must be said that, although Storm does not judge these usages, he is remarking on them in the light of their being different from British English, so he does not go so far as to describe American English completely in its own terms in the way the structuralists would later advocate. However, within the constraints arising from the fact that American English was a relative novelty in European scholarly publications, Storm must be given credit for what little he achieved. He attempts to describe Standard American English objectively. As he remarks, 'the American differences of pronunciation have not yet been made the subject of an exhaustive investigation' (p. 340). With nothing very solid to base his comments on, his discussion of the pronunciation of American English is impressionistic and sketchy. He provides phonetic explanations for some of the general impressions made on Europeans by American English, such as 'the nasal pronunciation' ('it stems from the incomplete opening of the nasal cavity' (p. 339)) and the articulation of /r/ in American English. On this latter point he disagrees with Ellis's analysis. It seems unlikely that Storm would have had much opportunity to hear American English, although he insists (rather too forcibly?) that he did. He bases his comments on the close phonetic observation of President Grant (from Missouri), and states: 'I have observed in many Americans the characteristics noted here and in the text' (p. 340, n. 3). Whatever the case may have been, Storm was not an expert on American English, compared with his enormous insights into British

English, but his attempts to deal with American English as fully as he could do tell us certain things. The *Englische Philologie* is far from being a dry list of rules, something he found so abhorrent in other language works. It rather attempts to deal with real language in use, and real language that the book's readers will encounter: colloquial and vulgar forms, and above all American forms. Storm is not afraid of taking on new areas of the English language, and nor is he afraid of criticising the views of established scholars.

2.2.3 *The Final Version*

2.2.3.1 Storm's letters to Thomsen during the first half of the 1890s are full of complaints about the preparation and publication of the final version of *Englische Philologie*. He found it extremely hard work. He complained that reading through and taking notes from the relevant literature took up a great deal of time. He complained that he was dissatisfied with the structure of the work because it covered too many areas and was therefore disjointed. He complained that the really irksome part of the whole process was having to reach the publisher's deadline. All these problems are interrelated, and they all self-evidently result from Storm's modus operandi. He once wrote of Moltke Moe, the first professor of 'the Norwegian popular language' in Kristiania: 'I am sorely afraid that he is one of those unfortunate folk, who are *never* finished with *anything*' (letter to A. B. Larsen, 5 January 1886, NBO Brevsamling 385). Storm may himself have been a fairly productive publisher, but in truth none of his publications constitutes a fully finished product. His unwillingness to write the final full stop led to serious arguments with the publisher, Reisland, arguments which left a very bitter taste in Storm's mouth. In fact these disagreements spoiled for him what was otherwise interesting, if not satisfying, work. The rather complex situation, whereby the publisher of the 1881 edition (Henninger) was bought up by Reisland ('I was, without my knowing it, sold like a slave'), who in Storm's view was a money-hungry tyrant, a furious philistine forcing Storm's hand all the time, is recounted in a letter of 15 March 1896 to Thomsen. One of Storm's favourite terms of criticism is 'one-sided', and this version of events is nothing if not 'one-sided'. Knowing how Storm worked, I think we can feel some sympathy towards a publisher trying to run a successful business, regarding Storm as some sort of infuriatingly ponderous family retainer he has inherited from Henninger. Anyway, the final version of the *Englische Philologie* did not have a painless birth, and Storm still bore the scars a year later:

> I rejoice, despite the fact that I am approx. six years older than you, in excellent health, especially now that I am free from the constant pressure which Reisland's pestering kept me under, until I finished my *Engl. Phil.* Otherwise I have derived a great deal of pleasure from this book. (11 April 1897)

This final revision is an immense work – two volumes embracing 1098 pages – but in terms of formal coverage of the language Storm did not get much further than he had done in 1881, or for that matter in 1879. Thirteen years and 700 more pages only really resulted in more detail. Chapter I ('General phonetics') is now longer than the entire book had been in 1879. This is quite an extraordinary process of development. Why did Storm fail to develop the final chapters, the stunted sections on literary history and grammar apologetically stuck on the end? Would it not have been better for the marketability of the book, not to mention the good of the students for whom it was intended, if he had completed the enterprise and produced a balanced study of the state of the art of English philology? Here again we are reminded of Rask's work (see also sections 1.6.1 and 2.1.1.2). Rask too followed his own interests to the detriment of his career and reputation. Storm's reputation was not in danger, but some dissenting voices could be heard amongst the reviewers of this new edition of *Englische Philologie*. There was the usual praise from colleagues, but Moritz Trautmann (1842–1920), writing in *Anglia*, saw the 1892 volume for what it was:

> As one can see, Storm's book is no systematic treatment of its object of study. He says what he has to say in two vast sections – a general and a specific – and this is almost all that can be discerned in the work by way of a plan [. . .] he just wants to say everything he knows and thinks about matters phonetic [. . .] but the contents of the work often bear a very loose relation or indeed no relation at all to the title *Englische Philologie*. (Trautmann 1894: 291)

It is true that much of the chapter on *Allgemeine Phonetik* concerns languages other than English (see section 2.2.4), and the excursuses on Serbo-Croat and Mandarin tones do seem highly irrelevant to the job in hand. On occasion Storm justifies the inclusion of an excursus on languages other than English, but the justifications are not very convincing:

> As the phonetics of the *Scandinavian* languages is of the greatest importance for English philology and for Germanic philology in general, I will discuss the most recent findings in this area and, where possible, complete them. (1892a: 221)

Despite the irrelevances, the third version of the *English Philology* is a tour de force, and we cannot dismiss it simply as the eccentric self-indulgence of a "phonetic fanatic". As the anonymous reviewer in the newspaper *Verdens Gang* (14 March 1896) put it, the 1892/1896 version is 'a veritable treasure trove for English linguistics'.

2.2.3.2 Vorwort

The preface is as always where we find major insights into the nature of the work. Here Storm answers in advance a number of the objections Trautmann and I raised in the last section. Storm's reasons for not undertaking a full revision and rewrite of the book are practical. He states that bringing such a book up to date is a 'difficult thing' (p. v) and, since the previous version received 'the approval of the new philology's public' (p. v), a rewrite was neither feasible nor desirable. I suspect that Storm did not realise what a monster *Englische Philologie* had become, so immersed in the detail was he, and that he had lost sight of the practical usefulness of the book which, full indices notwithstanding, remains hard to use. The disproportionate length of the phonetic chapters is due to Storm's having 'to work through, explain and, where I was able, complete the hugely expanded and fruitful phonetic literature' (p. v). The phonetic literature had really blossomed during the decade since the previous version of *Englische Philologie*, and Sweet too wrote that this literature 'becomes more and more indigestible every year' (Sweet 1890: p. v). It was Storm's hope 'to have made entry into this difficult science a little bit easier' (p. v). To this end he found it desirable to compare the sounds of English with the sounds of other languages, a procedure which he maintains elucidates them better than mere description. All this reads like an attempt to justify his failure to undertake a proper revision and to justify his obsession with phonetics. He complains that 'other work prevented me preparing a new edition straightaway' and that 'even now I have succeeded in doing this work in the face of many difficulties' (p. v). Storm was an incredibly busy man, and it is quite amazing that he managed to read as much as his works testify that he did read. He worked very quickly, as we know, and the pressures on his time must have caused him to work with greater haste still, hence the stream-of-consciousness style and the disorganised structure of the comments and discussions. However, he nowhere pretends that the various versions of *Engelsk Filologi/Englische Philologie* are anything other than what they were, 'a Guide to the Scientific Study of the English Language'. Storm was temperamentally unsuited to writing a traditional grammar or textbook, and in fact none of his "textbooks" were in the traditional mould. Sweet could write the short primers and grammars, but Storm's skills lay in other directions. We (and Trautmann) are undoubtedly right to criticise the *Englische Philologie* for its failings as a textbook, but we are wrong to criticise Storm for failing to write a book that he never intended to write anyway.

The *Vorwort* to the 1896 volume is subtitled 'Afterword to the whole work', and it provides an interesting counterbalance to the religious fervour of 1879. What did Storm believe he had achieved in all these "annotated bibliographies", these nearly 2,000 pages of commentaries and excursuses? He made a phenomenal contribution to the burgeoning study of English philology, to the understanding of the modern language, its history and its literature, but what did he see as his achievement, as his contribution to linguistics?

His aim in 1896 remains the same as it had been in 1879, indicating again the remarkable single-mindedness that he demonstrated throughout his career in adhering to his vision of philology. Looking back on what he has achieved from his vantage point in 1896 (or, more accurately, October 1895, when he wrote the preface), Storm points to more coherence in the book as well as to some of the areas in which he has made the greatest contributions to the discipline:

> I just want to note here briefly that my principal task was to present the language as it really is, in speech just as much as in writing, and to present its different forms according to place, time, learning and style. I have placed particular emphasis on the relationship between the written language and the spoken language, between English and American, and between the modern written language and that of the eighteenth century. (Storm 1896a: v)

As well as indicating the characteristics of the living language in all its varieties, Storm is able with hindsight to see these various comparative axes in the book. However, even having written 1,098 pages on the subject, he does not feel he has achieved his goal. A full understanding of English ('the truth') can never be arrived at. There are always unanswered questions and unsolved problems, and there is always more to read. Interestingly, Storm measures his achievement in terms of how much he has read. The most complete knowledge of the language is to be achieved, in his view, by absorbing as much information about it as possible, rather than by trying to formulate some general theories to explain it. Data is everything, as it has to be with pioneers in a particular discipline, but Storm does take this approach to extremes. A substantial part of this preface is consequently a statistical overview of how much Storm has read in preparing this version of *Englische Philologie*. By the time he delivered the manuscript to the publishers in August 1894 he had managed to read around 100 new volumes of modern English literature and around 30 from the eighteenth century, as well as around 200 volumes of newspapers: 'This proved to be inadequate. Many questions still remained unanswered, many decisions dubious' (1896a: v).

So the constant searching went on. During the year between submitting the manuscript and publication he managed to read another 100 or so volumes, and the fruits of this reading appear in the *Nachträge*, the appendices. Was Storm disappointed? In 1879 he had been so full of zeal: 'when we remain faithful to the truth, we have cause to hope that continued research will open up new vistas to us and cast light on many dark points.' He had certainly engaged in 'continued research', but, he writes in the 1896 version, he was forced to finish the book 'before these investigations were concluded' (p. v). His wish for the reader is certainly a great deal less extravagant than it had been in 1879, when he had wished the reader 'joy' in seeking to understand the English language, the same joy that he had felt in writing the book. Now in 1896 he simply wishes that the reader may find 'more learning and greater explication [. . .] than were available in the first edition'. This is the voice of the mature scholar. As a younger man maybe he had thought that he had the answer, but now he knows that he simply has some knowledge. As a younger man maybe he thought he could spread joy, but now he knows that he simply possesses facts, and lots of them. So was he disappointed? No, I think not. As *Englische Philologie* matured, so did its author. As he told Thomsen: 'Otherwise I have derived a great deal of pleasure from this book.'

2.2.3.3 *Contents*

We noted in section 2.2.2.3 that one way in which Storm tidied up the 1879 version in 1881 was by providing a clearer table of contents; and this process continues into the final revision. The 1896 table of contents which covers both 1892 and 1896 volumes (there was no table of contents in 1892), now lists all the authors Storm discusses under the relevant chapter headings, and this dramatically improves the usability of the work. The 1896 table of contents ('Table of contents for the whole work') also clearly outlines the general structure of the whole work and is, in Trautmann's words, 'all that can be discerned in the work by way of a plan'.

The first volume (1892a) is subtitled:

1. Abteilung. *Phonetik und Aussprache* [Phonetics and Pronunciation]

In singling out phonetics, Storm makes the distinction which would go on to become generally accepted in the twentieth century: that phonetics and linguistics are separate and distinct courses of study. Nineteenth-century phonetics did grow out of work in anatomy, physiology and physics, but, even in applying phonetics to the humanities, to language change, to language teaching, to language description, Storm, Sweet and others tended to treat phonetics as something separate. Yes, Sweet famously and regularly described phonetics as the 'indispensable foundation' for language study of all sorts, but it was a prerequisite, rather than part of the system of language: 'Phonetics is the *science* of speech-sounds' (Sweet 1890: 1). Storm shares the view that the contents of volume 1 and the actual language are quite different things: 'The first section deals with *sounds*, the second deals with the language formed from them, so a markedly different field of enquiry' (Storm 1896a: v). Sounds on the one hand vs. language on the other.

The second volume (1896a) is subtitled:

2. Abteilung. *Rede und Schrift* [Speech and Writing]

'Speech and Writing' is not what would normally be expected in a book which, having despatched the phonetics of the language in a previous volume, treats the language itself. Conventionally such a volume would have covered phonology, morphology, syntax and possibly a few other levels of linguistic structure such as prosody and word formation – not dictionaries, practical resources, literature and various varieties of the language, with grammar as an afterthought along with literary history and (according to the table of contents) the Bible. The *Englische Philologie* is in the words of its subtitle a '*Guide* [*Anleitung*] to the Scientific Study of the English Language' (my emphasis), and, as I remarked above, we must be careful not to criticise *Englische Philologie* for failing to be something it never intended to be. However, Storm never wrote a traditional grammar. For him the essence of language study does not lie in its formal system, its grammatical and phonological structure, but in its *variety*. Consequently an investigation of the varieties of English *was* for Storm Language (*Die Sprache*), alongside Sounds (*Die Laute*). The nearest Storm got to a traditional grammar, for which he was unsuited in both temperament and philosophy, was the *Større fransk Syntax*; but, as we shall see, this was much more like *Englische Philologie* in content, style and structure than any more conventional grammatical presentation.

The principal difference between the 1892/1896 version and its earlier incarnation is of course the greater number of texts discussed, and the correspondingly greater number of commentaries and excursuses, but the material has also been reorganised to reflect the relative importance of the material. In 1881 the extensive, original and (for Storm) central material on colloquial, vulgar and American English was, bizarrely, included under chapter 5, 'Reading and the study of literature', the long stream-of-consciousness chapter. Now these have their own chapters, and American English, which was divided up under three different sections in 1881 (*Amerikanische Literatur*, *Amerikanismen* and *Amerikanische Aussprache*) is now simply *Kap. X: Amerikanisches Englisch*. English dialects are still rather apologetically and sparsely treated ('I can't go into the dialects fully here [. . .]' (1896a: 832)), but they now have a separate (5½-page) chapter dedicated to them. Part of this brief chapter is a new section on *kolonialisches Englisch*, showing that Storm really was aware of all the most recent work being carried into English, and, uncharacteristically for his day, really interpreted the living language in its fullest sense. The final new chapter to appear in the 1896 volume is another interesting one: *Sprachrichtigkeit* (Correctness), subheaded 'Die Grenzen der Umgangssprache und der Vulgärsprache' (The boundaries of colloquial and vulgar language). Here he includes the lengthy discussion of the Alford/Moon controversy, as well as other popular prescriptive works, ranging from the relatively formal

(Cobbett's *A Grammar of the English Language in a Series of Letters*) to the irrelevant (J. Barter's *How to Speak Correctly*) – nothing lies outside Storm's *Sammlermanie*. The chapter concludes with a section – as so often, *ad hoc* in its contents and paratactic in its structure – showing that Storm had a clear notion of what constituted Standard English, despite his interest in and respect for non-standard usage: 'Characteristics of some English writers' (pp. 766–772). *Die Vulgärsprache* is next, but before embarkation Storm offers this warning:

> In this section I provide some brief and (due to lack of time and space) incomplete notes on the characteristics, carelessnesses, freedoms, archaisms etc. of some of those English writers most read by foreigners. (1896a: 766)

Englische Philologie was more than a static 'treasure trove'. Through it Storm had a pioneering influence on one of the most vigorous pan-European linguistic movements of the late nineteenth century, namely the language teaching reform movement. Many of the major linguists of the day were involved in this movement, and it is no exaggeration to say that Storm was the leading light amongst them, although this light faded as the movement gathered momentum. Sievers and Sweet, the other two "Great S's" in the establishment of modern phonetics, recognised his status. Sievers, in his review of the 1892 volume, wrote:

> Storm's *Englische Philologie* is in a position, like no other book, to initiate a reform in the teaching of modern languages in Germany, and we hope that it will fulfil its calling abundantly, although at the moment it seems as though the auspices for a successful reorganisation of this branch of education are very bleak. (Sievers 1893: 267)

Sweet for once was less negative in his evaluation of the state of affairs, hoping that *Englische Philologie*:

> will lend a strong fillip to the hopefully imminent reform of the still dominant mechanical, workman-like methods in this field. (Sweet 1881: 1400)

Englische Philologie was, according to Sweet, 'epoch-making for language-teaching most of all'.

2.2.4 Phonetik und Aussprache *(1892) and Beyond*

2.2.4.1 *Storm and the New Science*

2.2.4.1.1 In 1888 the first volume of a new phonetic journal appeared. That journal was *Phonetische Studien*, and everyone who was anyone in the growing field of phonetics was on the editorial board. The very first article of that first volume, Lundell's 'Die phonetik als universitätsfach'[5] (Lundell 1888),[6] was a manifesto for the new science, charting what phonetics was all about and proclaiming its importance for science in general. For Lundell, the Neogrammarians, who had launched themselves with great bravado only a decade before, were now the "Old School":

> Not only Bopp and Grimm, but Schleicher and Curtius too are already old-fashioned – which cannot in the least diminish the honour due to these brilliant scholars. The younger generation stands on the shoulders of the older and has a broader horizon because of it. (Lundell 1888: 4)

It is evident that Lundell sees his article as the new manifesto, since he explicitly dismisses the old manifesto, 'Leskien's 1876 dissertation'. This 'dissertation' was *Die Declination im Slavisch-Litauischen und Germanischen* (Leskien 1876), where the doctrine of the exceptionlessness of sound-laws was first drafted. That doctrine and the publication in which it appeared are now insufficient, maintains Lundell, to provide the basis for a new science of language. So what has been lacking in the world of linguistic scholarship that phonetics can now provide?

Phonetics, Lundell announces, is about studying the living language, not only the language of good society but also the language of the farmer and the urchin ('des bauers und des strassenjungen' (p. 4)) and it provides the means to do so scientifically. So phonetics can allow access to a previously uncharted linguistic landscape. Storm's pioneering work on non-standard varieties of English is an example of this particular application of phonetics. Furthermore, an understanding of the nature of speech sounds will shed new light on the history of languages, as phonetics penetrates the hallowed halls of historical and comparative philology. Phonetics will also revolutionise the process of language teaching, it will resolve orthographic debates throughout Europe, it will revolutionise the teaching of reading and it will revolutionise teaching for the deaf and dumb. 'Phonetics is constantly gaining greater significance, both scientifically and practically' (p. 6). These are the claims of an enthusiastic supporter, but the introduction of phonetics across Europe as an autonomous area of study during the second half of the nineteenth century must have been very refreshing for the new generation of linguists, weaned on a rather indigestible diet of classical and Indo-European philology. Lundell was in his mid-30s when he wrote 'Die phonetik als universitätsfach', but he was only 30 when in 1881 he held up the new science against the old philology at the Kristiania Philologists' Meeting (Lundell 1881). The new generation of linguists had a different way of looking at language, what Jespersen later called 'a philology of the ear instead of the eye' (1933: 5), a practical approach which had applications in

---

[5] It didn't use upper-case initial letters in nouns.
[6] Published as an offprint in 1887.

the real world, and an approach which was at the same time tangibly scientific with its affinity to anatomy, physiology and acoustics. Some of the earliest phonetics was allied closely to these parent sciences. Eduard Sievers's best-known phonetic work started life as *Grundzüge der Lautphysiologie* (Sievers 1876), and only in its second edition was it renamed *Grundzüge der Phonetik* (Sievers 1881). Phonetic research in Germany tended to remain close to the parent disciplines, at the level of theoretical physiology or acoustics. Sievers was an exception, and Lundell categorises him accordingly as a member of the 'englisch-skandinavische schule', of which more anon (section 2.2.4.2.3).

Given the importance of phonetics, argued Lundell, it had every reason to claim its rightful place on the university curriculum. Lundell was himself reader (*docent*) in phonetics at the University of Uppsala, but the apparent support shown by the university to phonetics in appointing Lundell to such a position was not borne out by the faculty regulations. When Lundell wrote this article, phonetics was still not permitted as part of the traditional examinations. He notes that he has, since his appointment to the readership in 1882, 'taught privately' in the area of general phonetics. He compares the situation at Uppsala with the situation for phonetics at other universities throughout northern Europe. It emerges from Lundell's comparison that the teaching of topics related to phonetics went back as far as 1867 and lectures in Berlin on the principles of orthography. Other lecture courses followed in the various universities, covering topics like orthography and the physiology of speech, but the first lectures in Lundell's overview of university-level phonetics (1888: 10–11) to include the word 'phonetik', are Storm's.[7]

Lundell reports that, in the academic year 1883–1884, Storm lectured on 'phonetics with particular emphasis on the Norwegian dialects' (p. 11). In the following two years, this series was succeeded by 'Norwegian phonetics', and 'Norwegian and general phonetics'. The emphasis on Norwegian is in part explained by Storm's being much occupied with the sounds of the Norwegian dialects at this time, but it would have been unthinkable for him to have lectured simply on general phonetics. No matter how posterity may have labelled him, he was not a phonetician. He was a student of the living languages, and the principles and methods of the new science of phonetics were an indispensable tool for the study of living language, but he was not interested in the science of phonetics as an end in itself. Storm may have been able to persuade Sweet to write his *Handbook of Phonetics* (Sweet 1877), but Sweet's repeated requests that Storm write a general study of prosody fell on deaf ears. Storm didn't do "general". In the unpublished *Kort fonetisk Kursus for Lærere i Eng. og Fransk* (*Short Course in Phonetics for Teachers of English and French*) (Storm 1890b), he opens with the statement that

---

[7] See section 4.1.1.3 for more on Storm's lectures.

phonetics is 'ikke Maal, men Middel', not an end but a means. Lundell was as much a dialectologist as Storm, but he was also more interested in the discipline of *die Phonetik*. It is not surprising then that Storm's greatest and most focused contribution to phonetics should come in a work dedicated to a particular language – English.

2.2.4.1.2 So Storm was not a phonetician in the modern sense of the word, in that it cannot be said that his subject was phonetics. He used phonetic techniques where they were useful, but was sceptical about phonetics being the answer to all linguistic problems. We shall see in section 2.3 how Storm was much more cautious and dubious about the use of phonetics in the teaching of foreign languages than, for example, Sweet and Jespersen. He was broad-minded enough to see the value in theoretical and instrumental approaches to speech sounds. He professed himself to be no expert in such matters, but he was very positive about the experimental work of the eminent American Romanist, Charles Hall Grandgent (1862–1939), and of R. J. Lloyd, and realised that such work represented the future of phonetic science. Of Lloyd he wrote:

> I am not enough of a scientist to make a conclusive judgement about the results, but this much seems to me to be certain, that here is an epoch-making achievement [. . .] Lloyd's work belongs to the phonetics of the future. (Storm 1892a: 343–351)

He was also intrigued by the potential applications of new instruments. From the newspaper *Aftenposten* he cut out a description of Amadeo Gentili's *Glosograf*, and he writes enthusiastically of Edison's *Phonograph*, and of his own few experiments with one (1892a: 351). He notes that his work on comparative intonation would have been more satisfactory had he had more time with a phonograph (Storm 1892a: 214, n. 1). Storm is more forward-looking than Sweet in this respect, who expresses his distrust of machines in his letters to Storm. But Storm had either insufficient opportunity or competence to explore the new scope for instrumental studies towards the end of the century. This is by contrast with, for example, Jespersen. Juul (2002: 104) reports that Jespersen was carrying out experiments using X-rays as early as 1897. Storm even found technical writings difficult to read, and he complained to Thomsen: 'I had earlier tried to read Helmholtz, but it just wouldn't work' (Letter of 2 February 1883).

The point is that Storm was not himself a theoretical or experimental phonetician. For him the only necessary instruments were the ear and the mouth of the linguist, instruments which could, with practice and with skill, be honed to perfection. Consequently, if we were to take away the detailed descriptions of the sounds of specific languages, there would be very little phonetic substance left in Storm's writings. This is not to belittle the value of Storm's research. All his contemporaries were in awe of his practical facility with speech sounds, and, in a largely pre-instrumental era, his findings really are as good and as accurate as they get. There is no better body of data on late nineteenth-century Norwegian sounds, and his contribution to the material on English of the same period remains invaluable.

2.2.4.1.3 So Storm never wrote a general phonetic textbook, by contrast with Bell and Sweet and Soames and Sievers and Viëtor and Jespersen and Lundell. In short he was not a phonetician in the same way. However, the first 484 pages of the final revision of *Englische Philologie* constitute a compendium of his life's work on the study of speech sounds, as he told Thomsen:

> I have for several years busied myself with my favourite subject, phonetics, in that I have been working on the second German edition of my *Engl. Philol.*, where the phonetic section is *greatly* expanded, actually *disproportionately so*, but I find it most convenient to collect together all my phonetic studies from these years, rather than spread them across different places. (Letter of 23 November 1890; Storm's emphasis)

The first volume of the final revision of *Englische Philologie* is, as we have seen, an annotated bibliography of all the important pieces of phonetic literature currently available. The first part of the book deals with the literature on *Allgemeine Phonetik*, although much of this in fact concentrates on the phonetics of individual languages. Storm begins with German scholars, principally with the work of Karl Ludwig Merkel (1812–1876), Ernst Wilhelm von Brücke (1819–1892), Hermann Berthold Rumpelt (1821–1881), Sievers, Viëtor and Trautmann. Next come the British "Big Three": Bell, Ellis and Sweet. Up to this point Storm has concentrated on works of general phonetics, since, he argues at the beginning of his presentation:

> One cannot achieve a scientific knowledge of the sounds of a foreign language without knowing something of general phonetics or the physiology of sounds. (Storm 1892a: 35)

The works discussed and the excursuses stemming from these commentaries are, then, of direct background significance to a student of English philology. From here on, the relevance of the works presented, and of Storm's often lengthy original remarks, becomes more tenuous, and we see the familiar Storm in action. The "stream of consciousness" exhibited elsewhere in Storm's writings is perhaps most strikingly in evidence here as Storm allows his vast knowledge of speech sounds to lead him freely from one point to another, from one language to another, with scant regard for the reader, who is likely to be a university student of English. Although undoubtedly true, Storm's argument for a presentation of Passy's *Les sons du français* (Passy 1887), and a 30-page excursus on the phonetics of French, strikes me as somewhat unconvincing:

I now proceed to some more recent presentations of the pronunciation of French. As the phonetics of French is extremely important for modern philologists, as well as in and for itself, on account of the stark contrasts with Germanic sounds, I have devoted particular attention to this subject. It is particularly true in this area that one's own is only properly elucidated by means of the foreign. (1892a: 158)

Discussion of French intonation here leads Storm's thoughts to prosodic matters more generally, and to probably the most original and significant part of the book, and the nearest thing Storm ever came to Sweet's longed-for general study of prosodic phonetics and phonology. We will return to these sections on tone and intonation in a variety of languages in section 2.2.4.3. From French the reader floats on Storm's stream-of-consciousness to the Scandinavian languages, of which inevitably the section on Norwegian dialects, flowing from a presentation of his own *Norsk Lydskrift med Omrids af Fonetiken*, is the longest.

One hundred pages after Storm meandered off into French, we get back to the job in hand.

Having thus gone through some specialised topics, we return to general phonetics, in that we at last discuss some of the most recent researches, especially those that try to break new ground, either by means of sharper scientific analysis of the speech organs and the formation of sounds, or through more precise definition of the sounds themselves. (p. 260)

The ground-breaking studies Storm goes on to address are principally anatomical, physiological and acoustic. Storm's treatment of these fills getting on for 100 pages more, and again demonstrates his interest in and respect for the new methods and approaches, even if, for whatever reason, he could not or would not get involved with them himself.

The second part of the book, and one quarter its total length, is given over to works on the pronunciation of English. Storm begins this section by presenting his own semi-phonemic transcription system for English (pp. 356–361). It employs symbols from his *Norvegia* script, and, as he remarks, is 'not always strictly phonetic, but adequate enough' (p. 355). An overview of pronouncing dictionaries leads to the central part of this section, namely presentations of and excursuses from the works of A. M. Bell, Henry Sweet and Laura Soames. The *New English Dictionary* (later becoming known as the *Oxford English Dictionary*), then with only the first three fascicles published, comes under the Storm microscope, and the book ends with surveys of works by R. J. Lloyd, August Western and a handful of more minor scholars.

This volume is on the surface more about people and books than it is about phonetics. It sets up a canon of phonetic literature and of phoneticians; so, before going on to consider the most significant original phonetic work in Storm (1892a) – on prosody – we will first consider his academic relationship with other groups of contemporary phoneticians, as it emerges in these pages. His *personal* relationships with other scholars, especially with Henry Sweet, Laura Soames, Vilhelm Thomsen, Otto Jespersen, August Western and Amund B. Larsen, are amply covered elsewhere in this book

2.2.4.2 *The Phonetic Schools*

2.2.4.2.1 *The German School*

Storm, in common with his contemporaries, divided the phonetic world into a German School and an English School. The English School (which included a Scot, resident in America – Alexander Melville Bell) came to form part of a wider Anglo-Scandinavian School, referred to by Lundell in his 1888 overview of the state-of-the-art of phonetics. Storm saw himself as being on the side of the English School, and others saw him as one of the most prominent members of the Anglo-Scandinavian School, probably the next most prominent member after Henry Sweet. However, Storm's allegiances, like the division between the Schools, were not clear-cut.

Storm expressed his dissatisfaction with much German phonetic research on a number of occasions, and the grounds for his dissatisfaction are summed up in *Englische Philologie*:

> Above all the Germans are characterised by too strong a theorising tendency, a treatment which is far too abstract without adequate under-pinnings in the facts. (1892a: 81)

Any approach to language which did not take linguistic data, and a detailed description of that data, as its central concern would never meet with Storm's approval. He was not naturally inclined towards the construction of theories and systems; this was not where his strength lay. However, his objection to theorising and systematising linguists was not inspired by the negative reason that he could not compete with or indeed fully understand their work. In Grandgent, Lloyd and others, he was quite capable of seeing the importance of linguistic work which he did not fully understand and with which he did not feel completely comfortable. No, his objection to linguistic work which focused on systems and theory rather than on data was born, like all his linguistic ideas, from love for the living language, the real utterances of real people. But Storm judged everything on its own merits. As we shall see, he did not object to *all* radical reform work on the Norwegian language. He objected to any instances of reform he perceived as badly done or as artificial, and he always provided data to support his objections. He was no bigot, and nor did he reject all German phonetics, despite the apparently sweeping nature of his comment about 'the Germans' quoted above. In Storm (1892a) he shows himself to be an admirer of

Sievers's work, 'even though a simpler, more practical and clearer presentation were to be desired, backed up by fuller examples from the author's rich experience' (p. 91). Storm's and Sievers's mutual support and respect is expressed in Storm's review of Sievers (1881):

> Getting to know a draft of my work by chance, Prof. Sievers did me the honour of making contact with me and reading through the phonetic part of my book. Thus there arose between us an exchange of views, which will always be fruitful between phoneticians of different nationalities. (Storm 1881d: 886)

As we know, the contact and the correspondence between scholars working on speech sounds in the late nineteenth century was very striking, and since there was in reality a continuum of approaches rather than two distinct national schools, it would be nearer the truth to talk, as Sweet did, of one truly 'International School of Phonetics' at this time, one which had an impact on all sorts of practical and theoretical issues, but which had at its heart practically oriented scientific linguists like Sweet, Storm and Sievers. Indeed Sweet felt that the three of them together had laid 'the foundations of international phonetics' (letter of 27 December 1880). That Lundell has to treat Sievers as a sort of honorary member of the English School shows that the national types were not as stereotyped as Storm sometimes made them out to be in his publications and in his lectures. In *Engelsk Filologi* (Storm 1879a: 31) he admits: 'Sievers for sure suffers less from this error [too much abstraction without basis in the data] than all his predecessors'. In *Englische Philologie* (1892a: 103–111) Storm also writes very favourably of the phonetic work of Wilhelm Viëtor, a scholar who, like Storm, had spent time abroad and was passionately committed to language-teaching reform. Viëtor's *Kleine Phonetik des Deutschen, Englischen und Französischen* was, like Storm (1892a; 1896a), published by O. R. Reisland of Leipzig. A glance through the advertisements in the back of Viëtor (1903) shows that, amongst other things, Reisland also published Western's *Englische Lautlehre für Studierende und Lehrer* (Western 1902), Felix Franke's *Phrases de tous les jours* (1900)[8] and Passy's *Le français parlé* (1902). This was a cosy, mutually supportive and truly international little milieu. Sweet was of course notorious for his professional jealousies, and it is remarkable that this milieu was not more rife with mistrust and bitchiness. But its members were on the whole not in competition with each other, since they were based in different countries. More importantly, there were next to no posts available in phonetics, so there was no rivalry there. Phonetics was for most of the protagonists a hobby or a means to improving their principal area of work or study. In this respect the phoneticians of the late nineteenth century were rather like today's historians of linguistics.

[8] For Franke, and specifically the correspondence between Jespersen and Franke, see Kabell (2000).

2.2.4.2.2 *The English School*

The so-called 'English School' really meant Sweet, standing on the shoulders of Ellis and Bell. Raudnitzky (1911) called it 'Die Bell–Sweetsche Schule'. After Thomsen, Sweet was the professional colleague to whom Storm was closest. Throughout the present book reference is made to Sweet's letters to Storm, and this is because they are so numerous and revealing. They are especially revealing in what they show us of phonetics in the making, of what real linguistic pioneers thought and aspired to. Their correspondence appears to have terminated abruptly in 1892, possibly on account of Storm's favourable opinion of Laura Soames, of whom Sweet disapproved utterly. In this light, H. C. Wyld's dedication at the beginning of his edition of Sweet's collected papers (Sweet 1913: iv) is rather confusing:

To
Professor Johann [*sic*] Storm
of Christiania
The Veteran Linguist, Phonetician,
And Scholar
this Collection of Henry Sweet's Shorter Papers
is dedicated
In Memory of their
Long and Unbroken Friendship
and
Of many Happy Days of Kindly Companionship

'Many happy days of kindly companionship' there certainly were, but 'their long and unbroken friendship' would appear to be something of a myth, at least its unbrokenness. Because their friendship was both long and productive, perhaps it seemed to Wyld that it had been literally lifelong. This issue is destined to remain mysterious for the time being. Whatever happened, they were in close contact from their first meeting in England in 1876 at least up to the middle of 1892. Sweet treated Storm as a sort of honorary Englishman. In reviewing *Engelsk Filologi*, he compared Storm's 'living language' approach favourably with the 'chaotic mess' of 'the German school' (Sweet 1879: 269). In reviewing the first German edition of 1881 he went further, describing Storm's *Geist* in one review as 'above all practical and conservative, and in that too he is pure English' (Sweet 1881: 1407). In another review Sweet alludes to the existence of an Anglo-Scandinavian School, a body of intellectually like-minded scholars, under the leadership of Storm:

We see, in Storm's work, how closely akin the Norwegian scientific spirit is to the English. Although the Norwegians partially resemble the Germans in possessing genuine universities and an organised system of scientific training, yet their work distinctly shows the more practical

character of that of England; and this is proved most unmistakeably in the
way in which the results of English phonetics have been taken up by Storm
and his young disciples. (Sweet 1882: 472)

Storm on the other side saw himself merely as tending towards the English
School, not as an uncritical member of it. He wrote to Thomsen (2 February
1883) that, while Thomsen approached the Germans, he, Storm, approached
the English. Approached, but not joined.

Storm was never blindly partisan. While he sympathised broadly with the
empirical, practical British tradition, as exemplified by Bell, Ellis and Sweet,
and its concentration on detailed and precise phonetic description, he was far
from uncritical. In general terms he felt that 'English phonology' tended 'to
see things piecemeal' (letter to Thomsen, 8 November 1874), the inverse of the
German tendency, but equally worthy of criticism. More specifically, Storm
had two major objections to the practices of the British phoneticians. The first
concerned Bell's Visible Speech transcription system, championed by Sweet
and the subject of some rather violent disagreement between Storm and
Sweet, and the second concerned the phonetic categories 'wide' vs. 'narrow'.

Alexander Melville Bell's (1818–1905) Visible Speech system was set out in
1867, and the philosophy behind it is self-evident from the title of the book
in which it was presented: *Visible Speech: The Science of Universal Alphabetics; or Self-Interpreting Physiological Letters, for the Writing of All
Languages in One Alphabet. Illustrated by Tables, Diagrams, and Examples.*
In short, it was intended as a universal phonetic alphabet. Bell may have
failed to get public backing for the system, a fact he recounts with the same
bitterness that Storm felt over his failure to get public backing for his
Norwegian project in 1877 (Bell 1867: vii–x), but the system did find a
vigorous champion in Sweet. Bell explains the system thus:

The fundamental principle of Visible Speech is, that all Relations of
Sound are symbolized by Relations of Form. Each organ and each mode
of organic action concerned in the production or modification of sound,
has its appropriate Symbol; and all Sounds of the same nature produced
at different parts of the mouth, are represented by a Single Symbol turned
in a direction corresponding to the organic position. (Bell 1867: 35)

Bell had the same sort of high hopes for Visible Speech that Lundell had for
the science of phonetics in general. He foresaw ten 'special uses' for the
system:

I. The teaching of the ILLITERATE in all countries to read their Vernacular
Tongue in a few days.
II. The teaching of the BLIND to read.
III. The teaching of the DEAF AND DUMB to speak.
IV. The communication of the exact sounds of FOREIGN LANGUAGES to
learners in all countries.

V. The establishment of a STANDARD of the NATIVE PRONUNCIATION of any language.
VI. The Prevention and Removal of DEFECTS and IMPEDIMENTS of Speech.
VII. The TELEGRAPHIC communication of messages in any language, through all countries, without translation.
VIII. The study, comparison, and preservation of fast-disappearing DIALECTS, and the universal tracing of the AFFINITIES OF WORDS.
IX. The speedy diffusion of the language of a mother country throughout the most widely separated COLONIES.
X. The world-wide communication of any specific sounds with absolute uniformity; and consequently, the possible construction and establishment of a UNIVERSAL LANGUAGE.

(Bell 1867: 20–21)

Bell sets the agenda here for the practical application of phonetics, and many of these applications were subsequently picked up by members of the Anglo-Scandinavian School.

Bell was aware of the potential difficulties inherent in his system, and of its being potentially off-putting by virtue of the unfamiliarity of its symbols. In 1897 he published a phonetics primer, which did not use the symbols, as a gentle introduction to Visible Speech:

> Some beginners are apt to be repelled at sight of [*sic*] unknown symbols, under the impression that the latter must be difficult to learn. But this idea soon gives way, before the lucidity and simplicity of the exponent symbols of Visible Speech. (Bell 1897: 5)

Sweet and his cousin and co-worker, Henry Nicol, were far less compromising. Sweet had no sympathy for those whom he thought too lazy to learn the Visible Speech system. Nicol wrote vehemently to Storm in 1877 that 'those people who have not mastered both the theory and practice of V.S., are scarcely competent to judge either of its practical difficulty, or its philological value' (NBO Ms. 8° 2402 J^{iv}). Sweet wrote most comprehensively in support of the system in his 'Sound notation' of 1880, where he also suggested various revisions (Sweet 1880). He was still vigorously commending its adoption ten years later in his *Primer of Phonetics* (Sweet 1890):

> So also by the retention of the main features of Bell's 'Visible Speech' terminology and notation – with the few modifications set forth in my *Sound-Notation* [. . .] – I by no means pledge myself to rigid conservatism. But I feel convinced that the path of progress lies through the Visible Speech analysis, and that the first duty of the very few who have a practical command of it is to do what they can to spread the knowledge of it. (Sweet 1890: vi)

Since, in Sweet's view, the Visible Speech system constituted the 'path of progress', there was no need for any other systems of transcription, and rival systems were no more than a waste of time. Storm's Norvegia system (see section 4.3.3) was one example:

> Prof. Storm, again, in his *Engelsk Filologi*, seems in some respects to ignore the results of English experience, and has special types made for an alphabet whose limited range and want of elasticity makes it useless to anyone but himself, even if it were generally accessible. (Sweet 1880)

It was however Storm's system which found disciples and survived where Bell's didn't. So what was Storm's problem with *Visible Speech*, which brought him into disagreement with his friend and guru, Sweet?

Despite Nicol's insinuations, Storm had studied *Visible Speech* very carefully and he respected Bell's work, calling 'the presentation epoch-making for its time' (1892a: 406), but he admits in a letter to Thomsen (5 August 1875) that he does not find the system attractive. As so often, it is a stiffness and artificiality he finds objectionable, a systematisation that does not do justice to the real variety to be found in living languages. Storm's criticism is that Bell's system describes not the sounds themselves but the mouth positions adopted for those sounds:

> In this I cannot agree with [several of the most modern phoneticians]. For me the highest principle is the quality and characteristic of the sound, i.e. the *acoustic principle* [. . .] The English School, with Sweet at the helm, goes so far as to confuse the sound with the formation of the sound, without any further ado. (Storm 1890b: 4–5)

This seems a narrow distinction to make, but for that student of living languages it was an important one. In this same letter he explains that Bell's descriptive labels are too mechanical and fail to capture the quality of particular sounds, and that Bell's 3×3 system for categorising vowels is arbitrary and does not allow for enough nuances of vowel quality. (Storm would doubtless have objected in the same way to Daniel Jones's system of Cardinal Vowels.) In *Englische Philologie* Storm gives a full account of Visible Speech, since it had remained little known outside the circle of its adherents, Bell's pupils, and he reiterates his chief objection, unmoved by the vigorous defence of Sweet and Nicol: 'My chief objection to the book is that the presentation is much too dry and schematic, and explains too little' (1892a: 112).

Storm's other objection to the English School concerned their penchant for the vowel categories 'wide' and 'narrow' (see Raudnitzky (1911: 132–133) for a discussion of this problematic contrast), and it was more forcibly and fully argued even than the objection to Visible Speech. He actually accepted much of the "English" system for vowel categorisation, and much preferred it, with its practical articulatory basis, to impressionistic German auditory methods of vowel categorisation. Bell's 'wide' embraces the parameter 'lax', and 'narrow' the parameter 'tense'. These categories have remained problematic, ill-defined and inconsistently applied, from one linguist to another and from one language to another, so Storm's problems with this corner of phonetics were not merely pedantry or failure to understand the categories properly. Certainly in Bell's and Sweet's day the idea of different degrees of muscular tension corresponding to clearly defined phonetic outcomes was highly subjective, and Storm was right to worry about this. Sweet defines 'wide' and 'narrow' as follows:

> The distinction depends mainly on the *shape* of the tongue. In forming narrow vowels there is a feeling of tenseness in that part of the tongue where the sound is formed, the surface of the tongue being made more convex than in its natural 'wide' shape, in which it is relaxed and flattened. This convexity of the tongue naturally narrows the passage – whence the name [. . .] The distinction between narrow and wide is not so clear in the back vowels, where the convexity of the tongue seems to be accompanied by tension and consequent advancing of the uvula. (Sweet 1890: 18)

Storm felt that this was not a satisfactory explanation, and that nobody had satisfactorily understood or explained these parameters. He felt (rightly) that different parameters for vowel contrast were being mixed up under the one label, since the contrast between narrow [ʌ] (as in English *but*) and wide [ɑ] (as in English *father*) or between narrow [e] (as in Norwegian *fe*) and wide [ɛ] (as in Norwegian *hest*) was as much a property of tongue height as of tongue tension. After much puzzling in his correspondence and in his lectures, Storm realised:

> What renders this definition unclear is that two different principles are mixed up here, two principles which cannot always be collapsed the one onto the other: *height* and *tension*. The whole tongue can be more or less tense without any associated partial arching, except that which necessarily follows from the position of *i*. (Storm 1890b: 78)

Storm uses the terms 'tense' (*spændt*) and 'lax' (*slap*), and is essentially happy with this phonetic feature, particularly as a property of English vowels. He expresses the view that English phoneticians have got particularly hung up on the distinction between narrow and wide because of the close relationship between tension and height in English vowels. Passy, by contrast, a native speaker of French, viewed all English vowels as wide and all French vowels as narrow:

> We other phoneticians, from nations which do not know of these extremes, tend more to accept this distinction as a necessary component of the system. (1890b: 82)

A detailed study in the *Kort fonetisk Kursus for Lærere i Eng. og Fransk* of a range of exceptions to the narrow/wide distinction leads Storm to conclude that:

> All these inconsistencies naturally contribute to an increase in the vagueness surrounding this distinction, which we can therefore for the most part disregard. (Storm 1890b: 84)

Storm, standing on the European sidelines, the practical linguist, with his profound and precise knowledge of the sounds of so many different languages and dialects, does not accept a theoretical distinction if it is not fully supported by the facts of the living languages. So he may have felt greater sympathy and respect for the 'English' approach to understanding speech sounds than to the German, but, as always, the data has the last word.

2.2.4.2.3 *An Anglo-Scandinavian School?*

If Storm was not a loyal disciple of the English School, that is to say if he did not accept some of Bell's and Sweet's central doctrines, could he be said to have been a member of an Anglo-Scandinavian School? On the face of it, no. But Storm was not a joiner or a follower. He never fully accepted the tenets of any school or group or movement. He formed his own views based on his own experience. This mistrust of other people's findings, and trusting no data but his own, smacked of arrogance, but he was uncompromising in his search for linguistic "truth". He was a merciless and unceasing critic of both sides in the Norwegian language-reform debate (see Chapter 4), and he avoided active involvement in the Quousque Tandem movement and the nascent International Phonetic Association.[9] To look for other linguists or groups of linguists whom Storm could be said to have followed is a waste of time. He was a pioneer in all he did. His solitary life as Norway's one professor of modern languages and first champion of phonetics made him feel like a pioneer. He was never going to follow, but was he a leader? Was there such a thing as an Anglo-Scandinavian School with Storm at its head?

He certainly had his followers. Amund Bredesen Larsen (1849–1928) and August Western (1856–1940) were his disciples. They learnt their enthusiasm for phonetics, for the contemporary languages and dialects, and for Norwegian Riksmål from him. Larsen's life was dedicated to Norwegian, and we will return to him in section 4.3, but it is worth remarking here that, prior to receiving a state salary from 1901, he worked, like Western, as a provincial schoolteacher.

Western spent his entire working life in the same Fredrikstad school, well

---

[9] Storm may not have sought involvement in these societies, but others sought it for him. He was one of nine 'membres onoraires' of the Assosiasion [*sic*] Fonétique des Professeurs de Langues Vivantes (the International Phonetic Association) on its foundation, and his (lack of) involvement in the Quousque Tandem movement is discussed in section 2.3.2.

away from the capital and from the academic environment provided by the university; but he nevertheless managed to be highly productive in the tradition of his teacher and mentor, Storm. He responded to his own working environment by writing language-teaching materials in the spirit of the Quousque Tandem movement, of which he was a co-founder (see next section). His 1893 doctoral thesis was on *De engelske Bisætninger* (*English Subordinate Clauses*), and he also published significant work on the 'be -ing' verbal construction in English and on the use of modal verbs. It was, however, to Norwegian that he dedicated the greatest effort, again very much along the lines taken by Storm:

> Throughout his entire life Western continued to be an adherent of Norwegianisation and of a maximally phonetic orthography, but his position is characterised throughout by cautiousness and by an understanding of the different language varieties we have in this country [Norway]. (Lundeby 1983: 67)

Like Storm, Western was as active in the publication of programmatic reform writings (such as Western 1907) as he was in the publication of serious scientific studies of the language. His *magnum opus* came in 1921, *Norsk Riksmåls-Grammatikk*, described by Lundeby in 1983 as 'to date the most magnificent work in Norwegian grammatical literature' (Lundeby 1983: 68). Lundeby notes that Western was, by his own admission, influenced by Jespersen in this presentation of Norwegian grammar, giving further credence to the notion of at least a Scandinavian School. But the influence of his teacher Storm is amply evident too, both in what Western worked on and in the approaches he took. As Storm's disciple, phonetics was of course high on Western's agenda, and he wrote a 'Kurze Darstellung des norwegischen Lautsystems' (Western 1889c). In Storm (1892a) Western is described as 'the excellent [*treffliche*] Norwegian phonetician', and in the preface to Western's *Engelsk Lydlære* (English Phonology) (Western 1882), Storm himself wrote:

> W. has wedded himself closely to the modern English School, even in points which are dubious to me. There is scarcely anyone outside England, who is as familiar with the results of the School as W. is. (quoted in Storm 1892a: 466)

If Western was Storm's disciple, then he was at least equally a follower of Sweet's. Western visited England from 1880 to 1881, where, according to his letters home to Storm, Sweet showed him much personal and academic kindness. Sweet explained to Storm:

> I see Western once a week. He seems likely to have a good influence on Norwegian phonology and the teaching of English pronunciation in Norway. (Letter of 27 December 1880)

These weekly meetings made a very favourable impression on Sweet, a man not easily impressed. Following Western's departure from England, Sweet told Storm (in a letter of 10 April 1881):

> I saw a good deal of Western, and thought him very promising. He is clear-headed, firm + modest – in fact, a true Norwegian. With him and Brekke you ought to found a good school.

Where Storm was not a follower and a joiner, Western was. Besides his involvement in the Quousque Tandem movement, he was a member of the committee of L'Association Phonétique Internationale from 1888 and a founder member of the Norsk Retskrivningssamlag (Norwegian Orthographical Association) in 1892. This was all in addition to the spectacular amount of work he undertook as a member of, and leading light in, a variety of local educational and other committees (Lundeby 1983: 69). Temperamentally different from Storm, and in fact 'ein ähnlicher "uncompromising character" wie Sweet' (Storm 1892a: 466), Western, at the confluence of Storm, Sweet and Jespersen, is certainly a good argument for the existence of a School embracing "new philologists" from Britain and the Scandinavian countries.

It is nearly as shocking that there is as yet no full study of Western's work and influence, as it is shocking that, until this moment, there has been no comprehensive study of Storm. Perhaps one day Western will receive such a study. Less well-known internationally even than Western is another productive linguist who is a very clear candidate for membership of an Anglo-Scandinavian School, Knud Olai Brekke (b. 1855). Brekke studied at the university with Storm and, like Western, spent time studying in England and in France, spending some of his time in England with Sweet, on whom he too, to judge from the quotation above, made a good impression. Like Western, then, Brekke can be said to be a disciple of Sweet as well as of Storm, and Storm saw Brekke as a close adherent of the English School (Storm 1892a: 241). Again like Western, he dedicated his working life to the teaching of English in the schools, and, also like Western, he was an enthusiastic and active committee man. He was a vigorous proponent of revised teaching methods, and the materials he wrote himself were immensely successful, being used and reprinted until the 1960s and translated into Danish, Swedish and Finnish, 'something which occurs very seldom with teaching books' (Sigmund 1925: 171). By the 1960s the hand of Storm would have been felt very lightly indeed here, but all the same the views and practices in language matters of that same School were still influential. These linguists were often characterised by their linguistic and methodological diversity, and Brekke is no exception. Concern for the living language also led him to the phonetics of his own language and to a *Bidrag til dansk-norskens lydlære* (Contribution to the Phonology of Dano-Norwegian) (Brekke 1881),[10] in which 'the author deals with the language of the capital

---

[10] Reprinted in Jahr & Lorentz (1981: 17–78).

as the most important source for educated Norwegian' (see Storm 1892a: 241).

There are other candidates to consider for membership of an Anglo-Scandinavian School. We have barely touched on the work and influence of the other "stars", the other leaders, such as Ellis, Sievers and Lundell, not to mention some of the minor players. The idea of an Anglo-Scandinavian School needs proper investigation, but we can reach some tentative conclusions which, if nothing else, might serve as the basis for further research. First, the School we are considering was nothing like the Geneva School of linguistics or the Generative School. First of all, the Anglo-Scandinavian School did not spring from the cult of the individual. Sweet and Storm were certainly the School's highly respected pioneers, but followers like Jespersen, Western and Lundell were independently minded scholars. They worked in a variety of language areas – indeed the heart of the matter, the living language, necessitated such variety. The disciples worked in different parts of northern Europe,[11] some of them remote from universities, so fossilisation did not occur as it did in Geneva, where Saussure's circle adhered strictly to the principles laid down by the School's founder. Perhaps because of its healthy variety and productivity, the Anglo-Scandinavian 'Living Language' movement (and maybe "movement" is a better label than "School"), has not appeared like a School, like the Saussurean or the Chomskyan. Secondly, contemporary phonetics, as Sweet saw, was truly international and did not divide neatly into a German School and an English School. The fact that the three founding figures of modern phonetics (the three Ss) were all of different nationalities supports this. Thirdly, I believe that we can in fact point to an Anglo-Scandinavian School of applied linguistics, rather than simply phonetics, chronologically situated between the Neogrammarians and the emergence of Structuralism, running from the 1880s to the 1910s. True, phonetics was central to the School's philosophy, but it was a philosophy of the living language more generally. This philosophy led those involved out into the real world to *apply* scientific linguistics to it. To the living, spoken language, to dialects. To language reform of one sort or another, whether that was orthographic, standardising or the creation of new artificial languages. To the classroom. With the Anglo-Scandinavian School, applied linguistics came into being. As the twentieth century has progressed, applied linguistics grew far larger than any branch of theoretical or experimental linguistics, and seen in this way, the impact of Sweet and Storm and Jespersen has been far greater than that of any Saussure or Chomsky. Their impact has not been properly acknowledged in the main-stream historiography of linguistics because practical language study (applied linguistics) has not had the sex appeal and stature within universities that theoretical linguistics has had, and the figures involved have not

---

[11] Even southern Europe, if we include Paul Passy, as there might be grounds for doing.

been professors in Geneva or Massachusetts. They have been Scandinavians, language teachers, worker linguists, on the margins. Admittedly, the history of linguistics has elevated Jespersen to the gallery of stars, but Jespersen, like all "big name" scholars, was able to make his name by systematising, popularising and promulgating the ideas of a previous generation of pioneers. Jespersen was, like Storm in my view, one of the few really brilliant polymaths of linguistics, and I would never belittle his achievement; but he stood on the shoulders of the previous generation, a fact he fully acknowledged in 1920 before the MHRA, as its president:

> Among the first who took the study of living speech seriously, I must mention the German Eduard Sievers, the Norwegian Johan Storm, and especially Henry Sweet. My own work, and that of many others, would have been nothing were it not for the initiation and inspiration due to what these three eminent men wrote in the 'seventies and 'eighties. (Jespersen 1920a: 87)

Deep inside a book about Johan Storm is probably not the best place to try to rewrite a chapter in the history of modern linguistics, but I hope that these few observations about Storm's place in that history might persuade others too to give the Anglo-Scandinavian School a closer look.

2.2.4.3 *Prosody*

2.2.4.3.1 Tale og Accent i Forhold til Sang *(1860)*

Johan Storm's very first publication appeared in 1860 in the weekly newspaper *Illustreret Nyhedsblad*. The full title of the newspaper was:

> *Illustreret Nyhedsblad. Ugentlige Efterretninger om Nutidens vigtigste Begivenheder og Personligheder, samt Dagens Nyheder, offentligt og selskabeligt Liv, Videnskab og Kunst etc.* [Weekly Information about the most Important Events and People of the Time, together with the News of the Day, Public and Social Life, Science and Art etc.]

It was an impressive publication, which came out each Sunday morning to provide gentle intellectual stimulation for the well-to-do folk of Kristiania, for those who had the leisure to peruse such a journal. Storm was in exalted company when, at the age of 23, he went into print for the first time. Other contributors to *Illustreret Nyhedsblad* that year were the folklorist Peter Christen Asbjørnsen, 'Theatre Director' Henrik Ibsen, 'Advocate' Jonas Lie (1833–1908), and the leading authors Aasmund Olavsson Vinje (1818–1870) and Johan Sebastian Welhaven (1807–1873). Why publish 'Tale og Accent i Forhold til Sang' ['Speech and accent in relation to song'] in a Sunday newspaper? First, *Illustreret Nyhedsblad* was no tabloid: it was a dignified learned journal with around 1,400 subscribers. Secondly, there simply weren't the specialist journals available for the publication of phonetic treatises that there would be later, and certainly not in Norway. Thirdly, the readership of *Illustreret Nyhedsblad* was educated and interested, so why shouldn't they wish to read about sounds? Paul Botten-Hansen (1824–1869), the editor, evidently thought that readers would welcome it, since the two instalments of Storm (1860) occupied the front page on 30 September and on 14 October respectively.[12]

'Tale og Accent i Forhold til Sang' is one of the best things Storm wrote. It doesn't have the scholarly bravura of *Englische Philologie*, nor the passion of *Det nynorske Landsmaal: En Undersøgelse*, but its tone is perfect, in a way that he rarely achieved again – with the possible exception of the 1887 version of *Franske Taleøvelser*. For all their brilliance, Storm's publications rarely made any concessions to their readers, but 'Tale og Accent i Forhold til Sang' (*ToA*) is beautifully clear and concise, full of insights, yet demanding no specialist knowledge, in fact the perfect accompaniment to a Sunday morning cup of coffee in the villas of Kristiania West.

Storm opens with a general question, and one which may have occurred to some of his readers: 'What is the relationship between these articulated sounds which constitute speech, and singing?' (p. 169). After a brief discussion of the difference between actual music and a "musical" voice, he goes on to explain the processes of initiation, phonation and articulation in terms of an organ pipe. This he does simply and clearly; the explanation could still be of benefit to a beginning linguistics student nearly 150 years later. In his discussion of pitch he moves over to the violin as a model, and in so doing does exactly what many phonetics teachers still do today when explaining the basics of speech to intelligent but non-specialist audiences. Having explained how pitch variation is achieved, he then explains what lies behind ordinary people's perception of "singing" speech, the Danes' perception of Kristiania Norwegian, or Eastern Norwegians' perception of the dialect of Bergen. It is this seamless interweaving of popular philology with simple metaphor and explanation that makes *ToA* so satisfying to read. It is popular science.

Assuming that the reader is still on board, Storm now becomes slightly more detailed, drawing a distinction between *Tonefald* (intonation) and *Tonelag* (tone). These Danish words were often used indiscriminately to refer to speech "melody" in a general way, so Storm's distinction (borrowed in fact from Knud Knudsen's 1856 *Haandbog i dansk-norsk Sproglære*) is a technical one. He points out the two different tones of Eastern Norwegian (the variety of Norwegian he always took as his model and the variety his readers would have expected to see as the model) by giving examples, and

---

[12] Botten-Hansen was, according to Hoel (1996: 288–290), the only editor of a national journal who supported the Landsmål project and who was sympathetic to national linguistic reform.

then weaves in the next musical metaphor. He explains what he calls the *even tone* (the single tone) by reference to the notes of the tonic (major) root-position chord, the first, third and fifth notes of the musical scale. He describes this chord as 'the resting one, complete in itself' (p. 169) and compares the single tone to it, the natural tone rising approximately a major third from the tonic. The 'uneven' (*ujævn*) tone (the double tone, found by and large in bases of more than one syllable) he exemplifies by reference to the four notes of the dominant seventh chord, the second, fourth, fifth and seventh notes of the musical scale:

> The first harmony has an inherent rest, by contrast with which the second is unsatisfying and requires the first for closure or resolution. It is in fact inherently disharmonious, which can be seen from its position in the sequence – 2, 4, 5, 7 – where two notes appear next to each other. (1860: 169)

This isn't rocket science, as they say, and the musical metaphors simplify the situation a great deal, but it would have been an informative read on the morning of Sunday 30 September 1860. Storm would go on in later publications to develop this musical model of tone and intonation (see section 2.2.4.3.2).

Two weeks later Storm returned to his theme and moved on to intonation in Norwegian by reference to the sentence *han negtede at bede om Forladelse* ('he refused to ask for forgiveness'), pointing out that the weight falls on 'those ideas which are to be emphasised, on *refusal* and on *forgiveness*' (p. 177). This is a brief and simple explanation of what we would now call tone units. Storm doesn't go into intonation in more detail, taking the view that 'it seems to be impossible to get a real grasp of it and to describe its movements with mathematical accuracy' (1860: 177). In this largely pre-instrumental age this was an insoluble problem for Storm, but he persevered, using just his ear, and attempted a quite detailed comparative study of intonation, using his musical system of notation, in Storm (1892a: 214–221).

The rest of this second instalment involves a comparison of tone in the urban varieties of Kristiania, Bergen, Denmark and Sweden. Storm notes that the musical notation of the tones in other Norwegian dialects is perfectly possible, but he prefers, given their variety, to stick to *Hovedstædernes Udtale* ('the pronunciation of the major cities'). He returns to the issue of why speakers of one form of Scandinavian can regard another form as more "singing", and explains it in terms of the musical parallel he set up in the first instalment, showing, for example, how the tones of Bergen involve greater pitch variation than those of Eastern Norway. Based on this he begins to construct the idea of greater pitch variation as a positive property, and therefore of the superiority of Swedish over Eastern Norwegian. Furthermore:

Danish prosody provides a sharp and unfavourable contrast with the Swedish. Our language does not perhaps sound as fulsome as Swedish, but it is nevertheless always better than Danish. (p. 177)

Well, this would have been true music to the ears of bourgeois, royalist Norwegians in a free Norway. It would not have been possible to make a comparison favouring Sweden over Denmark in 1860s Norway without distinct political overtones. It gets worse:

When the Danes pronounce a stressed syllable, it as if though they cut themselves off half way through. There is something stuttering, something reticent about it, which gives a very disagreeable impression. There is about it a weakening of its own force [. . .] and amongst men the Danish language in general gives the impression of something insipid and unmanly [. . .] (1860: 177–178)

You can almost hear the 'Hurrah for Storm!' go up at this point. Given this proposed weakness in Danish, its less vigorous use of tone such that, Storm claims, foreigners are not even aware of it, it is, in his view, regrettable that Danish prosody should be adopted by Norwegians to give Norwegian speech an air of solemnity. Storm writes that this feature of speech is something which will gradually disappear as Danishness is driven out of the country. Storm's patriotism is not quite complete because, based on suprasegmental phonological criteria, Swedish appears to be "better" than Norwegian, but the readers of *Illustreret Nyhedsblad* had no reason to choke on their coffee. The best is reserved to last:

If the original Norwegian language had been allowed to develop into an educated language and a written language without being influenced by Danishness, it would without doubt have become the most beautiful of all the Scandinavian languages, as its tone would thus have maintained its original fullness, and we would have the advantage over the Swedes of having our ancient sonorous diphthongs [. . .] But Danish influence has deprived our language of these advantages and rendered it from all points of view something in between Swedish and Danish. (1860: 178)

Surely this is completely tendentious: politics masquerading as phonetics. So why did I claim *ToA* to be the best thing Storm wrote? At the very beginning of his publishing career he did not have the immense knowledge he was unable to control later. Being so young, without authority, he needed to make a good impression by writing unselfishly and for his audience. His popular writings were always much more digestible than his scientific ones – he had a real popular touch. He had three-and-a-half columns on both occasions, so he was forced to be succinct. Coupled to all these positive points is his (not yet) famous phonetic ear and brilliant insight. The musical model of tone wasn't just a piece of juvenilia, but something he went on to develop in subsequent publications up to and including the 1892 volume of *Englische Philologie*, where musical notation is used to a great extent and where there is the 'Exkurs über Sprachmelodie' (1892a: 205–221).[13] Indeed 'Om Tonefaldet (Tonelaget) i de skandinaviske Sprog' (Storm 1875a) was reprinted in 1983 as one of the cornerstones of Norwegian prosody.

2.2.4.3.2 *Subsequent Work on Prosody*

Storm built on the 1860 work in 1874, when he gave a lecture in the Academy of Science on the subject of tone in the Scandinavian languages. This was published the following year in the Academy's *Proceedings* (Storm 1875a). In the published version there is a footnote acknowledging that this is indeed a development of *ToA*, and that it is also a preliminary to 'a more detailed work'. This latter, like a lot of Storm's plans, never came to anything, at least in terms of an autonomous study. The 'Exkurs über Sprachmelodie' of 1892 is a distillation of Storm's life's work on prosodic phonetics. However, it is buried deep in *Englische Philologie*, so it cannot really be said that Storm ever wrote the 'comparative tonology' that Sweet wanted him to write, and which, it seems, he did himself plan to write.

It is in the 'Exkurs über Sprachmelodie' that Storm fully develops his musical notation system. We know him to have been a singer throughout his life, and his theoretical knowledge of music was evidently good. He used musical notation with ease and with subtlety. Thus some of his notations of intonation, in addition to the careful recording of pitch, include dynamic and tempo markings. We learnt that in 1884 he was not completely satisfied with his musical system for intonation, and that he had an idea for a revised, more abstract system of notation, a system very like those which subsequently became the norm, indicating relative movement rather than absolute pitch:

> I should like to note here that some time ago I worked out a more precise notation of movement in the voice by means of curved lines instead of notes. Stress would then be indicated by the thickness of the line. I limit myself here to this brief mention, which I hope to be able to put into practice on another occasion. (Storm 1884/1902/1908: 55, n. 1)

This is another of Storm's never-to-be-completed undertakings. It is a shame Storm never moved over to a relative system like this. His ear for intonational difference was evidently remarkable, and he was held back in presenting his findings by the stiff musical system he adopted. He did go as far as he could in his analysis of intonation using only his ear and conventional notation. He knew that a different system of notation and a

---

[13] 'Om musikalsk Tonelag, især i Kinesisk' (Storm 1893b) is by his own admission very similar to the 1892 presentation.

different method of analysis (instrumental) were needed, but in practice he was just too firmly rooted in conventional methods to make the leap himself.

This is not to say that he did not undertake original work. He did, and in fact his prosodic work, next to his dialect alphabet (see section 4.3.3), is the most groundbreaking phonetic work he undertook. He begins 'Exkurs über Sprachmelodie' with his usual distinction between the melody produced by the singing voice and speech "melody", a distinction first explained in 1860 and returned to in the unpublished *Udkast til Oldn. Sproghistorie* of 1869, where the first section is entitled 'Sprogets Musik' ('the Music of Language') (NBO 8° 2402 A^i), and in lectures. In 1892 he deals first with tone, describing the systems used in Lithuanian, Latvian, Serbo-Croat and Mandarin Chinese. He had heard Serbo-Croat and discussed its tone system with native speakers, and he had heard Mandarin, but only from the mouths of Europeans who had spent time in China (1892a: 212). However, he had not heard the Baltic languages spoken by native speakers and his presentation of their systems of tones is based on the *Grammatik der littauischen Sprache* by Friedrich Kurschat (1806–1884) (Kurschat 1876) and *Die lettische Sprache* by August Johann Gottfried Bielenstein (1826–1907) (Bielenstein 1863/1864). This is quite out of character for Storm, who usually only trusts his own primary observations. However, the originality of a comparative presentation of tones necessitates unusual measures:

> Admittedly I have not been able to observe these languages equally thoroughly, and Lithuanian almost not at all; here I am by and large just giving a report. However, in this difficult area any contribution, no matter how humble, will probably be welcomed. (1892a: 208)

There is some evidence that Storm was familiar with Lithuanian, however, and this evidence is from a rather peculiar little episode. On 31 March 1884, one Sydney Holland of London sent a letter to the 'Editor of the Standard' entitled 'A linguistic puzzle'. The letter told the story of a young girl who had arrived in London docks and been taken to Marylebone Workhouse. Attempts to discover her nationality had failed. She had been spoken to in a variety of languages, including French, German, Italian, Swedish, Russian, Romany (falteringly), Polish and Yiddish, all to no avail. In the end she was asked the name of a number of common objects in her own language. These words were inexpertly transcribed and included in the letter to the *Evening Standard*. Somehow or other the letter ended up in Storm's hands. His reputation as the foremost practical linguist in Europe must have filtered through somewhere. Storm retranscribed the words and made a number of notes, before living up to his reputation and pronouncing that 'the girl must be from Prussian Lithuania' (UBB Ms. 743c)!

From tone languages he moves on to intonation languages, specifically English, French, Italian and Spanish, and here he feels very strongly that he is entering uncharted waters: 'The *Comparative Melodics of Language* [*Die vergleichende Sprachmelodik*] is still *terra incognita*' (p. 214). An idea of the originality of this little study, as well as the difficulty of the task for Storm, is to be gained from the preface (by Alan Cruttenden) to *Intonation Systems: A Survey of Twenty Languages* (Hirst & Di Cristo 1998):

> Books which have presented systematic comparisons of many languages or of grammars or of phonologies have been available for at least the last decade. But the enormous problems to be faced in achieving anything comparable for intonation have meant that no-one has dared to take on this task. Indeed the editors probably did not initially realise the enormity of this task [. . .] (Hirst & Di Cristo 1998: xi)

Storm did not have the instrumental resources available to the contributors to Hirst & Di Cristo (1998), nor did he have the benefit of several decades of research into intonation behind him; but he attempted what no one else dared to do for another century. To be fair, Storm's presentation is brief and it is impressionistic, but it is, as he suggests himself, a start. His attempt to notate English intonation is also a big step forward, compared with what had gone before.

Storm's strong and lifelong interest in all aspects of prosody, in stress and in length as well as in tone and intonation, is certainly an outcome of his linguistic background and his language passions, in short an outcome of his being Norwegian. Jahr & Lorentz (1983: 9) make this observation:

> Many Scandinavian linguists have taken an interest in prosody. This interest has to do with the fact that the Scandinavian languages, compared with other languages, have relatively complicated prosodic systems at word level, where length, stress and tone are used distinctively.

Few languages could generate an anthology of major writings on prosody like Ernst Håkon Jahr's and Ove Lorentz's 1983 collection of 29 studies of Norwegian prosody. Aasen and Knudsen both mention the existence of two separate tones in Norwegian, but the first study which goes beyond the superficial, and the first of the articles reprinted in Jahr and Lorentz's anthology, is Storm's of 1875.

2.3 LANGUAGE TEACHING REFORM

2.3.1 *The Reform Movement*

2.3.1.1 The language-teaching Reform Movement of the late nineteenth century was an extraordinary chapter in the history of linguistics. It united an entire community of people professionally concerned with languages, in universities, academies and schools, in a way that few linguistic concerns have done before or since. And the 'new philologists' were amongst those most actively engaged. An evangelistic zeal for phonetics at this time went hand in hand with an evangelistic zeal for reform in language teaching methods, a reform based at least in part on the application of phonetics in the language classroom. We have just been looking at Lundell's article, 'Die phonetik als universitätsfach', which appeared in the journal *Phonetische Studien* (Phonetic Studies). This journal was subtitled *Zeitschrift für wissenschaftliche und praktische Phonetik mit besonderer Rücksicht auf den Unterricht in der Aussprache* (Journal of Scientific and Practical Phonetics with Particular Emphasis on the Teaching of Pronunciation). In 1894 it was renamed *Die neueren Sprachen* (Modern Languages) with the new subtitle *Zeitschrift für den neusprachlichen Unterricht. Mit dem Beiblatt* Phonetische Studien (Journal of Modern Language Education. With the Supplement 'Phonetic Studies'). Sweet, Storm and Jespersen were all active in the Reform Movement, but it transcended the Anglo-Scandinavian School.[14] The linguist most usually credited with starting the movement is the German, Wilhelm Viëtor (1850–1918) through his anonymous propagandistic pamphlet, *Der Sprachunterricht muss umkehren!* (1882), which appeared under the pseudonym of 'Quousque Tandem', the name subsequently adopted by the Scandinavian movement for language teaching reform (see next section). (Subsequent editions of *Der Sprachunterricht muss umkehren!*, following the success and fame of the first, confessed the true identity of the author, with whom Storm corresponded in the period from 1888 to 1892.) Many of the contributions to the debate appeared in newly established German journals, such as *Englische Studien* and *Anglia*, and many were from schoolteachers like August Western and Knud Brekke in Norway. Sweet devoted an entire book to the question (1899) which goes way beyond practical issues involved in the successful teaching of foreign languages, and in which he 'endeavoured to give a comprehensive general view of the whole field of the practical study of languages' (Sweet 1899: v). Jespersen too devoted an entire book to the subject, the 1901 Danish original (*Sprogundervisning*) appearing in an English translation three years later (Jespersen 1904). Sweet and Jespersen both note the pioneering role in the movement played by Storm. Paul Passy in France was also actively involved, and, through his editorship of *Dhi Fonètik Tîtcer* (subsequently *Le Maître Phonétique*), took the issues involved to a wider audience still. It really was an international *movement*, not just a debate, and a movement which resulted in (some) change. As Jespersen wrote:

[. . .] at present it may be said that the reformed method is well on the way to permanent favour, at least as far as younger teachers have anything to say in the matter. (Jespersen 1904: 2)

---

[14] The editorial board of *Phonetische Studien* in 1888 included Bell, Ellis, Jespersen, Klinghardt, Lundell, Noreen, Passy, Storm, Sweet, Techmer and Western.

Internationally the contributions to the movement from phoneticians, Anglists, foreign language teachers and educators alike were so extensive that it is not possible to deal with them in full here. Consequently I shall just give an outline of the direction the reforms took, prior to considering Storm's contributions to and role in the movement. (For more detail about the movement in general, see Howatt (1984: Part III) and Howatt & Smith (2002).)

2.3.1.2 Essentially the Reform Movement came about because linguists concerned with the synchronic study of modern languages at last provided an academic basis for both teaching and studying foreign languages. (One of the many myths of the history of linguistics is that the notion of studying language synchronically didn't occur to anyone in the nineteenth century, and that all was diachronic until de Saussure swept away the perversity of previous generations.) Until the likes of Storm, Sievers, Sweet and Jespersen, there had been nobody professionally qualified to judge language-teaching methods and materials from an informed, linguistic point of view. When these linguists began to consider currently available methods and materials in the light of their own insights into language and languages, they were horrified. It should be stressed that there was nothing patronising about this. Many of the university folk active in the Movement, and many of those most vehement in their criticism of existing practice, had themselves worked as teachers in the schools, so they were not simply preaching from their ivory towers. To use Storm's own distinction, they came at the problem from both a scientific and a practical angle. Viëtor, Storm, Jespersen and Passy in their different national contexts had all worked as schoolteachers. Interestingly, those who proposed the most radical reforms were those with the most recent experience of school teaching, such as Western and to an extent Jespersen; Storm and Sweet were more cautious.

There were three basic tenets of the Reform Movement. Those involved were not in full agreement on every detail of reform, and we shall see Storm's disagreements in a moment, but, as Howatt (1984: 171) observes, 'the Reform Movement was founded on three basic principles':

> the primacy of speech, the centrality of connected texts as the kernel of the teaching-learning process, and the absolute priority of an oral methodology in the classroom.

Sweet, as usual, states the phonetic case in the strongest manner, although he held much more moderate views in other areas of proposed reform. Unlike the other linguists I have just mentioned, Sweet did not work as a schoolteacher, so was perhaps more idealistic in his phonetic-based approach: 'all study of language must be based on phonetics' (1899: 4). There were few amongst the reformers who would disagree with this, but not all would be so categorical about the use of phonetics in the early stages of language learning. Sweet of course begins with phonetics and would never have done otherwise. Jespersen by contrast leaves phonetics until he is nearing the end of his *How to Teach a Foreign Language*, and then states:

> I have now for many years advocated the use of phonetics – yes, even of phonetical transcription, in the teaching of foreign languages, and have to a large extent put my theories into practice both in dealing with children of all ages and with grown persons. New things always frighten people; they think with terror that here the pupils are to be burdened with an entirely new and difficult science and with a new kind of writing [. . .]
> (Jespersen 1904: 142)

Jespersen was an urbane man of the world, whereas Sweet was a fanatic. Where Storm stood on this we shall see in due course.

Sweet goes on in his *The Practical Study of Language* to insist that 'the second main axiom of living philology is that all study of language, whether theoretical or practical, ought to be based on the spoken language' (p. 50). It was by now commonplace to insist that the spoken language is the true object of linguistic study and the written language merely a secondary version of it. Viëtor spends part of *Der Sprachunterricht muss umkehren!* painstakingly explaining this point. However, three decades later we find de Saussure still lamenting the fact that people in general still insist on basing their observations about language on the written form:

> As much or even more importance is given to this representation of the vocal sign as to the vocal sign itself. It is rather as if people believed that in order to find out what a person looks like it is better to study his photograph than his face. (Saussure 1983: 25)

A century more of phonetics and of reformed language teaching has still largely failed to impress this difference upon the popular mind.

'The absolute priority of an oral methodology in the classroom' for the reformers meant a move away from the despised *readers* of the previous generation. Storm was possibly the most outspoken of all the reformers on the subject of textbooks based on the study of meaningless constructed bits of language. He vents his spleen in the preface to *Franske Taleøvelser (Mellemtrin)*:

> The methods hitherto employed have all proved inadequate for the purpose [. . .] The ordinary primers, textbooks and books of exercises, with their disconnected and often difficult sentences, are dull and tedious, and give no facility in the use of the language. (Storm 1892b: vii)

This sounds outrageously general and possibly unjust. But Storm felt very strongly about this, as we shall see, and he does go on to more specific criticisms, describing the language teaching method of Franz Ahn (1796–1865) and Heinrich Gottfried Ollendorff (1803–1865) (see Howatt 1984:

138–145 for a description) as 'exceedingly unpractical', 'often erroneous', 'ill-arranged and so overloaded with unnecessary details and with incorrect, stilted and uncommon expressions' (Storm 1892b: pp. viii–ix). Sweet is generally less extreme in his condemnation, agreeing with the 'continental reformers in condemning the practice of exercise-writing and the use of a priori methods such as Ahn's', but he 'refuse[s] to join them in their condemnation of translation and use of grammars' (Sweet 1899: p. vii), as in fact does Storm. So, while there was disagreement over the detail, as to how much reform was required and how radical that reform should be, none of this extensive network of scholars, teachers and educators was in any doubt that 'der Sprachunterricht muss umkehren'.

2.3.2 Quousque Tandem

2.3.2.1 On Thursday 12 August 1886, Lektor A. Drake from Nyköping in Sweden gave a talk at the third Scandinavian philologists' meeting, held in Stockholm, with the title: 'Huru skall en praktiskt och psykologiskt viktig anordning af och metodik för språkundervisningen vid våra läroverk kunna ernås?' (How can a practically and psychologically significant system of and methodology for language teaching be achieved in our schools?). It was decided to postpone the subsequent discussion until the following morning, Friday 13th, inauspiciously enough. Lundell, Passy and Western all took part in the debate. Further discussion was needed, and so an extra session was arranged for some 50 delegates, with Lundell in the chair. This time, it is reported (Jørgensen 1893: lxviii), Jespersen, Noreen and Storm, amongst others, also contributed to the debate. The chief outcome of these meetings was the foundation of the Scandinavian Quousque Tandem movement (QT), and a letter was sent out inviting like-minded people to join. The letter, dated September 1886, signed by Jespersen, Lundell and Western and printed in parallel Danish and Swedish versions, contained the invitation:

> in connection with the discussion of language teaching methodology, which took place at the third meeting of Scandinavian philologists in Stockholm this year, we the undersigned take the liberty of inviting male and female colleagues to join the society
> QUOUSQUE TANDEM
> Scandinavian Society for Improved Language Teaching

During the following period a number of articles appeared, setting out the programme adopted by the 'Quousquisterne' and explaining to school teachers why a reform of language teaching along these lines was desirable. The four lines along which reform was proposed by QT are set out in the letter and repeated in Jespersen (1886):

1. It is not the written language which is taken as the foundation for teaching, but the real, living spoken language. In those languages whose orthography differs significantly from the pronunciation, we therefore begin with texts in an appropriate phonetic script.
2. From the very start teaching is based on connected texts, not disconnected sentences.
3. Grammar teaching is wedded to reading to the extent that the pupil, with the help of the teacher, is guided into gradually working out the laws of the language from the reading. Only later should a systematic textbook be used for revision purposes.
4. Translation both from the first language into the foreign language and vice versa is limited, and replaced partly by written and spoken reproduction and free production in the foreign language in conjunction with what is being read, partly by more cursory reading.

A radical reform in teaching methods and materials was inevitably going to meet with a negative response from conservative teachers of the older generation. The three founders of QT were all young and idealistic (Jespersen was 26 in 1886, Lundell 35 and Western 36), and this cannot have helped their cause amongst older traditionalists. In fact Storm, although in many respects on the same wavelength as QT (see section 2.3.3), found the attitude of the individuals involved repellent (he regarded them as arrogant). As expected, there were some rapid counter-attacks, dealt with by Western in his 1888 article in *Vor Ungdom*. He dealt summarily with the first two *Modstandere* (opponents), C. Michelsen and J. Vising,[15] displaying some of the arrogance of which Storm and others accused him. However, the third opponent was Storm (in Storm (1887b) – see next section), and responding to the great man was, for Western, a much more sensitive problem. Storm was the pioneer, and he was Western's mentor. How should he deal with an attack on the movement from this quarter?

> Far from regarding Prof. Storm as our opponent, we regard him as our greatest ally, despite the fact that disagreement about the means to the end is still apparently so great that it has hindered a closer alliance. We have welcomed his contributions to the discussion as the most significant yet to have been made, and we are even grateful for the statements which go against us, as they have partly contributed to a clarification of our own views, and partly shown that there are points on which our own statements require greater clarification. (Western 1888: 53)

The fact that Western changes from a superior tone in discussing Michelsen's and Vising's objections to one of humility in dealing with Storm's indicates the status Storm had in this particular milieu. Western concludes his mollification of Storm with an exhortation for the great man

---

[15] Johan Vising was the Swedish translator of *Franske Taleøvelser* (Storm 1887a & 1897a).

to join, nay lead, the movement of which, in Western's view, he is the rightful leader:

> So if I could contribute to Prof. Storm's adopting his own child and taking on its continued upbringing and, where necessary, discipline, then not only would my goal with these lines have been achieved, but I would regard it as the best job of work I have yet done. (Western 1888: 58)

What Storm's position was we shall see in due course, but we must first consider the subsequent development of the movement.

2.3.2.2 A newsletter (*Revy*) was started in 1888 as an offprint of the Swedish journal *Verdandi*. It was not a particularly ambitious publication and was, according to the opening letter 'to the readers', produced on a tight budget. Its aim, in the words of the same letter, was 'to enter into more regular contact as much with our members as with the pedagogically interested general public than has been possible up to now' (p. 1). It contained brief reports and reviews and ran until June 1891, appearing in 15 rather irregular issues and covering a total of 120 octavo pages. It provided, amongst other things, a list of members. Issue no. 3 listed 169 members, and new members were added at a steady rate, if in declining quantities – there were 32 new members in October 1889 and only 10 in June 1891. It appears to have been a reasonably flourishing society, compared with similar special-interest societies, and the majority of members came, as one would expect, from the Scandinavian countries: Denmark, Finland, Norway and Sweden. A number of well-known names appeared on the list of members – Vilhelm Thomsen, Adolf Noreen (1854–1925) and the Swedish phonetician Hugo Pipping (1864–1944) for example – and there was a handful of members from outside Scandinavia, notably Passy and Hermann Klinghardt (1847–1926), the latter possibly the most active contributor to the European debate on teaching reform. Perhaps the most noteworthy cluster of members was the group of three *Æresmedlemmer* (honorary members) placed at the top of the list: Storm, Sweet and Viëtor.

The *Revy* fizzled out in 1891, and the movement seems to have been little more than an idealistic experiment, soldiering on another five years until 1896. This is not to say that it had no impact. There is no evidence as to how many members left between 1888 and 1891, but it can be assumed that there were around 200 members for much of that period, teachers who to some extent subscribed to the movement's reform programme and who carried on teaching in its spirit after the movement faded. Klinghardt adopted a thoroughgoing QT teaching programme in Reichenbach in Germany and was visited by several Swedish teachers (see Brate 1891).[16] According to Brate, Klinghardt had notable success in teaching English using this method:

[16] For more detail on Klinghardt's experiment, see Howatt (1984: 173–175).

I had the opportunity to receive a testimonial outside school as to what
fine results Dr Klinghardt's teaching achieved. A pupil had for some time
been absent from school on account of a contagious illness in his family.
He returned to the town while I was there and visited Dr Klinghardt in his
home, before rejoining the school. On that occasion Dr Klinghardt spoke
with him in English about his work and absence and all manner of other
things, for which he was not in the least bit prepared, and the boy not only
understood everything Dr Klinghardt said, but also replied to his
questions in English without faltering or stammering. This pupil was in
the third year of English at the time. (Brate 1891: 74)

Whatever else, as Western began his defence of the movement by saying:

If the Quousque Tandem society has achieved nothing else, it has at least
quickened tempers and generated some discussion. It has hopefully made
it clear to many that the excellence of our current teaching method is not
beyond doubt. And that is something. If the young society dies, it can't be
said that it was silenced to death, and hopefully it won't be spoken or
written to death either. (Western 1888: 40)

2.3.3 *Storm's Role*

2.3.3.1 Anyone who doesn't know Storm's work but reads Sweet or
Jespersen on the subject of language teaching will realise that he is a
seminal figure in this area. Although Storm did not write anything specifically devoted to language teaching reform until 1887, his concern for a
reform dates back at least to 1872. The source in question is a review which
appeared across several editions of *Morgenbladet* (Storm 1872b), in which
he wrote that 'all these practical methods miss their mark because they are
so killingly boring'.[17] He goes on to propose in general terms that reform in
practical methods must consist in rendering them less 'dull' (aandløse): 'The
more lively the child, the more destructive such a litany of disjointed
trivialities.'

The first formal, readily available treatment of these issues was in *Engelsk
Filologi*. This was published three years before Viëtor's pamphlet, but
Storm's opinions could not even then have had much impact on the
international community as they were yet to be translated from Norwegian.
Storm takes the relevant sections in *Engelsk Filologi/Englische Philologie*,
along with the preface to *Franske Taleøvelser (Mellemtrin)*, as well as other
smaller publications, as the basis for his principal contribution to the
Reform Movement, namely 'Om en forbedret undervisning i levende

---

[17] Holter (1986: 25) cites Bjørndal (1959: 77) to suggest that Storm may have been influenced
by P. Voss in these ideas, since Voss was formulating new language-teaching methods in 1872,
when Storm was working as a teacher in his school.

sprog'. This article appeared in two parts in the journal *Universitets- og skole-annaler (ny række)* for 1887, and it is this version of Storm's views that we shall use in what follows.

2.3.3.2 The first part of 'Om en forbedret undervisning [. . .]' (pp. 161–198) is concerned with method, with the faults to be found in existing methods of language teaching and with the faults to be found in the reforms proposed by QT. As elsewhere, Storm shows himself to be a moderate reformer, with one foot in the conservative camp and with the other foot in the reformers', not wishing to discard what is valuable from the past, but seeking reform where it is needed. As elsewhere, hindsight shows his approach to have been the right one.

He opens with his regrettable findings as an assessor for the school-leaving exam, the *Examen Artium*, that the standards achieved in English and French were unacceptably low. He had, rather embarrassingly, rehearsed the same point in his *Morgenbladet* article of January 1883. If 'we have numerous able teachers' and 'those methods which were regarded as the newest and the best have been employed' (1887b: 161), what is the problem? In the words that Storm repeats rhetorically in this article: 'Hvad er der dog i veien?' As he had already argued in the earlier *Morgenbladet* article, part of the problem lay in the school system, whereby 'one learns a little bit of everything and nothing in depth' (p. 167). Storm does not waste much space discussing this problem, since it would take a complete revision of the education system to put it right, and such a revision is unlikely. The other part of the problem lies in the teaching methods employed, and not just that they are in some way old-fashioned:

> The thing is that, despite all the improvements in language teaching, the old methods are by and large being adhered to, and not all changes have been for the better. (p. 167)

Something can be done about this, and the first thing to rectify is the overemphasis on the study of rules to the detriment of practical language skills. In this proposal Storm is fully in line with what Howatt calls 'the primacy of speech' as a central plank in the Reform Movement. Storm insists that the spoken language learnt be natural, that it be practised through the use of natural-sounding, connected sentences. He is, as we saw above, merciless in his criticism of the Ahn/Ollendorff method of learning a foreign language through the use of disconnected, absurd sentences. Sweet had his stock absurd sentence *The philosopher pulled the lower jaw of the hen*, supposedly found in such a book. Storm's examples, whether genuine or invented, are if anything even more amusing:

> Har De seet min pennekniv? Nei, men jeg har seet min gamle tantes grønne paraply. Hollænderen har flere fluer end franskmanden, og saa

videre *in omnia sæcula sæculorum*. [Have you seen my pen-knife? No, but I have seen my old aunt's green umbrella. The Dutchman has more flies than the Frenchman, and so on *world without end*.] (p. 170)

Storm rightfully asks, 'where in all the world do sensible people speak such a language?' His polemic seems strong, but methods like Ahn's and Ollendorff's and any number of imitators were readily available, entered many editions and were very popular with the general public. They gave their users the impression of learning a foreign language, but, as Storm remarks, when those users actually try to employ their new found language skills with native speakers, they are completely lost. The language they have learnt is artificial, not spoken by any native speaker anywhere. It is not the living language, 'just a bad selection of literary language' (p. 170).

If these materials are to be avoided, as Storm quite unambiguously argues they must be, what should the language learner use in their stead? The answer is: coherent sentences or reading passages of the sort found in Storm's own *Franske Taleøvelser*. Storm, with Sweet, does believe that 'a reaction against the disconnected sentences can be taken too far' (p. 178). Many natural sentences occur in isolation, but plausible examples of the living language are needed, rather than depressingly convoluted artificial scraps. In conjunction with this sort of reading book, Storm argues, simpler grammars are needed, and his campaign for simpler grammars is one he waged throughout his life. Traditional grammars, he argues, are off-putting, unnecessarily complicated and unhelpful for the learner in the early stages of study:

> A brief outline with paradigms and short, clear principal rules will in general be sufficient. The rest should be left to practice, emerge from reading and systematic exercises. (p. 176)

Simplicity is of the utmost importance to Storm, in grammars, in readers, in books of exercises, so as not to overburden the learner in the early stages. In this he is very much in sympathy with Viëtor, who addressed the issue of language-teaching reform precisely in response to the current debate on whether schoolchildren were overburdened. The subtitle of *Der Sprachunterricht muss umkehren!* is *Ein Beitrag zur Überbürdungsfrage* (A Contribution to the Overburdening Question). This issue was also a live one in Norway:

> In the [parliamentary] debate of 1889 there were some who directed fierce attacks at senior schools because they overburdened their pupils with work. The accusation was certainly exaggerated. (Høigård & Ruge 1963: 188)

Towards the end of his discussion of the faults to be found in existing materials Storm sets out the two foundation stones of his proposed reform, stones hewn from his own experience. The first of these is that 'living languages are learnt more by imitation than by rules' (p. 180). This shows Storm's heartfelt agreement with what Howatt called the reformers' 'absolute priority of an oral methodology in the classroom'. His second foundation stone is: 'Almost everyone who knows a lot of languages has learned them from books from the outset, not by reading long-winded grammars, but by studying simple connected texts' (p. 182). His point is not that the written language should be the focus of language study. Quite the contrary, but Storm (unlike Sweet) lived in the real world of language learning, of ordinary people with ordinary resources, and he realised that 'to try to learn the language *exclusively* via the ear, simply by mixing with native-speakers, is simply a waste of time' (p. 182). Instead he emphasises Howatt's third plank in the Reform Movement, 'the centrality of connected texts as the kernel of the teaching-learning process'. He concludes this section by asking the question again: 'Hvad er der dog i veien?' We now know the answer: 'Neither more nor less than that the entire method is misguided' (p. 184).

Storm was, then, in full agreement with the three main tenets of the Reform Movement, and we can certainly regard him as one of the central figures in that movement. He was a very early proponent of reform along these lines, maybe the earliest, but his influence was probably limited, despite Sweet's and Jespersen's advocacy, by *Engelsk Filologi* and 'Om en forbedret undervisning [. . .]' being in Norwegian.

Although he was essentially a card-carrying Reformer, he was nevertheless surprisingly at odds with the Scandinavian QT movement and with the radical use of phonetics in language teaching.

2.3.3.3 Storm declares himself a supporter of Sweet on most issues, but he does not agree with Sweet's use of detailed phonetic transcription in the first edition of his *Elementarbuch des gesprochenen Englisch* (Sweet 1885b). Whilst he was a great advocate of phonetics, Storm was much too rational to believe that phonetics was the answer to all the problems, at least without any evidence that it really helped language learners. He thought that it was worth trying, but confessed that he did not hold out much hope of it making language learning a great deal easier. He was happier to accept the use of phonetic script alongside traditional spelling, but he was still aware of its potentially confusing rather than clarifying influence:

When on the other hand there is talk of using phonetic script alongside conventional orthography, as Franke and Passy do in their books, and as Sweet does in the second edition of his *Elementarbuch*, then I can go along with it more easily. I dare say that the two systems can have a disruptive impact on one another, but this is a disadvantage which can probably not be avoided. (pp. 195–196)

Over-enthusiasm for phonetics in the early stages of language teaching is one of the objections Storm has to the QT movement. He quotes the four theses of the movement laid down at the Stockholm meeting, quoted above:

1. It is not the written language which is taken as the foundation for teaching, but the real, living spoken language. In those languages whose orthography differs significantly from the pronunciation, we therefore begin with texts in an appropriate phonetic script.
2. From the very start teaching is based on connected texts, not disconnected sentences.
3. Grammar teaching is wedded to reading to the extent that the pupil, with the help of the teacher, is guided into gradually working out the laws of the language from the reading. Only later should a systematic textbook be used for revision purposes.
4. Translation both from the first language into the foreign language and vice versa is limited, and replaced partly by written and spoken reproduction and free production in the foreign language in conjunction with what is being read, partly by more cursory reading.

We have already seen that Storm, although in total agreement with the basic premises of thesis 1, did not accept the practical suggestion resulting from it without any evidence to support its usefulness. Thesis 2 was quite acceptable to him, but with caveats as to the use of connected texts for all learning purposes (pp. 190–192). Similarly, Storm does not object in theory to the third thesis that the formal learning of grammatical rules should be kept out of elementary teaching, but again he objects on practical grounds. He maintains that the study of grammar need not confuse language learners through its abstractions. If a grammar is written in the right way, if it is brief and clear, and if grammar is studied in the right way, if it is closely supported by practical application, the formal study of grammar can, in his view, save a lot of time. Why try to work out the declensions of German from reading the language when they can be found neatly arrayed in grammar books? Storm's approach to language learning is eminently practical. He does not condemn particular methods or approaches *on principle*. He condemns methods where there is evidence that they do not work and should be replaced by more effective methods, whether they be old ones or new ones. As to thesis 4, that the learners' first language be avoided at all costs in the language-learning process, Storm is again sceptical. He can see the advantages. He agrees with Sweet that such an approach lessens the danger of interference from the first language (p. 190), but in normal school situations, where a second language is being learnt, it is practically impossible to insulate learners completely from their first language. Anyway, reference to the native language aids linguistic reflection and in some cases is the most practical way of teaching a word's meaning. Why, asks Storm, cite Walker's *Pronouncing Dictionary* in order to teach a Norwegian child that the English word *flea* refers to 'a small insect of remarkable agility', when the explanation could be achieved simply by using the Norwegian word *loppe*?

Storm was not just an old cuss, although he can sometimes appear that way in his writings. In 'Om en forbedret undervisning i levende Sprog' we do not simply find the mature scholar perversely attacking the enthusiasm of the younger generation. Storm was 'dhi grétest pràktikal liNgwist in dhi world' and was therefore always concerned with what would work in practice. This concern underpinned his attitudes towards reform in Norwegian. It made him seem conservative, but he wasn't conservative simply for its own sake, rather as (he thought) the QT advocates were being radical almost for the sake of it. In his own words:

It seems to me on the whole that the new school behaves much too dogmatically, in that they resolve a whole load of questions in advance, questions which remain unresolved. It is not much use abandoning the old, when it is not certain whether the new is so much better. It is better little by little to adapt what's already there and to feel one's way forward. Only lengthy experience and many attempts will be able to provide decisive answers here. In this question I have proceeded according to my own experience, acquired during a long period as a student and nearly 30 years as a teacher. (p. 198)

This sums Storm up.

2.3.3.4 In the second part of 'Om en forbedret undervisning [. . .]' (pp. 305–351) Storm applies the general views expressed in the first part to the specific situation of the modern languages in Norwegian schools. He takes the languages in the order in which they are studied, starting with German. Teaching should begin with a primer, but the teacher should speak the language with the pupils as early as possible, with the proviso that this is practically possible (p. 307). Storm is not dogmatic in his reform proposals. After a while the majority of the teaching can take place in German, but the best introduction to the language will always be 'systematically ordered, connected books of exercises' (p. 308). (It should be obvious already where this advertising campaign for the benefits of 'connected books of exercises' is leading!) Anything archaic or irrelevant should be discarded from the teaching and learning environment.

Moving on to English, he again expresses the need for a good primer. He then discusses the practical advantages and disadvantages of phonetics in the Norwegian classroom:

Sounds come in first of all via the ear, and only then do they appear on the tongue. The pupil learns more here by imitation than from rules and explanations. However phonetics should only be used as an aid *where it can make things easier*. Not that phonetics should be pursued in school.

On the other hand it is becoming more and more imperative that teachers study phonetics and are able to teach on a phonetic basis. (p. 321)

A complete phonetic system is not in itself beneficial. He explicitly criticises Western's *Engelsk Lydlære* (Western 1882), where the formation of sounds is more important than the sounds themselves, a fault of the *English School*. The phonetician Storm, who is first and foremost a practical linguist, writes in his characteristic aphoristic fashion: 'Language is sounds, not articulations' (p. 323). Having shown that other decent materials for the study of English are still needed, he moves on finally to French and perhaps his main purpose in this section of 'Om en forbedret undervisning [. . .]':

> Conversation exercises in French can be carried out in much the same way as in English but, on account of the current status of French in this country, will necessarily be more limited. The best way to achieve practical proficiency and skill in applying the laws of the language is, here too, a good practical textbook. I have above set out the principles for the structure of such a book, which I have tried to put into practice in my *Franske Taleøvelser*, printed in Copenhagen in 1887. In the preface, of which the present work is partly a further development, I have explained the structure, arrangement and deployment of the book in detail. (pp. 348–349)

He has begun to show how reform can be implemented in Norway, and now he leaves the reader to experience reform in practice through the use of his own book. Storm's views were taken up officially in reforms of 1896. From now on language teaching in the schools came to rest on pronunciation skills and conversation rather than grammatical skills and written exercises. It is clear that the reforms took Storm's line rather than the more radical QT line, since Høigård & Ruge (1963: 261) report:

> On one point the plans were cautiously restrained: translation of foreign-language texts into Norwegian would continue to be a regular component of the work.

2.3.4 Bennetts Practiske Lærebog i det engelske Sprog *(1862)*

2.3.4.1 As his career progressed, Storm actively opposed traditional language teaching materials of the grammar translation type (see Howatt 1984: ch. 11). He objected to their use of meaningless sentences, to their random introduction of grammatical rules, in short to their failure to address *det levende Sprog*. However, his first publication on English was just such a work, a work which explicitly adopted Ahn's method, regarding Ahn's 'method' as 'highly to be recommended'. This was *Bennetts Practiske Lærebog i det engelske Sprog* of 1862. Its principal author, Thomas Bennett (1814–1898), was one of the great entrepreneurs of nineteenth-century

Norway. He was born into a wealthy family from Shropshire on the Welsh border, educated at Westminster School and then spent much of his early adult life travelling. In 1848 he arrived in Copenhagen, from where he undertook travels throughout Norway, settling in Kristiania the following year. When he arrived in Kristiania he set up a sort of Anglo-Norwegian agency, arranging the sale and purchase of goods in both directions and providing practical advice and assistance for British tourists coming to Norway, thereby establishing the world's second travel agency (see Hoemsnes 1999: 9). The travel side to his enterprise grew rapidly, and he eventually opened branches in Bergen (1887), Stavanger (1889) and Trond-heim (1890). The concern soon became international with offices throughout Europe and North America (see Steen 1923) and it was still going strong in 1995 when it was taken over by the Hogg Robinson Group.

Sweet noticed the rapid growth in Norwegian tourism. In 1890 he wrote to Storm that there was now 'no sense o [sic] rest or quiet' in a Norway 'overrun w [sic] tourists' (letter of 1 June), compared to how he had found things during his earlier visits. Bennett did a lot to improve the travel situation within Norway, amongst other things starting up the first taxi service in Kristiania and opening boarding houses on the main routes across the country. He worked hard for the expatriate British community in Kristiania, was a leading light in the building in 1883 of St Edmund's Anglican church in Møllergate, was the author of a number of books of an Anglo-Norwegian character, and even worked as a teacher of English as a foreign language, from which Henrik Ibsen benefited (Hoemsnes 1999: 60). He was at the very heart of Anglo-Norwegian life, and it is not surprising that the young anglophile Storm was attracted to Bennett and his world. According to his diary, Ivar Aasen attended St Edmund's four times, and Venås (1996a: 498) follows Djupedal in presuming that this was in order to hear the English language being used. Derry (1975: 44) notes that significant numbers of Norwegians attended the church to learn English. The substan-tial expatriate English-speaking community in Kristiania (referred to in Storm 1892a: 417) centred on this church, and we can assume that Storm also found his way to Møllergate, as well as to the earlier temporary homes of the Anglican congregation. Before St Edmund's Church was completed, the Anglican congregation was permitted, free of charge, to use the university's ceremonial hall, and it is not unreasonable to assume that Johan Storm may have been behind this arrangement.

Storm's reputation as a scholar of English was established by the early 1860s, and Bennett engaged him to revise his *English Primer*, improving the grammatical sections and adding an appendix on pronunciation. Storm's involvement is plain to see. This is an elementary work, but the footnotes sometimes extend over several pages. They are often historical and frequently comparative. Sometimes they address a reader who is unlikely even to have opened a book as elementary as this. For example, rule 61 concerns class 6 of the strong verbs, verbs of the *fall–fell–fallen* or *blow–blew–blown* type. To this paragraph Storm adds the footnote:

> For the benefit of philologists it is noted here that this is the original reduplicating class. See Munch's & Unger's *oldn. Gram.*, pp. 28, 29. (Bennett 1862: 188)

The numerous footnotes were not enough detail for Storm, and his own copy of the book (in Bergen University Library) is full of notes, written round the margins of the pages and on extra sheets gummed into the book. He couldn't just take *Bennetts Practiske Lærebog* for what it was, a resource whereby ordinary people could learn some English; he needed to get as close to "the truth" as possible. Consequently he frequently notes that a rule or explanation is 'incomplete' or 'unclear' or 'unnecessary' or 'poor' or 'imprecise' or 'insufficient'. Some of these marginal notes are motivated by the arrogance of youth, of which he would later accuse Jespersen and Western. Storm, although only 26 (compared with Bennett's 48) and, unlike Bennett, not a native speaker, thought he knew best. Invariably, of course, he did know best. Bennett writes:

> Hos is realised in English as *at the house – family – shop of*; e.g. hos min Broder *at the house of my brother*. (Bennett 1862: 34)

Storm describes this as 'poor', which it is. With his attention to detail and his obsession with *det levende Sprog*, unarticulated here but a lifelong driving force nonetheless, he must have found involvement with *Bennetts Lærebog* a deeply unsatisfying experience. It did not damage their relationship, as nearly twenty years later they collaborated again on *A Selection of Phrases for Tourists Travelling in Norway* (Bennett 1881).

2.3.4.2 A positive outcome of Storm's involvement with the *Practiske Lærebog* was at least the appendix on English phonetics. This is an impressive analysis by any reckoning, but it is particularly impressive considering that Storm was still a student and had not yet visited an English-speaking country. It is original at this time for being a proper *phonetic* analysis, while the treatment of pronunciation in works on English as a foreign language was (and remains) typically *phonological*. The use of 'phonetic' and 'phonological' is anachronistic. Storm put it thus:

> The following treatise on pronunciation is mostly aimed at describing and explaining the sounds themselves, as it is this which is most lacking in the grammars that have been available up to now. For the sake of space only the most important rules for the use of the sounds are included. Otherwise the reader is referred to other grammars and those dictionaries in which pronunciation is notated according to *Walker's method*. (Bennett 1862: 197 n.)

One might wonder how useful such a presentation would be for the readership of *Bennetts Practiske Lærebog*. However, as we have seen and will see again, relevance and accommodation to the readership were seldom concerns to get in the way of Storm's pursuit of *det levende Sprog*.

Certain elements of the 'Appendix on Pronunciation' are old-fashioned, such as the division of consonants into *Læbelyd*, *Tungelyd* and *Ganelyd* (Labials, Linguals and Palatals), a system which does not allow for [h]. Apart from a few symbols borrowed from Walker, Storm does not employ a phonetic transcription here, thus [ŋ] = *ng* and [ʒ] = *zh*. The presentation may be somewhat old-fashioned formally speaking, but it contains some interesting and original elements. The extent of Storm's understanding of the diphthongal articulation of the long vowels is unusual for the time, and his comparison of the articulation of the sounds of English with those of Norwegian is both original and of practical value.

As his concern for *det levende Sprog* grew, Storm must have looked back at the grammatical sections of *Bennett's Practiske Lærebog* in horror. It is little wonder that he later wrote his *Franske Taleøvelser*, responsible as he had himself been for the furtherance of a pedagogical technique he saw as unacceptable. 'Those methods used up to now have all shown themselves to be impractical,' he wrote in 1887 in *Franske Taleøvelser (Mellemtrin)* (p. i). 'There has been too much theory and too little practice.' Entire pages of footnotes, perhaps?

> The regular primers, textbooks and books of exercises with their disconnected, often difficult sentences make for apathy and aversion, and give no skill in using the language. (1887a: i)

I wonder if he was thinking of examples like these from a book which may not have borne his name, but . . .:

> The day after tomorrow we shall cut the grass in the meadow. (p. 150)
> We talk of going to Paris early im [*sic*] the spring, if the weather be convenient. (p. 177)
> The water springs from the rock and runs into a small trough opposite to the inn. (p. 180)
> He struck the slave with a thick stick. (p. 186)
> This piece of iron is much too bent. (p. 195)

3

ROMANCE LANGUAGES

3.1 BACKGROUND

3.1.1 *Storm's Knowledge of the Romance Languages*

3.1.1.1 Storm's reputation as a Romanist was as impressive as his reputation as an Anglist,[1] and we already have some testimonials from his contemporaries. As with English in the last chapter, we are entitled to ask where Storm picked up his legendary knowledge and ability. It is not clear what formal study of French Storm undertook as a boy, and there would have been even less opportunity in mid-nineteenth-century Norway for him to study the other Romance languages. In 1869, prior to visiting Italy and Spain, Storm felt his knowledge of the languages of those two countries to be inadequate. He wrote of the need to 'prepare myself to obtain a sufficient competence in Italian and Spanish':

> Here I placed the strongest emphasis on Spanish, because I was weakest in it, and within the course of a few months I made really good progress. (Storm 1871: 19)

In 1858 he visited Belgium and the Netherlands to study French, Flemish and Dutch. It was after this period abroad that he changed his university course of study to Classical philology, inspired by this exposure to foreign languages. According to the 1877 application to parliament he also studied some Russian and Polish, as well as 'Old Slavonic (Old Bulgarian)' (1877a: 3). It is not generally recognised, but Storm did also boast a fair knowledge of Slavonic languages, which he was able to use in his work. His unpublished papers in Bergen University Library contain notes from his study of Russian, some as late as 1897, as well as letters in Russian from Georges de Peretz, *Secrétaire d'Etat de sa Majesté l'Empereur de toutes les Russies*, and letters to Thomsen in 1875 contain comparative Slavonic observations. His knowledge of Lithuanian came in useful, of course, when he received the call from Marylebone workhouse (see section 2.2.4.3.2).

He benefited as much as he could from Unger's teaching at the university. As we noted in the last chapter (2.1.2.2), C. R. Unger, professor of Romance and Germanic philology during Storm's student days, did undertake some Spanish and Italian teaching, but this was hardly his speciality or main interest. However, there is a notebook amongst Storm's papers, now in

---

[1] The labels "Anglists" and "Romanists" sound a bit foreign, but they are much neater than any competitors (e.g. "scholars of English/Romance studies").

Bergen, dated 1863, containing a list of words of Romance origin found in Shakespeare's *Romeo and Juliet*, 'after Prof. Unger' (UBB Ms. 740o). The result of this patchy training in Romance languages was that Storm was not terribly confident when he arrived in France in 1869. His linguistic insecurity – although in the case of a linguistic talent like his, this is only relative – comes across in *De romanske Sprog og Folk*:

> But if I could not acquire the language completely in that short time, I could nevertheless study both its sounds and expressions, both the physical and the spiritual aspects of the language. (Storm 1871: 5)

This humility doesn't do credit to what Storm managed to achieve during his stay in southern Europe from an academic point of view. Although he took in the sights and experienced the culture of France, Italy and Spain (see section 3.2.1), this was no holiday. He attended lectures, he spent time in libraries studying Old Romance documents, he recorded non-standard forms as he encountered them, and he met with linguists and other people interested in discussing language issues. He carried out such a detailed study of the history of Italian that he was even able to produce a publication contributing to the debate on its historical relationship with the ancient languages of Italy (Storm 1870) – see section 3.3.2.1.2 below.

3.1.1.2 Storm's professional career began and ended with large-scale Romance works. It began in 1871 with *De romanske Sprog og Folk* (The Romance Languages and Peoples), and it ended the year before his death with the final volume of *Større fransk Syntax* (Comprehensive French Syntax). There was plenty of Romance work in between, much of it in the form of shorter articles on narrow philological topics. We shall discuss later why he never managed a Romance *magnum opus* to set alongside *Engelsk Filologi/Englische Philologie*.

Thanks to *Større fransk Syntax*, and thanks even more to *Franske Taleøvelser* (French Dialogues), Storm is remembered specifically as a French scholar rather than as a general Romanist. As we shall see, however, he was as skilled in Italian as he was in French, and his knowledge of other earlier and non-national Romance varieties was extraordinary. He never showed quite the same enthusiasm for Spanish as he did for French and Italian. This was partly because there was not the same call for the teaching of Spanish, and partly because French and Italian philology were better established at that time than was Spanish philology. (He remarked in *De romanske Sprog og Folk* that 'scientific comparative language research seems still to be virtually unknown in Spain' (Storm 1871: 82).) His practical abilities in Spanish were nonetheless impressive, as this story indicates:

> In the evening we arrived at Zaragóza, where my new friend, who was called Felíz Fernández, invited me to spend the night at the military

hospital, where he was well known. There I got to know several of his colleagues, who asked Fernández whether I was Catalan. 'No', answered F., 'I think he is from somewhere in France'. Now, I didn't want to be taken for a Frenchman and explained that I was from *Noruéga*, but since this country was completely unknown, I took a way out by saying that I was from the Land of the Dried Fish, *el país del bacaláo* [lit. *the land of the cod*]. Unfortunately there are several countries that produce dried fish, and I therefore had to accept that the final outcome was that I was from America. (Storm 1871: 81)

It is probably fair to say that his Romance work made him better known to more people in his own lifetime than his work on English or Norwegian did. He had the respect of the international community of Romance philologists, which was larger than the community of Anglists, and *Franske Taleøvelser* was a huge commercial success. However, Storm's Romance work has not outlived him, as *Norvegia* and *Englische Philologie* have done. Eighty years after his death he is barely remembered in Romance circles at all. A 1982 overview of Romance studies in Scandinavia (Spang-Hanssen 1982) does not mention his name once. One purpose of this chapter is then to resurrect the work which was so widely admired and used less than 100 years ago. This is not to say that it will all have stood the test of time, but some of it can still tell twenty-first-century linguists a thing or two. We shall also be asking why this corpus of original contributions to Romance studies by a Romance linguist of Storm's standing could disappear from the canon so quickly.

First, however, we must provide a little more background to Storm's work, teaching and researching Romance languages in Norway.

3.1.2 *Romance Languages at the University*

3.1.2.1 There is no need for us to give as much detail on the background to Romance studies in Storm's day as we did on the background to English studies in Chapter 2. The main reason for this is that much of the history of the study of English on the one hand and the history of the study of Romance languages (specifically French) on the other, up to and including the nineteenth century, is shared. We have already seen that English and French together constituted group 4 of the linguistic-historical teachers' exam and that they were regarded as an academic unit. Certainly in Norway in the later nineteenth century it was felt that the modern foreign languages could be divided into English and French on the one hand, and Norwegian and German on the other. English was cut off from the other Germanic languages since it belonged with French on socio-political grounds. Romance languages other than French were a luxury rather than an integral component of university study. The selection of modern foreign languages taught during the early years of Det kongelige Frederiks Universitet was dictated more by the linguistic abilities of the personnel involved than by any carefully thought-out curriculum. Modern-language teaching came to be better organised with the appointment of Unger in 1851,[2] but it was only with the arrival of Storm that the university began to look like a serious part of the European scene in English and Romance philology. (The situation regarding modern languages at the university prior to Storm's appointment in 1869 is dealt with in section 2.1.2 above.)

3.1.2.2 It is instructive to look briefly at Storm's legacy. The picture of *English* philology at the university painted by Sandved (1998) is one of gradual improvement during Storm's period of office, such that the university had an excellent international reputation in the field by the turn of the twentieth century, thanks almost entirely to Storm's work. With his retirement and death, the situation changed radically in the new century, which witnessed a gradual decline in standards up to the Second World War. This shows just how much the reputation of Kristiania in this field had rested on the shoulders of the one man. Sandved writes:

> The research in English language and literature which actually went on was not up to the standard one was entitled to expect in a subject of such central significance to the Norwegian school system and to Norwegian society at that time. Of six doctoral theses from the period 1936–43, as many as four were rejected and the remaining two were to an extent accepted with grave doubts. It actually gives a very good indication of, or – were it necessary – a further confirmation of the crisis English was in during these years. (Sandved 1998: 307)

Did the fame of Romance studies rely equally heavily on the brilliance of one man, or was Storm's legacy kept alive by other scholars?

Storm's successor as professor of Romance philology was Oluf Eilert Løseth (1858–1945). He was a student of Storm's and, after taking the linguistic-historical teachers' exam, he travelled to Paris on a scholarship to study for a number of years with Gaston Paris and Paul Meyer. In 1892, having returned to Norway, he was first appointed research fellow in Romance philology and then later docent, prior to taking the chair in 1913. During his time in France Løseth developed an interest above all in

---

[2] As Hovdhaugen et al. (2000: 265, n. 15) point out, 'the term *modern languages* has, somewhat misleadingly, evolved to refer to German, French and English only, to the exclusion of the native languages of the Nordic countries, Russian etc.' I don't agree with this. From the British university angle at least, the term 'modern languages' refers to all currently used European languages except English (the "home" language). I agree that the term is used to refer exclusively to European modern languages and not others, but, to avoid the ponderous phrase 'modern foreign languages', I shall use 'modern languages' to refer to all those currently spoken European languages with which Storm was professionally involved, except the "home" Scandinavian languages and their varieties.

Old French, and his 1888 doctoral thesis – the fruit of his stay in Paris – bore the title *Tristanromanens gammelfranske prosahaandskrifter i Pariser-natio-nalbibliotheket* (The Old French Prose Manuscripts of the Tristan Romance in the National Library in Paris). Although he functioned as lektor in French from 1897, and although he was ultimately responsible for the first Norwegian-French dictionary (published in two volumes in 1936 and 1940), it is fair to say that Løseth's interests were of the traditional, literary variety, and that his work did not constitute a continuation of the direction taken by Storm.[3]

There was only one applicant for the post following Løseth's retirement, and that was Peter Hjalmar Rokseth (1891–1945). Rokseth had also studied in the Romance-speaking areas as a young man and maintained close links with southern Europe throughout his life, but, as professor of Romance philology and literature from 1929 onwards, he is remembered chiefly for his contributions to the administration of the university rather than for his academic output (Haakonsen 1952). His 1928 doctoral thesis – *Den franske tragedie. I: Corneille* – is the only substantial work he published.

Rokseth's successor in 1946 was one of the most eminent Norwegian linguists of the twentieth century, Hans Kamstrup Vogt (1903–1986), but his eminence was not as a Romanist. He published almost nothing on Romance philology (see Hovdhaugen et al. 2000: 475); his main contributions lay in the study of Caucasian languages and of the North American language Kalispel. From 1964 to 1966, and again from 1967 to 1969, he was rektor of the university (see Thordarson 1977).

Vogt had studied in France. He had taken his *baccalauréat* at the Lycée Corneille in Rouen in 1921 and studied Romance philology at the Sorbonne and at the École des Hautes Études in Paris (Amundsen 1961a: 448). After the death of Rokseth, who had himself been the only applicant for the chair, there were this time no applications:

> Nobody here at home was at that time qualified in Romance philology, and, out of the difficult situation which arose for French Studies, there came the happy outcome that Vogt – with his eminent linguistic skill and his complete familiarity with spoken French – took up the position. (Amundsen 1961a: 448)

Vogt occupied the chair in Romance linguistics from 1946 to 1962,[4] when he was translated (as a worthy successor to Alf Sommerfelt (1892–1965), also educated in Paris) to the chair in general linguistics. Despite this 'happy outcome', a quarter of a century after Storm's death, university French studies were in crisis. As was the case with English then, Storm had been a bright flame which had burned out very quickly, leaving no more than a few

---

[3] For information about Løseth, see Bødtker (1938).
[4] A separate chair in 'French and other Romance literature' was established at this time and filled by Carl Vilhelm Holst.

sparks behind. The situation for the other Romance languages was worse still. The first lektor position in Spanish arrived only in 1960.

3.1.3 *Further Afield*

3.1.3.1 We will not embark on a journey across Europe to see the full context for Storm's work in Norway, as we did in Chapter 2, again because we will be covering much of the same ground. There are just two final pieces of background information we need before we deal with the contributions Storm made to Romance studies in his publications. Firstly, it is important to be aware of the development of Romance philology at the University of Copenhagen, in many ways the parent institution to Det kongelige Frederiks Universitet in that it was where Norwegian students tended to study prior to the 1811 foundation of the Norwegian university. Although Copenhagen University was a much more venerable institution than its sister (or rather daughter) institution in Kristiania, it did not boast a professor of Romance philology until the appointment of Thor Sundby (1830–1894) in 1887, so, in the person of Storm, Kristiania got there first. Thanks to Storm, Kristiania could really be said to have been *the* centre for modern philology in Scandinavia. The other background information we need briefly to provide concerns the tradition of 'language masters' in European universities, the stream of badly paid, badly treated, practical language teachers who passed through the university cities during the centuries before the establishment of a scientific philology in the later nineteenth century. The reason why they are important is because, even when scholars of the stature of Unger and Storm, and even Jespersen, had taken over their role, something of their nature lingered on and tarnished working conditions for Storm and his colleagues.

First of all to Copenhagen.

3.1.3.2 As in the early years of Det kongelige Frederiks Universitet in Kristiania, the first teaching of Romance languages in Copenhagen was ad hoc and depended on the abilities of the individuals who happened to present themselves. The university had been founded in 1479, but the first teacher of Romance languages of whom there is any record was Carlos Rodriguez, born in Madrid in 1618. He was appointed language teacher at Sorø Academy in 1669, but that institution closed the same year, and he was appointed professor of French, Spanish and Italian at the university. This title means nothing in modern terms, and 'professor' cannot be taken to imply any scholarly pretensions. He published a brief Spanish grammar in 1662, *Fundamenta lingvæ hispanicæ*, which appears to be his only published work (Høybye and Spang-Hanssen 1979: 232).[5] That Rodriguez got his position at the university because he happened to be around and looking for

---

[5] This section is based closely on Høybye & Spang-Hanssen (1979).

work, and that he was made responsible for teaching in three separate languages, is typical of the arrangements for language teaching at northern European universities at this time (see next section). It is also typical that, when he died in 1689, he was not replaced for over 40 years. His was an accidental appointment, rather than something central to the work of the university. Rodriguez's successor was also a native speaker of a Romance language who ended up in Copenhagen. Isac Briand de Crèvecœur (1664–1747) was, like many language teachers in northern Europe in the sixteenth and seventeenth centuries, a Protestant refugee. He lived and worked in several countries sympathetic to Protestantism and appears to have arrived in Copenhagen in 1725. Nothing is known of his teaching or publication while professor of geography and the French language during the period from 1732 until his death. He was succeeded by his son, which once again bears witness to the informal arrangements for modern-language teaching in the university at this time.

In 1754 a rather more impressive figure was appointed lecturer in French: the Norwegian Hans von Aphelen (1719–1779). Five years later, in 1759, he became professor in the same subject, but without pay, another fact typical for those in the language master tradition (see next section). He is first and foremost remembered as a lexicographer, and Hovdhaugen et al. (2000: 98) describe him as 'the most important scholar of modern language studies in the Nordic countries before 1800'. He published a number of books for the teaching of French, a *Méthode d'apprendre à écrire correctement le François* in 1756, a lengthy *Fransk Sproglære* in 1775, and a *Fransk Sprogøvelse* in 1777 (see Høybye and Spang-Hanssen 1979: 236). Much more important was the French–Danish *Dictionnaire Royal* of 1759. His dedication of his language works to the royal family reminds us of the English–Danish work of his contemporary, Charles Julius Bertram (1723–1765) (see Linn 1999).

As a non-native speaker, Aphelen was the exception prior to the nine-teenth century – (being Norwegian, he was a citizen of the Danish kingdom). He remained professor of French until his death in 1779 and was succeeded four years later by Étienne Fumars (1743–1806). Fumars was born in Marseille and, not unusually for this type of language teacher, had a peripatetic life before coming to Copenhagen, by virtue of being a member of an aristocratic household, as Crèvecœur had been. He left a professorship in Kiel to accompany the marquis de Vérac to Copenhagen and was professor at the University of Copenhagen from 1783 until his death. The Swiss-born Marc Nicolas Puerari (1766–1845), who came to Denmark as a teacher in merchant and aristocratic households, took over the post after the death of Fumars. Like Fumars he provided practical teaching in French, as well as going through various major works of literature, notably the great seventeenth-century tragedies and comedies. Puerari returned to Geneva in 1822 and the post stood empty for seven years, indicating that as late as 1829 it was still an ad hoc post, filled where possible, but not as a priority. By this time Det kongelige Frederiks Universitet had been founded in Kristiania and Messell was on its payroll, teaching English, French and Italian.

However, from now on Romance studies take on a more serious, academic appearance in Copenhagen. Nicolai Christian Levin Abrahams (1798–1870) wrote his master's dissertation on the *Roman de Brut*, based on the study of manuscripts in Paris, and he worked on French medieval manuscripts in the Royal Library in Copenhagen. He was appointed lektor in French in 1828 and professor in 1832. It is noteworthy that no Romance language other than French had been specified in the title of posts at Copenhagen University since Rodriguez. Abrahams had good practical skills in Italian as well as French, but it seems that his teaching remained in the field of French. Like Messell's teaching in Kristiania, it was wide-ranging, covering literature and the history of the language as well as practical language skills. Here we can see the germ of the philology that Storm would later teach. Abrahams's successor, Vilhelm Jacob Bjerring (1805–1879), had even stronger historical interests. He is remembered more as a politician than as a linguist (see Høybye and Spang-Hanssen 1979: 240), but he was lektor in French from 1852 until 1879. Kristoffer Nyrop (see section 3.3.1.6 below), who in 1894 succeeded Sundby as professor of Romance philology, was a pupil of Bjerring and summed up the latter's contribution in these words:

> His lectures mainly covered the language in its modern form, but from time to time he also dealt with older periods, and he knew how to awaken interest in both the Middle Ages and the Renaissance. It is without doubt the case that his university activity provided the impetus for Danes beginning to deal in a much more thorough way than previously with the historical development of the French language. (Cited in Høybye and Spang-Hanssen 1979: 241)

Bjerring was followed by Thor Sundby (1830–1894), who was initially docent in French language and literature (from 1880), but who seven years later (in 1887) became professor in Romance philology. So, fourteen years after his appointment as professor in Kristiania, Storm finally got an opposite-number in Copenhagen. Storm's great friend, Vilhelm Thomsen, was an extraordinarily wide-ranging linguistic talent, truly one of the few contemporaries capable of being Storm's linguistic confidant. Although he was professor of comparative linguistics he lectured on a range of subjects, reflecting the breadth of his knowledge, and in 1879/1880 he gave a series of lectures on the history of Romance. Storm had great respect for Thomsen's abilities as a linguist, and a week after Storm's own appointment as professor of English and Romance philology (in a letter of 8 July 1873), he reflected on Thomsen's place in the circle of Scandinavian Romanists:

I am amazed at the wide range of your lectures. I expect you are as good a Romance scholar as both Thor Sundby and all us others? By the way, I thought that Thor Sundby was more of a literary historian and textual critic than an actual linguist. Scandinavia is not rich in Romance scholars, and nothing else is to be expected. Lidforss in Lund is not of the first rank, and barely of the second [. . .][6] What is the situation regarding Romance scholars in Uppsala? I never hear anything from that neck of the woods. Our Unger is superbly well read in the literature and lexicon of the Romance languages, but has not produced anything in that field. On the other hand, Sophus Bugge, who can do everything, has recently tossed off a whole pile of highly ingenious etymologies, particularly such words as Littré has left unexplained.

Charting the history of the teaching and study of Romance languages in Copenhagen, we can see how what would become Romance philology in Scandinavia evolved. It was assumed that one person could look after a number of languages from the Romance family. This might have been possible when all that was required was practical language teaching, but it was a lot more difficult when philology had taken on its nineteenth-century shape. Even more hopeless was Unger's task as professor of Romance *and* Germanic philology. Initially literature was added to practical language teaching, and in the nineteenth century along came the historical dimension too, in addition to the call for teachers of the Romance languages to exhibit scientific as well as teaching ability.

3.1.3.3 In section 2.1.3.2 we saw how the teaching of English during the seventeenth and eighteenth centuries in Swedish universities was provided by the so-called language masters. The principal task of language masters was usually to teach French, thanks to the status of French as the European language of culture at the time, so it is now the moment to consider these people. The working conditions and status of the language masters varied from person to person, from university to university and from country to country, but it is possible to make certain generalisations about the group as a whole.

First, most of them were native speakers of Romance languages employed by northern European universities to provide practical language teaching to those students who wished for it. Aphelen was unusual in this regard, and in Uppsala, where language masters were employed from 1637, country of origin varied, but most came from France, Switzerland and Italy. Lund, by contrast, tended to employ Scandinavian nationals, including the Dane Ifvar Kraak, whom we encountered in the last chapter as a gifted teacher of English too. Given the impermanent nature of their contracts and the

[6] Edvard Lidforss (1833–1910) was professor of modern European languages in Lund from 1878, and an Old French specialist.

unpredictability of work, many of the language masters led a peripatetic lifestyle, taking employment where they could find it. The Italian Blasius Ludovicus Teppati, language master in Uppsala from 1671 to 1672, for example, had spent two years in Denmark and probably some time in Germany before arriving in Sweden in 1667. He became official language master in French and Italian for two years, but after that the language master's salary was given to the stable master instead, whereupon Teppati appears to have moved to Stockholm (Hammar 1981: 95).

Secondly, conditions were often poor. The language masters were not treated as members of the academic staff of the universities. Knowledge of French (and any other modern foreign language) was seen as a practical skill, desirable in people of noble birth, alongside, and on a level with riding, dancing and fencing. Hammar (1981: 87) writes:

> Despite the growing and increasingly widespread need, language masters maintained their position as instructors for the nobility throughout the whole of the period investigated [up to 1807], outside the real work of the university.

Consequently many of the language masters had very little status. They were given permission to offer teaching within the university, but their income from this was pretty wretched, was not always forthcoming, and, as we have seen, was sometimes simply redirected to somebody else. In Uppsala from 1656 to 1664 the salary was redirected to the professor of theology, who had nothing to do with the teaching of modern languages, and for 11 years the stable master received the income which had been due to Teppati. In Lund there was a reason for redirecting the language master's salary, but it was a pretty dubious reason. It was assumed that the professor of mathematics was qualified to teach French on account of the amount of mathematical literature written in that language, so he received this income from 1682 until 1703 when a considerable fight ensued to redirect the money (Hammar 1981: 88). Language masters took private pupils outside their university work, and this helped their financial circumstances, but it was not predictable income, and was sometimes denied by circumstances beyond the teachers' control. Following the British bombardment of Copenhagen in 1807, Danish teachers of English, for example, found themselves in dire straits:

> Nobody dared to speak English in public places [. . .] One almost dared not let it be known that one read or understood English, and in the period immediately after the [British] attack, English language teachers were in great hardship since their students utterly forsook them [. . .] (Werlauff 1873/1874: 348)

Thirdly, the quality and level of the teaching was very variable, and there were few, if any, systems in place to set and maintain standards. Hammar (1981: 93) concludes:

The standard of French teaching at the university was on many occasions no higher than in the schools; however, the methods could be different. When the teaching provided by the language masters is discussed, often nothing other than 'parsing' is mentioned, which was viewed as sufficient in some cases, but too little in others.

It is not possible fully to generalise the nature, conditions and quality of the language masters, but we can safely say that these broad characteristics applied. Surely by Storm's day things were quite different in Scandinavian universities, so why is it necessary to spend time on the misfortunes of earlier generations? As we saw in the last chapter (2.1.3.3.1), it was imperative for modern linguists in nineteenth-century German universities to be seen to be a different breed from these earlier language masters, to be seen to possess scientific competence in a subject which could be recognized as susceptible to scientific study. The intellectualisation of modern languages filtered up to Scandinavia too, and we can be sure that the new breed of Danish philologists were just as keen to distance themselves from their humbler predecessors. The language master tradition never really existed in Norway in the same way, as the university was not founded until philologists were beginning to replace language masters anyway, and nobody for a single moment questioned Storm's scientific standing. However, some of the features of the language master tradition lingered on to plague the modern philologists.

It was still assumed that one person could cover several different languages. It was all right for Rodriguez to be professor of French, Spanish and Italian, but when this meant the breadth of teaching detailed by Storm in the 1877 application to parliament, it was no longer possible. We have earlier witnessed the fight Storm had to persuade the university to take on additional teachers of practical skills. This fight came about partly because Storm was assumed to be a *language teacher*. A university teacher of modern languages teaches students how to speak modern languages, doesn't he?

Storm's financial worries were not specifically connected to the subject of his professorship. The problem was academic pay in Kristiania in general. His employment terms were those of any other *professor ordinarius*, but the status of the modern languages (for so long the bedfellows of dancing and fencing) as university subjects could not yet be taken for granted. It was certainly to Storm's advantage that the teaching of modern languages in Kristiania was established along with the university itself. He did not have to justify it in quite the same way that colleagues introducing modern languages to established universities were frequently forced to do. For example, the first professor of modern languages (as distinct from the language assistants) at Oxford University was appointed in 1848, but the teaching of modern languages remained on a weak foundation, not least because:

The active hostility of many of the teachers of the old subjects, and the indifference of the majority of the University, had prevented the growth of the new subject by refusing it an adequate place in the examination system. (Firth 1929: 53)

It should be noted that at Kristiania, while there was no principled objection to the *study* of modern languages, the non-classical subjects as a whole were not universally embraced by the classical establishment which did regard them (rightly) as a threat to the status and popularity of the Classics. By the end of the century a traditional Classical school education was very much a thing of the past. From the 1830s the battle lines had been drawn in the schools between the Classics on the one hand and the modern subjects on the other (see Høigård & Ruge 1963: 95–137). The fact that it was so much of an issue in the schools meant that the university did not need to be involved to the same extent as in other countries with longer traditions of university Classics; but what went on in the schools clearly had repercussions in the university:

A modern sixth form [*realgymnas*] without Classical languages was something quite new in the European school system, and the university fought against the modern students as much as it could by introducing preparatory tests in Latin in the various faculties [. . .] The law of 1869 is the first great fissure in the wall of Latin surrounding the university, and there is not much left of that wall now. (Høigård & Ruge 1963: 136–137)

The situation was eased by the fact that Storm had a Classical education himself, frequently expressed his support for the study of the Classics, and had considerable documented knowledge of the Latin language.

3.2 POPULAR WORKS

3.2.1 De romanske Sprog og Folk *(1871)*

3.2.1.1 Having learnt what modern foreign languages he could in Norway, Storm set off on 5 February 1869 on his linguistic odyssey of England, France, Italy and Spain. The day-to-day details of his journey and its costs are documented in UBB Ms. 740q. His first expense was a tip for the steward on board ship, en route to Shields in north-east England. The final outcome of the journey was *De romanske Sprog og Folk*.

De romanske Sprog og Folk: Skildringer fra en Studiereise med offentligt Stipendium (The Romance Languages and Peoples: Depictions of a Publicly Funded Study Tour) started life, as its subtitle indicates, as Storm's official report on his funded study-tour of southern Europe. For publication in this form he spiced the work up a bit to make it appeal to a wider public: 'While I was preparing it I wanted to talk about this and that, which I thought could be of interest to a wider public' (Preface). Storm's aims are unashamedly popular. He expresses the hope that he will not put readers off with the philological observations which crop up throughout the book, and appeals to 'a not insignificant sector of the educated public, who, without being able to devote themselves to specialist studies, wish to take part in the most general and interesting scientific results'. This is the same readership he had in mind with 'Tale og Accent i Forhold til Sang' 10 years earlier, and it is a readership for which he had a particular feel. *De romanske Sprog og Folk* bears the scars of its authorship history, in that there are plenty of references to the studies Storm undertook, the libraries he visited and the lectures he attended. In short, it reveals its history as a formal report. However, it is Storm's comments on the countries and the peoples of France, Italy and Spain which leave the strongest impression on the reader – these and the amusing stories he recounts. In fact it is the humanity of *De romanske Sprog og Folk* which really singles it out amongst Storm's publications. As rarely again in Storm's *opus*, we get to know the man, the shy man, the disapproving man, the humorous man, the sheltered northern European trying to come to terms with the very different world of the nineteenth-century Mediterranean. Storm hopes that a second edition might be possible, which would be more lively and of yet more popular interest:

> Should this book receive a favourable reception from the public, I have available the material for a comprehensive travelogue, which would come into its own in a second edition. Here I would also include depictions of nature, in which I have a great interest, but not the space in this edition. Furthermore, the last traces of the official report would then disappear. (1871: Preface)

As with so many of Storm's publication plans, nothing ever came of this second edition. As to whether *De romanske Sprog og Folk* (*DrSF*) received a 'favourable reception', there is insufficient evidence to say, but of all Storm's publications it is probably the one which most warrants rereading 130 years later. The linguistics is not profound and the attitudes are biased and sometimes bigoted, but the book remains a joy to read.

3.2.1.2 So Storm's journey began with a boat journey from Stavanger to Shields. He travelled from there to London, where he spent a few days and formed a highly unfavourable view of English manners, at least as encountered in the staff and other guests of the Salisbury Hotel in Fleet Street. As soon as he embarked on his journey from Dover to Calais he noticed a difference between English and French politeness, the former being cold, the latter warm. On 9 February 1869 he arrived in Calais and travelled immediately to Paris, arriving there on the evening of the same day, and he booked into a hotel, which he described as 'simple, but decent' (p. 4). He got on well with the other guests at the hotel, who were for the most part students, but he was shocked by their ignorance and the looseness of their ideas. With one or two exceptions he was not impressed by the level of learning in France, Italy and Spain, and he was particularly shocked by what he perceived to be an unacceptably low level of philological scholarship. But, 'despite a general superficiality, one cannot fail, in such a large country and amongst such brilliant people, to find real scholars of the first rank' (p. 11).

Émile Littré (1801–1881), the lexicographer, and Gaston Paris (1839–1903) are the two French scholars Storm mentions favourably. He is particularly vigorous in his praise of Paris, whose lectures on the history of French Storm attended and described as 'a masterful presentation'. Looking back on his seven-month stay in Paris, it was the eponymous philologist Storm valued above all:

> It is him I have to thank for the real benefit I derived from my stay in Paris. His lectures completely balanced out the advantages of spending some months in Germany, where I would have had less opportunity to study the living Romance languages. Having heard him, I was certain that I had made the right decision in choosing France over Germany. The best of what is produced in Germany in the Romance field can be read here at home, but the living language cannot be read. In addition to this there is the fact that Gaston Paris has moved French philology on, and in several places has corrected Diez as well as Littré. (1871: 21)

The 'living language' is, as always, the primary consideration. Storm maintained contact with Paris, and they corresponded for many years after this first meeting. In a letter of 6 January 1872 (NBO Ms. 8° 2402 J^x) Paris is as complimentary about Storm the student as Storm was about Paris the teacher.

Storm's academic activities did not begin and end with attendance at lectures: 'the important thing for me was to pick up everything' (p. 14). It is a cliché to say so, but Storm was throughout his life hungry for knowledge. It was this insatiable hunger which prevented him stopping to organise, systematise, theorise, and in *DrSF* we find the breathless Johan Storm running around after knowledge. He visited libraries, he took practical classes and he went to the theatre. When the summer came and there were no more lectures or classes to attend, and despite a temperature in the city of 27° C, he turned his attention to the study of Spanish and Italian to prepare himself for the next legs of his journey. As I write this, I too am sitting in a library, benefiting the while from a research award. I imagine some people use their research grants to full advantage, whereas others squander the munificence of their benefactor. In Storm's case, the benefactors must have deemed they had had value for money.

On 6 September Storm left Paris and travelled via Lyon to Marseille.

3.2.1.3 From Marseille he travelled to Livorno, where he developed an interest in the Genoese dialect, and from Livorno he moved on to his first major port of call in Italy, Florence. In Florence he stayed with Professor Francésco Dall'Óngaro (Storm's system of accents), who Storm describes as 'a well-known Italian patriot and poet'. Storm claims that he found no real difficulties with the language, that 'the Italian language proved to be so easy, that, even when I arrived, I understood most of what was being said' (p. 23). This is a good example of the innocent arrogance of youth Storm sometimes exhibits in *DrSF* but which has been replaced by a measured, mature humility by 1879 and *Engelsk Filologi*. However, we can take this statement at face value. Storm was an unusually talented practical linguist. He knew Latin and French to a high standard, so we can assume that Italian genuinely posed no difficulties for him. This statement also shows that Storm had little or no knowledge of the language from before, over and above what he had managed to learn in Paris during the summer, and that he had not learnt any Italian in Norway as a boy. Since he had no practical problems with the language, Storm, ever hungry for more linguistic knowledge, focused his attention on the Italian dialects: 'The main thing for me was to acquaint myself as well as I possibly could with the living language' (p. 23).

Probably the most important linguistic contribution of *DrSF* is the comparative, parallel text samples of Italian dialects (pp. 33–39). Admittedly they are intended for a popular audience, and admittedly they are in Storm's adapted orthography, but the same text given in the dialects of Venice, Milan, Turin, Genoa, Naples and Palermo, with Italian and Norwegian translations, was a real service to Italian dialectology, especially since that discipline was 'still rather neglected':

> There are indeed fairly complete dictionaries for most of the dialects, although most of these are not written from a scientific point of view, but rather to disseminate knowledge of Italian, which, for northerners and southerners, is to be regarded as a foreign language. It is one of my dearest wishes one day to be able to return to Italy to undertake detailed investigations of the dialects, which would reap benefits here as in no other Romance country. (p. 49)

Is this just the sort of thing one writes in a report to a funding agency, in the hope of further funds being forthcoming? In any case, this was yet another project destined to remain unrealised.

As in France, Storm had little respect for native scholarship. He singles out Graziadio Isaia Ascoli (1829–1907), whose work he would present to the Scandinavian public three years later (Storm 1874b), and whom Storm here describes as 'one of the most brilliant cultivators of comparative linguistics' (p. 48), which of course he was. Storm's disrespect for Italian scholarly work extends to his views of the Italian work ethic in general. He supports the stereotype of a busy, productive North ('from the North proceeds Italy's vitality' (p. 48)) counterbalanced by a lazy South. As we saw in the last chapter, Storm has little time for Roman Catholicism, and the staunch Protestant expends disproportionately many words on the shortcomings of the Catholic faith: 'Italy is the least faithful country in Christendom. The nearer to the Pope, the further from Christ' (p. 51). He is eager to recount tales of hypocrisy amongst the Italian Catholic laity and priesthood, and his rather extreme reactions to the beliefs and practices of Roman Catholicism can only be explained by appealing to his childhood and the impact of his father, the Lutheran pastor. Regretfully Storm writes, 'I do not think that Protestantism has any real future either in Spain or in southern Europe generally' (p. 93).

As in France, Storm attended lectures, visited museums and galleries and went to the theatre, in short did as much as he could to immerse himself in the life and language of the country, although the immersion stopped short in religious waters. As we shall see later, there were also other traditional aspects of Mediterranean life he was simply too northern European to come to terms with, but he made the effort, in a way he believed his compatriots otherwise failed to do. If Norwegians found the French unfriendly, it was probably because they were themselves too stiff, he wrote (p. 20).

After Florence Storm moved to Rome together with Vilhelm Thomsen who had just arrived from Germany (February 1870). Sandfeld (1983: 505) describes this meeting as accidental (*tilfældigt*), but I find this hard to believe. Storm stayed in Rome for a month, visiting Naples, Pompeii, Sorrento and Pisa, before parting from Thomsen and returning to Marseille via Florence and Bastia to continue his journey to Spain alone.

3.2.1.4 Storm arrived in Barcelona on 27 March 1870 and stayed there for a week in order to study Catalan, before moving on to Madrid. His Catalan studies got off to a fortuitous start, when he met Joán Montserrat,[7] president of the Catalan language movement, *La jóve Catalúnya*, in a bookshop. Through Montserrát Storm got to attend a meeting of the society and was able to make contact with other Catalan speakers. This exposure to Catalan resulted in another important feature of the book from the linguistic point of view: a series of Catalan songs with Castilian and Norwegian translations. These must have been the first of their kind available to Norwegians. For comparison's sake Storm also provides a biblical excerpt in Provençal, Catalan, Castilian Spanish, Portuguese, Italian and Romansch. Although *DrSF* is a popular work, intended to give a general picture of the Romance languages and peoples, it could have served as a (very) elementary guide to the Romance languages, some of their dialects and some of the ancient languages of the area. As we would expect, Storm also gives brief guides to

[7] I have maintained the accents Storm provided to help readers with the pronunciation of names and other words.

the phonetics of the languages. It is fair to assume that the parallel texts in *DrSF* had a pedagogical intent, since it was the parallel text format that Storm chose in his model texts for the study of French, the *Franske Taleøvelser*.

On Sunday 3 April Storm left Barcelona, after a short but very productive visit – he also visited the university and met the vice-chancellor. He then stayed in Madrid for just over a month. By contrast with his stays in other southern European cities, he seems to have had less academic stimulus here and more time and inclination for leisure activities. He did not encounter any comparative Romance research, and it appeared that the philological advances being made in Germany were of no interest to the Spanish (p. 83). There seems to have been little formal information available on the dialects, and 'here', wrote Storm, 'the foreign researcher has to set up investigations off his own bat' (p. 83). As Storm was less familiar with Spanish than he had been with Italian, he was forced by this fact, and by the brevity of his stay, to concentrate on Castilian. He does point out, nonetheless, that his preparatory work in Paris had served him well, and that 'from the very first day I arrived in Spain, I had no difficulty in understanding the natives' (p. 118). The lectures he attended at the university were of little academic interest, and he was far from impressed by the level and nature of Spanish education (p. 111). On the other hand, he was full of praise for the Spanish museums, which made up in the richness of their collections for their lack of system.

The Spanish section is the longest of the three sections of *DrSF*, perhaps because this was the country least known to the book's potential readers, and Storm comments much more on national character, traditions and so on than he does for France and Italy. We learn Storm's views on Spanish family life and chivalry, Spanish literature, politics, religion, racial characteristics and work ethic. It is also in this part of the book that we get to share Storm's own experiences as a tourist most fully. The story of how he was nearly tricked by two conmen in Valencia at the very end of his trip (pp. 98–103), and the distaste he felt at his first (and last) bullfight (pp. 104–108), are brilliantly told.

3.2.1.5 On 12 June Storm left Madrid and made his way via various tourist destinations back up to Marseille, where he arrived on 17 June. From Marseille he travelled to Lausanne, and so, via Basel, Frankfurt, Marburg, Hamburg, Kristiansand and Stavanger, back to Kristiania to take up his post at the university. The detour from Kristiansand to Stavanger probably means a visit to his wife's family. He concludes the description of his travels in *DrSF* thus:

> And so I returned to my dear fatherland, where I try, in so far as the narrow circumstances allow, to cultivate science. I want particularly to record the result of my studies in detailed works, which could be of benefit

to students and perhaps to science more generally. But, on account of the difficult times [Tidernes Pinagtighed], little headway is being made.

Under these circumstances I must be all the more grateful that I have been permitted to be able to dedicate myself to my studies for getting on for a year and a half, and to hear the three most beautiful of Europe's languages being spoken. (p. 123)

He felt it to be his duty to make his findings available to the academic community, to students and to the community of scholars. We shall see in the rest of this chapter that this sense of duty seems to have guided his publication career. 'You can take a horse to water, but you can't make it drink', as the saying goes. Storm may have spent one-and-a-half years in Mediterranean Europe, but his own Protestant work ethic remained as strong as ever.

3.2.1.6 *DrSF* is a popular presentation, and has no pretensions to be anything else, but some of Storm's linguistic comments are nevertheless surprising, coming from a descriptive linguist of Storm's calibre – comments which might have been expected 100 years earlier:

In general the different impressions the three principal Romance languages make on the ear can be characterised thus: French sounds to be the most delicate language; Italian the most beautiful and sonorous; Spanish the most powerful. The sound system bears a certain relationship to the character of the people. (pp. 121–122)

Instead of being shocked by such impressionistic ideas, by such vagueness, I think we should find it refreshing that a "serious" linguist felt able to write this way. Storm, who stood on the margins in so many ways, did not feel compelled to toe the party line in terms of scientific writing. For him languages were living things, they were alive, and to describe languages like people as 'delicate' or 'powerful' was the most natural thing in the world. It was also the most natural thing in the world to write a book which intertwined descriptions of people, of customs and of languages. This may smack of Romanticism lingering on from the early part of the century, but National Romanticism was alive and well in Norway in 1870. (In one piece of linguistic Romanticism Storm was prophetically sort of right: '[the English language] of all languages probably has the greatest universality, the most qualifications for becoming a universal language' (pp. 126–127).) In the Storm of 1870 the Norwegian National Romantic meets the European new philologist. The scientific linguist also meets the travel writer, and in *DrSF* this is to everybody's mutual benefit.

Storm was the Norwegian and the European at the same time, with all this meant in terms of contrasting ideologies, and in *DrSF* those two sides to his character clashed head on, more so than in any of his other publications.

The question of who won, the Norwegian or the European, is an irrelevant question. The point is that it is the complexity of the man which makes the work so fascinating, original and refreshing. We can say, however (as elsewhere), that Storm's obsession with Norwegian often seems to underpin his thoughts and writings about other languages. The Preface contains an explanation of the orthographical principles to be followed in the book, and the question of a revised Norwegian orthography is clearly at the root of comments like:

> Just as the process by which the language develops goes unnoticed, so should that of the orthography also be. (p. 128)

If we were simply to replace Spanish with Norwegian, Storm's views on his own language would be perfectly represented in the following as well:

> Castelárs language is reminiscent in a less than pleasant way of the dialect of his home region, Andalusia. The pure Spanish language is that which is spoken in Castile, and particularly by the educated classes in the cities. (pp. 110–111)

All things considered, DrSF is a successful book, marrying the popular and the scholarly, the scientific and the practical in a way that the young Storm was so good at. In terms of commercial success, however, it was no competition for the books of French dialogues, the Franske Taleøvelser.

3.2.2 Franske Taleøvelser

3.2.2.1 Mellemtrin (1887)

3.2.2.1.1 We dealt with Storm's views on language teaching reform in the last chapter (section 2.3.3). The debates on language-teaching reform which were current in the late nineteenth century tended to be rooted in the teaching of English first and foremost. There are two related reasons for this. The teachers, like Klinghardt, Jespersen, Western or Brekke, most actively involved in Quousque Tandem and similar activities were primarily teachers of English. The second, related reason for English teaching being a more central concern than French teaching was that English had a much stronger position on the school curriculum at that time. Following the reforms of 1869, German was the first foreign language to be studied in Norwegian schools. English teaching began in the fourth class of the Middelskole (at the age of 12) with five lessons per week, and five lessons per week were allocated to the subject all the way through school thereafter, with the exception of the first year Gymnas (sixth form), where the number of hours was reduced to four per week. As Storm remarks, 'ample time is dedicated to this subject' (1887b: 312). French lessons started a year later, with two a week. In the first semester of the Realgymnas the allocation rose to four per week (at the expense of English), but two a week was the norm throughout a student's schooldays. Storm concludes: 'under current circumstances the outcome of the teaching of French can scarcely be anything other than unsatisfactory' (1887b: 337). It is no surprise that he should reach this conclusion here, since the second part of the publication where he writes this – 'Om en forbedret undervisning i levende sprog' – is, as we saw in the last chapter, one long advertisement for his *Franske Taleøvelser (Mellemtrin)* (French Conversation Exercises (Intermediate Level)) (*FT*[1]), published the same year.

Storm's greatest scientific success was his *Engelsk Filologi/Englische Philologie*, but his greatest popular success, and indeed his greatest commercial success, was *Franske Taleøvelser*.

3.2.2.1.2 *Franske Taleøvelser* (*FT*[1]) really was an immense success by any publication standards. *Engelsk Filologi/Englische Philologie* gained Storm the respect of the scholarly community, but it never set the market alight. *FT*[1], by contrast, had no scholarly pretensions, yet the bookshops could not keep pace with demand. The first Norwegian edition appeared in February 1887 and was sold out some three months later, such that Storm was called upon to produce a new edition, which he finished in October that year. A number of eminent French speakers from both Scandinavia and France, including Michel Bréal (1832–1915), author of *Essai de sémantique* (1897), and Passy, are credited with assistance in preparing the first edition, and Passy went through the whole draft of the second edition too. So *FT*[1] came with impressive credentials; but it wasn't just the fact that it had the imprimatur of Bréal and Passy that assured it such a tremendous reception and the need for a third Norwegian edition in 1895 (Storm 1895b).

FT[1] pressed the right buttons with the Norwegian public, but its success was not limited to its home country. By 1895 two Danish editions, two Swedish, two German, two Dutch, a Finnish edition and an English edition had appeared too. Seip is right to state that 'people learnt French from Storm in many countries' (Seip 1966: 79).

The various editions of *Franske Taleøvelser* were reviewed widely in journals and newspapers across Europe. Robert's measured admiration in *Taalstudie* is typical. He wrote of this work 'to which I do not hesitate to assign pride of place among the better works which have appeared in recent times' (Robert 1887: 145). The left-wing Norwegian newspaper, *Verdens Gang*, was not a natural supporter of Storm, perhaps, but it included the most extravagant claim about *Franske Taleøvelser*. In reality, though, this observation was not too far from the truth. *FT* really was one of Norway's greatest cultural exports in the 1880s and 1890s:

Professor Johan Storm's *Franske Taleøvelser*, which has now appeared in its third Norwegian edition from the Gyldendal publishing house, has gained the international reputation of one of Ibsen's plays.

3.2.2.1.3 In FT^1 Storm practised what he preached. In fact most of those involved in language teaching reform, at least those associated with QT, were not (just) arid theorists. They were eager for there actually to be a reform in language teaching and to this end they tried out the new methods themselves. Thus Jespersen (1901), for example, is full of practical advice from his own experience, and the second part of Western (1888) is entitled 'The new method in practice', where Western gives realistic consideration to the implementation of QT's principles:

> Under the present examination regulations and with the available text-books it is impossible to execute all four of Quousque Tandem's points, and thus I am unable to present practical results of, for example, the use of phonetic texts. On the other hand there is nothing to prevent starting to use connected texts straightaway, or learning grammar by the inductive method, or limiting translation from the first language. (Western 1888: 58)

As we know, Storm was not an enthusiast of thoroughgoing "Quousquist-ism", but he had his own programme, set out in the preface to FT^1, and put it into practice in the actual contents of that book.

What persuaded Storm to write this book was the misery for teachers and pupils alike caused by the failure of the existing methods to achieve a satisfactory level of competence in foreign languages. Storm was not personally involved with teaching in the schools by this time, but each year he had to deal with the products of that teaching, and he had to send teachers out into the schools to do that teaching:

> The result of the methods and textbooks used up to now is that pupils study French for five or six years without learning it. They can only read it with the greatest of difficulty, never mind write it. It has to be admitted that this result is depressing. It is wretched to spend such a long time learning so little. Reform is needed. (1887a: i–ii)

We already know what sort of reform Storm wanted (see section 2.3). How did he plan to achieve it in this book of French dialogues?[8]

3.2.2.1.4 As we would expect, the emphasis is on learning the spoken language. A knowledge of the written language will flow naturally from it: 'The written language is only a more artificial, to an extent older variety of the spoken language' (p. iv). However, the written form of the language is a model of usage, according to Storm, and should therefore be studied closely. Here is a dilemma. On the one hand the spoken language is the natural form, and is the variety which should be studied and learned. On the other hand, 'no literature can boast greater masters of prose style than

---

[8] The book had a parallel French title page, and the French translation of the title was: *Dialogues Français. Enseignant la grammaire et la phraséologie du français parlé.*

precisely the French' (p. iv). Storm overcomes this dilemma by presenting dialogues which are based on literature, thus combining practice in speaking with exposure to good French style. All the dialogues are of his own devising, but: 'I have collected the material over a lengthy period, partly via direct observation, partly from literature, particularly dramatic literature' (p. iv).

Western, although generally more radical in his approach to language teaching, took a more conservative line when it came to the use of the written language:

> I regard being able to read the foreign language as the most important [. . .] only the very few have a need for this skill [the ability to speak the language], while everybody has more or less use for the ability to read the language. (Western 1888: 47)

Both agreed that speaking and writing should be studied, but Storm's insistence on *det levende Sprog* led him to a more radical position as to their priority.

Storm's views on the other principles of QT emerge in the preface to *FT*[1] as well. He does not reject the use of phonetic script in language teaching, but does not think it would be useful here, 'since this would take up too much space and seemed less necessary in a book for advanced students' (p. v). Storm's approach is rational rather than fanatical. He was always in full agreement with QT as to the use of connected texts, and indeed this book is precisely a compendium of connected, natural-sounding dialogues. He was much less sceptical about formal grammar teaching than partisan QT members, and these dialogues in fact 'follow by and large the structure of ordinary school grammars, in that as much as possible is collected under shared viewpoints' (p. iv). Again practicality overrides the adoption of a radical position for its own sake. Finally, his view on the fourth principle of QT, on the role of translation in the learning of French, is again a rational one. He presented his views on translation in language teaching theoretically in 'Om en forbedret undervisning . . .', which he was writing at the same time, and in *FT*[1] he puts them into practice:

> I have accompanied these dialogues with a translation into the mother tongue, in which I have tried to remain as faithful to the original as was compatible with idiomatic usage. Some will probably deem the translation superfluous. However, I have added it deliberately, so that the reader might grasp the meaning without difficulty and thereby enter into the spirit of the French text, immerse himself in it and become familiar with it. Pupils should, as a rule, only use the translation where it is necessary for understanding or for noting the characteristics of the language. Nothing heightens the impact of idiomatic turns of phrase so much as comparison with expressions in the mother tongue. (p. v)

Western was strongly against this approach. The two approaches correspond in fact to different fashions in foreign-language teaching, and I am certainly not going to arbitrate over which one of them is "right". However, the differing points of view do demonstrate that Storm had no programme other than *det levende Sprog*. He was not so much a conservative or a radical as a rational student of languages who knew from experience what worked. His application of the scientific to the practical in *FT*[1] was a huge success in a way that QT cannot be said to have been. QT stirred the interest of language teachers, but *Franske Taleøvelser* hit home where it really mattered, with actual language learners.

3.2.2.1.5 Storm had a specific audience of language learners in mind. This was not a book for beginners, hence the subtitle *Mellemtrin*. He did have plans for an elementary textbook too, but, like a lot of Storm's publication ambitions, it was never realised:

> If I am granted the time and the capacity, I have also thought about developing a primer with indications of pronunciation, since the primers published to date do not accord with my principles. (p. vi)

FT[1] was aimed at students of French who had already acquired a basic knowledge of the language. It was not in the first instance intended for school use, but rather for adults, for students at *Gymnas* or university level, and for the general public. It could be used with a teacher, who would first read an entire dialogue, the students then taking roles and repeating the dialogue, Storm suggested, or the dialogues could be learned by heart for performance in the classroom. Alternatively, the dialogues could be used for self-study. I imagine that the majority of sales went to people intending to study French on their own, wanting to learn a natural, idiomatic, spoken French from such an authority on the subject as Storm.

There was another potential audience: French learners of Norwegian. I can't believe that there would have been many in this particular group. A review of *FT*[1] in the Danish newspaper *Avisen* was quoted in *Morgenbladet* on 4 March 1887, and the reviewer took a somewhat disparaging view:

> It is the intention that it could also be used by Frenchmen, if they wished for once to make an exception to the rule and go in for foreign languages.

3.2.2.1.6 The book is divided into 12 chapters, each with the title of a grammatical category, as follows:

Kap. I   Les articles défini et indéfini.
          Den bestemte og den ubestemte Artikel.
          [The definite and indefinite article]
Kap. II   L'article partitif. Delingsartikelen.
          [The partitive article]

None of the chapters is dedicated to the major parts of speech; they focus instead on those areas of the grammar which learners of French as a foreign language might find difficult. Storm explicitly treats the morphology and syntax together, being more motivated by presenting *det levende Sprog* than by the traditional structure of a grammar book. (As we saw in the last chapter, he did not have the interest or the temperament to write a traditional grammar.) His concern for the living language transcends the conventional structure of the language into first morphology, then syntax, since 'there is little point in learning the forms when you don't learn what they are used for' (p. iv).

Each chapter has the same basic structure. The bulk of a chapter is made up of short dialogues, varying in number and length from chapter to chapter, and designed to rehearse the grammatical category under consideration in as natural and unobtrusive a way as possible. Dialogues are presented in parallel-text format, the French text in roman script, the Norwegian in Gothic. Here is an example from the chapter on comparison:

Ah, mon ami, je ne sais plus ce que je fais. Je n'ai plus la tête à moi.

Il faudra faire un emprunt. Alors il faudra rendre (rembourser) le capital plus l'intérêt. On peut aussi toucher le capital

Aa, min Ven, jeg ved ikke længer hvad jeg gør. Jeg er ikke rigtig ved mig selv længer.

De faar optage et Laan. De maa da tilbagebetale Kapitalen *plus* Renterne. Det gaar ogsaa an at hæve Kapitalen *minus* Renterne;

moins l'intérêt, c'est ce qu'on appelle l'escompte; mais cela ne vaut pas mieux. Le mieux sera de prier vos créanciers d'attendre. Je travaillerai à réparer mes pertes.

Le travail est le meilleur consolateur. Je sais que vous êtes un travailleur infatigable; le plus souvent, vous travaillez jusqu'à minuit, jusqu'à une heure; et vous sortez le plus rarement possible. Mais il ne faut pas travailler trop non plus. Donnez-vous des distractions; vous n'en travaillerez que mieux. (p. 71)

det er det, man kalder Diskonto; men det er ikke bedre. Det bedste bliver at bede Deres Kreditorer vente.

Jeg skal arbeide paa at gjenoprette mine Tab.

Arbeide er den bedste Trøst[er]. Jeg ved, De er en utrættelig Arbeider; som oftest arbeider De lige til Midnat, lige til kl. ét; og De gaar saa sjelden som muligt ud. Men De maa ikke arbeide for meget heller. Und Dem nogle Adspredelser; De vil da arbeide saa meget bedre.

To twenty-first-century eyes and ears this may not appear to be the world's most spontaneous dialogue, but it really must have been a welcome relief from the sort of drivel more commonly encountered in readers and phrasebooks, against which Storm and the QT linguists justly fulminated. What is more, it is a (brief) conversation between adults on an adult subject. It is not necessarily a topic that Norwegian learners of French would wish to discuss with native speakers, but at least it is a relevant, grown-up topic. (Given Storm's financial difficulties in early adulthood, this particular dialogue could have sprung from reality.) The dialogues do vary, but we can gain a sense of why FT^1 was such a relief in a market flooded with this sort of crap, taken at random from an 1876 beginners' English book:

The humming bees flew to the tallest tree of the garden. By assisting each other, we were happy enough to gain the shore. Every one wondered at my having been able to defend myself so bravely with my father's heavy sword. (Mathesius 1876: 58–59)

After the dialogues in each chapter come two more brief sections. Storm explains their function:

A number of common proverbs and sayings are given at the end of each chapter, particularly ones that have not found a place in the dialogues, and finally there is a short practice piece to be translated from the mother tongue and into French. This constitutes a course of revision for consolidating and checking what has been read. (p. v)

There are no model answers to the translations, but there are detailed footnotes, offering hints for an idiomatic translation.

3.2.2.1.7 There are in fact footnotes throughout the text. Robert (1887: 144) judged these footnotes to be inappropriate:

[. . .] it seemed to me, since it is a classic work, that the footnotes containing quotations in support of certain forms used in the text, would have been better placed in an appendix at the end of the book.

Storm's concern for "the truth" meant that he found it hard to simplify things for the benefit of the learner. If qualification or amplification was called for, he appended a footnote. Often these are useful, suggesting alternative forms to those in the text for use in different registers or situations. On other occasions, however, Storm's stream of consciousness takes over, providing historical or comparative information really quite irrelevant to a learner of French. On page 103 the French 'si je ne le lui donne pas, il m'en voudra' is translated as 'dersom jeg ikke giver ham den, vil han blive vred (vond[1]) paa mig'. The footnote explains:

The form *vond* is usual in colloquial Norwegian, notably in expressions like: „være *vond*", „det gjør *vondt*", „li[d]e *vondt*". By contrast: „onde Mennesker", „den onde Verden". (ON. *vándr*, Icel. *vondur*, Dan. & Swe. *ond*).

The historical, comparative detail is irrelevant enough, but the omission of the ⟨d⟩ in 'lide' is positively confusing, especially to the putative French learner of Norwegian. Six pages later there is another footnote to the Norwegian:

Often „angre sig" in colloquial Norwegian, reflexive like Fr. *se repentir*, Germ. *sich reuen*, OE *he repented him[self]* (The Bible, Shakespeare). (p. 109)

A comparative reference to earlier varieties of English does seem quite out of place in a book intended, at least partly, for the general public. But Storm can't help himself. These glosses on the Norwegian further support the impression we formed earlier, reading the preface to *Engelsk Filologi*, that he is always thinking about Norwegian, whatever other language he is writing about. He actually indicated 10 years before that this was his modus operandi. In the 1877 application to parliament he wrote that the proposed *Værk over det norske Sprog* would be 'the first in a range of works on modern languages, for which research into the mother tongue will form the basis and starting point' (Storm 1877a: 6).

Criticisms though are hard to find, and it would be unfair of me to go on looking for them. This was Storm's greatest success, a success he deserved, and one he found in a rather surprising area. Surprising it is that the man who could cover 1,098 pages with examples and scholarly comments on English could at the same time limit himself to 200 pages of (relatively) unencumbered, practical exercises. But he was 'dhi grétest pràktikal liNgwist in dhi werld', and if anyone in the 1880s knew how to learn foreign languages to a very high standard in unpromising circumstances, it was Johan Storm.

3.2.2.1.8 The third Norwegian edition of 1895 is nearly 30 pages longer than the second edition. This is partly because it takes into account improvements that have been made in other editions of the book, through its translation into other languages. The most obvious area of expansion is the footnotes. There are considerably more footnotes in 1895, and they are substantially more detailed, drawing on comments made to Storm, or on further reading carried out since 1887. The footnote expansion would certainly have made Storm happier, but I very much doubt that it improved the usefulness of the book. In the programmatic preface to the first edition, Storm had written:

What we need is more practical methods and textbooks [. . .]
We need more practical *primers* [. . .]
We need easier *readers* [. . .]
We need shorter and easier *grammars* [. . .]
It is just such a systematic book of exercises I have tried to write. (p. ii)

The increase in learned footnotes seems rather to militate against the battle for shorter and easier materials. Yes, he was a great practical linguist and he had produced a great practical resource. At the same time, however, he was a scientist, striving after a true picture of French, and this striving, this scientific Mr Hyde to the practical Dr Jekyll, resulted in 1895 in a less practical and more scientific publication. It's a shame that an equivalent to 'If it ain't broke, don't fix it' wasn't among the many proverbs he included in 1887.

Other small changes made in 1895 include renaming the *Ordsprog og Talemaader* (*Proverbs and Sayings*) sections *Fraseologi* (which corresponds better to the French version of the section title) and numbering the dialogues. There is now an 'alphabetic index of the contents of the dialogues, together with the most important words, phrases and rules', which certainly improves the usability of the volume. However, as with subsequent editions of *Engelsk Filologi*, more is not necessarily better, and there were no more Norwegian editions of *Franske Taleøvelser* (*Mellemtrin*) after this one.

3.2.2.2 Høiere Trin *(1897)*

3.2.2.2.1 The preface to the first edition of FT[1] is reprinted in the 1895 third edition, but the vague promise of an elementary course is now replaced by an apology: 'I have had to abandon my plan to produce a primer as well due to lack of time.' A primer which met with Storm's approval did, however, appear the following year, namely *Lærebog i Fransk for Begyndere* by Adam Trampe Bødtker and Sigurd Høst. This was produced in Landsmål and

Swedish editions too, and the original entered its seventeenth edition in 1954. Another commercial success. By way of compensation in 1895, Storm is able to announce a new set of *Franske Taleøvelser*, which would appear two years later, in 1897:

> The Advanced Level (*cours supérieur*) will contain a more specialised treatment of verbs and particles, by far the most difficult side to the language's forms and relations, but limited to those which occur in the real spoken language. (1895b: vi)

The advanced dialogues are a continuation of the *Mellemtrin* dialogues in terms of the grammatical material they cover. They are not laid out under specific grammatical headings as was the case before, but Storm has chosen them to provide general practice in the use of the verb and its conjugations, and in the use of prepositions, as he had promised in 1887. The presentation is less systematic – the adjective *systematisk* [systematic] is now missing from the title – because, instead of composing dialogues which specifically include certain parts of speech and certain usages, Storm has selected the dialogues from French literature, from reading several hundred volumes of the stuff. He explains that he has gathered the richest harvest in the works of Alexandre Dumas Fils (1824–1895), 'whose mastery in handling the French language, notably in his plays, is universally recognised', but other authors are represented as well. He writes that he, Johan Storm, spoke himself in the first volume, and in this volume he has let the French speak. He has had to plough through a lot of potential sources, since he has (as we would expect) a very specific type of French in mind. The word *levende* is of course at the heart of his explanation of what sort of French he has tried to give:

> The aim was to find pieces which were *grammatically* and *phraseologically* instructive, written in a *good* and *natural spoken language*. The content had to be, as far as possible, complete in itself, presented in a lively [*levende*] and clear manner. It had to be universal, not too specialised, the sort of thing which more or less concerns and touches humanity, preferably from the day-to-day sphere, preferably trivial things, but always "a little bit of human life". (p. i)

So *Franske Taleøvelser (Høiere Trin)* (*FT*[2]) contains 50 dialogues, the majority taken from French literature, on a variety of *almenmenneskelige* (universal) topics. What counts as *almenmenneskeligt* depends on what sort of *menneske* (person) you are. 'L'amour' (from *La Souris* by Edouard Pailleron (1834–1899)), 'Le travail' (based on *Sans Famille* by Hector Malot (1830–1907)) and 'Une maison à vendre' (based on *Ceinture dorée* by Émile Augier (1820–1889)) all deal with issues faced at some time by most adults, or at least most of the adults likely to be reading *FT*[2]. Plays about phonetics and grammar seem unlikely, but Storm managed to find

extracts which reflected these aspects of his own daily life, if not the daily
experiences of most other people. Dialogue 39, headed 'La phonétique', is a
pronunciation lesson from *Le bourgeois gentilhomme* (Jean-Baptiste Molière
(1622–1673)), and dialogue 45, 'La grammaire', is based on scenes from *La
Grammaire* by Eugène Labiche (1815–1888).

The book received good reviews, and it is a good reader, presenting clear
samples of French from that difficult Stormian ideal of usage which is
literary yet popular. One review captures Storm's spirit particularly well.
'S.H.' (presumably Sigurd Høst), writing in *Morgenbladet* on 14 September
1897, remarks that 'what more than anything else characterises Professor
Johan Storm as a writer and as a university teacher is an intense realism, a
never-faltering faithfulness to reality'. There are footnotes, of course, but
they are not like the outrageous excursuses in *Bennetts Practiske Lærebog*.
They are synchronic, for the most part, and brief. Sandfeld Jensen, writing
as a Romanist with a very similar approach to languages as Storm, particularly praises the 'numerous comments' (1888–1889: 36). The book was aimed
at a particular reader, as all Storm's books were. Making money had always
been important to Storm, so he had a good eye for the market. FT^1 had
sought (and found in abundance) 'adult learners, Norwegian sixth-form
pupils, young students and the general public' (1887a: iv). The *cours
supérieur*, however,

> addresses the *advanced* public [. . .] first and foremost those who do not
> have the opportunity to spend time abroad [. . .] I am thinking in
> particular of academics, teachers male and female, linguistically interested
> ladies, officers, technicians and business men, in short any members of the
> general public who wish to "learn a bit more French" in a relatively easy
> and pleasant way. (1897a: vi–vii)

The book achieved what it set out to achieve, but from the point of view of
the history of linguistics, its interest lies not with the French dialogues but
with their parallel translations into Norwegian.

3.2.2.2.2   After FT^2, which was anyway the completion of a project started
10 years earlier, Storm concentrated his energies on Norwegian, on the
Norwegian language and on Norwegian institutions (see Chapter 4). There
was of course *Større fransk Syntax*, a peculiar appendix to Storm's life and
work (see section 3.3.1), but it is fair to say that in the last two decades of his
life, he returned to his first love. This change of direction is already evident in
FT^2 where the programme is in fact a Norwegian and not a French one. As
far as I know, this is the only place Storm actually adopted a revised
Norwegian orthography, and he used the collection of French dialogues
above all to make a point about Norwegian language reform. He claims that
his revised orthography is 'no language struggle' (*intet Maalstræv*) (p. ii), but
the 1897 dialogues followed hot on the heels of *Norsk Sprog: Kraakemaal og*

Landsmaal, and Storm was never able to carry out his linguistic projects in isolation from one another; he could not hermetically seal them. *Det levende Sprog* bound them all together, and, as we noted above, there is always the impression that the practicalities of Norwegian language reform lay at the heart of the matter. Most of his effort in writing *FT*[2] went into the Norwegian parallel texts:

> It was not easy in all cases to come up with the best Norwegian form, and it was particularly difficult to come up with it straightaway. Here I adopted the strategy I always adopt: I didn't give up until I had found the best expression I could in every case. Sometimes I could mull over a single word for hours, before I found something which satisfied me. From time to time, having pondered long and in vain, and having given up on finding something good, the right word could pop up of its own accord an hour later. (1897a: iv–v)

So why was it so difficult? What was Storm trying to do in the Norwegian translations that demanded so much time and effort?

He modified the written Danish of the translations in the direction of that variety of Norwegian he always took as his model (see next chapter), namely the educated speech of Kristiania. He claims that in so doing he did not intend to provide a model for the written language, although he did believe that the written language would, with time and if left alone, adopt such modifications. Instead what he has wished for is 'simply to present the *true, living, idiomatic spoken language*' (p. iv). He states that real French must be translated by real Norwegian:

> The challenge was to present the language as we think and speak by nature, so that the translation could be taken for the original and the original for the translation.

We will return to Storm's views on the reform of written Norwegian in the next chapter, and will look at the forms he used in the translated dialogues in that context. However, for now we are entitled to ask whether Storm was really simply dedicated to reflecting 'living' French with 'living' Norwegian for the good of the reader. He wanted the texts to be perfectly parallel in style as well as form, because, according to Storm, the main question for the reader was: 'When I say so-and-so in Norwegian, how is that rendered in good French?' (p. iv). Alternatively, was Storm being completely disingenuous in using a reformed written variety? Was he flagrantly introducing his own written variety alongside all the others that had come (and gone) during his lifetime, while pretending to help the Norwegian public towards a better understanding of French idiom?

Storm was strongly against individual Norwegians undertaking to reform the written language unilaterally, so when he states in 1897 (p. iv) that 'by using this form I have simply intended to present the living *spoken language*, not to put forward any model for the written language', we should believe him. In both volumes of *FT* his goal is a more natural method of learning the language than was to be found in previous books. Part of this programme is a more natural-sounding form of French than had typically appeared in language-teaching materials. On the other side of things, he had dedicated a great deal of his skill and energy to 'natural' Norwegian, to its sounds and to its style above all, so it was simply not within him to have mirrored 'natural' French with a written Danish, which, for all its qualities, could not be said to be coextensive with natural Norwegian. If his motive was 'naturalness', why did he not also use a Norwegianised form of Danish in 1887? He was after all actively working on Norwegian at that time too. *Om Maalsagen* appeared in 1885 and *Det nynorske Landsmaal: En Undersøgelse* in 1888. His main concern – his programme – in 1887 was, however, teaching reform. The 1887 dialogues were linked to 'Om en forbedret undervisning . . .' rather than to any of the studies of Norwegian. The very first words in *FT*[1] were simply:

> The need for reform in the teaching of modern languages (*levende Sprog*) has long been felt.

After the initial preamble about the contents of the book, the first programmatic statement in 1897 is, by contrast, this:

> The French text is accompanied by a Norwegian translation, with which I have taken special care, in that I have tried to represent the *educated spoken language of the capital*, which is by and large the only common spoken language of the towns and cities, indeed of the whole country.

There it is. That's what FT^2 is really about.

Yes, Storm is using FT^2 to play a card from Norwegian language politics, but it is not a cynical attempt to introduce a new written language via a book Storm's sharp-eyed enemies would be unlikely to read. Teaching reform and language reform are just two points on the spectrum of 'the living language'.

3.2.3 Encyclopædia Britannica

3.2.3.1 When Storm visited Edinburgh in April 1884 to collect his doctorate and take part in the tercentenary celebrations of the university, he stayed with the Revd John S. Black. University records indicate that Storm was proposed for his honorary degree by Black, as well as entertained by him during his stay. The description of Storm in the list of 'Persons on whom the Honorary Degree of 'Doctor of Laws' is to be conferred' is interesting. He is described as 'Professor of English and Philology in the University of Christiania'. I think we can assume that the omission of 'Romance' was a clerical error, especially as it was Storm's Romance skills that turned out to be of especial interest to Black. Black was, amongst other things, an assistant editor of the ninth edition of *Encyclopædia Britannica*, which was currently being published. Storm of course had a very fine reputation as a Romance scholar, although *Franske Taleøvelser* would not appear for a few years, so he wasn't quite such a "household name" as he would become later. However, that it was a Norwegian who ended up writing the article on Romance languages in *Encyclopædia Britannica* probably had more to do with the fact that he had met Black and owed Black a favour than with his scholarly standing. Certainly his fitness for the task, from the point of view of being able to write an article of the right length at the right level for a popular reference work, was doubtful.

Black originally asked Storm to write the article on Scandinavian languages. It is likely that Storm was the only Scandinavian linguist Black knew, as Scandinavian linguists were not thick on the ground in 1884. The request arrived in Storm's letterbox the month after he had met Black in Edinburgh. In October that year, the request to write the entry on Romance languages also arrived:

> Will you do us the favour of writing the general article *Romance Languages*? I mean a brief conspectus, the shorter the better, perhaps not exceeding five of our pages, and of course not impinging more than is absolutely unavoidable on the special articles on the languages of France, Italy +c [. . .] (NBO Ms. 8° 2402 J[vii])

Black also asked Storm in the same letter if he could cover Provençal, or if he could recommend anyone else to do it. Storm suggested Paul Meyer, one of the co-editors of *Romania*, who did undertake the work. Further correspondence followed, and a year later Storm eventually declined the original request to write about Scandinavian languages. Instead he suggested Adolf Noreen who, like Meyer, accepted. Storm completed the article on Romance languages in the spring of 1885, and the editors of *Britannica* were very pleased with it. We will go on in a moment to look at the article in some detail, and we shall see that it is a rather odd publication, but we can assume that Black was not being sarcastic when he described it in a letter of 13 August as 'a perfect model of liveliness, perspicuity, exhaustiveness and condensation'. The editors' satisfaction must have been genuine as they (via Black) tried to persuade Storm to write more language articles for the *Encyclopædia*. This gives an interesting insight into how this vast, prestigious reference work was put together. It seems that commissions were ad hoc and last minute. While volume 20 (Pru–Ros) was being put together, the editors were still looking for contributions on Provençal, Romance, Saxo, Scandinavian, Snorro, Spanish and Portuguese, and Speech Sounds. These are just the subjects mentioned in the correspondence between Black and Storm, so we can assume that the search was still going on for plenty more topics for this volume and subsequent ones. Black dangled Spanish and Portuguese in front of Storm in November, but Storm declined. He had acted as a broker for Black in securing the involvement of Meyer and Noreen, and he tried to tempt Thomsen with Spanish and Portuguese, but to no avail. He had more luck in persuading his brother, Gustav, to write the article on Snorro.

One might think that Storm would have regarded it as an honour to be asked to contribute to a work like *Encyclopædia Britannica*. Despite all his private complaints about the work, in letters to Thomsen and Amund B. Larsen, I think he probably was secretly quite satisfied to have been asked. He mentions the *Britannica* work unnaturally often, as if he is perhaps boasting about it while pretending to regard it as a chore. The truth is though that he did regard it as a chore, since writing brief overviews ran counter to his intellectual nature. In November 1884 he wrote to Thomsen about this difficult· job he had taken on, about which 'I have perhaps told you'. He was still telling in January 1886, when he explained to Larsen what it was that caused him such difficulties in this task:

> Last year I wrote the article *Romance Languages* for Encyclopædia Britannica, for which I first of all had to write a whole book and then take an excerpt from it. But I managed however to get down the most important elements of what I had in mind to say, and the editors were quite extraordinarily satisfied. It is one of the most difficult things I have done, to compress so much material into such limited space [. . .] (NBO Brevsamling 385)

It is typical that Storm should have to write 'a whole book' first. Black had been quite precise about length from the beginning, so Storm was under no illusion when he started the work, but the data simply flowed out. Even in its final, shortened form, 'Romance Languages' is still fairly indigestible fare for a popular, non-specialist encyclopedia.

3.2.3.2 Black had asked for a 'general article', but what Storm wrote was in the event a rather specialised article, concentrating on the development of the sounds of Romance. A historical study had not been commissioned, but that was inevitably the approach a linguist of the 1880s would take. The detail of sound change could potentially be rather uninteresting for a general reader, but Storm begins the article by generating an infectious enthusiasm for the process:

> As the literary language of the ancient Roman civilization died out, seemingly extinguished by the barbarism of the Middle Ages, all the forms of the old classical language being confounded in the most hopeless chaos, suddenly new, vigorous, and beautiful tongues sprang forth, ruled by the most regular laws, related to, yet different from, Latin. How was this wonderful change brought about? How can chaos produce regularity? The explanation of this mystery has been given by Diez, the great founder of Romance philology. The Romance languages did not spring from literary classical Latin, but from popular Latin, which, like every living

speech, had its own laws, not subject to the changing literary fashions, but only to the slow process of phonetic change and dialectic variety. (Storm 1886a: 661)

This is compelling writing, presenting historical linguistics as the unfolding of a great mystery, and it is the sort of popular science that Storm had already shown himself to be good at. It is little wonder that his popular lectures were a success with the general public, if he was able to generate this sort of enthusiasm for the wonderful and mysterious ways of language change. The notes for his lectures in the first semester of 1886 on the history of the Romance languages indicate that he enjoyed this style. They contain a string of questions and answers, and even some humour:

But was Latin always so stiff then? Did the Romans never wear a smile? Did they never write (speak) in short, interrupted sentences? Of course they did! It is just that there is so little left in this style. If we read Plautus, then we find a Latin which is somewhat related to the Romance languages. (UBB Ms. 740c)

Most of the rest of the article is taken up with the detail of sound change, for which Storm, the data collector, felt the greatest of enthusiasm, but which would, I'm sure, have gone over the heads of most readers. He states explicitly at the outset that much of the general history of Romance has been covered in the article on Latin, and that 'only some points, especially phonetic, which need a fuller discussion, are taken up again here' (p. 661).

He proceeds historically, then, following a conventional periodisation:

I.   *First (Pre-Classical) Period: to c. 80 B.C.* (Cicero).
II.   *Second (Classical) Period: 80 B.C. to 100 (150) A.D.*
III. *Third (Post-Classical) Period: 100 (150) to 300 (350).*
IV.   *Fourth Period: 300 (350) to 500 (550).*
V.   *Fifth Period: 500 (550) to 900 (1000).*
VI.   *Sixth (Last) Period*: 'For the sixth and last period – that is, for the history and distinctive traits of the great modern Romance languages – the reader is referred to the separate articles.' (p. 668)

To get an idea of his approach to Romance in each period, we will briefly consider the first and longest section.

He begins with his motto: 'Latin, like all other literary languages, began as a living popular speech.' As we noted earlier, he always viewed Latin as simply one living language amongst all the others, and this attitude informed his proposals for the use of Latin in university education (see letter to Sophus Bugge, 3 December 1876 (NBO Brevsamling 2)). This leads into an overview of the languages and dialects of Italy in the period. Then, as with the excursuses in *Engelsk Filologi/Englische Philologie*, Storm adopts a smaller typeface to go into the detail. The phonetics of Old Popular Latin fill 5 columns. He begins with the consonants, their occurrence and behaviour, including changes which occurred during the period to 80 BC. Next the vowels are treated systematically, in their long and short forms, paying particular attention to variants of them. Next comes stress and quantity in early Romance, before the higher levels of linguistic structure are addressed. 'Vocabulary' fills a column, but Storm merely provides 'a brief selection of archaic words, disused, vulgar, colloquial, or used with a disparaging sense, in the classical age, but reappearing later as quite usual and dignified expressions' (p. 664). In *Engelsk Filologi* he had pioneeringly demonstrated an interest in non-standard varieties and in the interface between standard and non-standard forms. This concern for all forms of the living language extends here to ancient forms. How useful this particular selection of lexicon would have been to readers, I don't know, but it is certainly interesting, and Storm's approach to the vocabulary is certainly original. The section concludes with a tiny selection of grammatical forms and an even shorter section on 'syntax and phraseology'.

Storm's approach is highly untraditional. His concern for the living language leads him to marginalise the traditional topics – grammar and representative vocabulary – and focus on the very new concerns of phonetics and non-standard forms. Fascinating, yes, and ground-breaking too, but probably not what readers would expect or hope for. The subtitle of *Encyclopædia Britannica* was *A Dictionary of Arts, Sciences and General Literature*. It was the over-inflated British equivalent of *Illustreret Nyhedsblad* (see section 2.2.4.3.1), designed to adorn the shelves of Victorian gentlemen – the spine was more highly decorated than the front cover. Storm was, as ever, caught on various sides of various fences: the populariser meets the data collector; the traditional philologist meets the new philologist.

Something which is definitely out of place in a popular summary, but which always makes popular summaries so much more spicy, is a dose of academic in-fighting,[9] and Storm's victim here is Emil Paul Seelmann (1859–1915), who would six years later receive a 'planing down' at Storm's hands (see section 3.3.2.4.4b). Storm did have some respect for Seelmann's work on the pronunciation of Latin, although you wouldn't guess it from his published comments. Seelmann's major publication, *Die Aussprache des Latein nach physiologisch-historischen Grundsätzen*, appeared while Storm was working on his *Britannica* article. Storm told Thomsen (2 October 1885): 'I have read quite a bit of Seelmann, of whom I have a really good opinion, although not about everything; I think that he is much too conclusive in doubtful questions'. Storm then listed for Thomsen the five points from his article where he disagrees with Seelmann. Unfortunately, the general regard he has for Seelmann's work does not emerge in the footnote

---

[9] *The Oxford Companion to Music* is a particularly entertaining hotbed of bitchy comments and camp asides.

on page 661 of *Britannica*, where he writes that Seelmann's book 'must be used with caution':

> Seelmann is superior to Corssen as a phonetician,[10] but is often obscure and given to elaborating strange theories. Thus he arrives at the absurd conclusion that the differences of quantity did not exist in the classical age, but that the poets judged of quantity by the close or open sound of the vowel.

So what are we to make of Storm's contribution to *Encyclopædia Britannica*? Although it was more or less anonymous (the 'J.St.' at the end is very low profile), although he found condensing his learning difficult, although he complained to Thomsen that the remuneration wasn't good, and although the selection of contributors to the encyclopedia was pretty haphazard, this was a prestigious international commission for Storm, and one of which I do think he was secretly rather proud. It was, however, a genre which did not really suit him. We have seen elsewhere how one of his greatest skills as a linguist, when things didn't get washed away in the tide of data, was dovetailing the practical and the theoretical, the popular and the scientific, but in his *Britannica* article popular and scientific sit uneasily side by side, unintegrated. This does mean, of course, that readers could, if they wished, simply read the popular sections, the sections in larger type, and ignore the linguistic detail in smaller type. However, Storm was right to turn down Black's request for further articles. He just wasn't temperamentally suited to this sort of thing.

3.3 Scientific Works

3.3.1 Større fransk Syntax *(1911–1919)*

3.3.1.1 On 27 December 1898 Storm wrote to Vilhelm Thomsen saying that, having spent so much time on the *Engelsk Filologi*, he wanted to do something to shed new light on French for the Norwegian public:

> I have therefore just studied Romance for several months, expanded my collections of Old French, Middle French, Vulgar Latin, and, most recently, especially *Italian* [. . .] It is above all *Romance syntax* that occupies me, and here there are surprising similarities between Italian and early French.

This interest in Italian did not lead to any publications, and the only serious publication during the last period of his life, in the field he was actually

---

[10] Corssen has not been mentioned before this point in the article. He is Wilhelm Paul Corssen (1820–1875) ('the quarrelsome German' (Storm 1871: 50)), whose prize essay for the Berlin Academy, *Über Aussprache, Vokalismus und Betonung der lateinischen Sprache*, was first published in 1858/1859 and entered a second edition in 1868/1870.

employed to study, was the *Større fransk Syntax* (*SFS*), which appeared in three volumes in 1911, 1914 and 1919, the final volume delayed by a typographers' strike. Less than a year later, on 17 September 1899, he told Thomsen that he had a major work on French syntax ready for launching (*på Stabelen*), but that it wouldn't be out until the following year. In the event, the introduction to the first volume was dated June 1910, when Storm was 73 years old, and the final volume is dated 1918, the year of his 82nd birthday.

His eyesight had been declining for years – indeed, his first apologies to Thomsen about the corresponding decline in the quality of his handwriting date from 1899. He appears to have been short-sighted at least as early as 1870, since he reports having to use a magnifying aid at the bullfight. After the turn of the century his handwriting becomes small and crabbed and often difficult to interpret, and it gets gradually worse. I have not seen Storm's manuscript of the 1919 volume, but the staff of the publisher Gyldendal must surely have had to overcome enormous problems of interpretation. In his letters to Thomsen Storm does explain that writing letters is the worst sort of writing to have to do, and that his handwriting is better when he writes more slowly in manuscripts, but nonetheless. . . . The preface to the 1919 volume is extremely perfunctory, not even in full sentences, and it certainly gives the impression that this is the work of a tired and elderly man:

> I hope too that the appended information will be welcome, comparisons with other languages etc. (Storm 1919: *Forord*)

Storm published *SFS* in three separate volumes, as he did not know whether he would live long enough to complete the whole text. In the first volume (1911a: xv) he wrote:

> If it should be granted that I complete it, what is published here will keep its value as an introduction to one of the most curious aspects of the language, in which it is most different from the ancient language.

At the beginning of volume 3 there is a note thanking Adam Trampe Bødtker for reading the proofs of all three volumes. All the same, it is clear that *SFS* was written too quickly and was inadequately proofread, the work of someone who was perhaps genuinely short of time. Volume 3 is particularly chaotic. The chapter after chapter V is numbered chapter IV. There are two §§ 22 (1919: 13–14). Chapter III is untitled, and its subsections are not given letters as elsewhere throughout the volume – and there's more. It is of course rare to find a published text completely without blemish, but it is sad that Storm's final work should be such a mess, and it doesn't even have the long list of *Tillæg og Rettelser* 'Additions and corrections' which characterise his other, earlier publications.

The first question to answer, then, is why did Storm, on the verge of retirement after nearly 40 years as a professor, embark on this large-scale study of French syntax? Why was he not beginning to take life more easily?

3.3.1.2 Part of the answer is that he had always intended to write a scholarly book on French for a Norwegian audience, but he had been prevented from doing so by other commitments. At the beginning of his career he had produced a number of highly respected learned papers (see next section), and later came two popularly successful books of dialogues, but there had been no *magnum opus* corresponding to *Engelsk Filologi*. So there was unfinished business to attend to.

The other part of the answer is that he felt a sort of duty to provide a book for which there was, in his view, a need. In fact Storm produced all his pedagogical works to fill an actual or perceived gap in the market. As the first professor of English and Romance languages in Norway, as the ultimate authority responsible for teaching and teachers in both schools and university, he felt he had to take personal responsibility for improving teaching and learning in this area. As we have seen, he was not just an ivory-tower scholar. He was as concerned about elementary foreign-language readers as he was about the phonetic distinction between 'wide' and 'narrow'. Accordingly he opens the 1911 volume of *SFS* with these words:

> We have got briefer and easier French school-grammars, but this is insufficient for the *teacher*. He needs information about the *laws* of the language and the reasons for these laws. He needs not only to *know* the language, but to *understand* it thoroughly. We have no large-scale grammars suited to our philologists. They are partly too diffuse and involved, partly too unscientific, partly full of dry and mechanical rules and exceptions, without any more profound penetration of the language's laws and their historical development. (1911a: v)

A lengthy, detailed, academic presentation of French syntax may seem (like the 1895 revision of FT^1) to go against the requirements he laid down in the preface to FT^1 for shorter, easier, practical teaching materials. However, his basic motivation is the same: to provide currently unavailable material for the benefit of Norwegian linguists. FT^1 had been intended for 'adult learners, Norwegian sixth-form pupils, young students and the general public' (1887a: p. iv), but *SFS* is written for 'philologists, students and teachers' (1911a: p. xiv), i.e. the next level up from the market for FT^2, which was itself more advanced than the 1887 market, and which included 'linguistically interested ladies, officers, technicians and business men'.

It appears then that *duty* compelled Storm to set about this substantial work (nearly 500 pages in total), duty to himself and duty to the community of Norwegian linguists. The next question to be answered is: why did the great phonetician write a study of syntax as his swan song?

3.3.1.3 It is true that Storm established his reputation as a phonetician, and, at least in *Englische Philologie*, seems to have been so absorbed in phonetics that he was incapable of focusing on other aspects of the language. Put another way, he went into such phonetic detail in *Englische Philologie* that he did not have space or time (under duress from the publisher, Reisland) to deal with much else. This is not the same as saying that he had no interest in or understanding of other levels of linguistic structure. The sounds were the most obvious surface manifestation of the living language, but syntax is as much a product of language being used, 'living' language, as phonetics:

> I have wanted to enable philologists to *immerse* themselves in the playful life of the living language with its laws and its freedoms, its different layers and its multifarious multiplicity. (1911a: xiv–xv)

Sandfeld Jensen (1911: 174) was of the view that Storm had succeeded in this aim 'to an exceptional degree'.

Another reason for turning to syntax relates to the point made in section 3.3.1.2 above. In Storm's view syntax needed a proper study, whereas French morphology was already adequately covered. The introduction to the 1911 volume is a mini version of *Engelsk Filologi*, a commented guide to the literature available to Norwegian philologists. In particular he recommends the fourth (1909) edition of C.-M. Robert's *Grammaire de la langue française* as 'the best modern French grammar by and for foreigners' (p. vii) and W. Meyer-Lübke's four-volume *Grammatik der romanischen Sprachen* (1890). About this latter he remarks:

> However the syntax does not contain much that is new and doesn't penetrate much deeper than is already the case into the features of the French language. (p. vi)

Storm praises a number of treatises on specific aspects of French syntax, but while 'a historical presentation of French *morphology* is to be found in several easily accessible works, French *syntax* needs a new treatment' (1911a: xv). Whether Storm was the right man for the job, or whether someone born in the first half of the nineteenth century was the best person to provide a treatment of French syntax for the twentieth, are questions we will return to below.

3.3.1.4 In a sense *SFS* was indeed the French equivalent of *Engelsk Filologi*. In the beginning Storm had intended *Engelsk Filologi* to include French, but soon abandoned this plan, as we saw in the last chapter. So by writing *SFS* he was finishing a job he had failed to finish (or even start) over 30 years earlier. The next question we need to address is to what extent *SFS* descends from *Engelsk Filologi*, to what extent it relates to the rest of his work, and, stemming from these questions, to what extent Storm's work on modern foreign languages constituted a coherent *opus*.

SFS was not written for quite the same audience as *Engelsk Filologi*. The latter was intended quite specifically as a textbook for students taking group 4 of the linguistic-historical teachers' examination, but *SFS* is intended to appeal to the slightly wider public of 'philologists, students and teachers'. It is not, then, a blood relation of *Engelsk Filologi*, so already it seems as though they can't be regarded as parts of a unified *opus*. However, when *Engelsk Filologi* of 1879, *Franske Taleøvelser* of 1887 and 1897 and *SFS* of 1911–1919 are considered together, important links between them begin to emerge. Through their differences they together add up to a whole, in that they cover everything, from phonetics through morphology to syntax, and from the near-beginner through the university student to the professional linguist. A further answer to the question of why Storm felt compelled to write *SFS* at a time in his life when other people think of putting their pens away is that he may have felt compelled to complete the symmetry, to round off his life's work shaping and enabling the study of English and French in Norway.

There *is* a notable symmetry here. At the heart of the enormous variety of linguistic publications Storm produced in the course of a 59-year publishing career, there is this decade-by-decade progression from *De romanske Sprog og Folk* to *SFS*, from the early ambition to the last full stop.

3.3.1.5 *SFS* and *Engelsk Filologi* may have focused on different levels of linguistic structure and on different readerships, but, if they were to lose their covers, it would not take the bibliographical detective long to realise that they were from the hand of the same author. The most striking similarity between the two works is their stream-of-consciousness style. Like *Engelsk Filologi*, *SFS* does not give the impression of having been carefully planned. Example follows example. Storm's encyclopedic data banks simply open and the data pours out. Thus, for example, paragraph 119 II of volume 3 – on the use of the infinitive with *à* (it is not clear how § 119 II relates to § 119 on the infinitive in comparative constructions) – eventually runs to § 119 II, subsection b, subsection β, subsection γ, as more and more examples occur to Storm (1919: 84–87). There is a table of contents, but no index, so this is not an easy text to use. To judge from the revisions of *Engelsk Filologi*, it can be assumed that, had Storm lived to revise *SFS*, the revision would only have resulted in more data.

A trait which indicates that *SFS* is from the same hand as *Engelsk Filologi* and *Franske Taleøvelser* is the relentless comparative urge. Although in essence a study of *contemporary* French syntax, this work 'rests on a historical foundation' (1911a: xv). It is only natural that a philologist of the nineteenth century would have one eye firmly on the *history* of the forms he is describing. In many instances the relevant history is the only way of explaining the synchronic state. For example, Storm gives a detailed account of the historical process whereby constructions like 'avoir faim/soif/besoin' lost the definite article, since the verb and the object 'together constitute a paraphrase of a verbal concept' (p. 136). His full account of the history of the partitive article from Old French onwards (1911a: 36–48) is particularly impressive. While the historical data is both expected and a valuable explanatory means, the comparative observations often seem superfluous, a product of Storm's hyperactive mental data banks. As with *Engelsk Filologi*, however, the stream of consciousness means that the presentation is certainly not dull. The reader is drawn along relentlessly by the burning quest for insight. What might be a criticism of *SFS* as a resource for the study of French from a purely structural point of view, is certainly not a criticism from the point of view of what Storm was trying to achieve in this particular work. If he had been trying to write a conventional, paradigm-based, pedagogical work, we could certainly criticise, but, like *Engelsk Filologi*, it is wrong of us to accuse Storm of failing to do something he never set out to do.

I quoted his intentions above, but this time I will complete that quotation:

> I have wanted to enable philologists to *immerse* themselves in the playful life of the living language with its laws and its freedoms, its different layers and its multifarious multiplicity – to replace the older generation's immersion in the dead languages and their harmonic regularity. (1911a: xiv–xv)

What Storm doesn't do in terms of systematisation, he without doubt does achieve in terms of bringing the language to life, of demonstrating 'its multifarious multiplicity'. Between the laws of the Neogrammarians and the systems of the Structuralists, we find Storm. In that no man's land between the nineteenth and the twentieth century, between Norway and Europe, between the practical and the scientific, unburdened by philological conventions, he simply loved languages for what they were.

3.3.1.6 Caught in this historical no-man's-land, Storm was the wrong person to write a study of this sort at this point in the history of linguistics. The brief Preface (*Forord*) to volume 3 (1919) clearly shows that he was looking backwards, no longer in the forefront of linguistic method and scholarship, and theoretically completely neutral:

> Greatest significance is accorded the selected examples from the widest variety of authors [. . .] This book, like volumes 1 and 2, is built upon a detailed study of ancient sources, so a truly historical foundation.

Other currents were being felt both within general linguistics and within Romance linguistics, particularly in Scandinavia. The *Cours de linguistique générale* (Saussure 1916) was published while *SFS* was being written, ushering in (though not in Norway) an approach to language very different to the one taken by Storm, and Jespersen began to publish his influential

Modern English Grammar on Historical Principles (Jespersen 1909–1949), which, despite its title, is mostly descriptive.

A detailed study of French syntax, based on numerous examples from the 'living' language, synchronic but with a firm historical foundation, written by an internationally acknowledged expert as the crowning achievement of his career. For such an apparently major work there were surprisingly few reviews. Storm's obituary in *Romania* (Långfors 1920) was particularly hazy about *SFS*:

> He published numerous phonetic and teaching works, amongst other things a two-volume French grammar, completed in 1915.

If this is the extent of the awareness of Storm's obituarist in a specialist journal like *Romania*, then the appearance of *SFS* must have gone largely unnoticed. None of the volumes even gets a mention in the 'Annonces et comptes rendus sommaires' section of *Romania*. It is true that Sandfeld Jensen reviewed the first volume in the Danish journal *Nordisk Tidsskrift for Filologi* (1911), but this would have reached very few contemporary Romanists. Why did it have so little impact?[11]

First of all, it was written in Norwegian for Norwegians, with plenty of references to Norwegian syntax and could not appeal easily to a wider audience. Secondly, Storm died the year after the final volume appeared and was therefore unable to oversee publicity. Thirdly, he was not the only Scandinavian at this time publishing detailed studies of French grammar, based on rich bodies of data. Høybye and Spang-Hanssen (1979: 241) write:

> For a period which stretches from the end of the nineteenth century and on into the 1960s, Romance philology in Denmark experienced an almost uninterrupted heyday. Several Danish scholars from that time are counted amongst the subject's greatest names.

Kristoffer Nyrop (1858–1931), Thor Sundby's successor as the second professor of Romance philology in Copenhagen, published the six-volume *Grammaire historique de la langue française* between 1899 and 1930. Unlike *Større fransk Syntax*, this 'is in constant use wherever people are occupied in the scientific study of French' (Høybye and Spang-Hanssen 1979: 241). The variety of Nyrop's work is comparable with Storm's. He had studied with Paris and Meyer in Paris and published editions of Old French texts on the one hand, and on the other hand he was a great populariser, the author of popular French language works and popular works of general linguistics. So what was the difference between him and Storm? Nyrop was not an isolated beacon in the wilderness. He had succeeded Thomsen and Sundby, and the "School" was set to continue to grow. Although published

---

[11] An idea of its lack of impact can be gained from the fact that there appears to be no copy in any British library and only one in a French library (Bibliothèque Nationale).

in Danish, Kristian Sandfeld's (1873–1942) *Bisætningerne i moderne fransk: En haandbog for studerende og lærere* (Subordinate Clauses in Modern French: A Handbook for Students and Teachers) of 1909 formed the basis for a string of monographs written in French on various aspects of French syntax, and Sandfeld's work was continued by Knud Togeby (1918–1974), pupil of Louis Hjelmslev (1899–1965) and occupant of the chair of Romance philology at Copenhagen from 1955 until his death in 1974. The elderly Storm was no match for this machine, although it should be pointed out that neither Nyrop's nor Sandfeld's work, nor the work of another internationally recognised Danish Romance linguist, Andreas Blinkenberg (1893–1982), was any more theoretically advanced than Storm's, and they tended to hark back to the Neogrammarians and to the sort of data-oriented studies in which Storm had excelled. In interests and methodology Sandfeld actually seems to have been very similar to Storm, to judge from the picture of Sandfeld painted in Skytte (1991). However, whereas Storm had been the right man in the right place at the very beginning of his career, at the very end of it he certainly was not. The new generation of Scandinavian philologists had taken over, and by 1911 Storm had been out of the Romance game for 14 years. This is a shame, since *SFS*, with its original but chaotic structure, is a mine of observations and examples on its subject.[12]

At the beginning of his lecture series on French grammar, begun in 1897, Storm explains why it took him so long to get round to this subject:

> For a long time I have wanted to lecture on French (and English) grammar, which has always been one of my favourite studies. But the situation has been such that nothing has become of it until now. Other sides of the language have pushed themselves into the foreground, partly phonetics [. . .] partly history of the language [. . .] partly practical applications, exercises in speaking and reading, the reading of authors and literary studies.

Had Storm's work on French grammar come to published fruition some decades earlier, its fate, and Storm's reputation in this field, might have been rather different.

It may not be possible to credit Storm with having started a School, and his spirit did not even live on in Norway in the persons of his successors to the Romance chair. However, Ebbe Spang-Hanssen (Spang-Hanssen 1982) identifies a characteristically Scandinavian form of Romance linguistic work in the twentieth century:

> Most Scandinavian philology bears the stamp of a certain empiricism or pragmatism, that is, a predilection for what, at the time given, is con-

---

[12] This is an expanded version of a discussion in Linn (2003a).

sidered linguistic fact. Scandinavian philologists are often more interested in palpable proofs than in brilliant and stimulating theories. (p. 251)

He goes on to discuss 'a hypothesis about language that seems inbred in Scandinavian linguists':

the hypothesis that language can be considered as a natural organism – or, if you prefer, as an organ like the heart or the liver – in the sense that it is a profoundly complicated mechanism *sui generis*, living its own life and having very little in common either with logic, or with normal social or cultural conventions. (Spang-Hanssen 1982: 252)

If this does not correspond to Storm's notion of *det levende Sprog*, then I am a monkey's uncle, as they say. Storm was a central figure in Romance philology in Scandinavia at the time when it was establishing itself as a serious scientific discipline. If we can't point to a Storm School inside or outside Norway, then we can certainly state instead that Storm's philosophy of language provided a foundation for this common Scandinavian 'stamp', 'a common stamp which has not been obliterated by the waves of European intellectual life' (Spang-Hanssen 1982: 251). Storm's last words were on syntax; as we have seen, they were not the most successful or prestigious words in the Scandinavia of their day, but perhaps *Større fransk Syntax* had an impact after all, as an early expression of the 'Scandinavian approach', of which Spang-Hanssen writes:

The Scandinavian approach appears perhaps in its most typical form in the syntactical studies which fairly can be said to have dominated Romance studies in Scandinavia in recent years [. . .] but it is impossible to pass over historical philology which counts many great achievements also in Scandinavia, and which is still a living discipline although it does not occupy the center of the scene anymore [*sic*]. (Spang-Hanssen 1982: 254)

3.3.1.7 Finally, after discussing the nature of *SFS*, its relation to Storm's complete *opus*, and its fate, it is high time I simply described what Storm covers in these three volumes. The structure is very conventional, theoretically speaking, although much original data is cited, and the syntactic phenomena are clearly and practically explained.

Volume 1 is subtitled *The Articles* and is divided up as follows:

De franske Artikler [The articles of French]
    Kap. I. Historisk Udvikling   (1–3)
    [Historical Development]

A. Den bestemte Artikel [The definite article]
    Kap. II – Kap. X   (3–31)

B. Den ubestemte Artikel [The indefinite article]
    Kap. I – Kap. III   (31–36)

C. Delingsartikelen [The partitive article]
    Kap. I – Kap. VII   (36–89)

D. Ingen Artikel [No article]
    Kap. I – Kap. VIII   (89–168)

Volume 2 (161 pages) covers *Prepositions*. After a very brief historical introduction, Storm works his way through the prepositions of modern French, alphabetically from *à* to *voici, voilà*. There is more evidence here of inadequate planning, of simply opening the data banks, as the strict alphabetical progress often breaks down. Usually this is because one preposition logically suggests another. Thus *près* and *proche* intervene between *auprès* and *chez*, for example. Storm follows his train of thought, which may or may not reflect the thought processes of the reader. Some of the insertions, however, seem to be less well motivated. *Selon*, for example, follows *le long de* because of a historical relationship between them, a relationship absent in modern French and unlikely to occur to a reader.

Volume 3 is by far the shortest of the three (96 pages), although it covers the most diverse categories: *Nouns, Adjectives and Verbs*. It is structured as follows:

Kap. I. Kongruens [Agreement]
    A. Substantiver og Adjektiver   (1–7)
    B. Verbets Kongruens   (8–9)

Kap. II. Konstruktion [Construction]
    A. Kasus   (10–11)
    B. Akkusativ   (11–18)
    C. Dativ   (19–29)

Kap. III. [No title]
    Verbum   (32–33)
    Moduslære   (33–35)

Kap. IV. Indikativs Tider; Konjunktiv
    A. Præsens   (35–37)
    B. Imperfektum   (37–38)
    C. Passé défini   (39–40)
    D. Perfektum   (40–41)
    E. Pluskvamperfektum   (42)
    F. Passé antérieur   (42–43)
    G. Futurum   (43–45)
    H. Førfremtid   (45–46)

It is worth comparing this structure with the structure of the syntax volume in Wilhelm Meyer-Lübke's *Grammatik der romanischen Sprachen*, the work that Storm praised in 1911, but found unoriginal. The syntax volume which appeared in 1899 (Meyer-Lübke 1899) is a grand undertaking of 815 pages, and is therefore directly comparable with *SFS* from the same generation. It was also published by Reisland, who, at the same time, was dealing with the final version of *Englische Philologie*. While Storm's work is completely word-based, starting with the word classes and later going on to deal with word agreement, and reaching a higher level of syntactic structure only briefly with subordinate clauses, Meyer-Lübke (1861–1936) belongs to a new generation where syntax is studied through the structure of groups. Meyer-Lübke (1899) has four sections: I: 'Die flexibeln Redeteile'; II: 'Die Wortgruppe'; III: 'Der Satz'; IV: 'Die Satzgruppe'.

3.3.2 *Shorter Works*

3.3.2.0 Many of the shorter publications Storm produced – articles, reviews etc. – concerned Romance languages. The series of treatises in the wake of *Englische Philologie* may never have happened, but, by contrast, from 1870 to 1893 he published short pieces on aspects of the Romance languages with reasonable regularity, starting with 'L'influenza dell'osco e umbro sulla lingua italiana' (Storm 1870). Why did he publish these short pieces on one side of his professional remit but not the other? There are two explanations. Firstly, it did not seem that he was going to publish the major work on French that had briefly been considered when he was planning *Engelsk Filologi*; it is interesting that the flow of short Romance works stops in the 1890s when he again takes up the idea of a longer work on French grammar. Most of what he wanted to say about English appears somewhere in the 1,098 pages of the 1892/1896 edition of *Englische Philologie*. His findings in Romance philology needed a different outlet. Secondly, he was closely involved with the foundation of the journals *Romania* and *Phonetische*

Studien, and of La Société de Linguistique de Paris, and probably felt a responsibility to help them in their early years. Storm was someone driven by a sense of duty. His contributions, excluding 'Remarques sur les voyelles atones . . .', were rather ad hoc and give the impression of having been thrown together for external reasons, rather than of being the outcome of focused, concentrated research.

It is not necessary for our understanding of Storm to go through all these shorter pieces in detail. Some of them now tell us little more than the breadth of his erudition. However, Storm's extraordinary reputation as a Romanist was built on these publications, so we do need to consider a representative sample.

3.3.2.1 *Early Reviews*

3.3.2.1.1 If we leave aside the brief etymological contributions to *Romania,* and 'Remarques sur les voyelles atones du latin, des dialectes italiques et de l'italien' which was the first high-profile publication he produced, Storm's first publications were review-type works. This is unsurprising; many young scholars cut their teeth on reviews before taking the risk of presenting original work to the academic community. It is more surprising that the first of these reviews was written in Italian and published in an Italian journal.

3.3.2.1.2 'L'influenza dell'osco e umbro sulla lingua italiana' (The influence of Oscan and Umbrian on Italian) was published in *Rivista bolognese di scienze e lettere* in 1870 while Storm was still abroad, and it is signed 'Giovanni Storm, Firenze'. It is a testament to Storm's linguistic talents that he was able not only to master the language from the practical angle during his stay in Italy but also to develop such an understanding of Italian and related ancient languages that he could contribute 27 pages on the subject to a thriving learned journal. For our purposes the fact that 'L'influenza dell' osco e umbro . . .' was written and published at all is really more significant than its contents.

Storm takes the 1869 publication, *Origine, formazione ed elementi della lingua italiana* by Fortunato Demattio of the University of Innsbruck, as the starting point for a series of observations on Oscan and Umbrian and the relationship between them. He demonstrates an impressive knowledge of the languages, particularly (of course) of their sound systems. His observations are rather loosely put together (again, of course), but he concludes tentatively, and contrary to contemporary Italian linguistic opinion, that modern Italian derives directly from Latin rather than from the other ancient languages of the region, languages such as Oscan and Umbrian:

Tutti le favelle italiane, tranne quella di Malta, sono figlie del latino volgare, ma sviluppate ciascuna con differenze individuali; tutte le sorelle sono differenti, ma pure si assomigliano nel tipo ereditato dalla madre. (Storm 1870: 276)

Storm made the same point in a popular form the following year in *De romanske Sprog og Folk*, where he wrote of the 'proud superficiality' (p. 41) of Italian views as to the history of the Italian language and its relationship with the ancient languages.[13]

3.3.2.1.3 In 1872 Storm published in *Morgenbladet* two brief reviews of elementary works dealing with French (Storm 1872b; 1872c), and in 1874 he published a more substantial scholarly review, of the first volume of Ascoli's *Archivio glottologico italiano*. Storm viewed Ascoli's work as 'the most significant work in the field of Romance Studies since Diez's grammar', and his review (Storm 1874b) was intended as an introduction to the study of Ascoli's work for Scandinavian Romanists. This review was written in Danish, in a new journal where Storm sat on the editorial board, and did little or nothing to advance his international standing as a Romanist. Despite the earlier publication date it was actually written in July 1873, after 'Remarques sur les voyelles atones'.

3.3.2.2 *'Remarques sur les voyelles atones du Latin, des dialectes italiques et de l'Italien' (1875)*

3.3.2.2.1 'Remarques' is dated January 1873 and forms the central trunk in the body of shorter articles on Romance topics from the early 1870s which established Storm's reputation. Although substantially written during 1872, it was not published until 1875. It appeared in volume 2 of *Mémoires de la Société de Linguistique de Paris*, where members of the society were also listed. *Membres perpétuels* included Joret, Meyer, Paris and Storm, and *membres ordinaires* at this time included Bréal, Littré, Tegnér, Thomsen and Wimmer. There was therefore a strong Scandinavian contingent in this prestigious society, but Storm had received the greatest honour of them all. His contributions to *Romania* and *Phonetische Studien* read as if they were produced out of a sense of duty to these new journals (see below), but the long gap between the writing and publication of 'Remarques' indicates that this work was not written to order, and it is superior to the other early Romance articles. In his 1877 application to parliament Storm describes 'Remarques' as 'the most significant scientific work I have so far produced' (Storm 1877a: 5), which it was.

He summarises the article's 63 pages like this:

---

[13] Storm also mentions a further article here, in which he attempts to 'introduce some serious research'. Its title was 'Sull' affinità dell' òsco al dialètto napolitáno', and it had been accepted by *Rivísta Bolognése* [Storm's own accents], but Storm writes that he had not seen it in print.

I have attempted here amongst other things to establish the connection between the older and younger popular language, Vulgar Latin and Italian, and to show that Italian (Tuscan) originally went the same way as the other Italian dialects and Romance languages, but that the language of Tuscany later approached Latin again in certain ways, to be precise via an influence from the South (from Rome). Umbrian showed itself here to be a predecessor of the Romance languages, while Oscan was closer to Latin. An earlier, more original form of Italian with regard to the unaccented vowels had been maintained in East Tuscan (Sienna) and in Venetian-Lombardic, of which dialects I have been the first to provide a scientific presentation. (Storm 1877a: 4)

Certainly Storm's command of both modern and older varieties of Italian is impressive, especially considering that this knowledge is based on work carried out during his relatively short stay in Italy a few years previously. 'Remarques' actually covers much more than the summary he himself gives. His reason for writing the article was in fact to examine the extent to which the different vowels are deleted in unstressed syllables, in response to a 'ladder of strength' for vowels proposed by P. Wilhelm Corssen in his *Über Aussprache, Vokalismus und Betonung der lateinischen Sprache* (second edition 1868/1870).[14] Most of the article is devoted to examples of 'voyelles atones' in language varieties closely related to Latin, and it is interesting (but expected) that for Storm, Latin is far from being a dead language. It is a living language with a pronunciation directly comparable with the sound systems of other living languages. For Storm 'dead' doesn't mean 'not living'! In 1886 he published an article advising on the pronunciation of Latin in Norwegian schools, indicating a continued interest and expertise in this area. As usual, his general advice was highly practical:

And so I consider that it is not practical to wish to implement ancient Roman pronunciation in the schools, but that the only practical thing is pretty much to stick to the traditional pronunciation. (Storm 1886b: 335)

He later wrote advising the National Theatre on the pronunciation of Greek names (Storm 1907), and his advice was the same: to adhere to the general European tradition, and not to try to reconstruct the ancient Greek pronunciation.

Although 'Remarques' sticks to one language family, and is not as wide-ranging as later publications, which would roam freely across language families, collecting data wherever and whenever it was to be found, it is nevertheless characteristically detailed, and Storm shows his characteristic unwillingness to stem the tide of data and reach a conclusion. He did not have access to some varieties, such as medieval Venetian, which caused him regret (Storm 1875b: 118), and he claims that some of the varieties (such as

---

[14] For more on Corssen, see 3.2.3.2.

thirteenth-century Milanese) only receive 'un coup d'œil rapide', when in fact the presentation, at least in the case of ancient Milanese, is rather full (pp. 138–144). Storm finishes that article by simply promising more data:

> Such is the Lombardo-Venetic form of the unstressed vowels: it remains to consider the developments of these sounds in the Emilian dialects. (p. 144)

3.3.2.2.2 All things considered, it has to be said that the findings which Storm summarised in his representation to parliament do not emerge very clearly or explicitly from this article; it is, however, certainly a good example of his extraordinary erudition and skill in assimilating language data, and it contains exemplary and original comparative work. It is not surprising that Storm was found fit to be a life member of the Société de Linguistique de Paris. However, the clear thesis of his summary has to be teased out of the data. His summary of what 'Remarques' achieves perhaps indicates that he was more of a theorist than we have assumed, but that the theories are hidden beneath the tide of examples. Making the theories explicit is what distinguishes the theorist from the practical linguist, and Storm remained the greatest practical linguist in the world, not the greatest theoretical one.

3.3.2.3 *Romania*

3.3.2.3.1 Gaston Paris reviewed 'Remarques' in volume 2 of *Romania*. Storm quoted this review in full in his 1877 application to parliament. Paris's words could perhaps not properly be called a review, amounting as they do to little more than a brief summary of this 'extremely important and highly valuable work' (Paris 1873: 375). However Paris's final words served Storm particularly well in his application:

> [. . .] it testifies from beginning to end to a prodigious memory, extensive study, an unusual capacity for thought and very sound philological sense.

The journal *Romania* was founded in 1872; and Storm contributed to the very first edition, and to a number of the other early volumes of it, his last contribution being in 1876. He obviously felt a commitment to this new journal, probably based on personal loyalty to Gaston Paris, who, along with Paul Meyer, was one of the editors. In the 1877 application to parliament Storm describes himself as a *Medarbeider* (collaborator) in *Romania* (p. 6), but, as the members of any editorial board are not actually listed, it is hard to know exactly what he means by this. His relationship with the embryonic *Romania* was in any case a reasonably close one. The subtitle of the journal was *Recueil trimestriel consacré à l'étude des langages et des littératures romanes* (Quarterly Journal Devoted to the Study of Romance Languages and Literatures), and predictably the language and literature it was devoted to was historical. Storm's initial contributions came under the section *Mélanges* (Miscellany), which involved (and still does involve) brief comments on specific narrow philological questions. The majority of these *mélanges*, in the early stages at least, were from the pens of Meyer and Paris; but Storm was one of the small group of scholars who helped prevent the entire journal becoming uniquely the work of its editors.

3.3.2.3.2 The contribution to volume 1 of *Romania* was very brief indeed, barely more than a page, written in French like all contributions (Storm 1872a). It was typically wide-ranging in the language data it drew upon. The narrow question Storm addressed was whether the parent form of modern French *trop*, *troupe* and *troupeau* was related to Gothic 'þaurp'. By citing a range of Germanic and Romance languages, including Norwegian dialect forms from Aasen's *Ordbog over det norske Folkesprog* (Dictionary of the Norwegian Folk Language), he showed that it was.

This brief piece demonstrates a characteristic practice of Storm's. He encounters an etymology he finds troublesome and throws his immense knowledge at it, his knowledge both of languages and about languages based on his encyclopedic reading. He concludes by noting that Diefenbach, in his *Vergleichendes Wörterbuch der gothischen Sprache*, arrived at the same conclusion, but states: 'it was however only after having arrived at this derivation independently of him that I got to know of his article' (1872a: 491).

3.3.2.3.3 In volume 2 there was an even briefer piece on the word *musgode* as found in the eleventh-century *Vie de St Alexis* (Storm 1873), and in 1874 *Romania* contained another brief note from Storm, again on a narrow topic, but this time specifically a question of historical phonetics: 'Remarques sur le vocalisme des Serments de Strasbourg' (Storm 1874a). He encountered the manuscript in 1869 during his stay in Paris. Storm addresses the question of how the front vowels found in the ninth-century *Serments de Strasbourg* would have been pronounced. This particular Old French text attracted Storm, as it is the earliest surviving example of a text written in the French vernacular, and was therefore an attempt to find a system for representing the vernacular without a tradition to base it on, rather as Storm would do in *Norvegia*. In short, the living language was reflected in writing without any of the obfuscation which creeps into a written language as it develops.

Storm takes the vowels represented by ⟨a⟩, ⟨e⟩ and ⟨i⟩ in turn and discusses their probable pronunciation in various phonetic environments. 'I selected this group because it encompasses the most difficult forms in the text' (p. 287). As usual, his evidence ranges widely across different languages and language varieties, but he sticks on this occasion to closer relatives of Old French, to early Romance varieties and to English.

3.3.2.3.4 Storm's longest contribution to *Romania* appeared two years later. It was still only *mélanges*, but since it ran to 23 pages, it warranted a place among the articles at the front of the volume. Although reasonably substantial, this, like so much of what Storm published, does not constitute 23 pages of developed argument. It is short notes on 38 Romance words, 38 brief observations from the non-systematising 'data processor', Johan Storm. In each case Storm uses evidence to cast doubt on an etymology which has been proposed previously, and in most cases to propose an alternative or revised etymology. In some cases his etymologies are new, where he has not found the word explained in any of the literature. The following (an explanation of the Spanish *sereno*) is an example of Storm's common-sense yet fully informed modus operandi:

> Prov. *seré*, Fr. *serein*, Nap. *serena*, evening dew, Sp. *sereno*, night-nurse. Diez wonders how the suffix *en*, so rare in Late Vulgar Latin, could be explained, and if perhaps a French *serein* for *serain* (*seranus*) could have been borrowed first in Provençal and later in Spanish. In my opinion we have here the Lat. *serenus*, whose meaning has been changed through popular etymology, because it has been seen, and very naturally, as a derivation of *sera*. This was how the popular mind derived Sp. *forense*, fairground, It. *forese*, peasant, from *foras*, preserved in Late Vulgar Latin, while Lat. *forensis* comes from *forum*, lost in Late Vulgar Latin. (Storm 1876: 182–183)

This example shows the difference between Storm, with his notion of the living language developing through use by speakers, and the evangelical Neogrammarians, with their single-minded appeal to language-internal laws. Modern Spanish *sereno* is indeed derived from Latin *serenus*.

Storm's detailed reference to other Romance scholars and detailed knowledge of European work in Romance philology, evidenced in this article, demonstrates the degree to which he was *au courant* with European scholarship. He was sent copies of work by his network of European colleagues, and the way in which scholars did send their work to other interested persons is perhaps one of the major differences between academic life then and now. In the twenty-first century we rely much more on inter-library loan schemes and on electronic resources, but both these routes to scholarship depend on our having known about the work in advance. Storm was recognised as one of the leading Romance philologists of the day, so aspiring linguists inevitably were keen for him to read their work. Some of his notebooks show how he took careful notes when he was reading new Romance works (see NBO Ms. 8° 2402 F[i]), and this was very necessary since he was not in a position to buy some of the more substantial works. When his personal library was donated to Bergen Museum on his death, it contained in the region of 6,000 volumes, so he did buy books, and plenty of them, and there is evidence of him going to

booksellers. Storm's presence at Bertrand Jensen's antiquarian bookseller's
is recorded in Myre (1943):[15]

> As well as Boeck and J. B. Halvorsen a string of other city Riksmål
> adherents often visited the lair of language activism and radicalism at the
> Triangle, amongst others the great language scholar, Professor Johan
> Storm, he who knew the English language better than most Englishmen!
> What Storm was after was of course all manner of English books,
> especially Tauchnitz editions. He was a courteous, even-tempered and
> pleasant man. However, to begin with he would only be served by the boss
> himself. If, as an exception to the rule, Bertrand Jensen was unavailable,
> Storm went on his way, as quietly as he had come. As time went on he got
> to know the other staff too, after Bertrand Jensen had informed them that
> the professor was allowed the Tauchnitz books at half price (80 øre per
> volume). Johan Storm's brother, Gustav Storm, the historian and
> antiquarian, on the other hand never honoured Bertrand Jensen with a
> visit. (Myre 1943: 21)

However, in the 1877 application to parliament, written the year after these
Mélanges étymologiques, he lamented that he was 'probably the only
professor of Romance in the world who cannot afford to buy *Littré's
French dictionary*! This is typical of Norwegian conditions.' Local library
resources were not among the greatest in the world, so Storm's encyclopedic
and up-to-date knowledge is not something that was easily achieved.

With *Mélanges étymologiques* Storm's active involvement in *Romania*
came to an end. He travelled abroad later in 1876. The following year
came the *Værk over det norske Sprog* debacle (see section 4.2.1.2), and then
he got down to *Engelsk Filologi*. By the time he returned to shorter scientific
works on French, *Phonetische Studien* had been founded, and by that time
Storm's interests were better reflected by the ethos of the newer journal.
Engelsk Filologi and the second edition of *Englische Philologie* both received
enthusiastic announcements in *Romania*, and by the early 1890s the
Romance world had still not forgotten Storm:

> This magisterial study may serve as an introduction to the grammar of
> any language at all, and, in fact, all who would seek to write a grammar
> should begin by immersing themselves in the sound ideas and precise
> observations of the wise professor from Christiania, and this applies
> particularly to Romanists, amongst whom he also occupies an eminent
> position. (*Romania* 22: 334)

The brevity of Storm's *Romania* obituary (see 3.3.1.6 above) and the
inaccuracies in it – 'Tale og Accent i Forhold til Sang', for example, is

---

[15] My thanks go to Gudmund Harildstad for alerting me to this reference.

described as 'un livre' – indicate that 30 years further on (1920) he had been largely forgotten by the Romance world.

3.3.2.4 Phonetische Studien *and the Philologists' Meetings*

3.3.2.4.1 We made reference to the influential journal *Phonetische Studien* in the last chapter, the journal which was later renamed *Die neueren Sprachen* as the emphasis moved from phonetics to language teaching reform, and which had everyone who was anyone in the field of phonetics/language-teaching reform on its editorial board. The list of contributors reads like a *Who's Who* of late-nineteenth-century linguistics, as many of those on the board took an active role in filling the journal's pages. Storm was no exception, although one feels that he was deliberately finding things to publish rather than using the journal as an outlet for work he had ready for publication.

The first volume (1888) opens with Lundell's article 'Die phonetik als universitätsfach', surveying the state of the teaching of phonetics in European universities (see section 2.2.4.1.1), and Storm's first contribution appears in volume 2 (Storm 1889). It seems rather out of place. Lundell had set the trend for practical and synchronic studies. Other contributions to the first two volumes were Passy's 'Kurze darstellung des französischen lautsystems', Viëtor's 'Beiträge zur statistik der aussprache des schriftdeutschen', Western's 'Kurze darstellung des norwegischen lautsystems' and H. Hoffmann's 'Die phonetik im ersten sprechunterricht der taubstummen'. In this company Storm's historical and comparative study of quantity in Romance looks decidedly fusty. Yes, it is a phonetic topic, but not in the same spirit as the other studies surrounding it. The reason for this is that it is 13 years old and was written for a quite different context.

In 1876 the first Scandinavian philologists' meeting was held in Copenhagen. Storm attended as part of his publicly funded foreign tour in the summer of that year. He would later visit the Netherlands, Belgium, England and France, but the philologists' meeting was where it started. (Although Storm himself got further than Copenhagen, the *Diary on my Foreign Travels*, from which we have already quoted in Chapter 1, did not.) It seems from a letter to Thomsen written on 6 July, shortly before Storm's departure from Kristiania, that he stayed with Thomsen's brother while in Copenhagen. That, at least, was the plan. On 21 July Storm gave his paper on quantity in Romance, and this was first published in 1879 in the conference proceedings, edited by Ludvig Wimmer (1839–1920) (Storm 1879b). It is the published version of that paper which forms the basis for Storm's first contribution to the new, forward-looking *Phonetische Studien*. I cannot help feeling that he just pulled this out of the drawer in order to have something to send to *Phonetische Studien*, although he does himself give a more carefully reasoned explanation. He notes (Storm 1889: 139, n. 1) that the contents of the 1879 paper have received little notice abroad, on account of their being written in Danish. Consequently he has taken the opportunity to translate the paper into German to ensure it a more widespread readership. Some of the observations, particularly those concerning French, had in fact already appeared in an international language in *Englische Philologie* (Storm 1881a), but 'I did not however want to tear them out of their context, and I leave them in here.' The relative lack of revision in this 1889 version further points to his having spent as little time as possible on this piece of work. Rather than simply criticising his motives, I should instead describe briefly what 'Romanische quantität' is about.

Although he is addressing an academic audience, Storm opens with the same technique he had used in 1860 in 'Tale og Accent i Forhold til Sang' (see section 2.2.4.3.1); he presents a linguistic phenomenon that everyone is in practice aware of, and then sets about explaining it. This is another example of the way in which the practical and the scientific mix, or rather the way in which they are undistinguished in Storm's approach to language and languages:

> What strikes us first of all when we hear the Romance languages spoken, is the extraordinary clarity and purity with which all parts of the words come out, the equilibrium they are in. (1889: 139)

Conversely, speakers of Romance languages feel that 'the Germans and the English "swallow half their words"'. 'This contrast is based on the different treatment of quantity.' We also find a good example here of the way in which the living language cuts across conventional distinctions between standard and non-standard, between written and spoken. Even though this paper is addressing a phonetic and therefore (one would have thought) uniquely spoken phenomenon, Storm is nevertheless able to draw in examples from written living language, specifically dialect-oriented writings. By drawing examples from all sorts of varieties of Italian, Storm concludes that:

> The whole scale is therefore represented in Italy, from the greatest of equilibrium between stressed and unstressed vowels to the greatest weighting of stressed ones. (p. 145)

He is aware, however, that the admission of all varieties of the language will inevitably lead to such an unsystematic conclusion, and prepares to look further to find 'the original and the normal'. After bringing in data from French and Spanish, he is able to state:

> the normal and original situation in Romance [is] [. . .] *that the stressed vowel only really predominates over the unstressed by virtue of the stress, not at the same time by virtue of length.* (p. 155)

This leads into a comparison of metre in the verse of the three languages, a comparison which demonstrates that, although Storm by his own admission did not have the same skills in literary studies as he did in linguistic ones, he nevertheless had a good knowledge of Romance literature. His findings are not particularly dramatic, but his evidence as to the remarkable similarity between the rhythm of the three languages is certainly interesting. He goes on in the second part of the paper to use his findings about the relative lack of quantity distinction in Romance to shed new light on the historical development of the three languages. He is quite aware that his findings are no longer as original or striking as they had been when the paper was delivered to the Copenhagen conference, and he concludes with an apology to this effect, hoping that he might be able to return to the question of quantity in Romance and study it again based on more recent scholarship (p. 177). Storm often took these hostages to fortune, promising work which as often as not never came to fruition. The elementary French course is one such example. There was so much to do in the search to understand the living languages, and he could never have achieved everything he wanted to achieve, but he was willing to try.

3.3.2.4.2 The second Scandinavian philologists' meeting was held in Kristiania in 1881. Storm was not himself involved in the planning of it, but he returned the compliment and invited Thomsen, promising that he would arrange accommodation for him. In a letter of 8 July that year Storm wrote to Thomsen, discussing these arrangements and clearly looking forward to the meeting, and to getting together with Thomsen, Lundell and Noreen to discuss dialects – as Storm wrote, this was an opportunity which would not arise again in the near future. He writes that he is himself planning to give a paper on the dialects of Telemark.

3.3.2.4.3 In 1886 Storm attended the third Scandinavian philologists' meeting, the one at which Quousque Tandem was founded. He clearly enjoyed it. On 23 November 1890 he wrote to Thomsen, hoping that these meetings would continue, not so much because of their academic value but because of the personal contacts made and renewed on such occasions. He went on to say that 'we had such an extraordinarily good time in Stockholm in 1886'. His presence there was first and foremost to give a paper entitled 'Nogle Bemærkninger om Diftongdannelsen i de romanske Sprog', which he did at 10 o'clock on Wednesday 11 August. It was published in 1893 (Storm 1893a) in a slightly revised form. In Storm's notebook at NBO Ms. 4 1285 F[xli] there is an incomplete draft of a different lecture, with the comment 'which was not held'. This aborted presentation is entitled 'Nogle korte Bemærkninger om bløde Konsonanter for haarde i Norden' (Some short comments on the use of soft consonants for hard in Scandinavia). In August 1886 Storm had just returned from a dialect trip in Norway, so Scandinavian dialects were on his mind. In the event he clearly decided that a Romance topic was more suitable.

As we have come to expect of Storm, his discussion here is not limited to Romance languages, but ranges quite freely via English, Old and Modern, and Frisian, to Norwegian dialects, particularly those of Setesdal. His question is why, according to evidence presented by Gaston Paris in *Romania 10*, certain Latin vowels, both long and short, later diphthongised on their way to the modern Romance languages. The reason for citing such a range of languages and language varieties in his 'Bemærkninger' on this question is this:

> My studies of living dialects have instead led me to a different view: with regard to the treatment of vowels, languages are divided into two groups: the monophthongal (monophthongising), which maintain the sound of a vowel without altering it, and the diphthongising, which tend to a greater or lesser extent to alter the vowel, notably a long vowel, at a certain point, such that it ends differently to how it began. (p. xxxix)

Few besides Storm could safely make a generic statement of this sort, based on first-hand knowledge of Romance, Germanic and Slavonic varieties, ancient and modern, standard and dialectal. Close comparison in particular with the dialect of Valle in upper Setesdal (as distinct from the dialect of Bygland further south in the valley, which he also discusses) leads Storm to his conclusion as to why diphthongisation occurred in certain Romance vowels:

> The growth of stress in Romance occasioned, as in most modern languages, an upheaval in the quantity relations, whereby originally short vowels became similar to originally long ones. Now the capacity for splitting, dormant in most languages, came to the language's service for the sake of distinctiveness, and the vowels came to be distinguished by different means, as the old ones disappeared. (p. xlvii)

His general finding is certainly useful, but this method is highly original, using data from modern Norwegian dialects to shed light on sound changes evidenced in Old French. If this paper had been more widely accessible, his method would have met with some scepticism. He is certainly aware that such wide-ranging comparative methods and findings are unusual. He compares raising of Latin *a* in French (e.g. *talis > tel, carus > cher*) to a raising in English, Frisian and Danish and to developments between Southern Italian and Modern Greek, and between Spanish and Arabic. Storm defends these observations by referring to:

> The mysterious influence of neighbourliness throughout so many centuries [. . .] There is something, shown to be the case so often, about neighbouring languages getting closer to each other with respect to certain features of the sounds, even though they are not more closely related. (p. xxxvi)

He was not, as we know, a dedicated Neogrammarian. If he found certain features in living languages, then the data was enough for him, and his enquiries were not limited by the expectations of previous explanatory mechanisms. Storm's findings should not be belittled by our own age, obsessed as it is with theoretical underpinnings and sceptical of creative analysis. His approach, coupled to the vast store of data in his head, meant (if the theory wood was visible for the data trees) that Storm was undoubtedly one of the most challenging and original linguists of his day.

The next philologists' meeting was held in Copenhagen in July 1892. Storm wasn't sure whether to attend this conference or to speak at a meeting of the British Association in Edinburgh. In the event he went to Copenhagen and returned to the topic he had first written about in 1860 and which continued to fascinate him throughout his life – tone. The 1892 paper resulted in the published form 'Om musikalsk Tonelag, især i Kinesisk' (Storm 1893b). As in 1886, Storm evidently had a very good time – although, being a shy person, he was initially nervous about travelling to Copenhagen without his friend Sophus Bugge (letter to Thomsen, 25 July 1892).

In 1898 the meeting returned to Kristiania, where it was held from 12 to 15 August, Storm being part of the organising sub-committee (see Falk (1899) for the abstracts of the papers and other conference details). A month prior to the meeting Storm suffered probably the greatest tragedy of his life: the death, after a protracted illness, of his son Gunnar. Accordingly he had no wish to take part in the philologists' meeting a month later. He informed Thomsen of his intention in a letter of 11 July, and he also wrote to his brother Gustav and to Sophus Bugge with the same news. In the event he did attend the meeting, although he did not give a paper himself and his name is not given in the impressively long list of participants. By 1898 Storm was one of the "grand old men" of Scandinavian linguistics and he had many academic friends. Hearing some papers and meeting 'good, old, faithful friends' (letter to Thomsen, 27 December1898) did him a great deal of good and cheered him up at a time when life was difficult.

3.3.2.4.4a Storm never wrote a "proper" article for *Phonetische Studien*, and his next two contributions were both reviews, but they were substantial and contain interesting things for us as we seek to understand him. In 1892 he published a review of Passy's *Étude sur les changements phonétiques* in *Phonetische Studien* (Storm 1892c). Dealing with this review here in the chapter on Romance languages, rather than in a section on phonetics, shows how unsatisfactory it can be to divide Storm's work up into discrete categories. On balance, this review belongs with the other contributions to *Phonetische Studien*, and Passy's work is about the sounds of French, but both Storm and Passy devote at least as much attention to general phonetic questions, and the full title of what was in fact Passy's doctoral thesis is *Étude sur les changements phonétiques et leurs caractères généraux*. Storm's review of it is in many ways an ordinary review, summarising the contents of the chapters, elaborating and correcting some of Passy's observations, generally praising the quality of the work. The way to find out what Passy says here is to read the original, rather than to read A. Linn summarising J. Storm, summarising P. Passy, but some of Storm's comments do help us to understand his intellectual character and his linguistic views and therefore need to be looked at.

Storm is quick to praise Passy for achieving something Storm himself found difficult. This often happens in reviews. Reviewers make a point of criticising when the work under review does what the reviewer does him- or herself. The reviewer feels the need to demonstrate their own standing or protect their own reputation. Consequently Storm corrects small errors or questionable statements concerning Scandinavian languages. Passy quotes Jespersen's support for Verner's view that there is a fixed musical interval associated with Danish *stød*. 'To me this new theory is very dubious', writes Storm (1892c: 205), 'despite Jespersen's approval', and evidence from Thomsen is used to support this. Storm is certainly not inventing evidence to score a personal point, but it would probably have suited him for Thomsen and himself to be able to lob balls of data at the opinions of the younger generation. Later Storm also corrects Passy's citation of a view of Sweet's on the pronunciation of the word *falla* in Norwegian dialects. By contrast, though, Storm is extremely impressed by Passy's ability to systematise:

> Passy's dissertation covers the field of general phonetics as much as specifically French phonetics, and deals with one of the key questions of language history, namely the problem of HOW and WHY sound changes actually occur, in a thorough and systematic fashion. (1892c: 199)

Storm goes on to laud Passy for not just being a phonetician 'but also a real language scholar'. This distinction is an interesting one, and shows that even in the early days a gulf was perceived between language study proper on the one hand and phonetics on the other: that it was rare to find people for whom the study of speech sounds was part of the larger picture of philology. Storm was of course one of those for whom phonetics was indeed a key to the living language, but for whom the living language meant more than just phonetics. There are two other places in this review where Storm shows himself to have been a rational linguist who dealt with real language facts and consequently avoided the extreme positions.

Ascoli and Sweet are two of the scholars cited here who espoused the view that *climate* influenced the phonetics of individual languages. Passy suggests that the raising of [ɑ] in the Germanic languages, which is 'almost unknown in the Romance languages', could be 'an effect of the cold and damp climate'. Storm describes this as 'a completely madcap field' (*ein sehr spinöses gebiet*) and provides data from a variety of languages exhibiting similar phonetic developments but spoken in very different climatic conditions. The relationship between climate and language was evidently an attractive one, but it is too simplistic for Storm, who is forced to doubt the theory through finding contradictory data. While he might not have had much time for theories linking language change with climate, he evidently believed in a relationship between climate and national character. In a letter to Gustav (9 May 1875) he discusses the amount of work required of professors in different European countries. He takes the view that Germans have 'a much greater capacity for work than us', due to their climate and geographical location. He fears that, if a university were to be established at Hammerfest (in the far north of Norway), 'one would find that even less was done there than here' (NBO Brevsamling 86). Storm would have worried about the productivity of the University of Tromsø!

Passy is typical of 1890s linguists in stressing the idea of constant and regular phonetic change, and again Storm finds the current notion of exceptionless sound laws very problematic, in that there is data that simply doesn't fit the picture. For Storm this doesn't mean that there must be another law to explain the rogue data. It means instead that languages are more interesting, varied and unpredictable than theories or laws allow. He expands this view in the draft of an unpublished review of Seelmann's *Die Aussprache des Latein*. (He would return to attacking Seelmann the following year in the same journal – see next section). In this draft review he writes:

> The author shares with most Germans the fault of being too much of a theorist, too doctrinaire. He sets up his theories and the language just has to obey them. In a word, he doesn't always pay sufficient regard to the facts. Thus he professes the Neogrammarians' teaching, that sound laws within the same dialect admit of no exceptions, are absolute laws of nature. When however irregularities are found, these are written off as analogical formations. This is however simply a case of giving human frailty another name, and it is not always enough [. . .] I think, despite the Neogrammarians, that one still has to accept that there are sporadic sound changes, in which the individuality of people or peoples expresses itself. Changes do not always begin all along the line, but with individual words. (UBB Ms. 739c)

Storm was not the only conservative (or radical) in this matter, not the only linguist drawing attention to the 'conservative', stable phonetic elements. He insists (rather vaguely, but forcibly): 'In stark contrast to the theories advanced here stand the views of several other recent language scholars' (p. 211). The community of linguists at the end of the nineteenth century was certainly not as uniformly Neogrammarian as the canon of linguistic historiography would have us believe, and nor was the sound system of language uniformly understood in terms of exceptionless laws. At the other extreme stand views like those Storm quotes from the 1890 *Geschichte der*

schwäbischen mundart by Friedrich Kauffmann (1863–1941). Kauffmann
maintains in effect that there had been no change in the pronunciation of
Swabian since the fourteenth century. Storm's final paragraph is important.
His moderate, objective position, standing on the touchline of European
linguistic argument, is one that linguists today would benefit from heeding.
True understanding lies, boringly enough, somewhere in the middle. As we
have remarked already, Storm was not a stick-in-the-mud conservative. He
was simply rational, and that is different:

> It would be interesting if a discussion between two such contrasting
> approaches were to take place. From my point of view I don't believe
> that the entire sound system of a language can remain completely
> unaltered for several centuries. On the other hand I believe that the
> basic phonetic character remains the same for a long time and does not
> become another one without violent disruptions. Characteristic differ-
> ences such as the weakening of voicing in southern German and the
> aspiration of the *tenues* [voiceless plosives] in northern German are
> without doubt very old. (Storm 1892c: 212)

There is a specific point being made here about phonetic change, and one
which is not as straightforward as I or Storm have made it appear; but the
general point is one which characterises Storm's approach and which makes
him a linguist whose views survive the vagaries of philological fashion.

3.3.2.4.4b Storm's review in volume 6 of *Phonetische Studien* (Storm 1893c)
covers exactly the same pages as the review in volume 5, also running from
page 199 to page 212, but the similarity between the two reviews ends there.
While the review of Passy was predominantly positive, this one is predominantly negative. While the review of Passy systematically worked through the
publication it addressed, this one would have surprised a reader expecting to
see a review of the work named at the beginning. It is nominally a review of
Kritischer Jahresbericht über die Fortschritte der romanischen Philologie, but
Storm only deals with the phonetic parts, so the review ends up rather like a
reduced version of the opening of the final version *Englische Philologie*,
which had been published the previous year, that is to say a commented
bibliography of recent phonetic literature. We could accuse Storm of
jumping on his hobby-horse, but this review is intended for a journal
entitled *Phonetische Studien*, so for once we must allow that Storm has
had his audience in mind. It is not a simple bibliography though, but rather a
critique of the phonetic bibliography given in *Kritischer Jahresbericht* by
Seelmann (see also section 3.2.3). In fact the review is simply a critique of
Seelmann's competence as a phonetician. We learn towards the end of the
review that Seelmann has criticised Storm, unfairly and in excessively strong
terms accusing him (indirectly) of having insufficient knowledge of Latin
grammar and of consequently adopting fantastic theories. As we know,

Storm did not respond well to criticism, and we might expect him to be less than amicable towards Seelmann in this review. As we saw in section (3.2.3), however, Storm's public criticism of Seelmann actually dates back a number of years.

Storm makes his views on Seelmann's phonetic ability perfectly clear from the very beginning:

> he can [. . .] scarcely be regarded as a competent authority. He is too lacking in phonetic schooling and in thorough knowledge of the sounds of living languages and dialects for that [. . .] He lacks not only competence, but also the objective distance proper to the critical reporter. He does not know how to observe to the appropriate extent. (1893c: 199–200)

We get the picture. The rest of the review is spent in correcting the reputation of contemporary phoneticians unjustly criticised or praised by Seelmann. There is not a lot to be learned about Romance philology here, but this is Storm at his most formidable, armed with his encyclopedic knowledge, mercilessly setting the record straight, placing philological truth above personal etiquette. Storm was not a lone voice railing against Seelmann, but Seelmann was only doing what Storm did . . . without the knowledge to back it up. The lesson remains: don't attack Storm in print. Many on the Norwegian as well as on the European front suffered for doing so.

3.3.2.4.5 Storm's publications fall into groups. The pursuit of knowledge of the *levende Sprog* underpinned them all, but the focus of his attention shifted from one period to the next. The contributions to *Phonetische Studien* are a surprisingly ad hoc little group of works and an exception to the generally focused publication programme Storm adopted. The only explanation for this can be that they were not part of Storm's publication programme at all, but extras, produced either through a sense of duty to the new journal or through Storm having his arm twisted by the editor, Viëtor. Editors short of material do that sort of thing. Certainly the massacre of Seelmann was encouraged by Viëtor. On 2 January 1893, Storm sent New Year greetings to Thomsen and told him that Viëtor had persuaded him to give Seelmann this *Afhøvling* (planing down). By volume 6, the list of members of the editorial team has been abbreviated to 'with the cooperation of numerous colleagues' and contributions are coming from all over the world, from Spain, Hungary and Chile as well as the traditional homes of philology. Maybe Storm now decided that he didn't need to help out any more. In any case, his mind was on other things. In the same New Year letter to Thomsen he complained about the hard work involved in finishing *Englische Philologie*, and proposed 'a Phonetics, particularly for Norwegians', another idea destined never to be realised. The shorter scientific works are all interesting and made important contributions to contemporary philology. They show us much about

Storm's way of working as well. For better or worse, they did not allow his ideas to develop in the same way as the longer works did. Storm actually found writing short works, reining in his thoughts, an uncomfortable experience, and nowhere more so than in the article on the Romance languages for *Encyclopædia Britannica* (see section 3.2.3).

3.3.2.5 *Practical Works*

3.3.2.5.1 In 1888 and 1890 respectively Storm contributed brief articles to *Universitets- og skole-annaler (ny række)* (University and School Annals (New Series)). They were really developments of 'Om en forbedret undervisning i levende Sprog', which had appeared in the same journal in 1887. However, since the 1888 and 1890 articles are both specifically focused on French, we will deal with them here.

The 1888 piece, 'Nogle punkter af den franske grammatik nærmere belyste' (Some points of French grammar more closely illuminated) (Storm 1888b), is a direct appendix to 'Om en forbedret undervisning . . .', and Storm opens by reiterating his reformist views in a nutshell:

> Everything that does not belong to the spoken language, but only to the literary language, everything old-fashioned, everything rare, all elevated style must be thrown overboard at the first level. (1888b: 1)

Most of this article is given over to examples of forms, lexical and grammatical, which Storm had maintained should be omitted from pedagogical materials on account of being archaic or rare in contemporary French, and therefore not part of the living language. He gives six examples, which he begins by declaring never to have encountered himself. This is not enough of an assurance, and he supports his own observations by appealing to French authorities too:

> I am in contact with some of the most brilliant French language scholars and find myself to be in close agreement with them. (p. 1)

He has, for example, Passy's direct assurance that the form *travails* 'must be a slip'. Passy also supports Storm's claim as to the unnaturalness of the forms *mol* (for *mou*, 'soft') and *plumail* (for *plumeau*, 'feather duster').

The purpose of this article is essentially to give credence to Storm's reformist programme of the year before. He needs to show that reform in pedagogical materials is not mere whimsy, but is based on real language data, verifiable by native-speaker authorities like 'the famous French language scholar and phonetician, Paul Passy' (p. 2). It is obvious that he is simply making a point rather than presenting some sort of thesis, as the article is so brief. He finishes by saying: 'That is enough for now. Perhaps more another time' (p. 6).

3.3.2.5.2 But there wasn't any more. The point had been made and Storm moved on. The next practically orientated publication in the same journal was a response to 'Schou Bruun's travel report'. At face value it is an amiable piece, written in the spirit of the journal in which it appeared, demonstrating how academic phoneticians and school teachers can be of mutual benefit to one another:

> Such an exchange of views will be the best means to pave the way for mutual understanding between teachers and phoneticians and to show teachers the practical significance of phonetics. (1890a: 258)

In reality, however, Storm's comments are little more than corrections of comments made by Bruun, and corrections made in a rather high-handed way.

Jens Schou Fabricius Bruun (1843–1919) was a teacher in Kristiansund in northern Norway and a specialist in Greek and French. In 1876 he wrote a *Græsk Grammatik til Skolebrug* (Greek Grammar for Use in Schools), which was very successful and really replaced the Norwegian translation of Curtius with which Storm had been involved as a young man. I can't believe that Storm would have been looking for an opportunity to get back at Bruun for this, and certainly not as late as 1890. Bruun made a study trip to Paris in 1889, which was publicly funded, and the *reiseberetning* Storm is responding to is the official report on this trip (Bruun 1890). In 1898 Bruun wrote a *Grammaire française par questions et réponses* which appears to have been popular too.

Much of Bruun's report is given over to phonetic observations, both those he made himself and those gleaned from his teacher in Paris, Charles Roussey. Bruun had initially sought out the teaching of the Scandinavians' favourite French teacher, Mlle Guemain,[16] but she had given up teaching due to ill health. Bruun's phonetic points are not profound. They are intended to be of practical value to Norwegian learners of French. Thus he discusses the difference between French [s] and [ʃ] and the Norwegian equivalents, the pronunciation of French ⟨ou⟩, of unstressed schwa and other aspects of the pronunciation of French which he, as a teacher, views as difficult for Norwegian speakers. In so doing he cites Passy's *Le français parlé* and other non-specialist publications on French phonetics.

Citing numerous very specialised authorities, including himself, Storm sets about putting right the pronunciation rules given by Bruun. He makes fairly extensive use of his *Norvegia* script and, it seems to me, achieves the opposite of his stated claim to wish for rapprochement between academic phoneticians and teachers. If this is the tirade of scholarship waiting for a teacher

---

[16] 'I took a few lessons with the well-known language mistress, Mlle Guemain, who was of no little help to me in doubtful cases; I got better information from her than from most men. She rightly enjoys general recognition from all Scandinavians for her solid skills and her intimate knowledge of the language and the literature' (Storm 1871: 14).

who ventures to enter the debate on practicalities of language learning, then
it must surely have served to discourage rather than encourage. There are
some interesting comments here, like Storm's recommendation that Norwegians whose dialect includes a front rather than a back *r* should not attempt
to pronounce the uvular [ʁ] of French, 'since they generally do not manage
to do it in a natural way; what matters is to pronounce *r* clearly' (pp. 259–
260). However, the really striking thing about this piece is the way Storm
uses it to demonstrate his authority in language matters.

Both these pieces, in the official Norwegian education journal, produced
as it was by the ministry, the *Kirke- og Undervisnings-Departementet*, are
about Storm stamping his authority on the schools. Why he should have felt
insecure enough to need to do this isn't clear. He did have enemies, or at
least opponents, in language circles. His views on Norwegian were politically
undesirable, and he was known in school circles to be a radical on the one
hand, yet sceptical towards Quousque Tandem on the other. He was not
held in awe at home as he was abroad, and maybe he just wanted to show the
Norwegian schools that Schou Bruun was all very well, but J. Storm was
better. He also takes the opportunity in 1890 to condemn some of the more
radical suggestions put forward by Passy in the teaching of French as a
foreign language:

> Teaching foreigners to pronounce *mam* for madame, *vla* f. voila [*sic*], *dja* f.
> déja [*sic*], *çuici* f. celui-ci, is just like us teaching them to say *mam Hansen*
> for madam Hansen or *åfno* f. hvad for noget [. . .] (1890: 258–259)

Storm was professor of Romance languages at the Norwegian university,
so he had authority anyway, but it is only human to feel insecure from time
to time, and he suffered from a lack of self-confidence, belied by the
authoritarian tone of his writings. If Storm's motives in these two articles
were as human as I think they were, he should not be condemned for being
human. 'Nogle punkter' and 'Nogle bemærkninger' did, after all, contain
practical observations about French grammar, lexicon and pronunciation
from which teachers of the language in Norway would have benefited.

4

NORWEGIAN

4.1 REFORMING THE LANGUAGE

4.1.1 *Storm's Role*

4.1.1.1 How best to teach the modern languages, as we saw in Chapters 2 and 3, was certainly a hotly debated question in late-nineteenth-century Norway, and one involving people at all levels, from schoolteachers up to members of parliament. However, it was a mere nothing compared with the big linguistic issue of the day, the issue which affected and involved every Norwegian, the issue which Einar Haugen described in 1966 like this:

> During the past century Norway has been the scene of a conscious effort to plan the development of a new national language. Ideas about language have reached out from the quiet studies of scholars to the public press and the halls of parliament. They have aroused vigorous discussion and compelled decisions affecting every citizen and his children. Little by little a linguistic avalanche has been set in motion, an avalanche which is still sliding and which no one quite knows how to stop, even though many would be happy to do so. (Haugen 1966: 1)

Storm himself reached out from his quiet study to the public press and the halls of parliament, and much of what he wrote about Norwegian appeared in the national newspapers, even if it later appeared in book form too. But what was Storm doing involving himself in the debate on reforming written Norwegian, the debate about how to devise and implement a written language distinct from the inherited Danish, and one worthy of the new nation? His area of expertise was English and the Romance languages. Wasn't he going beyond what he was competent to do?

4.1.1.2 No. First, the language issue in Norway was the property of everybody, as language issues often are. A native speaker is by definition an expert in his or her language and is consequently qualified to have "expert" views about the language, and language is something about which people hold particularly trenchant and emotional views. We are all identified by the language or type of language we use, but the question of reform in the national written language has an impact not only on personal identity but on group identity too. So, in a free society, Storm was as entitled as the next Norwegian to air his views on language reform.

Secondly, Storm was officially a language authority. He was professor of modern languages at the country's one university. He was recognised as a linguistic authority well beyond Norway's borders, and his international successes were reported in the Norwegian newspapers, so he was known to be an international language authority at home too, even if he did sometimes suffer the fate of prophets in their own land. Ivar Aasen was perhaps the National Linguist, if we can speak of such a thing, in that he was funded by the state from 1851 until his death 45 years later, to carry out linguistic work, but Aasen was himself responsible for one of the lines of reform. He couldn't enter the debate as an objective commentator and critic – not that many were capable of objectivity on this highly emotive subject 'which generates heated argument wherever Norwegians forgather' (Haugen 1966: 2). Aasen was anyway not a public person, unlike Storm. He did not seek public arenas, while Storm, by contrast, spent his entire life in institutionalised debate, in the schools, in the university, in newspapers, in learned societies and journals and in public lectures.[1] So, if anyone was in a position to enter the public, national debate on the big language question, it was Storm. He is not, in any case, the only Norwegian linguist to have contributed to the debates surrounding the mother tongue. Storm's is the first name in Haugen's list of 'distinguished scholars' who 'have made both theoretical and practical contributions to the issues of language planning' (Haugen 1966: 296), although Haugen goes on to note that 'it would be harder to name a Norwegian linguist who has not in some way contributed to the discussion'. Few, though, made such a far-reaching contribution as Storm did.

In 1907 it was decreed that there should be a compulsory essay in Norwegian Landsmål for the school-leaving exam, the *Examen Artium*. This provoked violent objection from those users of Riksmål, the language variety rooted in Danish, who were opposed to Landsmål, the language variety rooted in Aasen's work, and the way they perceived it was being imposed on the schools. The school students themselves, at least those in the capital, reacted vigorously to this new regulation, and around 2000 people attended a protest meeting on 7 April that year – 'the largest public meeting which until then had been held in Norway' (Langslet 1999: 42). One of the speakers at this meeting was the thunderous champion of Riksmål, the leading figure of late-nineteenth-century Norwegian culture, Bjørnstjerne Bjørnson (1832–1910). Amongst other things he said was this:

> Go no further with this until the authorities or the people have been asked! Up to now the authorities have not been listened to [. . .] Ask the highest authority on language as such, *Johan Storm* [. . .] (reported in Langslet 1999: 44)

---

[1] Krokvik (1996: 213–221) challenges the traditional view of Aasen as non-militant and non-political. Krokvik's evidence is convincing but too sparse to reinvent the modest figure who 'thrived best on peaceful research, writing and reading' (Krokvik 1996: 217).

It is noteworthy that the largest public gathering to have been held in Norway until that time concerned the language question: such was public feeling. It is also noteworthy that it was Storm who Bjørnson regarded as the language authority, the person fit to decide how the Norwegian language should develop and what strategies should be adopted. Storm was sympathetic to Bjørnson's cause, but, just as it is unarguable to state that Bjørnson was 'the leading figure of late-nineteenth-century Norwegian culture' (Storm described him as 'this mighty intellect, who burst all bounds' (1878a: 541)), so Bjørnson is simply stating a fact when he describes Storm as 'the highest authority on language as such'.

Thirdly, Storm was well qualified to state views about Norwegian, and not only as a Norwegian citizen and as a general linguist. He knew the Norwegian language probably better than anyone else at that time. Aasen was more deeply immersed in the popular language, and Unger was more of an expert on the ancient language, but nobody had an understanding of the Norwegian language past and present as profound as Storm's.

4.1.1.3 Some of Storm's earliest work had dealt with tone in Norwegian and other Scandinavian languages (Storm 1860; 1875a), and it is clear that, although fate provided him with a post in English and Romance languages, he was from a young age fascinated by Norwegian, and actively studying it. Neither of his two big Norwegian projects came to anything. There are notes and an incomplete draft from 1869 of an *Oldn. Sproghistorie*,[2] which was never completed or published thanks to Storm's departure to southern Europe, and we shall return to this and to his grand *Work on the Norwegian Language* in section 4.2.1 below. His failure to complete these projects was due purely and simply to lack of time. We have seen in the course of the last two chapters how demanding his day-to-day work was, teaching, researching and administering the modern languages at the university and overseeing their examination in the schools. It was his own passion for Norwegian which drove him to work on the language as an "extracurricular activity". His tours of the Norwegian countryside, collecting and recording dialect data, were carried out in his own time, during the summer vacations, although often with financial assistance from the university.

As well as possessing a detailed knowledge of the history of the language, based on the study of primary materials, and a detailed knowledge of the dialects based on primary and secondary research across the whole country, Storm was very well read in Norwegian literature. The 40 notebooks now housed in the Norwegian National Library (at Ms. 4° 1290 H) contain wordlists taken from Norwegian writings from the sixteenth century up to Storm's own day, mostly from serious literature, as part of an ongoing study of the style and lexis of Modern Norwegian. One outcome of this study of

---

[2] In: NBO Ms. 8° 2402 A.

literary language was 'De store Forfatteres Sprog og Retskrivning', serialised in *Aftenposten* between 20 September and 2 November 1900 (Storm 1900) (see section 4.2.3.2.2.2), where Storm wrote: 'there is something superior to form and spelling, and that is style, the tone of the language.' Another outcome was the article in the *Festschrift* for Ibsen's 70th birthday on 'Ibsen og det norske Sprog' (Storm 1898a), and Storm was further involved with Ibsen's works when he was invited to edit the commemorative edition of the collected works of Norway's leading author, following his death in 1906, and to write a linguistic commentary on Ibsen's language (Storm 1908a) (see section 4.2.3.2.1).

Storm may have been turned down by parliament in 1877 (see 4.2.1.2), but later, and particularly after the turn of the century, Bjørnson was right – he really did become *the* official authority on the language. In 1888 Storm was engaged as language consultant to the new translation of the New Testament, which would appear in 1904 (see 4.2.3.1). In 1902 he was appointed language adviser to the National Theatre, and in December 1903 *Aftenposten* was able to report:

> Professor Storm has been requested by the Ministry for the Church and Education to assist them as the ministry's consultant in matters concerning the Norwegian language and Norwegian orthography. Professor Storm has promised willingly to undertake this duty, which is unpaid. (2 December 1903)

To cap it all, a year later (1904) he was made Commander of the Order of St Olav for his services to science. We have come a long way since 1877 when not only was Storm *persona non grata*, but his biggest concern was financial insecurity. Here he is as the linguistic darling of the Establishment and doing work for free.

The first person to be appointed to a post at the university, which at least in theory covered the teaching of Modern Norwegian, was Moltke Moe in 1886. Ingebret Moltke Moe (1859–1913) was the first professor of Norwegian, or more accurately of *norsk Folkesprog* (Norwegian popular language), at the university. Such a post had first been proposed in the mid-1870s (see Venås 2000a: 35), but it took years of politically motivated disagreement (Venås 2000a: 35–38) eventually to arrive at the terms of the professorship. Storm discussed the terms of the post somewhat disingenuously in his lecture in the *Studentersamfundet* (Society of Students) in February 1885,[3] saying that he assumed, and that he assumed that the government assumed, that *norsk Folkesprog* was to be understood as *norsk Sprogvidenskab* (Norwegian linguistics). (Storm 1885a: 7). Moe was in the event the only applicant for the

---

[3] Storm delivered his lecture 'Om Maalsagen' in the *Studentersamfundet* on Saturday 21 February 1885, and this provided the basis for a discussion the following Saturday. The three main contributions to this subsequent discussion were published in a little book as Hertzberg et al. (1885).

post and was appointed with effect from 20 January 1886. His interests actually lay in the area of folklore, and he began his period of office with a year-long sabbatical to acquire the necessary linguistic skills, but even then, language teaching did not begin until the autumn of 1888. Moe must have been a disappointment to the great linguist and Norwegian expert Johan Storm, especially as Storm felt that Moe's appointment was politically motivated. On 7 June 1885 Storm wrote to Amund B. Larsen:

> It will probably be *Moe* who gets the popular language position. The radicals do not have anyone else they would put up with. Even with Moe they will have to live with the fact that he has expressly stated that he cannot undertake to lecture on Landsmaal. I can probably be satisfied with Moe, in so far as he has a sizeable general knowledge of the dialects, but he lacks, as he admits himself, *specific* qualifications as a linguist [Sprogmand]. In the terms and conditions they will probably attach folk traditions to the post to insure themselves against unwelcome right-wingers like, for example, you. That is in any case what I have been led to believe. (NBO Brevsamling 385)

Moe was then, by his own admission, no linguist, and a specialist in the language, a 'professor i landsmål og dets dialekter', did not arrive until 1899 in the person of Marius Hægstad (1850–1927) (see Venås 1992; 2000a: 40–44). There was no corresponding chair in Riksmål at the university until Didrik Arup Seip (1884–1963) was appointed in 1916, and this was after Storm's retirement. So Storm felt a responsibility (and a desire) to provide what teaching he could in the area of Modern Norwegian and its history.

In the autumn semester of 1875 he began a series of 'popular lectures' on the subject of *Modersmaalet* (the mother tongue). Although the surviving notes are incomplete, the first page of these lecture notes is entitled 'main points', and at least outlines what he intended to cover:

> The idea of *Modersmaalet*. The changeability of language. Dialectal variation. The musical element. The 4 Scandinavian languages. Our mother tongue not the orig. The artificial element. Our language of culture in relation to the dialects. The Landsmaal movement [Maalstræv]. Our language from a European standpoint, particularly the phonology. Vowels. Here orthographical questions arise like *e* or *æ*. Consonants. The physiognomy of the language. Overview and comparison. Prosodic accent variation. Romance and Germanic. (NBO Ms. 8° 2402 K)

This is just the sort of approach we would expect of Storm, focusing on the sound system of the language on the one hand and on dialects vs. the 'language of culture' on the other. It is not a presentation of *Modersmaalet* in its entirety, but rather *Modersmaalet* filtered through the 'living language' philosophy of J. Storm. Typically Stormian too is the paratactic ("stream-of-consciousness") structure, moving freely from topic to topic as they occurred to him. The lectures were evidently popular in the other sense of the word, since Storm reported that they were attended by an audience of around 100 listeners. A second series of popular lectures in 1883 seems to have been even more successful. Storm wrote to Thomsen on 7 May that this time he had an audience of nearly 200 at his lectures on 'The Characteristics of the Norwegian Dialect Groupings, with Several Linguistic Examples'. He also explains to Thomsen why he gives these popular series. He was not motivated by a love of the language alone:

> The fact is that I had made so many sacrifices to be able to devote my time to Norwegian dialects, that I became utterly bankrupt, and so I hit upon the idea of holding a course of popular lectures on language and dialects, and it surpassed expectations. I have had nearly 200 in the audience, and *earned* [. . .] roughly or a shade over Kr. 700 net, which happily has saved me from all my small financial embarrassments. I'm thinking later of continuing this business so as eventually to get rid of my debt.

There were indeed more popular lectures two years later, entitled *Language Development in Norway from the Middle Ages until the Present* and announced in *Morgenbladet* on 10 May 1885:[4]

> Professor Storm intends to hold in the immediate future a course of at least three lectures on 'Language Development in Norway from the Middle Ages until the Present'. The lectures will be held at the university, auditorium no. 4, Wednesdays and Saturdays from 6 until 7. First lecture Wednesday 13 May. Season tickets Kr. 2. Individual tickets Kr. 1, available from Cammermeyer's bookshop and on the door.

Later the same year (November), Storm went on tour and gave three lectures 'On the Norwegian Dialects and the Development of Language in Norway' in the neighbouring town of Drammen (see Storm's notes at NBO Ms. 4° 1285 F[xliv–xlv]), a shorter version of those given earlier in the year.

But these weren't the only lectures he gave on the Norwegian language. On 15 May 1878 he lectured on 'A bit of Old Norwegian language history' in the *Filologisk Forening* (Philological Union), and he held further lectures there (on Norwegian dialects) in October 1882. In January of the same year he held a lecture on 'Grouping the Norwegian Dialects' in the Academy of Sciences. His official lectures at the university also dealt with Norwegian. We can assume that his lectures on English and Romance languages made widespread use of Norwegian examples. He was, after all, addressing a Norwegian-speaking audience, and his publications, even those intended for an international audience, make frequent reference to Norwegian. But there were also scientific (as opposed to popular) lectures specifically focusing on

[4] Storm's notes are at NBO Ms. 4° 1285 F[xlvi].

Norwegian. Christen Collin's notes from Storm's lectures on phonetics, held from spring semester 1883 onwards, begin with Storm's statement of intent:

> So as not to get lost in the endless profusion of language data, it is most practical to start with our own language and use it for comparison with others. The sounds of the different languages are more or less never the same. (NBO Ms. forelesn. 1306:1)

(As we have seen in the previous chapters, this policy of 'starting with our own language' did not just apply to the teaching of phonetics.) Following a general introduction on human versus animal communication, language acquisition, reasons for language change and the relationship between the Scandinavian languages – a very similar introduction to the opening sections of his 1875 popular lectures – this lecture series goes on to deal essentially with historical Norwegian phonetics. Twenty years later *Aftenposten* announced a lecture series, which ran every Tuesday from 5 May until 24 November, explicitly dedicated to Norwegian phonetics (*Norwegian Transcription* – see notes at NBO 4° 1285 F[xxxviii]), rather than Norwegian phonetics masquerading as general phonetics, and again it is instructive to quote the description of the course in full:

> Professor Storm will in the coming semester begin a course on *Norwegian phonetics*. These lectures have long been anticipated by those interested in the subject, amongst other things because here for the first time complete and systematic guidance in the use of the transcription system composed by the professor will be given.
>
> Dr Amund B. Larsen will likewise use his *jus docendi* to hold a course of lectures on *The Development of Sounds in the Norwegian Dialects*. (14 January 1903)

Here the popular and learned meet, showing clearly how the distinction between practical and scientific language work did not really exist for Storm. Scientific phonetics goes hand in hand with practical language study, and it is for *everybody* – for 'those interested in the subject', yes, but worth announcing in a national newspaper too.

4.1.1.4 Storm's role in the language issue of the latter half of the nineteenth century was clear. He was better placed than anyone to consider the development of the language as a whole. He was recognised within and beyond the university as an authority. He understood language-internal variation in the dialects, and he could consider the language comparatively vis-à-vis Europe's other 'languages of culture' (*Kultursprog*) (an important concept for Storm); one of the 'main points' in his 1875 lecture plan was 'our language from a European standpoint'. He knew the history of the language and he had made a detailed study of its literary variety.

When Storm applied to parliament in 1877 for funding for the proposed

Værk over det norske Sprog, his opponents tried to belittle his competence to undertake such a study. It was 'G' (Arne Garborg) who expressed this scepticism about Storm's expertise in Norwegian most strongly:

It appears from looking at Prof. Storm's earlier publications that there is nothing in it which can be said to offer any guarantee whatsoever of his competence to write the linguistic history of Norway. One learns simply what one knew already: that Mr Storm is a distinguished Romanist, and that his speciality is phonetics. (*Aftenbladet*, 20 March 1877)

It is true that Storm had not published anything substantial on the language by this time, but Garborg's argument is really a front for his true objection to Storm's potentially being funded to write a historical study of Norwegian, an objection which emerges later in the article:

So not much more is to be expected than a treatment of the Dano-Norwegian urban language, viewed principally from the side of phonetics and explained in 'relation' to 'Danish' and 'Norwegian'.

Garborg's concerns about Storm's stance on the language were certainly well founded, but who else could have written such a work at this time? Gustav Indrebø (1889–1942), author of *Norsk Målsoga*, would not be born for another 12 years, and a sober study of the language and its history was, as Storm observed, needed to help contextualise the debates:

It is precisely at this moment that a history of the Norwegian language will be most timely of all, since there is so much dispute in language questions. (Storm 1877a: 1)

Little by little, as Storm published work on Norwegian, which he did with striking regularity from 1878 onwards, his authority came to be recognised. *Morgenbladet*, admittedly always Storm's most enthusiastic supporter, wrote in 1902 of 'the many and great services for which the professor has earned the gratitude of our language' (14 August).

So, despite his "official" expertise being in other languages, it was natural for Storm to take an active and influential role in the Norwegian language debates from early on in his career. He established his views early on too, and, as Holter (1986: 115) writes, 'Storm's views on Landsmål remained relatively unchanged from 1878 onwards'. What his views on Landsmål and the other varieties of Norwegian were, we shall see in due course.

So far in this chapter I have treated it as a straightforward fact that the Norwegian language was in some way in need of reform in the 19th century, and that there were heated debates on the subject to which Storm was an active and influential contributor. I do not intend to describe the language situation in detail, even though this book is not intended purely for an audience of Norwegian linguists who are already familiar with the ins and outs and ups and downs of nineteenth-century Norwegian linguistic debate.

There are summaries of the principal facts and figures available in "international" languages.[5] However, Storm was not a primary actor in the language question. Most of his contributions came in response to others' work or proposals. He was a commentator, an observer, a critic, as he so often was. We only have to think of *Engelsk Filologi/Englische Philologie* to see his preferred critical role in action, although he did devise and exemplify a reformed variety of Norwegian, as he did exemplify reformed methods of language teaching. Nonetheless, it was as critic that he was busiest. Consequently it would be unhelpful simply to present his critiques without at least outlining what he was responding to. Much of his critical writing on the subject of Norwegian language reform was directed quite specifically at the work and persons of two men, Ivar Aasen and Knud Knudsen, so we do at least need to hear from Aasen and Knudsen before we hear Storm's attacks on them.

4.1.2 *The Language Situation*

4.1.2.1 Once Norway became independent of Denmark in 1814, an independent Norwegian identity had to be established.[6] As we noted above, a common language is one of the most important markers of a shared identity. The common written language used in Norway up to 1814 was Danish, since until that time Norway and Denmark had a common political identity. The main thrust of cultural activity post-1814 was about showing how Norway was different from Denmark, how Norwegian culture was different from Danish culture, and, most important of all, how the Norwegian language was different from the Danish language – although naturally not all Norwegians advocated a complete break with the Danish tradition.

Various strategies were employed post-1814 to combat the fact that the written language was that of the foreign power to which Norway had been subjugated for 434 years. One of the more common solutions was to call the language *Modersmaalet*, the mother tongue, which was aimed to satisfy Danes and Norwegians alike. Løkke (1855), the first historical Danish/

---

[5] For historical background, Danielsen et al. (1991) is a detailed summary of Norwegian history, written in Norwegian. Also written (mostly) in Norwegian is the invaluable series of studies of the development of Norwegian national identity during the nineteenth century (*Utviklingen av en norsk nasjonal identitet på 1800-tallet*), culminating in Sørensen (1998). The chief English-language histories are still Popperwell (1972) and Derry (1973); Midgaard (1989) is an admirable brief history. Libæk & Stenersen (1991) also includes a wide range of illustrations and is specifically intended for foreign readers who know very little about the history of Norway, or for that matter about contemporary Norway. Skard (1967–1980), although incomplete, is a clear outline of the history of the language up to the twentieth century. Indrebø (1951) is more impenetrable, but more detailed (to c.1850 only), and Jahr (1989) is a readable account of events in the nineteenth century. Burgun (1919; 1921) is written in French, and an English-language history of Norwegian can be found in Haugen (1976). The history of Norwegian linguistics is covered in English by Hovdhaugen et al. (2000), Linn (1997) and Linn (forthcoming).

[6] Much of this section is adapted from Linn (1997).

Norwegian grammar, employed this technique. The principal grammarian in
Norway during the years following independence was Mauritz Christopher
Hansen (1794–1842).[7] In 1822 he adopted this solution, taking the title
Forsøg til en Grammatik i Modersmaalet for his Danish grammar, which was
published in Kristiania. The third edition had the revised title *Grammatik i
det norske og danske Sprog*, since 'nobody can determine whether a book is
Danish or Norwegian if the title or perhaps just the place of publication is
removed' (1828: 4). The fourth edition of 1833 had a new title again – *Norsk
Grammatik* – although the language described is indistinguishable from
Danish.

Tinkering with the name of the language was not enough, however, and
many felt that a more radical strategy was required, that a completely new
language system was needed to express the identity of the new nation. The
question of the appropriateness of Danish as the sole written language in
Norway had in fact been in the air for some time, even prior to independence.
The most explicit expression of dissatisfaction with the status quo was the
appendix to Gregers Fougner Lundh's (1786–1836) *Ny Samling af norske Ord
og Talemaader*, which was entitled *Hvorfor har Norge ikke sit eget Sprog?*
[Why does Norway not have its own language?]. Here Lundh proposes that
idioms should be collected in different parts of the country with the intention
of bringing this information together in a complete dictionary. This
programme of 1807 prophesies what would later be done by Ivar Aasen,
but, although there had already been sporadic work collecting dialect data in
Norway, and although there was a demand for reform, the political
circumstances did not yet allow such a reform to take place.

4.1.2.2 *Aasen*

The work of Ivar Aasen resulted in the variety of Norwegian known to
Storm as *Landsmaal* and renamed *Nynorsk* in 1929.[8] Storm would not have
been happy with the label *Nynorsk*. In polemical style he wrote that the
language was neither *nynorsk* nor *oldnorsk*, but 'an abstraction, a utopia, an
idea unsupported by reality' (1878a: 425). Aasen travelled around Norway
and collected dialect forms, which he later standardised in grammars and
dictionaries. His dialect work was very different to Storm's. Storm's
dialectology was underpinned by modern linguistics, and specifically by
the insights and methods of phonetics, whereas Aasen's work was much
more traditional. Aasen's methodology may have been unsophisticated from
the point of view of modern linguistics, but it was highly systematic, and he

[7] Hansen's first name is usually spelled with a final ⟨s⟩ – *Maurits*. However, as Storm points
out in 'Ibsen og det norske Sprog' (Storm 1898a), Hansen's preferred spelling was with a ⟨z⟩.
[8] More has been written about Aasen than about any other Norwegian linguist. Note, in
addition to Linn (1997), the three comprehensive works from the Aasen centenary year of 1996:
Krokvik (1996), Venås (1996a) and Walton (1996).

was able to draw out the common features underlying the variation exhibited by the dialects. Aasen looked for unity, for the common Norwegian which lay below the surface of the spoken language, but Storm was concerned first and foremost with data, with the facts of the living language. Having seen how Storm approached English and the Romance languages, it should not surprise us to find that his goal was to catalogue the *variety* in Norwegian dialects rather than discover a unifying system. Storm was fully aware that he and Aasen differed from each other in this respect:

> Every dialect is one key of a particular sort of sound. Aasen has selected the harmonious notes and unified them in a choir or a beautiful chord. We on the other hand let every dialect sing its own melody in its own register and compare the character of the different tone pictures. (Storm 1884a: 7, n. 1)

Aasen did more than record dialect data and systematise his findings. He went on to use the resulting language system, Landsmål, himself. The first attempt appeared in 1849, extraordinarily given that organ's later right-wing affiliations, in *Morgenbladet*.[9] This was the *Samtale imellem to Bønder* (Conversation between Two Farmers). His 1853 *Prøver af Landsmaalet i Norge* contained the first attempt to write in the new language in a published book.

Storm and Aasen had great respect for each other. We know that Storm respected Aasen because he says so repeatedly in his writings, and Aasen seems to have respected Storm. In 1878 Storm fulminated against the unscientific work of those involved in the Landsmål movement:

> Little is produced in the field of Modern Norwegian [*nynorsk*] philology. The Nynorsk movement, which is represented by the Landsmaal activists [*maalstræverne*] seeks in the main to write books in the newly created 'Landsmaal' and to get this recognised as a national language. (Storm 1878b: 3)

But then he singles out Aasen, 'the old master', as 'an honourable exception amongst the maalstræverne'. Aasen's work possessed 'all the conditions to satisfy the demands of science as well as beauty' (Storm 1885a: 3). Storm had little respect for linguists who were not scientific, who did not approach language in a serious, careful and informed spirit, but Aasen was evidently "one of us". Later, in his most programmatic writing on Norwegian philology, the *Introduction* to *Norvegia* (Storm 1884a), Storm ranks Aasen with the founders of Germanic and Romance philology:

---

[9] Krokvik (1996: 157) writes that '*Morgenbladet* has a mixed history behind it', and from 1831 to 1857 the paper was pretty much the organ of the radical rural left in parliament, with A. B. Stabell as editor-in-chief and collaborators like Henrik Wergeland and Ludvig Kristensen Daa. Later the paper became more conservative and supported the government and the bourgeoisie.

Just as the two great German linguists, *Jacob Grimm* for the Germanic languages and *Friedrich Diez* for the Romance, have provided the pioneering work, on which others have been able to build, so *Ivar Aasen* has done the same for the Norwegian dialects. He is the father of Norwegian linguistics. (p. 7)

This is praise indeed from Storm. If Storm could criticise, he certainly would, but he sets Aasen up on a plinth with the other 'fathers'. As Holter noted, Storm is absolutely constant in his view of Aasen and the language he created, and indeed some of his warmest words come in 1896 as a post mortem tribute to Aasen:

It is recognised by all parties that, with his death, a great man has passed away, a man of fundamental importance for the Norwegian people.

Ivar Aasen was great in everything he did. Even his Landsmaal was a magnificent experiment, great in its thinking and great in its formation. Although it cannot attain general validity, it will nonetheless stand for us as an ideal, a symbol to show us what is Norwegian. (Storm 1896c: Preface)

We shall see later why Storm thought that Landsmål/Nynorsk could not 'attain general validity', and we shall consider whether or not he was right in his predictions. But Vinje's (1978: 206) characterisation of Storm is too simplistic:

Johan Storm was Landsmål's most dangerous opponent. He was, moreover, a sticker. Right up to 1907 he was the bitterest opponent of the Landsmål movement and of the Norwegianising movement [*målmennenes og fornorskingsmennenes argeste motstander*].[10]

Venås's description of Storm as 'one of the hardest language-political opponents of Aasen' (Venås 1996: 1) also needs to be interpreted carefully. Dangerous he was, but not a single-minded danger to Aasen or his Landsmål. What Storm attacked was anything he saw as artificial in language, anything which went contrary to the idea of *det levende Sprog*. In some respects his views about the natural development of the language echo those of P. A. Munch from the 1850s (see T. Knudsen (1923) and Hoel (1996: 165–172)), but Storm's *levende Sprog* is a scientifically conceived entity, versus Munch's Romantic *Sprogaand* (Spirit of the Language). Storm was the

[10] This is a description of Storm which stuck to him. Mentions of Storm in the secondary literature are few, but they are nevertheless extraordinarily uniform. Longum (1989: 78) also calls Storm *en av målbevegelsens farligste motstandere* ('one of the language movement's most dangerous opponents'). Nygaard (1945: 95) describes Storm as *"nystavernes" argeste fiende* ('the worst enemy of the "new spellers"'). "Dangerous" and "bitter" are the epithets Storm has been saddled with in the literature on the history of Norwegian. They provide an interesting comparison with the "outstanding" and "highly gifted" Storm of the international literature (see section 1.8). See Linn (2003b) for a more detailed discussion of this issue.

'most dangerous opponent' of artificial, insensitive, ignorant intervention in language, any language. He was full of admiration for Ivar Kleiven's 1894 collection of folk texts written in the dialect of Gudbrandsdalen (Storm 1895c), and he certainly had nothing against Landsmål in the form in which Aasen created it. The section on Landsmål in *Norsk Sprog: Kraakemaal og Landsmaal* begins with praise for the language:

Norwegian Landsmaal is a beautiful language.
It is the language of the heroic ballads, of fairy tales and folk tales.
We read Vinje and Ivar Aasen, Garborg and Mortenson; we are seized by a strange power. (1896c: 70)

He used a disparaging name for Knudsen's language (*Kraakemaal*, 'crow language', 'gobbledygook'), but not for Aasen's Landsmål. Throughout his life he held the language and its creator in the highest regard. It was other Landsmål activists and official policy with regard to the language that made him see red. It was not only Aasen and Kleiven whom Storm respected. He was always enthusiastic about any good, scientific work on the Norwegian dialects. In 1896 he bore no unkind feelings towards Hans Ross (see section 4.2.1.2) and his continuation of Aasen's *Norsk Ordbog*, writing:

Only those who have engaged to any extent in similar studies will be able to appreciate what amount of unstinting love, devotion and patience is required to bring about such a collection. (Storm 1896b)

Storm, Aasen, Ross and even Kleiven were, in Storm's eyes, colleagues and not enemies.

It might surprise us to discover that Aasen and Storm did not spend more time together, when they had so much in common. However, they could not have been more different as people. Storm was the son of a priest, a professor, and firmly embedded in the bourgeoisie. Once Aasen became a published writer, an employee of the Establishment and a resident of the capital city, he took on the surface plumage of the bourgeoisie, but it only went skin-deep. Storm was married with a large family and had a demanding job within some of the leading Norwegian institutions. Aasen, by contrast, had no family or professional ties, and he had little or nothing to do with the university as an institution (see Venås 2000a). They were simply very different people and they looked at each other from a distance. In Aasen's case, he literally did look at Storm from a distance, as one of the audience at his 'popular lectures' of 1875 and at the phonetics lectures of 1883. Aasen's diaries and letters (Aasen 1957–1960) show that he visited Storm on several occasions and was also visited by him (see summary in Venås 2000a: 79). These social visits seem always to have been in the company of others, and there is no evidence that the relationship between the two men was anything more than polite. On 31 July 1877 Storm took Sweet to see Aasen. This visit was for Sweet's benefit rather than Storm's, and Aasen does not appear to have enjoyed it much either, his only comment on it being 'much delay' (Aasen 1960: 317). It is interesting to note that Aasen himself was a part of the 'Tour of Norwegian Curiosities' laid on for visitors from overseas. In a review of *Det nynorske Landsmaal* (Storm 1888a), published in the *Saturday Review* for 19 January 1889, Sir Edmund Gosse (1849–1928) recollects his 1873 visit to Aasen, to 'the tiny man in his tiny house'.[11] The only surviving correspondence between Aasen and Storm concerns the publication of the *Kortere Ordliste* (Storm 1884b). Storm wrote to Aasen on 14 June 1883, enquiring whether there was, from Aasen's point of view,

> anything to prevent my printing at the Society's expense a short *extract* from my Wordlist, containing in addition examples for the *Grammar* together with a short explanation of the *transcription system*. (NBO Brevsamling 174)

This is a very formal piece, exhibiting none of the personal style to be found, for example, in the letters to Thomsen. Storm needed Aasen's agreement to the publication of the *Kortere Ordliste*, since Aasen was one of those who had in 1881 founded the *Forening for norske Dialekter og Folketraditioner* (see section 4.3.2.1) and so had to agree to anything carried out under the name of and at the expense of the Society. Aasen's reply was equally formal, and in fact exists in two versions (Aasen 1958: 217), indicating that Aasen was at pains to formulate a correct response, a lengthy and formal 'OK':

> As to your plan for an interim presentation of a wordlist and collection of examples, I must say that I am not aware of anything to prevent it. I think on the contrary that it is a fortunate idea.

So Storm's relationship with Aasen was essentially a good one. They kept each other at arm's length socially, because they were not natural companions, but each showed respect for the other's work. They may have been in disagreement about what that work on the Norwegian language should be used for and how it could contribute to the development of the written language, but it is basically wrong to view them as having been opposed to each other. As Storm saw it, their dialect work was complementary.

4.1.2.3 Aasen's Landsmål rapidly proved to be an attractive model for those who wished to write a form of Norwegian closer to their own dialect than to Danish, and writers from those parts of Norway where Danish was a particularly foreign language followed in Aasen's footsteps. These included writers like Garborg and Vinje, whom Storm mentions with admiration in the quotation above (Storm 1896c: 70). Storm begins to part company from the Landsmål ethos at the point where it seeks to become a 'land' language in another sense of that word: not just the language of the countryside, but a

---

[11] Gosse assumes Aasen to be dead here, although he would live for another seven years!

language for the whole country. The early Landsmål writers used Aasen as a model, yes, but as a model for a written language based on their own dialects. Landsmål soon became, in Haugen's words, 'a plaything of idealistic linguists and poets' (Haugen 1966: 36), and, despite the presence of Aasen's 1864 *Norsk Grammatik* and 1873 *Norsk Ordbog* as yardsticks, Landsmål was in reality rife with variation and formal disagreement. The most extreme form of experimentation was in the Bergen School of language reform, and it found its most radical exemplification in Jan Prahl's 1858 *Ny Hungrvekja*.[12] Storm felt strongly that the practical reality of Landsmål, of a variety in which anybody was free to introduce their own forms, made it unfit to be a truly national language:

How is one to learn to write a language which does not exist in a spoken form, which is not based on any tradition and which is written differently by each and every language activist [*Maalstræver*]? (Storm 1878a: 422)

In this quotation we have the essence of Storm's objection, not to Aasen or to what in 1896 he called Aasen's 'grand experiment', but to the Landsmål *movement*. Storm was a member of the bourgeoisie, and Landsmål smelt very much like a Norwegian for the radicals, or at least like the language of the left wing, so Storm and the Landsmål movement were not likely to find an ideological meeting point. However, Storm's objections, often and vehemently expressed as they were, did not rest on ideological arguments. Storm had studied the history of other national languages, of some of the most influential and long-established European standard languages, and he knew what characterised a standard language. He knew that they grew from the spoken language, he knew that they developed via tradition and agreement. So his essential objections to Landsmål were not the red-necked rantings of a conservative. They were the measured arguments of someone who knew about languages and how they develop. Of course, since we know Storm to have been conservative, it is perhaps hard to disentangle the man from the linguist, but, as we shall see, there is little reason simply to label Storm according to a bipolar process of language reform. There were the reformers, loosely associated with the political left wing, and there were the language conservatives loosely associated with the political right wing. Storm was politically right-wing, but his linguistic views were not simply those of the Right. As with the question of language-teaching reform, he was a practical realist in matters relating to reform of the national language. He held no other position than his own. His practical, rational view (he always described himself as 'moderate') was the product of his intellectual schizo-phrenia. He was a Norwegian who loved the Norwegian language, but he

---

[12] For a contemporary assessment of the Bergen School from the hand of an opponent, see Mohn (1868). For a recent re-evaluation of the School, and of Prahl in particular, from a partisan hand, see Krokvik (1993).

was also the European, looking in at Norwegian with the eyes of a European outsider.

We need to put some flesh on these bones, and we shall do so by working through Storm's major publications on the language reform question. Before doing so, we must briefly complete the story of Aasen's Landsmål and see what happened to it after the first generation of disagreement and 'Dilettanteri' (Storm 1878a: 429).

4.1.2.4 Storm prophesied a gloomy fate for Landsmål (1896c: 114–115):

We do not wish for Landsmaal's demise; let those, for whom it is natural to do so, write it [. . .] but if it is forced on those for whom it is alien, then it will not be possible to conceal the fact that it is an artificial and randomly put together dialect language, and it will suffer the fate of all artificial languages:

it will pass quietly away.

If Landsmål had been left to its own devices, even with the support of its followers, it is doubtful whether it would have developed into much more than a 'grand experiment', a historical curiosity like *Ny Hungrvekja*. From the very beginning though, Aasen's Landsmål had had official support. Aasen received a personal stipend, and the publication of the 1864 grammar, the framework on which the new standard would hang, was financed by the Royal Academy of Sciences. The first two decades of Landsmål's life were, as we have seen, marked by experiment and deviation from the Aasen norm, but political events of 1884 led to further political support to advance the Landsmål cause. One of the first acts of the new left-wing parliament was to throw itself behind Landsmål. It moved that the government 'be requested to pass the necessary resolution for putting the Norwegian folk-language on the same footing as our normal language of writing, as the language of education and of public affairs' (*anmodes om at træffe fornøden Forføining til, at det norske Folkesprog som Skole- og officielt Sprog sidestilles med vort almindelige Skrift- og Bogsprog*) (*Storthings Forhandlinger* 1885: 17, 755). During the 1880s and 1890s a series of resolutions strengthened the official position of Landsmål, authorising its equal status in a variety of public forums. With 1905 and the independence of Norway from Sweden came a wave of national feeling 'which brooked no compromise with the foreign on any point, but craved the right of undiminished Norwegianness in all areas' (Nygaard 1945: 105). This helped bring public sympathy for Landsmål into line with the political sympathy of the previous decades.

Although Landsmål had public backing, it did not yet have a universally accepted standard. Aasen's norm was already felt to be archaic or exclusive, and writers continued to adapt Landsmål to suit themselves and to adapt it to their own spoken usage. Storm's vigorous and persuasive criticism of the lack of a Landsmål standard galvanised the government into action. A committee was set up, and this committee presented its report in 1899, the year in which Hægstad was appointed *professor i landsmål og dets dialekter* at the university. Hægstad was on the committee, and, despite his minority views, it was Hægstad's conservative spelling (in the direction of Aasen's norm) which was eventually sanctioned in 1901. For obvious reasons Storm was not involved in the official debates surrounding the standardisation of Landsmål, but his authority and the sheer volume of his uninvited contributions to the debate were such that his voice could not be ignored.

4.1.2.5 *Knudsen*

Knud Knudsen was badly treated in his own lifetime, not least by Storm, and posterity has been unkind to him too. In his review of Knudsen's *Unorsk og norsk* in *Morgenbladet*, Storm wrote:

> Knudsen has lived out his whole life for his one idea, the Norwegianisation of the language. To that end he has lived a lonely and frugal life. To that end he has sacrificed large amounts of his hard-earned savings. There is something moving about this faithful adherence to a life's goal. (Storm 1881b)

Worse was to come. We remember the fine epitaph Storm gave Aasen in 1896. Knudsen had died the year before, and this is what Storm finds it in his heart to write about him:

> There are certain natural talents, certain senses which are denied Knudsen: a taste for that which is beautiful; an eye for reality; an ear for the nuances of sounds and the euphony of the language. (Storm 1896c: 2–3)

Such a personal attack was quite unnecessary, and harsh even by Storm's standards. Knudsen has remained fair game in the secondary literature, and Haugen (1966), which is a classic account of the history of modern Norwegian, takes up the cudgels, describing Knudsen's untiring work for the cause as 'tireless and occasionally tiresome efforts' (p. 49). A cheap pun. If Knudsen's efforts did become tiresome, it was because he was forced to defend himself so frequently.

History has made Aasen into a national hero, but it has tended to ignore Knudsen, even though history has at the same time shown Knudsen's language programme to have been more successful and, at the same time, more extraordinary than Aasen's. The centenary of Aasen's death unleashed three substantial biographies, a touring exhibition, and much more, including a comic strip (Osland & Midthun 1996). The centenary of Knudsen's death a year earlier passed virtually unremarked. There were, as far as I am aware, just three brief articles: one, based, like my account below, very closely on Seip (1936), in *Språknytt* (Lundeby 1995), the journal of the

Norwegian Language Council; the others in newspapers.[13] A web search of Knudsen's name, turns up nothing. In his article on Aasen and Knudsen in the volume of *Språknytt* celebrating *Aasen's* centenary, Arne Torp wrote:

> There is scarcely any adult Norwegian who has not heard of Aasen, and most probably also know considerably more about him than just the name. If you ask after Knud Knudsen, there are by contrast many whose gaze begins to flicker, while others have the answer ready to hand: He was a good cyclist![14] (Torp 1996: 8)

Why has Knudsen become such a dim figure in the history of the Norwegian language, when the existence of modern Bokmål, the predominant written language of the modern country, is due to his vision and work? Knudsen slipped into the shadows the same way that Storm did. His views and his proposals tended to be regarded as conservative compared with those of Aasen and, particularly after the political events of 1905 and full independence, did not fit so well with the national mood. Furthermore, the ideas and work of men like Storm and Knudsen did not so readily inspire followers and supporters.

Since nineteenth-century Norwegian language reform was personified by the two men, Aasen and Knudsen, it is easy to conceive it in terms of Aasen at one end of the spectrum and Knudsen at the other. However, Knudsen was not a language conservative. He was a reformer just as much as Aasen. In fact the man Knudsen and the Knudsen programme had a great deal in common with their opposite numbers in Aasen. What is more, all three linguists – Aasen, Knudsen and Storm – representing three clearly different approaches to reform were in essence in agreement. They all agreed that an independent Norway needed an independent Norwegian language, which was distinct from Danish. They all agreed that it should have its basis in actual usage. In theory, then, they were of one mind. They parted company from each other on the question of what usage should be followed, and, more fundamentally, on the question of methodology. On the face of it, Knudsen and Storm did agree methodologically, that the written language should be reformed along the lines of what Knudsen, in his 1867 *Det norske målstræv* and elsewhere, called 'the educated spoken language [*det dannede talesprog*]' according to 'our nationally agreed pronunciation [*vår landsgyldige uttale*]' (see Knudsen 1867: vi), and what Storm called 'the living, educated spoken language [*det levende, dannede Talesprog*]' (1888a: 115). Storm's *levende* is the all-important difference in his formulation, but in essence they both meant the urban, supra-regional spoken standard:

---

[13] My thanks to Kjell Venås for help with these references. There may be other items which I have not found.
[14] The "other" (Knut) Knudsen (born 1950) was an international cyclist, and gold medal winner at the 1972 Olympic Games. My own gaze began to flicker until Arne Torp was kind enough to provide me with this information!

I have always agreed with the principle underlying Knudsen's language reform programme, that of basing the written language on the living, educated spoken language, which is becoming more and more Norwegian with each generation. It is just when he wants to move more quickly than the language itself that I part company. (1888a: 115)

As always, it was the artificial which really offended Storm, and which made him such a vigorous and offensive opponent of poor Knudsen. Any attempts to meddle with the natural life of the language were to Storm like a red rag to a bull. In passing it is worth quoting his own definition of his model variety, 'det almindelige dannede Talesprog':

By 'the general educated spoken language' I understand that which is spoken by the educated classes, not only in the towns and cities, but also round about across the whole country. (Storm 1896c: 7, n. 1)

Storm and Knudsen were not friends, and indeed any respect they may have had for each other in the early days soon evaporated. When Storm first began to write about the reform question, he certainly had his reservations about Knudsen's programme, but he also gave credit where credit was due. In 'Norsk literaturoversigt for 1877 og nærmest foregaaende aar' (Storm 1878b) he accused Knudsen of lack of consistency; this is an accusation which would reappear and reappear, but the accusation is tempered somewhat:

If the author had been consistent in this [in the use of voiceless plosives], his orthography would have been of philological interest by presenting the language as it really is [. . .] Despite this and despite a load of neologisms, the book contains many good observations. (p. 4)

Storm even allows himself a personal compliment:

By his dedicated endeavours for Norwegianness in speech and in writing throughout many years, Knudsen has exercised a great and a beneficial influence. (p. 4)

Three years later, however, came the review of Knudsen's *Unorsk og norsk*, and any generosity towards Knudsen and his programme has disappeared for good. So what went wrong? How did grudging respect turn into concerted attack in the space of three years?

It seems as though war was actually declared by Knudsen, who was very sensitive to attacks on his programme, as well he might have been. As we shall see, Storm's *Det norske Maalstræv* of 1878 dealt almost entirely with the Landsmål programme and only made brief and (relatively speaking) positive reference to Knudsen's programme towards the end (see section 4.1.3.1.5). However, Knudsen reacted very strongly to what Storm wrote, and published a rebuttal in *Dagbladet* in July 1879. He was made all the more furious because this rebuttal was not accepted by *Morgenbladet*. He immediately spotted a conspiracy between Storm and the right-wing press. He was not being wholly rational, but he was clearly very upset, and his 1879 *Dagbladet* piece, reprinted under the title 'Morgenbladet og Professor J. Storm mod Overlærer K. Knudsen' in Knudsen (1881b: 1–19), is rather pathetic, in the literal sense of that word. When Storm counter-attacked two years later with his review of Knudsen's *Unorsk og norsk* (Storm (1881b) – see section 4.1.3.2), they were sworn enemies. Had Knudsen not reacted so viciously in 1879, I suspect that Storm would have remained more support-ive towards his programme, and the two men might even have found common ground. Maybe not, but a personality clash here certainly made things much worse for Knudsen than they need have been.

Since Knudsen has been comparatively overlooked by the historiography of Norwegian linguistics,[15] I will take the opportunity here to say something more about him and his work, before, at last, going on to address in proper detail Storm's contributions to the debates, and specifically his engagement with Aasen's and Knudsen's programmes.

4.1.2.6 Knud Knudsen was born in 1812 in the parish of Holt, near Tvedestrand on Norway's south coast.[16] The external facts of his life are simply told. They comprise, as Seip (1936: 476) puts it:

> the not uncommon tale of the talented smallholder's son, who, by virtue of his own endeavours, and via support from well-to-do admirers who had noticed his talents, advanced by way of study to the realms of public service.

It was clear from an early age that Knudsen was destined to become a teacher, and most of his working life (from 1846 to 1880) was spent on the staff of Kristiania Cathedral School, in which capacity he taught the young J. Storm. Storm wrote to Thomsen (23 September 1880) that, because Knudsen had been his teacher, he did not enjoy writing the critical review of *Norsk og unorsk*. His was not, then, the romantic life of the lonely traveller, like Aasen's, but one of daily toil at the heart of one of Norway's principal institutions. By contrast with Storm, however, he had little time for the traditional classical education offered by his school and by the university, and he campaigned from the 1830s onwards for a weakening of the classical stranglehold and a strengthening of the position of the modern subjects. The school legislation of 1869, which provided Storm with his job, was something Knudsen regarded as a personal triumph. By 1870 Storm had much to thank Knudsen for.

---

[15] Published works in which Knudsen receives more than just passing consideration are Bleken (1956), Dahl (1962) and Hoel (1996: 61–225).

[16] See Knudsen's *Livsminner* (Knudsen 1937) and *Reiseminner* (Knudsen 2001). See also Seip (1936).

Knudsen continued to campaign for curriculum reform until his death, and he witnessed further battles won in this war. In place of the traditional classical education, Knudsen envisaged a 'national-humanist' curriculum with Norwegian (including Old Norwegian) as the principal subject. It was via his work for Norwegian in the schools that he became involved with the "language question". He was inspired by the proposals of Rask and Niels Matthias Petersen (1791–1862) in Denmark for a spelling system that better reflected the spoken language, and Knudsen's first linguistic publication appeared in 1845 in the journal *Nor* under the title 'Om Lydene, Lydtegnene og Retskrivningen i det norske Sprog' (On the sounds, symbols and ortho-graphy of the Norwegian language). Here he set out some of the proposals which would dog reform debate until into the next century, specifically the introduction of 'hard' (voiceless) consonants in those environments (post-vocalic) where written Danish had 'soft' ones (⟨b, d, g⟩ for ⟨p, t, k⟩), and short forms of various words (e.g. *Far* for *Fader*, *ta* for *tage* or *bli* for *blive*). These are all issues Storm is still addressing in detail in his *Norsk Retskrivning* 60 years later.

Knudsen was not an extremist, despite the spin Storm gave him, and drew the line at certain possible reform principles, such as using Old Norwegian as a model, which some of those in the more radical Landsmål camp advocated. Around 1850 he saw Aasen very much as his colleague, and welcomed the fruits of Aasen's labours as a source for the Norwegianisation of the written language, particularly in enriching the vocabulary. As the 1850s progressed, Knudsen's ideal rapidly became politicised via debate in the press (see Seip 1936: 482), and in the middle of the decade he published his major linguistic opus, the *Haandbog i dansk-norsk Sproglære* (Handbook of Dano-Norwegian Grammar) (Knudsen 1856), explaining and exemplify-ing his programme for the Norwegianisation of the language, based on the ordinary speech of the capital. His programme was beginning to move away from the Landsmål programme, and with *Det norske målstræv* (Knudsen 1867) he showed where the differences lay and where the two approaches – the 'norsknorske' ('oldnorsk-norske' or 'islandsk-norske') and the 'dansk-norske' (or 'skandinavisk-norske') (1867: 1) – had common ground. Much of *Det norske målstræv* concerns points of difference, but the essential goal remains a shared one:

All our language activists have in common the fact that they want the language of Norway to be as Norwegian as the language of Denmark is Danish, Sweden Swedish, Germany German, or – since these are not as national in their own countries as would be desirable – if possible even better, even more Norwegian and national. (Knudsen 1867: 3)

One of his major preoccupations was the replacement of foreign lexicon in Norwegian with more "native" vocabulary, and it was this "artificial" activity which provoked such ire in Storm. Knudsen's major publication in this field was the dictionary, *Unorsk og norsk*, which appeared in instalments from 1879 to 1881, and complete with preface and *Efterskrift* in 1881. Knudsen published other pamphlets throughout his life, expounding and defending his 'dansk-norsk' position, emphasising differences and commonalities between his own programme and the Landsmål one. He was not first and foremost a scholar, but he was passionate in his causes. This made him an easy target for unforgiving intellectuals like Storm, and much of Knudsen's life was spent locked in battle with protagonists on both sides of the linguistic–political divide, with Vinje, Garborg and Ross as much as with L. K. Daa, Storm and Western. Much of the preface to *Unorsk og norsk* is given over to Knudsen's responses to adverse criticism in the press. His very last published words appeared posthumously in *Morgenbladet* on 9 June 1895 (he had died on 4 March), headed 'K.K.'s sidste Ord om Maalstrævet' (K.K.'s last word on the language struggle) and entitled 'Prof. Joh. Storm, "Morgenbladet" og målstrævet' (Knudsen 1895). Here he wrote:

> I have probably not yet uttered my final word either on the subject of these double forms or on much more besides.

But he had. It is sad that Knudsen should have had to carry on fighting even unto death, especially as the form of Norwegian he fought for did ultimately find its supporters. His closing years were not all strife, however. He received a state pension of 3000 kroner per year, he was publicly feted on his 75th and 80th birthdays, and he was awarded the St Olav Cross for his work. He should be remembered for other contributions to nineteenth-century Norwegian life too. His role in the pan-Scandinavian movement was significant,[17] as was his role with Det norske Theater in its earliest years from 1852. He was responsible for training the actors to use 'det norske dannede talesprog', while the actors at the Christiania Theater still spoke pure Danish. Ibsen was artistic director at Det norske Theater, and Knudsen had a strong impact on Ibsen's language at that time.

What of his language programme? Knudsen was the pioneer in the programme which would eventually result in the Riksmål spelling reforms of 1907 (see section 4.1.3.6.1). The subsequent more radically Norwegianising reforms of 1917 and 1938, which by the 1950s had resulted in a Bokmål with pretensions to meet Nynorsk on the middle ground – the 'Samnorsk' programme – were Knudsen's legacy. In 1945, with the spectre of *Samnorsk* (Common Norwegian) hanging over Norwegian language politics, Nygaard wrote that Knudsen had:

> drawn up the foundation on which orthographic reform has built ever since. And if the goal is ever reached – one Norwegian written language in

---

[17] For an overview of the movement from a Norwegian perspective, see Sanness (1959) and Thorkildsen (1994). For a more general study, see Becker-Christensen (1981).

NORWEGIAN   235

Norway – Knud Knudsen must always be named as the one who laid the foundation for this programme and marked out the road it had to follow. Knud Knudsen did not live to see his plans carried out and the reforms officially sanctioned. But those men who fought through the orthography of 1907 operated in his spirit and felt themselves to be his disciples. (Nygaard 1945: 27)

More conservative tendencies in official Bokmål reform since 1950, and the fact that most writers of Bokmål today use very few of the Nynorsk-inspired grammatical or lexical forms available as alternatives in Bokmål, indicate that, 100 years on, and with decreased political engineering of the language, it is in fact Storm's legacy which has won through in the end. However, let us leave this evaluation until after we've seen what Storm's legacy is.

Aasen's work was impressive, but, according to Hovdhaugen et al. (2000: 240), 'Knudsen's work is even more remarkable, even unprecedented':

A parallel (suggested by Jan Terje Faarlund) might be that after the breakdown of the Soviet Union, the Ukraine had chosen not to use Russian or Ukrainian as its national language, but had chosen Russian as spoken by Ukrainians, adapted the orthography to this pronunciation and included numerous Ukrainian words, phrases, morpho-syntactic features which were widespread in this Ukrainian-Russian interlanguage.

A comparison of the five pages written to celebrate Knudsen's centenary in 1995 (Lundeby 1995) with the thousands of pages written about Aasen in 1996 points to a historiographical injustice. For better or for worse, Faarlund's rare linguistic bird is alive and well in Norway today. Perhaps its father and first champion will one day get the study he probably deserves.

4.1.3 *Storm's Position*

4.1.3.0 Storm stated his position on the reform of the language with his first publication on the subject, namely *Det norske Maalstræv* (The Norwegian Language Struggle) of 1878 (Storm 1878a), and that position remained constant throughout his life. His view was simple, and was based on the same linguistic philosophy which informed all his work, whether he was describing French syntax, providing language-teaching materials or writing a detailed guide to the study of English: the philosophy of *det levende Sprog*. Everything he argued about Norwegian and its development rested on the guiding principle that the language must develop naturally, that it must be allowed to live a normal life like other languages and that this natural development must not be stunted by any form of artificial intervention. His position was far from radical in any direction: it was one of moderation, of letting things happen in the fullness of time. Politicians and activists wanted change, however. They wanted the national standard language to be seen to be changed into Norwegian, as the nation had been officially seen to be transferred from Danish rule. Storm's position did not meet with much support in circles where it mattered, but he was too high-profile to be ignored, and he did have significant influence on the language movement – a constant, loud-voiced presence for 30 years. A hundred years on and it is time to review Storm's position in the light of the successes and failures of the Norwegian language reform movement. Was he right after all? We shall see.

Det norske Maalstræv – the same title as Knudsen (1867) – was not quite Storm's first word on the subject. He was already known to be an opponent of the contemporary Landsmål movement, and this is why, in his *Aften-bladet* article, Garborg had objected so strongly to Storm's 1877 application for public funding to write his proposed *Værk over det norske Sprog*. Storm's position was no secret, but it was often misconstrued, by Landsmål people and by Knudsen alike, as *arch-conservative*. The Landsmål camp and Knudsen felt themselves to be radicals in language matters, and Storm opposed their positions. Therefore he must be a language conservative, they concluded, but, as we shall see in greater detail in the course of the following sections, he wasn't. *De romanske Sprog og Folk* of 1871 had contained a few hints as to Storm's views on his native language, but the only statement there which explicitly deals with the reform of Norwegian shows him – rightly – to be a cautious moderniser:

> I shall give a brief account of my orthography. It is for the most part that which should now be regarded as the most general. In foreign loans I keep *c*, where it is pronounced as *s*, otherwise I change *c*, like *ch*, to *k*; *ph* I alter to *f*, but I keep *th*, though I write *t* after other consonants. (Storm 1871: Preface)

He began to argue more forcibly in his 1877 response to Garborg, also printed in *Aftenbladet*, and entitled 'Blind Alarm i Maalstrævernes Lejr' (Storm 1877b). Here he presented himself as the innocent scholar, dutifully trying to make an objective study of his beloved mother tongue, placed under ban by the *Maalstræverne*. Storm is being disingenuous here. Although he had not yet published anything on the subject, the language reformers knew they had good reason to fear Storm getting the opportunity to do so, and this is why (through their spokesman, Garborg) they were so keen to prevent Storm getting his public funding. The development of standard Norwegian in the late nineteenth century might have been very different if parliament had sponsored Storm's version of Norwegian language history, which would then have had the status of an official version, making Storm's position much harder to ignore (see section 4.2.1.2).

Perhaps the most effective means by which Storm had made his position known prior to 1877 was the popular lectures of 1875. The audience was substantial, and if Aasen was there, we can assume that other active linguists were there too, listening to him 'go at the Norwegian language activists or the reform programme (*Maalmænd eller Maalstrævet*), and considerably harder at that than the innocent programme seemed to promise', as *Verdens Gang* reported it on 10 April.

4.1.3.1 Det norske Maalstræv *(1878)*

4.1.3.1.1 Why did Storm make his first written statements about Norwegian language reform in 1878, when he was busy working on *Engelsk Filologi*? Both *Det norske Maalstræv* and *Engelsk Filologi* were written following the disappointment of 1877. As we saw in Chapter 2, with *Engelsk Filologi* Storm symbolically turned his back on Norwegian. This was the negative response, and *Det norske Maalstræv* (*DnM*) was a more positive one. We also saw in Chapter 2 how the young Storm of *De romanske Sprog og Folk* reached maturity through *Engelsk Filologi*, and the same maturing process is happening in *DnM*. Storm is establishing what he stands for.

DnM is in many ways the best piece that Storm wrote on the subject of language reform. It concentrates on the Landsmål movement and only deals with Knudsen's programme very briefly, so Storm has not yet covered everything he would go on to cover. Nevertheless, his position is laid out clearly and persuasively, with just enough detail to support his arguments. As with later revisions of *Engelsk Filologi* and of *Franske Taleøvelser*, more does not mean better. With subsequent publications Storm brings in more examples and more case studies, but the same basic points get remade. Its querulous tone notwithstanding, the 1902 article in *Den 17. mai* ('Johan Storm on the warpath') had a fair point to make:

> At least once every equinox he has to come out. And it's always the same notes that "blast" out of him. He knows that people have short memories, so the thing is to grind out the same thing over and over again.

DnM is also a significant piece because it demonstrates, through its appeal to the living language, how Storm's polemical Norwegian work relates to the rest of his output. On the face of it his involvement in the language reform debates seems like a sideline to his serious, academic work on the modern foreign languages and on phonetics, but it is all joined together by the same "red thread".

4.1.3.1.2 *DnM* was published in two parts in the first volume of the journal *Nordisk Tidskrift för Vetenskap, Konst och Industri*. Through his Romance publications Storm showed that he was keen to support new journals – a support which usually dwindled after the first few issues of the journal had appeared. In addition to the two parts of *DnM*, Storm also contributed a literature review, 'Norsk (filologisk) literaturoversigt for 1877 og nærmest foregaaende aar' (Storm 1878b), to this volume. *Nordisk Tidskrift* was a wide-ranging journal, a more academic version of the Norwegian *Illustreret Nyhedsblad* (in which he had published 'Tale og Accent i Forhold til Sang'), and it was a natural place for him to publish, given the lack of appropriate specialist journals in 1877. His brother Gustav also contributed a review of Norwegian historical literature.

DnM is in theory a review of Arne Garborg's 1877 book, *Den nynorske Sprog- og Nationalitetsbevægelse: Et Forsøg paa en omfattende Redegjørelse, formet som polemiske Sendebreve til Modstræverne* (The New Norwegian Movement for Language and Nationality: An Attempt at a Comprehensive Account in the Form of Polemical Letters to its Opponents). I don't believe it to be an accident that Storm's first published contribution to the reform debates was explicitly an attack on Garborg, smarting as Storm still was from the events of 1877 and from Garborg's public attack on him and on his competence to write about Norwegian. *DnM*, though, goes well beyond being a straightforward review of Garborg's book.

The first part of *DnM* (pp. 407–416) gives the background to the Landsmål movement. Storm opens with praise for Aasen ('our genius of a linguist' (p. 407)) and his work. Aasen's 1848 grammar ('this epoch-making work' (p. 408)), *Det norske Folkesprogs Grammatik*, is praised for its presentation of the Norwegian dialects and for the brilliantly clear system it adopts. Aasen may have concentrated on certain dialects at the expense of others, but Storm does not object to that. Neither does he explicitly object to the norm Aasen proposes via his 1853 *Prøver af Landsmaalet i Norge* being rooted in western Norwegian dialects; and yet, by means of his presentation of one of Aasen's best-known poems, *Dei gamle Fjelli* (The ancient mountains) (from the collection *Symra*) Storm begins insidiously to expose weaknesses in Landsmål. Criticism of Aasen's norm is implicit in the 17 footnotes to the poem. The implication is of course that Aasen's norm is not universally comprehensible, and that 17 of the words or forms need explanation for most readers. Later on in *DnM* he summarises his position on Aasen's Landsmål:

> Beautiful this language certainly is, but at best it is only appropriate for a small part of the country, namely the diocese of Bergen, whose population in 1875 was around 250,000 people. (p. 415)

Storm's method here is subtle. All his *explicit* comments on the poem are gushingly positive:

> Later Aasen published various writings in this language, and has even shown himself to be a poet of rank, as in that beautiful and atmospheric poem, *Dei gamle Fjelli*, which we here permit ourselves to reprint. (p. 410)

He gives the footnotes, and then he simply moves on.

Storm is not so full of praise for the first generation of Landsmål writers, but he is still very positive about their work. He describes Vinje as 'highly talented', and states that his poetry 'soars to quite a different level to Ivar Aasen's, but it is no simple national verse, it is cultured poetry' (p. 411). And herein lies the second problem for Landsmål. When Landsmål expresses higher or 'cultured' notions (*Kulturbegreber*), it alienates the people on whose language it is based and for whom it is intended as a more natural form of expression. So Storm has now implied that the putative new national language is incomprehensible for those who do not know the dialects on which it is based and incomprehensible for those who do. Storm exaggerates, but he had so much linguistic data at his disposal that he could find examples to support any position, and this first written statement of his views in response to Garborg's polemic is itself nothing if not polemical.

Lack of comprehensibility was not an issue as long as Landsmål remained a scientific experiment in the recording and use of dialect forms. Storm becomes an *Antimaalstræver*, as he described himself in a letter to Thomsen (31 May 1877), at the point where the private work of a few talented individuals becomes a *Stræv*, a movement, at the point where, with every new practitioner, there is a 'split in Landsmaal'. Being a member of the bourgeoisie, Storm did not like radical activity or "movements" in any shape or form. His dissatisfaction with the 'radical majority in parliament' once bubbled to the surface in his correspondence with Thomsen:

> The political situation is, as you probably know, wretched. The radical majority in parliament stops at nothing by way of dirty tricks, and does not or will not understand that we are losing more and more in the eyes of the civilised world. But enough of this. All our hopes are fixed on the new election. If this goes wrong, it will be intolerable to live here. (17 April 1894)

This is probably one reason why he so conspicuously remained outside societies which, like Quousque Tandem, represented movements. Temperamentally he didn't like radical activity, and this was one of the express reasons why he found the Landsmål movement objectionable. Something that started off as a scientific investigation into the dialects, and therefore close to Storm's heart, was soon, and regrettably, 'associated with political agitation' (1878a: 414). He is not anti-nationalist, and he is certainly not against the peasants being able to use their dialects in public arenas without shame or embarrassment. He is against the artificial reforms which are in danger of resulting from the political dimension. Change was already occurring – naturally – and that was, for him, exactly right:

> The dialects are moving towards the written language, and the written language is in turn moving towards the folk language, all down to the fact that the educated classes are being recruited from the ordinary people, and both estates are moving towards each other. All this is going on inexorably, here as in other countries, irrespective of all the shouting and all the theories. (p. 414)

So political intervention was one artificial, unnatural development in the life of the living Norwegian language that Storm could not tolerate.

4.1.3.1.3 His next argument is developed in section II (pp. 416–430), specifically in response to Garborg's statement that the Norwegian peasant has 'one single Norwegian language'. Storm views the situation in terms of 'living' data and argues that in reality ordinary Norwegian people speak in the region of 500 separate dialects, and that:

> If peasants everywhere had more-or-less the same language, Landsmaal would create itself, and the language movement would be no movement. The internal disagreement amongst the language activists is the best testimony to the fact that an artificial unity in the written language will not be able to be maintained when there is no unity in the spoken language. (p. 417)

There then follows a typically Stormian "case study", showing in detail how the dialects differ from each other and from Aasen's norm. He shows at length how dialect forms would have to be translated into Landsmål in order to be written down and would thereby lose their 'living' character. If Aasen's norm were to be introduced as a standard, Storm argues, the effect would be to kill off the variety which really exists in the dialects. He describes Aasen's norm as 'something dead, unreal, impersonal' (p. 417), by contrast with the 'living, individual, personal' dialects on the one hand and 'the real living Dano-Norwegian language' on the other. This latter may be remote from many of the dialects, but ordinary people, he suggests, have never had any difficulty learning and using this language which has developed naturally, and anyway, 'with each generation the peasant loses more and more of the dialect and even in speech moves towards the language of culture' (p. 430). This may be undesirable from a staunchly nationalistic perspective, but it is a linguistic fact. What is more, it would be artificial, and contrary to the way in which the written norm has developed in other languages, to introduce a written norm which was not actually spoken – 'Landsmaal is not spoken anywhere' (p. 425) – since the established written forms of European languages were all, he argues, based on the notion that you write how you speak. This same idea of course underpinned both Aasen's and Knudsen's programmes, but Storm chooses not to recognise this, and instead to concentrate on the artificial or unnatural aspects of the languages which have resulted from the ensuing programmes or movements. However, ' "Landsmaal" has taken a bit from each dialect and as a whole is foreign to them all' (p. 415). The alternative to adoption of the Aasen norm, and the alternative which Storm claims that Garborg actually favours, is for Norwegians to do precisely what has happened in the other languages Storm refers to, to write as they speak, and simply '*stick to the dialects*, since these have the advantage over Landsmaal that they really exist'

(p. 425). If Norwegians were to do this, then perhaps a proper dialectological study could be undertaken, as had happened in Sweden: 'Sweden has here as in so much else set us a shining example' (p. 429). (We remember that this was written for publication in a Swedish journal!) If Norwegian peasants were to write as they spoke, they would learn to respect the characteristics of the individual dialects:

> They would realise that the same principle that makes claims for the peasant's language aganst the Danish, demands that he shouldn't have to give up his language for an artificial Landsmaal either. Whatever happens, he will get no other national language than Dano-Norwegian, but in this way it will happen without dispute and discord [Strid og Splid] and with all forces working together in agreement. (pp. 429–430)

With this sentiment Storm concludes the first part of DnM. It has been worth looking at his argument in some detail and quoting a reasonable amount of how he actually expresses it. He was a merciless critic, proceeding via a series of circular arguments backed up by unassailable data. Landsmål is a brilliant linguistic discovery, the argument goes, and an admirable work of dialectology, but in practice it is a dead language which nobody actually speaks. Norwegian can only achieve a new living standard if Norwegians do what other nations have done in establishing a written standard: write as they speak. If Norwegians write as they speak it will become clear that there is no standard, but they will make a brilliant linguistic discovery and produce an admirable work of dialectology. How very neat! The science of the living language will have been advanced, which is fine by Storm, since, by implication, he is the man to spearhead such an undertaking – which he would later do, and which parliament should have realised the year before:

> Only by serious, scientific study of the living dialects will the language issue get onto a more sound track. (p. 429)

This study of dialectal variation will show that Dano-Norwegian is the only serious option for a national standard.

4.1.3.1.4 DnM continues on page 526, and the remaining two sections of the piece fill pages 526 to 550. Storm's theme is the same – the desirability and possibility of orchestrated reform in Norwegian – but he turns to some other questions.

In section III he addresses more fully the question he touched on earlier, of how the proposed means of standardising Norwegian compare with the means whereby other European languages were standardised. He begins with a technique we encounter elsewhere, and a technique which is really beneath him. Just as he used his superior knowledge of phonetics in 1890 to humiliate Schou Bruun and put him in his place (see section 3.3.2.5.2), so he uses his superior knowledge of the history of European languages to do the same to Garborg here. 'He only knows antiquated sources,' he writes of Garborg's version of the development of Standard English. Well, of course Garborg doesn't know the as yet unpublished edition by James Murray of the tenth-century *Rushworth Gloss*, showing Standard English to be descended from the East Midland English dialect. Once again, Storm is being disingenuous. I am not entirely sure why he occasionally resorts to humiliating his opponents by wielding his knowledge like a sword. However, he was genuinely and totally committed to discovering the truth about languages, and indeed this lust after "the truth" comes out very clearly in the *prekentekst*, the 'text of the day' which would open *Engelsk Filologi* the following year. Consequently he could not tolerate imprecision or lack of detail. Precision and detail were in the long run more important than scholarly etiquette. It has to be admitted, too, that he liked point-scoring. We have seen him relish scoring points off Jespersen, and, after what Garborg had written about him, he was probably glad simply to be able to knock Garborg down. Storm demonstrates how the development of a standard Norwegian could not be compared directly with the development of Standard English or Standard Italian, in the way that 'Maalstrævere' had claimed.[18] If a Standard Norwegian were to follow the model for standardisation seen elsewhere, 'it would have to be on the basis of one dialect':

> But I don't have much faith in the possibility of that happening. It has come too late, and the difference between the dialects is too great. Neither do I regard it as desirable, although I completely accept the patriotic idea at the foundation of the language movement. The fact remains that we have a written language in which our history and culture are entrenched. There can be no sensible talk of the educated classes giving this up. To deprive the peasants of it and thereby to cut them off and shut them out from European culture would be in my view 'to use violence on the peasants' [*at øve Vold mod Bonden*]. And the peasants will, to be sure, have none of it. (p. 533)

4.1.3.1.5 In the final section of *DnM*, he moves on to Knudsen. *DnM* is supposed to be based on Garborg's book, so Knudsen and the 'dansknorske Maalstræv' are only discussed briefly. But Storm needs to show his hand here, since *DnM* is essentially the manifesto for his position in the reform debate. He would go on to develop the individual points in more detail (of course!) later on, but for now he needs at least to show the entire hand.

His position vis-à-vis Knudsen is more or less the opposite of his position vis-à-vis Aasen. He has little respect for Knudsen or for his work, but he is in general agreement with Knudsen's programme (up to a point). The 'dansk-

[18] See also Western (1907) for another attack on the same argument.

norsk' programme is, Storm writes, based on a very logical and simple principle, Quintilian's Golden Rule '*to write as one speaks*' (p. 534). The Landsmål programme, he goes on, is not even built on the principle of writing how one *should* speak, but rather 'on writing how one does *not* speak'. So Storm finds general favour with the programme, as one would expect from someone who the following year (in *Engelsk Filologi*) would stress, as part of what I earlier called his 'linguistic manifesto' (*DnM* is his specifically Norwegian manifesto), that 'the spoken language is the source. It is that which decides what is idiomatic and what is not' (Storm 1879a: p. ii). So far so good, but now begins another of Storm's famous circular arguments. Knudsen is inconsistent in his application of Quintilian's Golden Rule. He follows pronunciation in writing *en man* ('a man'), but he follows existing (etymological) spelling in writing *et land* ('a country'), where there is no final [d] in spoken Norwegian. Conversely, 'the difficulty with the phonetic principle is drawing the boundary' (p. 534), and in places, Storm suggests, Knudsen is *too* consistent, failing to recognise that different registers require different styles of language. Some registers in late nineteenth-century Norwegian require a usage which is close to spoken Norwegian, but other registers require a "higher" style, one closer to the inherited Danish. Thus contemporary usage preferred *å vite* ('to know'), but *Videnskab* ('science') with voiced stops, the Danicised version corresponding to a different linguistic register; so simply to adopt a general form *Vitenskap* was, in Storm's view, too hasty:

> [. . .] to write pure Norwegian where speech is still half Danish, is too hasty. The written language in all cases follows the spoken language, and usually extremely slowly. (p. 535)

Following on from these two objections Storm comes back, extraordinarily and via an argument that is so circular as to be spherical, to the statement that Knudsen does indeed 'write as one speaks' (p. 536). Storm has begun to show some examples of how Knudsen's programme leads to artificial forms, forms which do not correspond with the real, living language, but he will have much more to say on the subject later. It is more important here to disagree with Garborg, and, against Garborg's accusation that Knudsen 'writes half Swedish', Storm is more than willing to side with Knudsen – although Knudsen did not exactly perceive what Storm wrote as the words of an ally.

Storm concludes *DnM* with a brief excursion through his other favourite Norwegian topic: the language of Norwegian literature. His point here is that 'Norwegian tone and colour is as ancient amongst Norwegian authors as Dano-Norwegian literature itself' (p. 536). As with Knudsen, he will return to this theme in much more detail later on, but he finds it sufficient simply to give a selection of examples of Norwegian forms and style in writings by Norwegian authors from the sixteenth century onwards. This is another case of throwing data at one of Garborg's statements, this time the statement that younger Norwegian authors write almost pure Danish. Storm always maintained that any changes in Norwegian must come in slowly and through the literature, that new forms needed to be properly fixed in the language by this means, before they could be said to be fully naturalised in the language. 'The spoken language is the source.' Storm had those words emblazoned on his shield every time he rode into battle, but the classical written language, as in English and French, was the filter. This pronouncement in *Engelsk Filologi* goes on: 'The written language is obviously the noblest form of the language, constituted by the nation's great authors and built up generation by generation.'

DnM leaves a lot of detail for later. It is a clear, unencumbered statement of Storm's position with regard to Aasen, the *Maalstræverne* and Knudsen. It gives the impression, unlike much of Storm's output, of careful planning. It is a well-rounded manifesto. The *Forord* to *Engelsk Filologi* is a rhetorical masterpiece, and some of the same rhetoric is evident in *DnM*. The circular arguments are in themselves rhetorical devices, finishing up where they had started, but the end of the argument in each case is subtly different from the beginning. Something has changed. The text as a whole works in this way. We began with 'Landsmaalet', Aasen's 'discovery', and we end up with Landsmål again on the final page, but by the final page this Landsmål is something different. Things have changed: *'The true "Landsmaal"* [language of the country] *is Dano-Norwegian'* (p. 550).

4.1.3.1.6 *DnM* was an impressive opening salvo in the forum of language reform debate, and its balanced treatment of the reform movements, from a non-partisan (i.e. not pro-Landsmål or pro-Knudsen) yet linguistically expert position, met with an enthusiastic response in some quarters. The folklorist Peter Christen Asbjørnsen would certainly have been pleased by *DnM*, since Storm praises him as 'the real reformer who has introduced authentic, sonorous Norwegian style into our literary language' (p. 540). Bearing in mind that he might not have been exactly objective, Asbjørnsen did describe *DnM* as 'the best account of the issue to have seen the light of day' (letter to Moe quoted in Venås (1997: 266)). It outlined Storm's position for all to see, and whether followers of the Landsmål programme or Knudsen chose to agree or not, it showed him to be not so much an enemy of reform as a supporter of moderation. He concludes by announcing that 'the truth lies in the middle' (p. 550): that the situation is best explained and understood by learning from extreme positions and by taking a middle ground between them. This was his approach to the question of regularity in language change and to language-teaching reform. The eternal watcher from the sidelines, he had that remarkable ability of seeing the strengths and the weaknesses in all positions and of taking up a standpoint in the middle, embracing what he saw as the strengths of all those positions and the weaknesses of none. Thus 'every serious movement has to have its exaggerations and hyperbolic twists and turns':

> But above all the language movement, both the Dano-Norwegian and the Nynorsk, has contributed to furthering the claims of Norse elements in the language in the face of foreign ones. If the Nynorsk movement never achieves its actual "goal", it will nevertheless have had its intended effect by strengthening the case for Norwegianness. (p. 550)

The Norwegian meets the foreign, and Storm knew all about that.

4.1.3.2 Unorsk og norsk (1881)

4.1.3.2.1 Knudsen's *Unorsk og Norsk, eller fremmedords avløsning* (Un-Norwegian and Norwegian, or the Replacement of Foreign Words) is a list of words, currently used by Norwegians in writing, which in Knudsen's view are foreign, un-Norwegian (*unorsk*). Alternatives are given for each word, alternatives which, again in Knudsen's view, are more native. Storm reviewed *Unorsk og norsk* ('Knudsen's chaotic book'[19]) in the columns of *Morgenbladet* immediately after it appeared. In fact he completed his review before the final volume came out, something for which Knudsen quite reasonably later criticised him. Storm's review, with the same title as Knudsen's book, was printed in the period 6 February to 5 March 1881.

4.1.3.2.2 Storm takes the opportunity here to flesh out the general objections to Knudsen's programme he had first aired in *Det norske Maalstræv* three years previously. His principal objection (*vor Hovedanke*) is that Knudsen 'has wanted to do too many things at once' (Storm 1881b). Storm's position, maintained throughout his life, was of course that Norwegian would change gradually. Norwegian lexicon and grammatical forms would slowly gain acceptability without any artificial intervention in the development of the language, as respected Norwegian writers took them up. In his review of *Unorsk og Norsk* he allows himself to make a prophecy:

> Although I am no prophet, I dare however to predict that Norwegian and Danish will never become mutually incomprehensible, not even difficult to understand. (Storm 1881b)

This is not the only place in this review that Storm attempts to tell the future, and elsewhere he gives examples of the sort of language that might be written in 1981 if Knudsen's reform proposals are adopted. Mutual incomprehensibility between Danish and Norwegian is just one of the regrettable outcomes foreseen by Storm in the event of Knudsen's programme being adopted. Norwegian and Danish have not become wholly foreign to each

---

[19] Postcard to Thomsen, 18 February 1880.

other, but it must be said that the difficulties in mutual understanding which
do obtain today are precisely in those areas where there has been the greatest
engineering in Norwegian.

The general objection to Knudsen's programme lies with the proposed
radical replacement of the existing lexicon in one raid, the 'too many things
at once' policy, but much of Storm (1881b) is taken up with specific
objections to the replacement lexicon suggested by Knudsen in his 1881
dictionary. Knudsen's spelling principles are inconsistent and hard to follow.
The forms he proposes are a mixed bag, borrowed inconsistently from a
variety of sources, from Landsmål, from Norwegian dialects in various parts
of the country, from non-standard Norwegian, from the other modern
national Scandinavian languages and from Old Norwegian. In addition to
these sources for replacement words, there are also the words that Knudsen
devised himself. Storm has less to say about these than might be expected.
His objection is more to the artificiality of the programme than to the
specific strategies adopted by Knudsen.

Storm's fiercest attack on Knudsen's alternatives is reserved for technical
vocabulary of various sorts, for artistic and scientific terms. His point is that
these are known words with specific nuances of meaning. The general public
would not make much sense of Knudsen's proposed *bok-avl* when it was
already familiar with the word *Literatur*. None of Knudsen's new forms
'expresses the whole concept'. They are, Storm maintains, 'poor words'
(*fattige Ord*), a phrase borrowed from another unfavourable review of
Knudsen (1881a) by the literary historian Hartvig Marcus Lassen (1824–
1897).

Having poured cold water on the principle behind Knudsen's programme
of Norwegianisation and on the specific strategies for devising replacement
lexicon, Storm sets about Knudsen's *Sprachgefühl*. One of Storm's major
preoccupations in his studies of modern Norwegian was the style of the
language and the use of different styles and different registers by authors. He
finds that Knudsen fails to distinguish the stylistic nuances of different
words. A final diatribe on the inevitability of foreign loans in a modern
language leads to what is perhaps the most interesting part of this review, a
part which actually has nothing to do with reviewing Knudsen (1881a),
namely a study of lexical developments in modern Norwegian. Storm's
reviews invariably serve as a springboard for some more general discussion,
and it is a shame that this particular discussion, unlike so many of Storm's
Morgenbladet contributions, was not later reprinted in a more permanent
form. Those articles and reviews which were reprinted directly related to the
question of language reform, whereas this discussion does not.

4.1.3.2.3 Storm begins this short study with the observation that 'even the
folk language has its antinational tendencies'. He goes on to list words which
have recently come into popular use from various sources, from German,

from Swedish and from Danish. Some of these modish borrowings he regards as good and useful – enrichments for the language – but others he regards as unnecessary and borrowed solely because they are fashionable. As a practical linguist, he does not have a blanket policy on foreign loans. Each one, each atom of data, needs to be considered on its own merits. However, there is a purist in Storm, as there was in Knudsen and in Aasen. Unlike Knudsen, the puristic Storm advocated light pruning:

> It is with regard to the superfluous or incorrect use of foreign words that a really clear-headed language purifier should step in, while the words are still new and foreign; cut off such excrescences and replace them with fresh national shoots; give us a single good word and not twenty bad ones. (Storm 1881b)

Storm also takes the opportunity to study the old-fashioned, so-called *Kancellistil* ('officialese') ('a relic from the Middle Ages') adopted particularly by lawyers and others whose responsibility it was to draft official or quasi-official documents. He argues for the desirability of replacing this style, a style adopted by many ordinary writers too, with a more modern, more Norwegian style, a style gradually adopted by following the model of 'our best authors'. In his response to Storm's review (see next section), Knudsen portrayed Storm as archaic, as yesterday's man, but he wasn't. He was as much a reformer as Knudsen or Aasen, insofar as he favoured and encouraged a reform in written Norwegian. But he was of the opinion that neither Knudsen's programme nor the Landsmål programme constituted the way forward to a more Norwegian written language:

> If bad really has to be, if languages absolutely must be created, we prefer the real thing, Landsmaal, to Knudsen's mish-mash language, as it emerges from his last work. Aasen's Landsmaal is undeniably "better done", much more harmonious. But not every linguist is blessed with being an Ivar Aasen. We must say, though, that we prefer the living dialects to Landsmaal. For a nationally acceptable written language we stick to the truly existing, living, educated language of the country, i.e. Dano-Norwegian. (Storm 1881b)

Here is the conclusion that will become very familiar to us as we work through Storm's publications on Norwegian language. Interestingly, though, we have here a hierarchy of Norwegian varieties, with the 'living' written language at the top, followed by the 'living' dialects, and with 'Knudsen's mish-mash language' at the bottom.

Knudsen was not happy.

4.1.3.2.4 As in the wake of Storm (1878a), Knudsen reacted violently to Storm's comments and penned a lengthy counter-attack. *Morgenbladet* at first refused Knudsen access to their columns, as had happened in 1879, and this reinforced Knudsen's sense of a conspiracy against him. *Morgenbladet* subsequently relented and accepted an abbreviated contribution from Knudsen (printed on 26 February 1881, so before Storm had completed his serialised review). *Aftenbladet* accepted some more (printed on 18 March 1881), but the bulk of what Knudsen had to say on the subject appeared in the book *Af Maalstriden* (Knudsen (1881b: 38–115)), which, like much of what he produced, was published at his own expense. Although Knudsen (1881b) is quite long, it is not a convincing retort. Storm's vast knowledge and skilful wielding of data are simply much more convincing than Knudsen's general and protracted arguments, consisting in many cases just of unsupported refutations of quotations from Storm. Knudsen may have known in his heart that he was right in many of his observations about Norwegian usage, but heartfelt claims were useless against Storm's head, that mine of detailed information.

Storm, like Knudsen, did not respond well to criticism. We saw in Chapter 2 what happened to 'Sproglærer Dahl' when he dared to question Storm's linguistic knowledge in his review of *Engelsk Filologi*. If only Knudsen had not entered into battle! Storm kept up the attack with a review of *Af Maalstriden* in *Morgenbladet*. Here he repeats (quite briefly) his objections to Knudsen and, indeed, the points on which he praised Knudsen in his previous review. Storm finds here that:

> it is regrettable that Mr Knudsen possesses characteristics which make it impossible to have any fruitful discussion with him.[20]

It must have come as a relief to all concerned that Knudsen did not counter-attack again, and here the matter rested until 1895.

4.1.3.3 Det nynorske Landsmaal: En Undersøgelse *(1888)*

4.1.3.3.1 *Det nynorske Landsmaal: En Undersøgelse* (The New Norwegian Landsmaal: An Investigation) (*DnL*), like *Unorsk og norsk*, started life as a series of articles in *Morgenbladet*, this time in May and June 1886. *Morgenbladet*, and the conservative press more generally, was Storm's favoured outlet for his contributions to debates concerning the Norwegian language, and, as Knudsen experienced so painfully, Storm did have a special relationship with this newspaper. The book version of 1888 is not long (116 pages), but it is a highly focused and (excessively) detailed development of one of the points he had first outlined 10 years earlier in *Det norske Maalstræv*. The argument is, then, not a new one, but, as with all Storm's later developments of previously presented ideas, it is supported by a mind-boggling corpus of data and examples. In 1878 the point – that

---

[20] Knudsen was not the only person with entrenched views on the subject of language reform with whom Storm found it impossible to have a reasonable debate (see Storm 1885a: 1).

Landsmål does not constitute a unified language system, but is in fact split – was made simply and quickly: Vinje's language was different from Aasen's, and 'with it a split in Landsmaal had already begun, which later deepened with each new language activist' (1878a: 413). By 1886 more Landsmål literature has appeared, giving Storm an expanded stock of examples, and *DnL* starts with a list of the literature from which examples are to be taken.

There was in reality a specific external motivation for Storm to return to this theme in 1886 and to explore it in such detail. In 1885, as we saw earlier, the so-called *jamstillingsvedtaket* (resolution on language equality) had been passed, placing Landsmål on an equal footing with *Dansk-norsk* in the schools. In support of this, Arne Garborg and Ivar Mortenson the same year brought out their *Lesebok i det norske folkemaal for høgre skular* (Reader in the Norwegian Folk Language for the Higher Schools). Storm felt very strongly that it was not practical in the schools to study or teach a language which did not at that time possess a universally recognised standard form, but was on the contrary used in different forms by many of those who wrote it. He believed in the facts of language. You could idealise or politicise a language or language situation until you were blue in the face, but there was no escape from the facts of the living language. The facts of Landsmål use were for Storm more persuasive than the political "dream":

It can be of no benefit to stick to shifting, commonplace colloquialisms. One has to go right to the heart of the matter, and "study" the linguistic form of Landsmaal in the available literature. One knew for sure that there were considerable points of disagreement, but scarcely anyone had imagined that the deviations were so great, the chasm so gaping between the different Landsmaal authors, as it now on closer investigation shows itself to be. (Storm 1888a: *Forord*)

The study of languages in the schools in general was at the forefront of Storm's mind in the period 1886–1888, since in 1887 he published 'Om en forbedret undervisning i levende sprog' (Storm 1887b). Storm's attack on Landsmål is no arid theoretical one. His argument is rather a practical one, which is only to be expected from that great 'pràktikal liNgwist'. Storm's views on Norwegian certainly came from the heart, and his objections to Knudsen's programme were of a more aesthetic nature, but their basis was always in practical reality, in the facts of the language:

What is sure above all is that it is everywhere difficult, very difficult, to teach schoolchildren to *write* Landsmaal. The great difficulties involved with this have not in any way been accounted for. Being able to write a language presupposes partly that one can speak it, partly that there is a literary tradition and a usage developed through it, a single, definite, established usage. Landsmaal fails on all these points. (pp. 2–3)

Landsmaal is not presented as ugly, or artificial, or tasteless, or any of the things Storm accused Knudsen's language of being – it is simply impractical.

4.1.3.3.2 Part I of *DnL* deals with Aasen. Storm again expresses his admiration for Aasen and his enterprise, as he had done a decade before, and as he would go on to do until Aasen's death. On this occasion Storm calls Aasen's work 'an astounding work of art' (p. 3), but he cites examples to show that Aasen's use of Landsmål exhibited formal variation as he developed the language. Storm does not criticise this, and in fact I don't think he had it in him to criticise Aasen and his work directly. Instead he describes the variation in Aasen's own use as akin to the variation which is to be found between the older and more modern stages of 'a historically developed literary language' (p. 9). Nevertheless, Storm uses his analysis of Aasen's usage to suggest that Landsmål had 'the seeds of division' – a phrase taken from his 1885 lecture (Storm 1885b: 5) – within it from the very beginning. In part II Storm does exactly what he did in *Det norske Maalstræv*, but in more detail and embracing more authors. He demonstrates the variety found in the subsequent generations of Landsmål writers. As he had done in 1878, he pays especial attention to Vinje, but new in 1888 is the detailed analysis of the language of Olav Jakobsson Høyem's (1830–1899) *Den helige saga og kjørkjesaga* of 1881.[21] There are two reasons for Storm being so interested in Høyem's version of the Bible story. First, 1888 was the year Storm was engaged as linguistic consultant to the New Testament, so he had a strong personal interest in Norwegian versions of the Bible. Secondly, there was a particular practical issue surrounding Høyem's work. Another of the acts of parliament for 1885 was to make funds available to distribute copies of Høyem (1881) throughout the country free of charge. On 10 January 1888 Storm received a letter from M. Walther, a Kristiania apothecary, containing work by Høyem. It is worth experiencing Walther's bile to show that Høyem and his programme were far from welcome amongst the Kristiania bourgeoisie:

> The language activist Høyem has sent me a copy of his most recent work. As I have absolutely no interest whatever in the language movement and do not care to waste my time reading the book, might I permit myself to send it to you instead of consigning it to the wastepaper basket. You are in duty bound to look at this sort of literature. I beg for forgiveness for helping on this occasion to secure this sort of reading matter for you. (UBB Ms. 743h)

It is little wonder that Storm, the practical linguist preoccupied with Bible translation and language teaching, was moved to write his articles in

---

[21] Of Høyem, Venås (1996: 387) writes: 'He was a teacher, a telegraph operator and a bank employee, and he wrote both articles and books – and in Landsmål. But Høyem wrote in his own way, close to the spoken language of Byneset, where he was from.'

Morgenbladet and then to make them available to a wider public in book form.

In part III of *DnL* Storm turns his attention to variation exhibited at specific levels of the language, rather than in and between the work of specific authors. He is determined to expose the practical 'division' in Landsmål from every angle. He deals first of all with the grammar, as 'all linguists agree that grammatical form is the most decisive for a language's character' (p. 39). Example follows example of 24 grammatical categories and the variety of forms of them evidenced by Landsmål writers. This exercise fills over 45 pages and is a prime example of Storm's tendency to take a hammer to crack a nut. The reader, reeling from the force of his onslaught of data, gladly enters part IV, which the relentless Storm opens by stating:

> There could well still be many grammatical points left to deal with, but the main points dealt with above will be sufficient to support our claim about Landsmaal's complete lack of certainty of form. (p. 85)

Without pausing for breath, he strides right on ahead:

> In addition comes the lack of certainty in the orthography and phonology, about which an entire book could be written.

The reader is left breathless, running to catch up. Almost more than anywhere else in Storm's published output, we get the physical feeling in *DnL* of his relentless striving after the truth, his unceasing journey of discovery and linguistic revelation, 'like stout Cortez when with eagle eyes he star'd at the Pacific'.[22] The wealth of material is too great and the structure too paratactic in *Engelsk Filologi* to give quite this same impression. There just isn't the same feeling of a headlong rush through a linguistic forest into the sunlight on the other side. We have seen elsewhere how Storm's unceasing collection of data led to appendices, the outcome of further discovery after the work in question had gone to press, and we find something similar here. *DnL* is a reprint of newspaper articles two years after they first appeared, but two years is a long time in the Stormian quest, hence the 16-page *Efterskrift*:

> In the couple of years which have passed since the above comments first appeared, the process of language division in Norway has continued without ceasing. (p. 100)

Eleven cases of orthographic and phonological 'division' lead (on page 98) to a brief comment on style and the tendency amongst Landsmål writers to use folk forms in an otherwise elevated style, and finally Storm has mercy on the reader: 'It is time to conclude these comments' (p. 98). What is the

---

[22] John Keats, *On First Looking into Chapman's Homer*.

conclusion? To what have all these examples led? What is the light beyond the forest?

> Only that which is common to the whole country can have any prospect of being accepted. But what form of language is common to the whole of Norway? The *Dano-Norwegian usage of the towns and the language of literature*. Only this language is by and large uniform throughout the whole country. No amount of theories, of wishes, of laws [. . .] can help in respect of this inevitable fact. (p. 99)

For Storm, the scientist, the rational student of language, the facts are where the buck stops. 'The language of the towns will continue to adopt Norwegian elements', but, in Storm's view, neither it nor the dialects can 'be suppressed by an artificial Landsmaal'.

The new *Efterskrift*, as well as giving examples of formal variation in the most recent publications – the most up-to-date is from 17 August 1888 and the *Forord* to the book is dated September 1888 – addresses variation in Landsmål from a different perspective.[23] While the main text of *DnL* discusses what we might call internal variation in written Landsmål, the *Efterskrift* discusses *external* variation, that is to say variation between Aasen's Landsmål (*Normalmaalet* or *Generalnævneren*) and some of the spoken dialects. Storm provides a series of parallel texts showing a passage in *Normalmaalet* next to the same passage in dialect, in most cases transcribed by Aasen (in Aasen (1853)). This is, like a number of Storm's rhetorical strategies, disingenuous. Aasen did not intend for his Landsmål to correspond directly to any of the dialects. It was designed to provide a bridge between them as well as a bridge between Old and Modern Norwegian, so Storm is asking Landsmål to be something it was never intended to be. All the same, the technique is a clever one: pitching Aasen against himself to show 'that Landsmaal itself deviates substantially from the "best" dialects, and that the difficulties involved in learning the normalised form will be neither few nor small' (p. 113).

An interesting feature of this *Efterskrift* is the seemingly pro-Knudsen stance it takes. Anyone reading *DnL* who had not witnessed the vitriol of 1881 would assume Knudsen and Storm to be of the same mind, which, to a point, of course they were. Storm can write completely honestly, 'I have always agreed with the principles underlying the Knudsen language movement, basing the written language on the living, educated spoken language' (p. 115). However, he lists Knudsen as just another example of whimsical variation in contemporary written Norwegian, no better, no worse, no different from Aasen, Garborg, Høyem or even Bjørnson.

---

[23] Despite finishing the book, the search for data went on. There is a notebook in the Norwegian National Library (NBO Ms. 4° 1285 F[xxxii]) entitled *Nye Slags Landsmaal* (New Forms of Landsmaal), dated September 1888.

4.1.3.3.3 So how does *DnL* fit into Storm's opus as a whole? It is a highly typical piece, exemplifying neatly many of the characteristics of Storm's work. With revision comes more detail. Detail is constantly striven for. Careful planning accedes to breathlessly presented bodies of examples drawn from here and there. Storm always wrote in response to external events. In his French and English work, he published things that responded to educational requirements and reforms. In his Norwegian work, he published direct responses to specific developments in the language question. It may have been a Storm-internal event which provoked *Det norske Maalstræv*, but thereafter he had his ear to the ground and, via the newspapers, he could respond swiftly and dramatically to others' pronouncements or acts. The critic was never off-duty.

Responses to *DnL* were predictable. Those who shared Storm's views responded enthusiastically, and those who didn't, didn't. It provoked a widespread reaction and was not only reviewed in national and regional newspapers in Norway, but abroad too. The British literary critic and poet, who had a particular interest in Scandinavian literature, Edmund Gosse, reviewed it in *The Saturday Review* and took the opportunity to cast scorn on the Norwegian language situation: 'It would be crazy in a large country; is it less than suicidal in a small one?' (Gosse 1889). The book was summarised approvingly in *Dansk Nationaltidende* on 24 August 1889. The only significant negative review appeared in the Norwegian *Dagbladet* on 17 February 1889, signed X.

One of the most interesting reviews, at least in terms of its form, was Western's in *Lə Mɛ:tr Fɔnetik*. Western was Storm's disciple in many ways, although they disagreed on the detail of language-teaching reform (see 2.3.2.1) and the Riksmål described and championed by Western was more traditional than Storm's. But Western's review is unsurprisingly positive:

> The objectiveness and passionless tone that goes through the book is especially admirable when compared with the violent language which has often been characteristic of what has hitherto been published on this subject.[24] (Western 1889a: 20)

The next review in this same edition of *Lə Mɛ:tr Fɔnetik* was Passy's review of the Landsmål organ, *Fedraheimen*, where he expressed his general support and enthusiasm for the Landsmål movement (Passy 1889). Western responded to Passy in the next month's issue of *Lə Mɛ:tr Fɔnetik*, claiming that Passy was quite incorrect in his view that the Landsmål movement had a good chance of success. The right-winger Western comes up face-to-face with the liberal Passy, and gets very hot under the collar!

Considering that the question of the adoption of Landsmål alongside Dano-Norwegian was a specifically Norwegian one, this book attracted

---

[24] Transcribed from the phonetic system used in *Le Maître Phonétique* in its early days.

significant attention beyond Norway's boundaries, all the more surprising
for its being written in a Scandinavian language. Storm's personal fame
and the network of scholars to which he belonged secured an international recognition that few other Norwegians of the day could have
commanded.

4.1.3.4 Norsk Sprog: Kraakemaal og Landsmaal *(1896)*

4.1.3.4.1 More *Morgenbladet* articles – another book. *Norsk Sprog: Kraakemaal og Landsmaal* (Norwegian Language: Crow Language and Landsmaal) (*NSKL*) also began life in the columns of *Morgenbladet*. In book
form the articles are divided up into two main sections, as indicated by the
book's subtitle. The first and longer of the two sections had its genesis in a
serialised review of Knudsen's 1894 *Norsk målvækst*, and its nine instalments
faced *Morgenbladet* readers during the period from the beginning of January
to the end of May 1895. Those readers would have encountered something
which, on the face of it, was an innocent review. But it was anything but
innocent. Storm's "data warfare" had become more and more concerted as
the years went by. The title 'Kraakemaal', though, is new with the book
version. Storm abdicates responsibility for any unfavourable association of
this description of Knudsen's version of Norwegian:

> The treatise now appears under the shorter name 'Kraakemaal'. K.K. uses
> this word to describe the existing Norwegian language, polluted with un-
> Norwegian words. Vicious tongues use it on the other hand of K.K.'s own
> newly constructed language. The discriminating reader may select the
> meaning he finds most appropriate. (Storm 1896c: Preface)

In case the 'discriminating reader' was not already aware that this term had
been used to describe Knudsen's 'newly constructed language', he is now.
This is merely the first of a string of abusive comments Storm throws at
Knudsen and his work. He notes in this same preface that Knudsen died
while the book was in press, but there is no attempt to retract or moderate
any of the negative comments. As we have already seen, this is in stark
contrast to the honeyed words Storm adopts in this book to describe the also
recently dead Aasen. This is another example of Storm placing the language
before people, linguistic truth before etiquette. This is no bad thing in some
ways, as we are often subjected to the most saccharine rubbish in the name
of collegial politeness. But once again we are forced to exclaim, 'Poor
Knudsen!'

The second section of the book, 'Landsmaalet', originally appeared as a
series of articles in *Morgenbladet* during the period June to August 1896,
under the heading *Landsmaal i Skolen* (Landsmaal in the Schools). It is
worth noting how quickly many of Storm's publications appeared. He had
his problems with the production of the second edition of *Englische*

Philologie, but many of his books rolled off the presses with extraordinary efficiency. The last of the newspaper articles appeared in the August of 1896, Storm's preface to the book is dated October 1896, and the title page shows 1896 to have been the year of publication too. Modern authors will marvel at the speed of this process. In the case of *NSKL*, there was a price. It is marred by an unusually large number of printing errors. A list of 'additions and corrections' (for once lacking here) is as much a part of a Storm book as is a table of contents, and these *Tillæg og Rettelser* probably bear witness to Storm's impatience, his constant striving for linguistic truth. He was undoubtedly a perfectionist at heart, but he was also in a big hurry.

  Landsmaal i Skolen, the original article series, 'has now been given the shorter name "Landsmaal"' (1896c: *Forord*). Typically, the original premise for writing serves as no more than a starting point, an excuse for something else, and there is very little here that specifically relates to the issue of Landsmål as an object of study and as a medium in the schools. It is only 10 pages into the presentation that we learn what has piqued Storm into action, 'the most recent manifestation of the language movement', namely 'that the language activists now unanimously (imagine!) want to have The Language introduced into the upper schools' (1896c: 80). The critic Storm, however, does little more than flex his rhetorical muscles, returning to and updating points made and remade before, so we do not need to spend long looking at the 'Landsmaal' section of *NSKL*.

4.1.3.4.2 Storm takes his long-suffering readership back to the old point that Landsmål exhibits great variety in its use, that it can therefore not be regarded as a unified language, and so cannot become a school language, a clear and discrete system that can be studied and taught. Here we are taken on the same journey through the Landsmål authors as in 1878 and 1888. This is Storm's decennial outing. The final outing would come in 1903 (see next section). In 1903 the terrain covered is more varied, but the speed (as we shall see) has become distinctly dangerous. Back to 1896.

  As earlier, Storm opens with praise for Aasen and his 'grand experiment' and for the work of those who early followed in Aasen's footsteps. Arne Garborg's *Haugtussa* is given a particularly close examination and found to be the work of a 'master's hand' (p. 75). But inevitably there is no reprieve for the Landsmål movement. The further away from the world of fantasy Landsmål strays, the less appropriate it becomes, and the further Landsmål writers stray from Aasen, the more split the language becomes. Thus Aasen, Garborg and Mortenson are subjected to a further demolition of their style, and this time Vetle Vislie (1858–1933), author and teacher, and Lars Eskeland (1867–1942), teacher and author of various Landsmål textbooks, join the gallery of victims. As usual much data is thrown around, and as usual it is presented as only the tip of the iceberg:

We have not been able to go through more than just a few Landsmaal authors, and have not considered anything other than the principal grammatical rules, but that is enough for our purpose. (1896c: 104)

At the very end Storm returns to his theme (1896c: 114):

Well, since Landsmaal is still unfinished and rife with division, to want to introduce it into the upper schools across the entire country can only have one outcome:

Chaos.

This layout is Storm's own. He has to resort to a different format to make his point now. He has been shouting at the top of his voice for so long, deploying dramatic rhetorical language, using written emphases of every available sort, that he has become hoarse. His voice has become weak and faint. His repeated formulation of the same point is losing impact. There are only so many times a point can be repeated, no matter how valid it is and no matter how strongly it is felt, before it begins to lose its force. Even his usual parting shot, that 'Dansk-norsk' is the real Norwegian, is becoming weak and needs propping up with extra typographical supports:

It will then be found that it would have been better to employ those 'fine wasted powers' [skjønne spildte Kræfter] on the harmonious development of the national language we have, and which, despite all language activism, we are going to keep: Dano-Norwegian, or, as it should now be called:

Norwegian.

4.1.3.4.3 'Kraakemaal' is the most concentrated attack on Knudsen to come from Storm's pen. It is true that Storm (1881b) pulled no punches, but that was then and this is now. In the early 1880s Storm had not developed the ramping and raging rhetoric, which came as he got older and felt that his warnings about the development of the standard language were not being heeded. He was a busy man with many irons in the fire, and he would not have spent his valuable time making the same points every decade or so, in detail and at length, if he had not thought it necessary to do so. This is certainly one of the reasons why he became so passionate on the subject. He believed himself to be right, and indeed, as we shall argue below, history has in general shown him to have been right. Nevertheless political motivations were leading the language in a direction which Storm, that ardent lover of *det levende Sprog*, could not tolerate. His style in the later writings is that of the religious agitators who were active in nineteenth-century Norway: 'Can you not SEE?' He cites the fact that 'the circumstances dealt with here remain in force' (1896c: *Forord*) as the reason for reprinting these *Morgenbladet* pieces in book form.

Amidst all the abuse, Storm does have a few grudging words of praise for Knudsen, but it is almost as though he can't bear to utter them, as they are always followed immediately by a further stinging attack. So he does admit that 'as to *style*, it cannot be denied that it is pure Norwegian' (1896c: 45). However, 'on the other hand his style also exhibits very significant disadvantages' (1896c: 45), and, even if it didn't:

> If we investigate Knudsen's language a little more closely, we find that his even style is after all rather uneven with regard to *tone* and *choice of vocabulary*. (p. 48)

Storm's objections to Knudsen's programme are not in essence different from his objections to the Landsmål programme. These are not specific attacks on specific language programmes. Instead Storm's "outings" are practical applications of the philosophy of the living language. Knudsen is attacked because his programme is artificial. Firstly Knudsen is proposing forms that are stylistically inappropriate to the register for which they are intended, which are artificially constructed by Knudsen or borrowed in an ad hoc way from a variety of sources.

> The worst thing about his programme is just this, that he shows no respect for reality, for the educated spoken language which exists in reality. (1896c: 3)

Secondly, his proposals have not been adopted by the authors. Despite an early enthusiasm for Knudsen's forms by Bjørnson, no respected writer has been inspired to provide a model for the use of Knudsen's variety of Norwegian. Thus it remains an unreal (unrealised) system, presented in Knudsen's publications, but not *living*. Thirdly, Knudsen is too consistent, and in the third part of 'Kraakemaal' Storm shows that there are a number of double forms in contemporary Norwegian, where one form is appropriate to one type of discourse and a different form is appropriate to another type of discourse. Thus the language exhibits a stylistic redundancy, which Knudsen attempts to iron out, and which Storm cannot accept his doing. Maybe Norwegian will one day have just one word for 'sea' (which it now does), but as long as the Danish form *Sø* and the Norwegian form *sjø* exist side by side, with different nuances of meaning, it is too hasty (and artificial) to give the entire functional load to *sjø* alone. Fourthly, how far should we go down the path towards Norwegianisation advocated by Knudsen, and what is our guide? Storm maintains that this path can only be followed with a guide, and that guide must be actual usage, the real forms of modern, educated spoken Norwegian, as mirrored by the best authors:

> If there is anything which recent linguistic research has clearly established, it is that the written language is in all cases rooted in the spoken language and develops with the spoken language. (1896c: 3)

Knudsen was no linguist. His heart was in the right place, and, like Storm, he was passionate for his cause. Beating him with the stick of modern linguistics is a not uncharacteristic cheap trick on Storm's part, although this observation can hardly be said to constitute the profoundest piece of linguistic theory, and it is in fact basically Knudsen's view as well.

Having attacked the premises for Knudsen's programme, Storm dedicates the fifth section of 'Kraakemaal' to the question: 'What does Knudsen's language actually look like?' (p. 30). Storm portrays his presentation of Knudsen's variety of Norwegian as objective, but it isn't. The statement 'We shall limit ourselves to drawing out some principal characteristics, and giving some examples, such that the general reader can gain an impression of the peculiar language of Knudsen [*det Knudsenske Særsprog*]' (p. 30) prepares the reader for some sort of unbiased summary, on the basis of which the reader can make up her own mind. The choice of label, *Særsprog*, does not bode well for an objective presentation, and Storm launches straight into an attack on Knudsen's inconsistent spelling principles. He uses this section of 'Kraakemaal' to rehearse further inconsistencies. It is typical of Storm that too little consistency on the one hand and too much consistency on the other can be called upon as criticisms when it suits. The 'dansk-norsk' that Storm championed, like all natural languages, was consistent in some respects and inconsistent in others. It was this unpredictability of language, this endless capacity to vary and yet communicate meaning, that so fascinated Storm and which provided him with a lifetime of tireless activity pursuing linguistic variety. *Det Knudsenske Sprog* was not a natural language, but nor did Knudsen intend it to be a new language. It was intended as the means of hastening the development of an existing natural language. Nonetheless, Storm's arguments do allow rhetoric to topple into simple injustice.

Storm's final point is another one which he had made vis-à-vis Landsmål: that the language needs foreign loans. Most of the foreign loans that Knudsen sought to replace, he maintained, were perfectly well understood by ordinary Norwegians and were in no way regarded as foreign. He demonstrates this at some length. Knudsen's energies were, Storm concludes, wasted (1896c: 68). He could have put all that effort into using the language as it was and helping it develop naturally via usage. This leads Storm to one of his favourite conclusions, that the only model to follow is not Knudsen, but Ibsen. It is of course interesting that for a while Knudsen's programme influenced Ibsen's own usage. However:

> That fine and subtle art, that sure feel for the language, that idiomatic flawlessness, which alone determines the true classical form of the language, and which furthermore fulfils the requirement for increasing Norwegian-ness, is after all only to be found in one person, *Ibsen*. (1896c: 69)

Nobody could accuse Storm of inconsistency on this score (see section 4.2.3.2.1)!

4.1.3.5 Landsmaalet som Kultursprog *(1903)*

4.1.3.5.1 Storm's involvement in the language debate reached a crescendo around the turn of the century. Landsmål became more and more widely used in more and more domains during the 1890s. In 1899 the report on the spelling of Landsmål, the *Framlegg til skrivereglar for landsmaale i skularne*, appeared, and in 1901 the new official spelling for the language was sanctioned. On the opposite side of the linguistico-political divide, *Rigsmaalsforeningen* (The Riksmaal Association),[25] the society for the further-ance of the inherited written language, was founded in November 1899, with, amongst others, Gustav Storm (but not Johan) on the committee. The names of both Storm brothers were amongst the 100 signatures under the statement by Bjørnson, constituting the open invitation to the November meeting, which was posted in the newspapers. This statement was a letter to parliament announcing the fact that the signatories

> are of the opinion that the ruling on Landsmaal in the legislation of 6 July 1892 concerning country and city schools, and in the legislation of 27 July 1896 concerning higher schools, is mistaken.

At the same time Bjørnson's statement contained the following qualification, which has a whiff of Storm to it:

> So as not to be misunderstood, we expressly bring it to your attention that our protest does not apply to work maintaining and developing the Norwegian dialects.[26]

There was a lot of activity going on as the end of the century approached, and therefore a lot for Storm the critic to react to.[27] Huge notebooks grew from all these external events as he obsessively collected, charted and documented. The notebook in the Norwegian National Library labelled *Norsk VIb* has 225 sheets in it, and other notebooks on Norwegian from the same period (the turn of the century) are similarly fat and battered. So Storm was at this time fairly single-mindedly concerned with Norwegian. The second set of *Franske Taleøvelser* had appeared in 1897, but from then on all Storm's original publishing effort was directed to Norwegian language issues until the appearance of the first volume of *Større fransk Syntax* in 1911. The reason for this single-mindedness, when his earlier career had been

---

[25] Renamed *Riksmaalsforbundet* in 1909.

[26] Letter and signatures reprinted in Langslet (1999: 30–33). Storm's own copy is filed amongst his papers in NBO.

[27] The offices of *Morgenbladet* received the views of J. Storm with increasing regularity. See also Storm (1897b; 1897c; 1898b; 1898c).

characterised by an ability to keep a number of different irons in the fire, is easily explained by the change of pace in the language question up to and beyond the great national moment of independence from Sweden in 1905. In December 1900 Storm wrote to Thomsen:

> Apart from a couple of German editions of my *Fr. Taleøvelser*, my work for the rest of the year has been a battle *pro aris et focu* for our Dano-Norwegian language, in that I have turned on both Landsmaal (here more in passing), and particularly on the *New Spellers* who want to upend our language at one fell swoop by writing, e.g. *kake, gate, tape, takk, kapp, hatt* and much more besides. (20 December 1900)

Storm was by his own admission in the midst of *battle*. He still regarded the Knudsen movement as the greater enemy, but *Landsmaalet som Kultursprog* (Landsmaal as a Language of Culture) (*LsK*) is directed at the Landsmål movement.

4.1.3.5.2 The individual sections of *LsK* also started life as newspaper articles, this time in *Aftenposten*. I suspect that the articles, which had appeared during the period from June 1900 to July 1902, were collected together and published in book form at the suggestion of, or at least in collaboration with, Gustav. *LsK* was published by *Rigsmaalsforeningen*, as number 8 in their collection of *Smaaskrifter* (Pamphlets), and Storm dedicated the book to that society, without indicating his full espousal of their cause:

> I present this publication to Rigsmaalsforeningen as a small contribution to staunching the tide which threatens to divide our people and which threatens to alienate him who would unite it. (Storm 1903a: *Forord*)

This is an unusually vague form of words. What did Storm mean by this? Well, he meant that he wanted to help stem the tide of 'artificial' reform and further the traditional, slowly Norwegianising written language – but why couch this polarity so explicitly in terms of the people? I suspect that he was appealing in part to the strongly nationalistic feeling of the period prior to independence from Sweden, and implying that the Dano-Norwegian route was the only truly national one. He had used this "unity versus division" image before. *Det nynorske Landsmaal* was all about *Splittelse* in written Landsmål, by contrast with the truly national, unifying Dano-Norwegian:

> Only that which is common to the whole country can have any prospect of being accepted. But what form of language is common to the whole of Norway? The *Dano-Norwegian usage of the towns and the language of literature*. (Storm 1888a: 99)

In the more nationalistic climate of the new century, a more marked statement of nationalism was a sensible political move on Storm's part.

This statement of national unity would get stronger later. In 1906 he described himself as a member of the 'linguistic coalition party' (*sproglige Samlingsparti*) (1904/1906: 176). It is rather unfortunate that the movement in Norwegian language politics which, in 1959, would most vigorously champion language engineering through unifying the two standards, would be called *Språklig Samling*.

The original newspaper articles are organised into three sections – *Landsmaalets Former* (Forms), *Landsmaalets Ordforraad* (Lexicon) and *Landsmaalet som Kultursprog* (Language of Culture) – of which *Landsmaalet som Kultursprog* is by far the longest. In the first section he develops the idea of unity versus division further. Storm again expresses the view that it is undesirable that there should be anything other than unity in the national language – one nation, one language – and he shows through detailed examples that there is a major gulf between the spoken language of eastern Norway and a Landsmål rooted in the dialects of the western part of the country. This is really a continuation of the 'Splittelse' argument developed in 1888. The second part of the book – *Landsmaalets Ordforraad* – is a very brief rehearsal of some of the points Storm has made elsewhere. Of the book's 89 pages, 69 are given over to the main point, indicated by the title of the book, 'Landsmaal as a Language of Culture'.

This final section is itself split into eight topics:

I   Landsmaal i Skolen [Landsmaal in the schools] (20–25)
II   Det nye Testamente [The New Testament] (26–33)
III   Vestlandsk-Oldnorsk [West Norwegian–Old Norwegian] (33–42)
IV   Lokale Udtryk [Local expressions] (43–49)
V   Dansk-tydsk [Dano-German] (49–61)
VI   Kulturord [Culture terms] (62–69)
VII   Abstrakter [Abstracts] (69–83)
VIII   Folkesprog [Folk language] (83–89)

It would be excessive in a general book about Storm to follow his arguments in detail here. Many of these pages are anyway filled with examples, as Storm, in characteristic fashion, sets about bringing the Landsmål house down by keeping up a constant barrage of data-missiles. As in earlier writings on Landsmål, he is concerned above all with demonstrating the inappropriateness or impracticality of Landsmål as a national language, and it can be guessed from the section headings what sorts of argument he employs.

His main source of data is the 1899 revised edition of Elias Blix's Landsmål New Testament.[28] As we have seen, and will see in more detail later, the language of the Bible and indeed of other key religious texts was important to Storm:

---

[28] His notes are at NBO 4° 1285 F[xxxi].

The first door to education, for children in town and country alike, the first vision to lift thought up to a higher sphere, is *religion*. The language of religious education is therefore of fundamental importance for the people's entire spiritual and intellectual development. (Storm 1903a: 26)

Having established the fundamental importance of Biblical language, and having described Blix as 'one of the most outstanding experts on Landsmaal' (p. 27), Storm's next task is to reveal weaknesses in Blix's language, by association weaknesses in Landsmål as a whole, and by association again in the 'the first door to education', which parliament has sanctioned. He finds examples to show that Blix's language is too obscure, too regional, too close to Old Norwegian, too artificial, too vulgar, too alien, too folksy, too learned, in short unequipped to fulfil the role of a language of culture.

While it is the Landsmål tradition and particularly Blix's New Testament, which is the object of Storm's attack on this occasion, Storm cannot help having a dig at Knudsen, and in a particularly unkind and unpleasant fashion:

K. Knudsen tried to "purge" the language of those foul foreign words by constructing hundreds of Norwegian "replacements". But these had something so constructed about them, they were so badly done, that they inspired only laughter and distaste, except amongst a few of the faithful. (1903a: 12)

The measured argumentation of Storm's earliest writings on the language reform question has changed by now into a rant. The "ranting" is manifested partly by the endless examples ('and another thing . . .!'), but partly also by the rhetoric, which doesn't feel to be fully under control. The language is more colourful, images more striking. Foreign loans in Landsmål are described as 'pseudo city finery on a chubby peasant girl' (p. 12). We read that 'the new Norwegian language of culture [. . .] appears as a *surprise*: a garden full of colourful flowers which have shot up overnight, as if by magic':

But look closer, and you find that all the flowers are *artificial*! It is a theatrical decoration. (p. 84)

A striking image, certainly, but, in a work from 100 years ago, somewhat hysterical with its emphases and exclamation mark. Hysterical too are the wild-eyed rhetorical questions which now abound. This is a Johan Storm we can imagine foaming at the mouth, and someone best avoided in a dark street. To be serious, however, reading *LsK*, we do sense Storm in the white heat of passion. The Victorian of the photographs often surprises us by his passion for *det levende Sprog*, and here he is at his most passionate.

Storm was conservative in so far as he was a completely undiluted member of the nineteenth-century bourgeoisie. There is no evidence for him being particularly reactionary or bigoted; in fact the opposite is true, notably in his views of the peasant classes, which were unromantic and rational. However a rather unpleasant note creeps into *LsK*, in the very definition of 'culture' and what is meant by a 'language of culture'. He writes that 'it remains to be seen':

> The peasant will not get far with his own culture. It is only urban culture that leads to the goal of full development and advancement in all directions. (p. 14)

This is perhaps not such a surprising view from someone as urbane as Storm, someone who had spent his entire adult life in the capital city and occasionally hankering after the greater "civilisation" of other European capital cities. But it wasn't a view that was in tune with Norwegian politics at the turn of the twentieth century. The extension of this sentiment to the linguistic level is that '*Landsmaal as a language of culture will be pure affectation* [*Knot*]; it is still-born from the outset' (p. 18). Storm's point here is that Landsmål is all very well as long as it knows its limits and sticks to appropriate spheres. He had written in 1896 that 'Landsmaal is superb as a poetic language, in verse and in tales, depictions of folk life. Here is its natural sphere and its proper limitations' (1896c: 72). Opponents of Landsmål/Nynorsk have used this patronising argument ever since, but Nynorsk has (with a little help from its friends) shown itself to be fully adaptable to all types of discourse.

4.1.3.5.3 Storm must have frustrated his opponents with his negative, critical stance, and his failure to specify in greater detail what he proposed instead of the Aasen norm, the Landsmål programme or the Knudsen programme. Aasen, Knudsen or any of the Landsmål writers could have argued that at least they got off their backsides and did something about the language. Had they said that, Storm would have replied that this was precisely his point: that the inherited language was already developing a Norwegian hue and that this colour would simply deepen with the passing of time; that Norwegians should emulate the good usage of the great writers and simply let the language live. However, from now on he did become more specific about his own views, and began to postulate an actual programme of his own, that of what in 1906 he would call the 'linguistic coalition party'. *LsK* was not Storm's only publication in 1903. He published an article entitled 'Modersmaal. Maallag' on 28 June that year, in honour of the foundation of *Bymaalslaget* (the Urban Language Club) the previous year (reproduced in Storm (1904: 103–110)). Here the lover of images gives a metaphorical account of what is to come:

> The only language reform work which is any good is the *moderate conservative*,[29] which builds on what is there, seeks to protect and *ennoble*

---

[29] He had been describing himself as 'moderate-conservative' at least since 1881 (Storm 1881b).

what we have by choosing the best and removing excrescences, adopting the new which takes hold and becomes generally accepted, in short working on a *good language*, not on a *new language*. It is the gardener's work we need, not the radical's.

This image of the linguistic gardener is one he developed *in Norsk Sprog: Kraakemaal og Landsmaal* and is a good example of the colourful style of his later writings. The image actually goes back further in Storm's writings, at least to 1881, where he wrote of the need to 'prune such excrescences and replace them with fresh national shoots' (see section 4.1.3.2.3). Only the true gardener, through loving care towards his garden, can hope to promote mature and healthy growth, encouraging plants which will last and grow stronger year by year. Landsmaal plants were artificial, beautiful in appearance but not the real thing. In Storm (1896c) we see how Knudsen's Norwegian fits into this extended image, this parable:

> [Knudsen], unlike the careful gardener, will not let the language grow of its own accord, weeding, pruning and protecting it with a gentle hand, but he wants to force up artificial plants and trees at one stroke; he shoves them down into the linguistic field with a hard hand and with a harsh: 'Go on then, grow, and make it snappy [*værsgo å gro, å det på flygende flækken*]!' The outcome is as expected: Growth is scant and poor: for each shoot which comes up, there are ten which will not grow. (1896c: 16)

The description of Knudsen's herbage as 'artificial' is a red herring in what is otherwise a neat extended metaphor. It is a good example of Storm's readability, his popular touch. The newspaper columnist and the dry lecturer inhabited the same body.

4.1.3.6 Norsk Retskrivning *(1904/1906)*

4.1.3.6.1 If *Landsmaalet som Kultursprog* represents the crescendo of Storm's written war on Landsmål, then *Norsk Retskrivning* (Norwegian Orthography) (*NR*) can be said to represent the crescendo of his written war on the Knudsen movement, on those who aimed to Norwegianise the inherited written language through language planning. This latter war was more vigorous. At the beginning of *NR* Storm writes that the *Nystaverne*, the 'New Spellers', constitute a 'greater danger to the unity of the national language (*Rigsmaalet*) than that threatened by Landsmaal' (1904: 2). Accordingly his attack is stronger than it was in *Landsmaalet som Kultursprog*, and his rhetoric more vehement. Emphases, rhetorical questions and colourful imagery characterise *NR* even more than they did *Landsmaalet som Kultursprog*.

NR is in two parts, two related parts but with quite different backgrounds and aims. Part I from 1904 is equivalent to *Landsmaalet som Kultursprog* in being a collection of *Aftenposten* articles, written during the preceding years, in response to external events in the process of language reform. The external events in question were the series of proposals and debates, notably 'The *New Spellers'* radical orthographical reform proposal of 1898' (1904: *Forord*), leading up to the first major piece of language planning in Norway, the Riksmål spelling reform of 1907. Storm attacks the radical forms used by the 'New Spellers', writers of Riksmål sympathetic towards and active in reform, thrashing his way through endless examples to show that a radical introduction of new forms via the schools would be impractical, undesirable and confusing. Nygaard (1945: 100) states that Storm's articles in their original form had a significant impact on the ongoing process of reform in Riksmål:

> Storm's articles created a wide sensation and made a deep impression. They are certainly one of the main reasons why the Ministry let the matter lie and did not take any decision in 1901.

Storm was not simply a theorist, and he decided that it was time to come forward from the sidelines and take an active role in the process of reform, rather than simply a critical one, hence a second part to *NR*. Volume 2 (part II, volume 1), also from 1904, contained the first instalment of his detailed reform proposals, and government decided to put reform on hold until he had had the opportunity to present them. Storm was not someone who could be ignored, and he was by now the spokesman for those Riksmål users, probably the majority, who were cautious about reform. In the 1904 volume he covered the question of adopting ⟨p, t, k⟩ in the spelling to reflect the voiceless Norwegian articulation of the voiced Danish equivalents, and the question of using double consonants in certain cases where Danish used single consonants. Thus he began his reform proposal with gusto; but he was unable to complete it in 1904 due to the need to finish his treatise on the language of the new translation of the New Testament (Storm 1906). The concluding volume did not appear until 1906, and this delay was, according to Nygaard, 'fateful'. Nygaard (1945: 104) maintains, and he is certainly right, that a great deal was expected of Storm's proposals, and he certainly seems to have had the political powers (Conservatives, 1903–1905, and Coalition, 1903–1907), on his side after the turn of the century. There was reason to believe that his 'moderate' proposals would in fact be the ones adopted when the reform was finally sanctioned. However, and Holter (1986: 152) agrees with Nygaard on this: Storm and his proposal arrived too late. The year between 1904 and 1906 was no ordinary year in Norwegian history. It was the year when independence from Sweden was achieved. Many Riksmål users, usually amongst the conservative in society, were, like the majority of Norwegians of all political colours, fired by national feeling, and were in the mood for a more national-looking spelling system. They were tired of vagueness and were simply glad to have a fixed set of rules. What is more, the final reforms were not as radical as many had at first feared. They were a sort of compromise between Storm's proposals and the more extreme programme put forward in the official report of 1898 – *Om en del retskrivnings- og sprogspørgsmål* – by Jacob Aars (1837–1908), Simon Wright Hofgaard (1843–1908) and Moltke Moe. Storm may not have carried the standard in the end, but by holding up the official reform for a period of nine years he certainly caused all those involved to think. The 1907 reform was a success in that it was accepted fairly readily by ordinary Norwegians. Had the more radical spellings advanced in 1898 been allowed to go forward uncriticised, then this transition to the 1907 spelling might not have been so smooth.[30]

4.1.3.6.2 Back to the first 1904 volume, subtitled 'Nystaverne og deres radikale Reform', a compendium of articles which first appeared in *Aftenposten* in the period 1901–1903. The first article (from 1901) is entitled 'Rigsmaal og Retskrivning' (Riksmaal and orthography). This is Storm's reaction to the official proposals for reform from 1898. He begins by making his usual point: that he is essentially in agreement with the Norwegianisation of the language, but disagrees with attempts to reform the language *immediately* and *via the schools*. He then goes on to make 11 'key points' (*Grundsætninger*) about the relationship between the written and spoken forms of a 'language of culture'. By 1904 he did not have much new to add to his basic philosophy of language, which had remained unaltered since its first statements in the 1870s; but with subsequent reformulations this philosophy had gained in smoothness and force, such that this 1904 version is a vigorous statement of Storm's position. The rest of the article is dedicated to the specific areas of reform proposed by Aars, Hofgaard and Moe in 1898: 'hard' consonants, double consonants (orthographic geminates), alternative (Norwegian vs. Danish) spellings in the norm, punctuation and morphology. Examples abound, of course, including a string of examples from the New Testament where Storm maintains that the radical Norwegianised spelling is inappropriate for Biblical style. He was writing his treatise on Biblical language at the time, and was unable to parcel his linguistic thoughts into separate packages. Storm's conclusion to his study here is:

> the new orthography, far from ushering in more orderly conditions, is much more likely to create new doubt, new disorder, new confusion [. . .] In my opinion this proposal has come at least three generations or a century too soon. (1904: 48)

This last point is an interesting one for those of us who know what Bokmål looks like 100 years further on. In 'Rigsmaal og Retskrivning' Storm

---

[30] The 1907 reform, and events leading up to and following it, are covered in detail in Nygaard (1945) and in Haugen (1966). Steffens (1991) is a fresh re-evaluation of language reform from Knudsen until the Second World War.

attempts to shock his readers by giving an extreme form of what would happen to one of Asbjørnsen's tales if translated into 'the language of the New Spellers':

> Marie satte seg i græsset under den gamle *ek[en]*, og vi fulgte eksemplet. Da *bølget* det pludselig en tonestrøm hen over os. Forundret *lyttet* Marie og *stirret* opp i hvælvet av den mørke skygge*rike* krone, som om hun *ventet* at få øie på alle *skogens* vingede sangere. Jeg kjendte *tonene*; det var den gulbrystede sanger[en] som *ga* os denne koncert[en]. (1904: 42) (Storm's italics)

Modern Bokmål has gone slightly further in the direction of Norwegianisation, but in essence this is pretty much the sort of written Norwegian that Storm prophesied would indeed be appropriate 100 years on.

The next article to be reproduced in *NR*, also from 1901, is 'Professor Moltke Moe om Retskrivning'. As the title suggests, this piece, printed originally in two parts, is a review of two publications by Moe, *Retskrivning og Folkedannelse* (Moe 1900) and 'Det Filos. Fakultets Minoritets-Indstilling i Retskrivningssagen' from 1901. This latter is Moe's response to the October 1900 comments of Storm and Alf Torp (1853–1916), and reproduced in this reprinting. 'Professor Moltke Moe om Retskrivning' is a typical Storm review. It is not a review in any traditional sense, but an attack on specific points in the work being reviewed, backed up by copious examples. Storm cannot resist opening with what must be a sarcastic reference to Moe's failure to produce in 1884 (see section 4.3.2.1). In general Storm did respect Moe's abilities, and this warmth comes through in the article; but he needn't really have raised the issue of Moe's dilatoriness 20 years on:

> I have held back before voicing my opinion of this publication, in the hope that the long promised justification, the great tabular overview of our authors' orthography, would at last appear. However, after nearly a year only a small part (1 – one – proof sheet) has appeared [. . .]. (1904: 49)

There is little new in the first part of 'Professor Moe om Retskrivning', and Storm's usual points are trotted out, points about a radical reform constituting a violent and unnatural change in the language, by contrast with the more desirable procedure of a 'moderate and gradual adaptation of the orthography according to the sounds, as also a moderate and gradual Norwegianisation of the written language' (p. 53).

The second part is more interesting in that it is a defence of the clearest statement of Storm's reformist position, namely the document, supposedly co-authored by Storm and Torp, but reeking of Storm in every letter. This document is itself a commentary (commentaries within commentaries . . .) on the official faculty pronouncement, authored by Storm, Torp and Bugge, which was printed in *Morgenbladet* and *Aftenposten* on 4 June 1901 and also reproduced in this reprinting. The Storm–Torp commentary would form the basis for the second part of *NR*, which was essentially a fleshing-out of the general principles enunciated there. Storm saw this document as the official distillation of his views:

> I believe that I have provided a *practical* and *moderate* proposal for a common Norwegian orthography in the report, authored by Prof. *Torp* and me, to which the Faculty of Arts majority refers in its recommendation on the orthography issue [. . .]. (1904: 62)

Much of this second part of the attack on Moe is devoted to demolishing his statement that the intention to introduce the new spelling forms via the schools is in line with recent reform practices in Germany and France. Storm the European mercilessly deploys his knowledge of linguistic matters in Europe, as he had done elsewhere with other victims, to pour cold water on Moe's well-meant parallels.

The next article (1901) is entitled 'Det moderate Fremskridt i Retskrivningen' (The Moderate Advance in Orthography), and is a detailed study of the use of 'hard' (voiceless) consonants by Norwegian authors from the sixteenth century onwards, but specifically by the two great national writers of the nineteenth century: Ibsen and Bjørnson. The usage, specifically the lexical choices, of Norwegian writers from the sixteenth century on was, as we know, one of Storm's great interests, and he used the material he first collected in little notebooks, now amongst his papers in the National Library, on a number of occasions to show what Norwegian forms and spellings had been adopted by the canonical authors. The notebook now in NBO Ms. 4 1290, on Bjørnson's forms in his 1894 *Nye Fortællinger*, introduces a special section entitled 'Haarde Kons.', and the bulk of this article is indeed devoted to Bjørnson. The tide of data from Ibsen and Bjørnson washes up the following conclusion:

> With regard to the moderation that our two greatest authors exhibit, it must be evident to all sober-minded people that the time for the implementation of the hard consonants in the schools *has not yet come* [. . .] For the time being the schools should put up with writing *vide, bage, kjøbe*. Exceptions could be made in Ibsen's and Bjørnson's footsteps. To write *knakende kaldt* [creakingly cold] could be permitted a sixth-former or university student, but middle school pupils are too young to judge what the different registers require. (pp. 99–100)

The final two articles are both from 1903, both responding to events which took place that year. As always Storm the commentator, Storm the critic, was very quick to react to events in the language debate. 'Modersmaal. Maallag' presents his views on the establishment of *Bymaalslaget* as a subgroup within *Det norske Samlaget*, according to the testamentary wishes of Knud Knudsen and using funds made available by Knudsen's executors. Storm was really becoming a little obsessive by now, fearing the worst in every new development. Perhaps he had reason to feel beleaguered, or perhaps his battle with Knudsen simply continued despite the fact that his enemy had been dead for eight years. His fear here is that the existence of an 'urban language club' to continue Knudsen's work, alongside the existing Landsmål and Riksmål, would lead to yet further disunity in the Norwegian language. Against this he repeats his own programme several times and even more colourfully and forcibly than before. This is the language of someone who is about to reach boiling point, and it will be a relief when Storm lets off some steam via his own concrete proposals of 1904/1906. Entire statements are now being emphasised (spaced), the written equivalent of red-faced rant:

> *The only right and realistic revision of the written language is that which takes place via the authors and literature.* (p. 109)

Storm's being at boiling point seems to be most clearly expressed here through his completely unnecessary and unkind recipe, given in Knudsen's spelling, for an authentic Knudsen 'sour slop' (*sursørpe*):[31]

> Gi bymålet et Knudsensk opkok av hårde medlyd og nystavermål. Slæng ind en tvilyd her og der, så det blir en passelig målgraut. Spæd så op med østlandsk vasvilling, og strø på nogen avløser-nøtter til atpåsleik og krydder. Så er Maalrøra færdig og kan smøres utover hele landet. (p. 109)

The final piece in this first volume of *NR* is simply a brief commentary on a commentary on the document reproduced as appendix I to the volume, namely 'Kirke- og Undervisnings-Departementets Spørsmaal vedkommende Skolernes Retskrivning' (Questions of the ministry for the Church and education concerning the schools' orthography) of 1900. (More commentaries within commentaries. The debate is getting very dense as 1907 approaches.) Storm uses this opportunity to point out that there is in fact considerable opposition to the reforms outlined by the ministry in this questionnaire, reforms inspired by the 1898 report. He must truly have been a thorn in the side of a government trying to do something about Riksmål. All these articles show that, despite his being what we would now regard as of pensionable age, his responses to all developments in an "unnaturally" radical direction were swift and devastating. The Stormian arsenal of data and of rhetoric was impossible to counter. It is little wonder, whatever *Aftenposten* actually meant by its announcement, that the ministry had had enough by the end of 1903 and invited Storm to assist them as consultant 'in questions concerning Norwegian language and Norwegian orthography' 'If you can't beat them,' as the proverb goes, 'join them'.

---

[31] *Sur-sørpe* is in fact the suggestion Knudsen makes in his *Unorsk og norsk* for a Norwegian translation of the English 'mixed pickles'.

4.1.3.6.3 Storm was not the right man to pen the detailed reform proposals on behalf of the 'moderate' Riksmål reformers. He was the right *linguist* in that he was the spokesman for this movement, and he had unparalleled knowledge of the language in all its historical and contemporary varieties, but temperamentally he was unsuited to the task, just as he was temperamentally unsuited to the task of writing a textbook on English philology or French syntax. Linguistic truth was to be found via the unceasing, uncompromising search for more and more data, more and more examples. A language could only be fully understood if it was fully known. Any reforms which were going to work would have to be clear, straightforward and predictable, as Storm had argued; but he was evidently nevertheless aware that his own proposals were too detailed, complicated and full of exceptions. On a number of occasions he remarks that these proposals will need simplifying if they are to be adopted in the schools:

> But of course the schools must limit themselves to the most significant and to the pedagogically correct. In any textbook for use in the schools the rules given above [on the use of 'hard' consonants] could be considerably simplified. (1904/1906: 89)

So Storm's proposals are in the event no more practically applicable than those of his opponents. The greatest practical linguist in the world is finally defeated by his philosophy of the living language just at the point when he could have made the greatest impact in Norway. Storm the European had gradually learned to play second fiddle to Storm the Norwegian, and this could have been Storm the Norwegian's finest hour, but he blew it. He blew it in part by failing to complete his proposal in 1904, but he also blew it because his proposals were too detailed and impractical to implement.

In 1904/1906 he repeated his four reform principles, first set out in the faculty pronouncement of October 1900:

(1) Changes in the existing orthography should be *few* and *small*.
(2) They must be *genuine simplifications*.
(3) They must be introduced via *general practice*, via *real life*, not via the schools.
(4) The schools have to abide by what is *established*, not *pre-empt* developments, not *force* anything *new* on the pupils.

This is an admirable distillation of Storm's principles, but once the examples and the data enter into the equation, the admirable clarity gives way to confusing detail. Rules and examples for the use of 'hard' consonants fill over 70 pages, and words are divided into (1) those where only ⟨p, t, k⟩ should be used and (2) those where ⟨p, t, k⟩ are allowed. This latter category is further subdivided into cases where 'hard' consonants are 'best', cases where 'soft' consonants are best, cases where 'hard' consonants should only be used for emphasis and cases where 'hard' consonants should only be used in cases belonging stylistically to 'pure folk language'. Vinje (2001) describes the learning of Nynorsk by first-language Bokmål students as playing 'a finger at a time, note by note'. This is a neat image, and, if Storm's detailed proposals for the introduction of ⟨p, t, k⟩ had ever been adopted in their original form, this is exactly how Riksmål writers would have felt, looking forms up, word by word, in order to identify their exact ⟨p, t, k⟩ status, and scratching their heads to decide whether what they were writing was an example of 'higher or more noble style', 'homely or day-to-day (familiar) style' or 'folksy (popular or vulgar) style', according to Storm's definitions (1904/1906: 9–10). More just didn't mean better.

4.1.3.7 Franske Taleøvelser *(1897) revisited*

4.1.3.7.1 As we noted in section 3.2.2.2, there was a Norwegian programme behind Storm's 1897 collection of *Franske Taleøvelser*. The book contains a series of French dialogues, mostly taken from the dramatic literature, together with Norwegian parallel texts, and Storm states in the preface that it is these Norwegian parallel texts which cost him the greatest effort in writing the book. This advanced-level set of dialogues was produced in what we could call his second Norwegian period, from 1895 onwards, and it is inevitable that he should focus on Norwegian and his Norwegian text as he wrote. His expressed aim in the Norwegian texts is to give a natural-sounding Norwegian to mirror the natural-sounding French of the original. He does not seek to give a full phonetic transcription of the Norwegian, and so this little project is not in the tradition of his dialectological work, nor does he aim to exemplify a revised spelling system. He is adamant on this latter point: 'It is no Maalstræv' (Storm 1897: ii). If anything, the way in which he presents Norwegian here is in the tradition of *A Selection of Phrases for Tourists Travelling in Norway*. He aims to provide a guide to the way in which Norwegian is actually pronounced, but in a practical and helpful way that can be of use to the average (non-phonetically trained) reader.

The variety of Norwegian Storm is trying to reflect is no surprise:

> [. . .] I have tried to present the *educated spoken language of the capital*, which is by and large the one single common spoken language of the towns and cities, indeed of the whole country. (1897a: ii)

4.1.3.7.2 The most striking feature of Storm's Norwegian text is the use of the apostrophe to indicate segments which appear in the written language but which are not realised in this spoken variety of Norwegian. Thus we have *no'n* for *nogen* (*nogle*) ('some' (pl.)), *ha't* for *havt* ('had'), *gi'* for *give* ('give'), *det fin's* for *det findes* ('there is'), and so on. The grammar is lightly Norwegianised, notably in those cases where the Norwegian and Danish plural forms differed from each other. Danish has *Heste* ('horses') while

Norwegian has *Hester*, for example. Storm is not, however, over-consistent in this respect, as he accused Knudsen of being. When a text demands a more elevated style, he chooses the Danish form instead, the form associated with more elevated, literary language. As well as a selection of phonological and grammatical features, he introduces some characteristically Norwegian lexicon, where appropriate. Thus in dialogue 9, where he notes that 'in the translation the language of the younger generation is emulated' (p. 30, n. 3), he gives *graate* ('to cry') alongside the Danish *græde*.

Storm's Norwegianisation or colloquialisation of written Danish is no more than slight stylistic colouring, and it is possible to read some sections of dialogue without realising that this is anything other than normal written Danish. He is quite clear about this not being a contribution to the reform process, and he certainly did not intend anyone to adopt this spelling as a serious alternative to the inherited written language. So why are we looking at it now in our section on Storm and language reform? First, it would be naïve to try to understand anything Storm wrote around the turn of the century without reference to his views on and his contributions to language reform. He was obsessed by it. Secondly, by appearing to have to work so hard at his Norwegian translations, he showed that 'the one single common spoken language of the whole country' is systematically different from written Danish. This was hardly news, but he suggests that some of these systematic differences may, in the fullness of time, be adopted by the written language:

> With this form I have only intended to present the living *spoken language*, not to set up any model for the written language. I certainly believe that the written language will change in this direction in the fullness of time. But the written language only ever follows the spoken language *slowly*; it takes a long time for all authors to come on board. And there is no rush either [. . .] What I have wanted is simply to present the *real, living, idiomatic spoken language* to the reader. (Storm 1897a: iv)

4.1.3.8 *Was Storm Right?*

4.1.3.8.1 Storm's involvement in the reform process was protracted, spanning three decades. It was concerted in that he kept making the same points in different contexts, points he believed in and points informed by detailed knowledge of the Norwegian situation and of the situation in other languages. It was devastating through being immediate and directed indiscriminately at radical "unnatural" reform proposals wherever they manifested themselves, irrespective of party colour or background ideology. It was not completely indiscriminate, though. Storm respected Ivar Aasen and he respected the basis for Knud Knudsen's programme. He respected much of what both Hans Ross in the one camp and Moltke Moe in the other had to say.

Storm was unavoidable. He was a mountain that was always there between radicals and their goals. Whenever they manoeuvred round the mountain, they found the mountain had moved too. Storm was most frustrating of all because he had the knowledge. He could destroy any ideological argument with a crushing data blow at any moment. In the end the man shouting from the sidelines was invited into the game, but it turned out that he didn't know the rules after all.

1907 was not Storm's moment, as it might have been if he had been able to handle the opportunity better. Actual reform, while certainly moderated by his influence, was based on forms in the spoken language rather than forms which had acquired status through use in the literature. What of the long term? Has history proved Storm right? The simple answer is 'No'. Riksmål, as Storm and the *Riksmålsforbundet* (the modern successor to *Rigsmaalsforeningen*) understand it, is not one of the two standard varieties formally taught and promulgated in Norway. However, the 'moderate conservative' Bokmål written by the majority of Norwegians today is in ethos closer to Storm's programme than to any of the other nineteenth-century programmes, and is in practice more or less identical in form to modern Riksmål. Venås (2000b: 336) writes that 'a normal linguistic eye cannot distinguish those two from each other'. To non-Norwegians this scenario must seem bizarre. There appear to be *three* varieties of standard Norwegian here, two of which are essentially the same, but with different names (not to mention Høgnorsk (High Norwegian) – see Linn 2003c). The scenario is as it is because, for the first half of the twentieth century, Bokmål moved away from Riksmål, as the Knudsen programme triumphed via political intervention over the Storm programme. During the last 50 years, as usage has been left more to its own devices, to develop through practice, Bokmål has increasingly swung back in line with Riksmål. This would, I suspect, have made Storm very happy. His prophecy of 1904 seems to have been fulfilled, although we can't undo the twentieth-century history of Norwegian. Whether it would have been fulfilled *without* language engineering along the Knudsen lines, we will never know:

> The New Spellers, K. Knudsen's successors and heirs, must first convert the *general public*, before they embark on converting the schools. If they can just get Ibsen, Bjørnson and all the other authors to adopt the new system, they will have won the game.
> If this doesn't happen, then it will probably be best to leave the language and the public in peace. Then the hard consonants and other Norwegian forms will come in over the course of several generations, first in the spoken language, and then, little by little, in the written language too. (1904: 31)

4.1.3.8.2 And what about *Landsmaal*, modern Nynorsk? Here Storm's prophecy that the language would 'suffer the fate of all artificial languages:

it will pass quietly away' (1896c: 115) was not fulfilled. The fortunes of the
language have risen and fallen over the past 100 years, but it is alive.
Without the political support of the 1890s and subsequent language engineering, what would have happened then? Would Storm have been proved
right? Here I will duck out of the debate. History isn't open to speculation . . .
However, even dyed-in-the-wool Landsmål supporters have had to admit
that Storm did utter many a wise word:

> Storm did not have an eye for the forces which drove language reform
> forward. But there was much that was right in the detail of his criticism,
> both of Knudsen's tastelessness and of the disorder and the affectation
> [*rotet og knotet*] in Landsmaal. (Liestøl 1920)

4.2 CHARTING THE LANGUAGE

4.2.1 *History of the Language*

4.2.1.1 Oldn. Sproghistorie *(1869)*

4.2.1.1.1 Storm made two serious attempts to write a history of the
Norwegian language. I have referred to both of these already and so will
not dwell on them here, but their stories do need to be told at this point for
the sake of completeness. They both correspond to the topics of his lectures
on Norwegian and, had they been written, would have focused on the
dialects and the history of Norwegian sounds. They would both certainly
have expounded Storm's views on language reform too. Storm's first
published work, 'Tale og Accent i Forhold til Sang' from 1860, dealt
with the sounds of Norwegian. His second publication, the revision of
Bennetts Practiske Lærebog, was a commission, or at least it was not work
Storm undertook purely of his own volition. The next attempt to write
something original was the first of his attempts to chart the Norwegian
language, the incomplete *Oldn. Sproghistorie* (History of the Old Norwegian Language) of 1869. Before he could finish this work, of course, he left
for southern Europe, and his attention turned to the Romance languages.
In the midst of all the Romance work, which grew from his travels and
from his appointment at the university, there appeared another work in the
tradition of 1860 and 1869, namely 'Om Tonefaldet (Tonelaget) i de
skandinaviske Sprog', delivered as a lecture in 1874 and published in
1875 (Storm 1875a). In 1874 (8 November) he wrote to Thomsen that he
had 'a real desire to write about the sounds of Norwegian and about many
other things':

> I have a great *compulsion* to produce, but in part lack the corresponding
> ability and especially the opportunity to do so, since one cannot anywhere
> get paid for such work.

So, it does appear that there was some truth in Storm's description of Norwegian as his 'first love', since he kept on returning to it whenever possible, and the 1877 application to parliament to write the *Værk over det norske Sprog* (Work on the Norwegian Language) was his attempt to return to Norwegian, if not once and for all, then at least without interruption from other work. Storm was the Norwegianist who never was, the Norwegianist *manqué*. Had he been born at a time when it was possible to specialise in Norwegian and to find a post in Norwegian studies which was not politically determined, I feel sure that this is the direction he would have chosen, rather than English and the Romance languages.

The notes for *Oldn. Sproghistorie* survive as NBO Ms. 8° 2402 A1. The introduction could have been written at any stage in Storm's career. His interests and his obsessions are evident from the very beginning. It opens with these words:

The main aim in this work is to describe the sounds of our mother tongue compared with the sound elements of other well-known languages, and particularly those characteristics of our sound system that are specifically Norwegian, in short the *sound physiognomy of the mother tongue* viewed from a European point of view.

This is interesting, because it shows Storm to have had a European perspective, to have been able to view Norwegian with the eyes of an outsider, even before he had travelled abroad to any great extent and gained a cosmopolitan outlook (leaving aside the brief trip of 1858). After this statement of intent to write a comparative phonetics from a European standpoint, Storm the Norwegian, his alter ego, immediately steps forward:

By mother tongue we here mean the common *spoken language* used by the *educated classes* around the country, not only as it is written, but also, and especially, as it really sounds, particularly in colloquial speech [*i den daglige Tale*].

So here is the complete Storm, in a sense, encapsulated in the opening words of a document written at the moment he was about to appear as an authority, the year of his appointment to the university.

After this introduction, like all Storm's introductions a little "manifesto" in itself, he moves on to plot the history of the language to the year 1400. Six incomplete notebooks, rich with examples and samples, cater for the vowels. Further notebooks deal with 'Oldnorske Konsonanter' and 'Dialektiske Forandringer i Oldnorsk'. By this stage the notes are very schematic, and they finally peter out. There are other notes from later which indicate that Storm made attempts to continue with this work, but, when it came down to it, he was simply too busy with other work. 'Time! Time! Time!', as he wrote to Thomsen in the same letter of 8 November 1874. Although incomplete, the *Oldn. Sproghistorie* remains a significant landmark in his intellectual development.

4.2.1.1.2 In 1875 Storm had a number of related Norwegian projects on the go, according to a letter to Thomsen written on 5 August that year. These projects would combine in the single undertaking set out two years later in 1877 (see next section), but in 1875 they are separate, as if he is doing a bit of this and a bit of that, unsure which direction to take. He mentions a *Norwegian Grammar* (with this English title) on which he had been working since the previous year. He also mentions a *Norse Phonetics* (again with this English title), which he had offered to the Philological Society for publication. This offer was turned down by Henry Nicol, writing on 21 July, on behalf of Ellis and Furnivall. With the lack of success of these individual projects, Storm is beginning to look ahead at something more ambitious, something he (mistakenly) believes will be more successful:

> I am thinking now about a more detailed work in Norwegian on the Norwegian or Dano-Norwegian language, and I have reason to believe that I will get a publisher for it.

4.2.1.2 Værk over det norske Sprog *(1877)*

4.2.1.2.1 This 'work' was the spiritual successor to the *Oldn. Sproghistorie*, the *Værk over det norske Sprog* (*Værk*). The wording of the opening of *Oldn. Sproghistorie* and the opening of the incomplete draft of *Værk* is almost identical. So important was this failed project that it has been subject to romanticisation in the secondary literature about Storm. Hambro (1937) is a retelling of the *Værk* saga, and one which turns Storm into a tragic hero, a hero who 'had suffered much' (p. 59), one of those who, despite being 'badly paid [. . .] highly educated, giving much and demanding little', 'bore Norway through the nineteenth century' (p. 75). This is all very colourful, and we have already seen that the events of 1877 had a significant impact on the direction Storm's work took, in that his early passion for the history and structure of the Norwegian language was rerouted into reform polemic and into concentration on the languages he was actually employed to study. However, we should not exaggerate the effects of the *Værk* business. Storm was a tough individual. He had had a tough youth and he was quite capable of riding the storm. He told Thomsen (31 May 1877) that he 'is not grieving over it particularly'. Well, it was a blow to him, but, as I say, he was made of stern stuff.

The *Værk* story has been told in little pieces throughout the course of this book so far, mainly because the application Storm sent to parliament in 1877 is such a fount of information about him, and the only real autobiographical account we have. In what follows, then, I will stick mainly to external events, rather than the contents of the application, and finish the story off. My account is based on that provided by Holter (1986: 28–36).[32]

In order to complete the work on Norwegian, begun in 1869 and continued through the public lectures of 1875, Storm decided to apply to parliament for 1,600 kroner per year for two years to give him the necessary freedom from other responsibilities and financial worries. Such an application had to be approved by the relevant university authorities before being sent on to the national level, and, as he reported in his application (Storm 1877a: 7), both the faculty and the *akademiske Kollegium* recommended that the application should proceed. The application continued smoothly through the bureaucratic machine, being approved by the appropriate government ministry (*Kirkedepartementet*) on 10 February, and by the budget committee three months later. Meanwhile Storm's opponents had started to express their views in the newspapers. We have already heard Garborg's objections in *Aftenbladet*. *Dagbladet* was cautious in its reaction, but hoped, despite some of the unfortunate aspects of the application, not least Storm's immodest statements of his own ability, that parliament would be sympathetic. An anonymous reviewer in *Verdens Gang*, like Garborg in *Aftenbladet*, was more negative, but also more offensive, casting doubt on Storm's competence and on the usefulness of phonetics, 'since parrots and crows can also fruitfully be taught phonetics' (17 March 1877).

Against the background of this sniping in the national press, Storm's case came before parliament on 9 May and, following a recount, was voted against by 51 votes to 50. The closeness of the vote was all the more frustrating for Storm since it appears that one of the members of parliament arrived too late for the vote, thanks to the bell not being rung. Had this member, Walter Scott Dahl (1839–1906), been able to vote, he would, he stated, have voted in favour, and, with the casting vote of Stortingspresident Bernhard Ludvig Essendrop (1812–1891), Storm would have got his money (*Morgenbladet*, 10 May 1877). If events were exactly as they were reported, then this was a cruel blow of fate. If the bell had rung and Storm had got the money, the subsequent history of the Norwegian language would probably have been quite different. This is no exaggeration, since Storm's *Værk over det norske Sprog* would necessarily have become a central plank in debates, and he himself a more central figure, leading to more cautious, less radical policies for both Landsmål and Riksmål. It is always tempting to write the history that might have been, but we must stick to what actually happened.

What actually happened next constituted a further blow to Storm. As *Aftenbladet* for the day in question reported it:

At the following vote, by contrast, the recommendation to grant kand. theol. Ross 2,000 kroner was approved unanimously and without debate.

---

[32] The story is also told in Longum (1989).

Hans Matthias Elisæus Ross (1833–1914) had shown an early interest in the dialects, an interest furthered by "dialect journeys" from 1866 onwards.[33] From 1867 to 1869 he had a grant from the university to investigate the Norwegian dialects. Aasen's *Norsk Grammatik* had appeared in 1864, so dialects and dialect study were very much on the agenda at this time. In 1870 his application for an extension of the grant was turned down, but he continued to publish folk literature and related studies. In 1877 Ross too applied to parliament, in his case for 2,000 kroner per year, and parliament agreed, although not, as *Aftenbladet*'s account has it, completely unanimously – there was one voice of dissent. This sum was raised to 2,400 kroner in 1880 and to 3,500 kroner the following year, and the amount was raised several times thereafter. Even when he retired from active work, Ross maintained a state pension of 3,500 kroner per year. Why was Ross successful, when Storm wasn't? The feeling, echoed by Hambro 60 years later, was that the respective outcomes of the Storm and Ross applications were politically motivated. As Hambro put it (1937: 69), 'Hans Ross was an ardent and active left-winger and one of the founders of Det Norske Samlaget; Storm was a conservative.' Be that as it may, but Ross was also a safer pair of hands, with proven capability in his field. Of course the ever-active newspapers were quick to debate this outcome, and the debates rumbled on into the new year and a piece in *Morgenbladet* on 5 January 1878, where, amongst other things, Storm reported subsequent developments.

He stated that, despite encouragements from others, he had not renewed his application, since 'one does not appeal twice in the same court'. The events of May 1877 had been a humiliation, and, understandably, he did not want to go through it all again. In this same *Morgenbladet* piece, Storm went on to write:

> I was on the other hand in no position to turn down a gift of 1,600 kroner from an anonymous donor, who described himself simply as an old pupil.

Somebody appreciated Storm, and this anonymous gift is really quite moving. But it didn't enable Storm to finish his major work on Norwegian:

> Despite the support I have mentioned I could not all the same continue my work on Old Norwegian [. . .] I have on the other hand started some works on *English philology* and *the history of the language*, which I hope to be able to complete in a shortish time, and which should hopefully in the form of handbooks be of benefit to students.

4.2.1.2.2 Both Hambro and Holter make much of Storm's defeat, and it is certainly tempting to see Storm as crushed by this blow. He had invested a

---

[33] See Seip (1952).

lot in the application. He had publicly aired his financial difficulties, something which cannot have been easy for such a private person, and he had been subjected to a very public humiliation, both in the newspapers and by the nation's parliament. However, events caused him to channel his energies and abilities into new areas. If he had produced the *Værk*, and if, as would have been possible, the period of funding had been extended, he might have devoted himself to the study of Norwegian, something whose outcome, as we postulated above, would have been fascinating to know. Just imagine the history of the Norwegian language over the last 100 years dictated by Storm! Modern Riksmål proponents may sometimes dream of this. But he might then not have become the internationally important linguist he did become. Storm the European might have acquiesced to Storm the Norwegian. More speculation. Nevertheless, I cannot fully agree with Holter that 'the rejection [. . .] delayed and reduced his opportunities for further research and for the publication of his results' (Holter 1986: 36), and I can even less accord with Hambro's statement that 'after parliament in 1877 had rejected Storm's application, there was a downward turn in the liveliness and elasticity of his output' (p. 72). In 1877 Storm had barely started his extraordinary, wide-ranging, passionate, international publishing career. Even from the point of view of Norwegian, the best was yet to come. The incomplete drafts of *Værk* still lie there in the National Library, but so does all the phonetic/dialectological work, which has been a treasure trove of information for Norwegian linguists ever since. And he was certainly not going to be silent on the subject of Norwegian in newspapers and books alike in the course of the next 30 years. 1877 was a blow, yes, an *annus horribilis*, but it had a positive effect. The idea of a major project, charting the history and structure of Norwegian, had been in Storm's mind for a decade or so. That year finally cleared his mind and settled him firmly on course: *Engelsk Filologi* appeared two years later.

4.2.2 *Advisory Work*

4.2.2.1 A Selection of Phrases for Tourists *(4th edition 1881)*

4.2.2.1.1 A decade or more after his first collaboration with the English entrepreneur, Thomas Bennett (see section 2.3.4), Storm worked with him again to produce another practical language book, this time a Norwegian phrasebook – the cover reads *Bennett's English–Norwegian Phrasebook*. As with the *Practiske Lærebog i det engelske Sprog*, Storm was engaged by Bennett to revise the book which had first appeared in 1870, and the full title is *A Selection of Phrases for Tourists travelling in Norway by T. Bennett, fourth edition enlarged and revised by Johan Storm, Professor of English and the Romance Languages at the University of Christiania*. Bennett made a great deal of money out of the Anglo-Norwegian tourist industry, and we can assume that this phrasebook was a successful part of his empire. Perhaps more than anywhere else, *A Selection of Phrases for Tourists* (*SPT*) demonstrates Storm's extraordinary skill in carrying out both highly scientific and intensely practical language work. That year was also the year of publication of the German translation of *Engelsk Filologi* and the year of foundation of the Forening for norske Dialekter og Folketraditioner. It was all part of the broad spectrum constituting *det levende Sprog*, of course, but few linguists are or have been able to dovetail the scientific and the practical like Storm, because few are able to obscure the distinction between the two approaches as he did. In his review of the third edition, Aars (1876) expressed his amazement at Storm's impressive linguistic schizophrenia:

> One notices everywhere the learned phonetician's fine observation, at the same time as the organisation of the whole, the disposition of the material, the applied transcription system and the representation of expressions and turns of phrase strike one as wonderfully practical.

4.2.2.1.2 The phonetic transcription is perhaps the most striking feature of this slim volume, and it would have been unthinkable for Storm to have been involved with a book on the spoken language without using phonetic transcription. However, the system used is a simple one, providing a small amount of extra phonetic information, just enough to help the non-specialist linguist get nearer to an authentic pronunciation. Knowing how Storm's practical publications developed, *Franske Taleøvelser* or the dialect wordlists for example, we can guess that any subsequent editions of *SPT* would have included greater (less helpful) phonetic detail. There weren't any further editions involving Storm, although a fifth edition did appear in 1891 and a sixth edition in 1899, the year after Bennett's death, so let us simply give Storm the credit on this occasion for hitting the right note with his intended readership. In fact the opening 'Remarks' indicate that 'in the present fourth edition the phonetic spelling has been simplified' since the third edition, with which Storm was also involved (Bennett 1881: 2).

In addition to regular Scandinavian graphemes (i.e. including ⟨æ⟩, ⟨å⟩, ⟨ö⟩ and ⟨ø⟩), Storm introduces a small number of other symbols. He provides ⟨ə⟩, and he provides ⟨'l⟩ and ⟨'n⟩ for syllabic consonants, both useful techniques for helping readers achieve the correct stress. To this same end he adds quantity diacritics to the vowel symbols. On the consonant side there are four extra symbols:

⟨*l*⟩ = italicised l for retroflex (*thick*) [ɽ]
⟨ng⟩ for [ŋ]
⟨sj⟩ for [ʃ]
⟨kj⟩ for [ç]

All these symbols are explained in the opening section on 'Phonetic signs' and, in my view, constitute an unthreatening, sensible middle ground between leaving the would-be Norwegian speaker to fend for him- or herself, and confusing and alienating the reader with too many "funny symbols". Tone is covered briefly in a footnote, where Storm honestly but comfortingly describes it as 'difficult to imitate, but essential to the understanding' (p. 5). He does include symbols to indicate the two tonemes, but for more detail the reader is referred to Storm (1875a), to Sweet (1877) and to Storm (1881a).

The phonetic transcriptions give the pronunciation of the written (i.e. Dano-Norwegian) form as it would typically be pronounced in the sort of Norwegian heard amongst educated inhabitants of the capital, Storm's preferred model variety. However, Storm also includes more Norwegian or more colloquial pronunciations in bracketed italics, where that form is likely to be encountered. The best way of showing Storm's technique is to cite some examples:

1 Hvad er [der] at faa her? | Va ær [der] at få hær (*va ær də å få hær?*)

2 Faar De meget Hø iaar? | Får di mē ʻgɔt (*møʻe*) hø (*höi*) i-år?

3 Er der [nogen] Hjerper i | Ær der [*nöˋn*] jerʻpər i skå'vən (*sköu' ən*)?
  Skoven?

4 Et stort, rundt Hoved | Et stort, runt hoʻvəd (*hōˋdə*, vulg. *hūə*)

Forms like 'hūə' and 'møʻe' are really quite surprising and would not have been common in normal educated parlance. Storm's inclusion of a lengthy excursus on the appropriate word for *toilet* (footnote to the headword 'Privy' on page 81) also shows a strongly realist programme behind this practical language resource. The book concludes with 'Some practical hints on the pronunciation', and again these are brief, unthreatening and practically useful. They chiefly involve notes on the articulation of certain vowel distinctions, but Storm's advice on the adoption of 'standard' vs. 'colloquial' variants is interesting:

As a general rule do not try the colloquial form except where this is indicated as the only one used. Norwegians are accustomed to hear the literal pronunciation used by foreigners. The colloquial form is given here chiefly to assist the *understanding* of the spoken language. But if you can manage a really good imitation of the latter, this is of course to be preferred. (Bennett 1881: 132)

This reminds us of his advice in Storm (1890a) to Norwegians learning French, where he advises that the uvular [ʁ] of French is best avoided unless it can be reproduced really well. Storm was himself 'the greatest practical linguist in the world' but he was practical in another sense too – he knew what in practice was right for the average language learner.

4.2.2.1.3 The bulk of the book is ordered alphabetically by headword, from 'About' down to 'Yours', and one or more English phrases or sentences is given next to each headword, showing how the word is used in context. The third column contains the 'Norwegian' orthographic form of the given phrase or sentence. This column is labelled 'Norwegian'. It is to all intents and purposes identical to Danish, but Storm is true to his cautious reform principles, and includes Norwegian written variants which are in regular use. Thus the Danish form *Er min Seng redet?* ('Is my bed made?') includes the Norwegian form (*redd op*) in brackets, and the English question 'Are there foxes here?' (perhaps one of the less practical phrases in the book!) is rendered as 'Er der (*det*) Ræv her?' The fourth column gives the phonetic transcription and, all things considered, English-speaking tourists arriving at Bennett's office in Kristiania, and equipping themselves for their stay in Norway, would have had access to a useful little book.

SPT concludes with a series of tables, designed further to improve the book's practical worth. Thus we find an overview of the days of the week, the months of the year, and cardinal and ordinal numbers. There are, of course, footnotes: the scientific linguist could not keep his nose out of matters completely. These footnotes tend to be of a historical and/or comparative hue, but they are not obtrusive, and in some cases would have been of real interest to the general reader. For example, an English speaker learning the word 'Mad (*Mat*)' would probably have been intrigued to learn that it is 'the same word as the English *meat* which formerly meant food or repast in general, comp. His *meat* was locusts and wild honey Matth. III. 4. Jesus sat at *meat* Matth. IX. 10 etc.' (p. 40).

Few linguistic works survive their day less well than phrase-books. Their style and their content are irredeemably wedded to their own time, so, while a twenty-first-century reader might well benefit from reading *Større fransk Syntax*, for example, an English-speaker planning to visit Norway today should probably look elsewhere. However, imitation, they say, is the highest form of flattery, and if this is true, then Storm's revision of Bennett received the ultimate honour.

4.2.2.1.4 In January 1888 Storm complained to Thomsen that *SPT* had appeared in a German version, and not a version that he had himself produced or approved. It had been 'completely plagiarised' by one Svend Christensen. Storm requested Thomsen to do whatever he could to find out who this Christensen was, since he appeared to be Danish. Thomsen did not have to do much research into the identity of Christensen, although he wouldn't have got very far, even if he'd tried. 'Svend Christensen' turned out to be the pseudonym of 'a poor literary devil' whom Storm was too diplomatic to name in his next letter to Thomsen (18 May). It seems that the offender came clean, presumably having discovered that Storm was on the warpath. He pleaded with Storm for forgiveness 'in such a moving way that I could not deny him'. And so ended that little episode, as abruptly as it had begun.

4.2.2.2 Lexicon Lapponicum *(1887)*

4.2.2.2.1 There are two other projects Storm worked on in an advisory capacity, revising the phonetic side of linguistic works written by others. Neither project dealt with Norwegian. The one dealt with Ancient Greek and the other Sami – not exactly Storm's usual areas – but in both cases it was his phonetic insights that the original authors wanted to make use of. As neither piece of work involved the Norwegian language, they should probably not be discussed in this chapter, but the nature of the work was the same as Storm's involvement with *SPT*, so it does make sense to consider these excursions into Ancient Greek and Sami – languages at opposite ends of the spectrum of nineteenth-century comparative linguistics – at this point.

4.2.2.2.2 Storm's colleague Jens Andreas Friis (1821–1896), professor of Sami and *Kvensk* (the Finnish spoken in northern Norway), seems to have used him as phonetic adviser to his *Lexicon Lapponicum* (*Ordbog over det lappiske Sprog*). This Sami–Latin/Norwegian dictionary came with a grammatical introduction. The grammatical sections proper are unremarkable from our point of view, but the first few pages – on 'letters and their pronunciation' (Friis 1887: xv–xvii) – have a familiar flavour. There are lots of comparisons with the sounds of a range of different languages, and there are plenty of footnotes giving references to *Norvegia*, to *Englische Philologie* and to Lundell. Storm is nowhere credited with any part in this work, but we don't need to be great literary detectives to spot his hand here. I imagine that Friis showed him the proofs one day and asked if he had any comments. Storm, being Storm, took the job more seriously than Friis had a right to expect.

4.2.2.3 Græsk Grammatik til Skolebrug *(1866)*

4.2.2.3.1 In his application to parliament in 1877 Storm claimed among other things that he had 'taken an active role in the revision of *Curtius's Greek school grammar*' (1877a: 4), and indeed he had. The translator and editor of this work, Valentin Voss, thanks a number of people in the preface, including 'cand. mag. Storm'. It is not clear why Storm's opinions were invited, but the Norwegian linguistic milieu at this time was very small, and there were not many language experts available. Twenty years later, when the milieu was somewhat expanded, it was still the professor of English and Romance who was called upon to advise on an official translation from Greek to Norwegian, the text that resulted in the 1904 New Testament. It is not so surprising, then, that the linguistic Wunderkind, J. Storm, was invited to comment on this prestigious and successful school grammar. It was used in the majority of Norwegian schools, and the first edition of 1859 had sold out its 1,000 copies by 1865.

4.2.2.3.2 Voss thanks Storm for his 'many interesting individual comments and comparisons with other languages' – 'above all in the grammatical sections'. In Storm's own copy of the book this last phrase is underlined in red with an exclamation mark. I assume this is because Storm's contributions were not so much to the grammatical sections (the *Formlære*) as to the sections on pronunciation, the *Lydlære*. Curtius's grammar is highly traditional, divided into two parts, a *Formlære* and a *Syntax*. The *Formlære* is in turn divided into a *Lydlære*, a *Bøiningslære* and an *Orddannelseslære*. Traditionally phonology, inflectional morphology and derivational morphology were subsumed under *Formlære*, comprising the *forms* of the language which could then be combined according to the rules of *syntax*, so Voss naturally thanks Storm for his help with the *Formlære*. Storm is one of the new generation of linguists, though, for whom the sounds constituted a completely independent object of study, hence his rather ungrateful exclamation mark next to Voss's words of thanks. Storm's presence is indeed keenly felt in the *Lydlære*, via comparisons with English, Old Norse, Modern Norwegian, Swedish and other languages too.

4.2.3 *Literary Studies*

4.2.3.1 *Biblical Language*

4.2.3.1.1 *Storm's Involvement*

4.2.3.1.1.1 It may seem an odd dismembering of Storm's *opus* to deal with his work on Biblical language under the heading of 'Literary studies', but there are good reasons for doing so. First, the Bible is firmly sited amongst English *literature* in *Engelsk Filologi/Englische Philologie*. In Storm (1896a) it follows on neatly from the section on Shakespeare, and the section on the language of the Bible is heralded by the words:

> After the secular writers of the seventeenth century, the language of the rightfully famous *Authorised Version of the Bible* probably deserves to be studied. (Storm 1896a: 995)

Secondly, Storm approaches the language of the Bible in exactly the same way as he approaches the language of Norwegian literature – as a corpus of data and a mine of examples. We have previously mentioned Storm's spiritual life, and noted some religious elements which are probably the result of his having grown up the son of a pastor. Religious language and Lutheran practices formed a backdrop to his life and work, although, as he told Thomsen in 1898 following Gunnar's death, he had always been too busy to develop this side of his life. Gunnar's death was of course a "life event" for Storm. It gave him cause to consider his spiritual dimension, and he vowed, he implies, to devote himself to it more vigorously from here onwards:

> [. . .] my Louise is so pious and devoted to God's will [. . .] I try too, as well as I can. I have never been a non-believer, but perhaps half-hearted, mortal, occupied with my studies. But this has shaken me. Now with God's help things will be different. (11 July 1898)

So Storm's principal contribution to Biblical literature (Storm 1906) was published in what we might call the religious phase of his life. He had been the objective scholar for too long though, and, apart from his evident devotion to duty, there is little to show that his involvement was anything other than scientific.

It might have been reasonable to look at *Bibelsproget* (Storm 1906) in the context of his reform work. *Bibelsproget* it was that interrupted his production of *Norsk Retskrivning*, and possibly prevented his reforms getting onto the statute books in 1907, and it is, as we shall see in a moment, essentially a reform document, detailing reforms adopted or not adopted in the new translation of the New Testament. When he was writing *Bibelsproget* – it is dated October 1905 – reform principles were at the forefront of his mind, but, despite its subject matter, *Bibelsproget* is not a direct contribution to the reform debate, to the question of the desirability or otherwise of the Knudsen programme.

4.2.3.1.1.2 On his retirement from the professorship of theology in 1870, Professor Jacob Frederik Dietrichson (1806–1879) was given the task of providing a new translation of the New Testament from first principles. Dietrichson was elderly and not *au courant* with recent Biblical scholarship or recent linguistic thought, and by the time he abandoned the project due to ill health in 1877, a new approach was called for. The work was taken up by Dietrichson's professorial successor, and from 1893 bishop of Kristiania, Frederik Wilhelm Klumpp Bugge (1838–1896), who completed the translation on the one hand and revised the work done by Dietrichson on the other. Bugge's original work was complete by 1887, and his revision of Dietrichson three year later.

Storm's involvement with the new translation of the New Testament went back as far as 1888. On 12 May of that year *Morgenbladet* announced the plans for publication of the new translation:

> The central committee of the Norwegian Bible Society has appointed a committee, consisting of Professors *Caspari*, *Johnson* and *F. W. Bugge*, on which Professor *Joh. Storm* has, at the request of the central committee,

joined the three men mentioned, as consultant with regard to Norwegian language issues [. . .]

The committee had begun work already on 1 February, and Storm was in august company. The other members were Carl Paul Caspari (1814–1892), Gisle Christian Johnson (1822–1894) and F. W. Bugge. Although Bugge was more or less the same age as Storm, Storm would outlive Bugge by a quarter of a century, and the other two committee members were of an older generation. Caspari was born and educated in Germany, and only moved to Kristiania in 1848 to take up a lektor post at the university. He became professor of theology in 1857. Although he only settled in Norway in his 30s, his reputation was formidable, and the *Norsk biografisk leksikon* describes him as 'founder of a scholarly Norwegian theology'. Johnson became professor of theology in 1860 and had a profound influence on Norwegian practical theology as the founder of the so-called orthodox-pietistic movement within Norwegian Lutheranism. Storm was the obvious choice as linguistic adviser. Whatever his views on the reform of the written language, he understood Norwegian like nobody else at the time, and, unlike Aasen or Knudsen for example, he had the appropriate academic gravitas. His 'moderate conservative' outlook matched the attitude of the rest of the committee towards the project, and the faith the other committee members placed in Storm's involvement was certainly repaid. Holter (1966: 406–407) is of the opinion that the committee did indeed have a lot of faith in Storm:

> The committee was soon convinced that in Storm they had found a man who was so valuable to the work that he should have the same status on the committee as they did themsleves. His annual fee of 800 kroner was therefore raised to 1,200, as much as for the others.

Storm, the only member of the committee to survive to see its work come to fruition, took the work very seriously. He set about a rigorous study of the language of the text straightaway. His working method emerges clearly from the notebooks now housed in Bergen University Library (Ms. 744). He began with the text of St Luke's Gospel and of the Letter of James: these were the two books dealt with first by the committee, and their translations were published as a sample of the project in 1891. Storm's linguistic commentary on the translation of these two books is dated September 1888, so he worked quickly as well as seriously. His working notes are (inevitably) contained in small notebooks, and are based on a handwritten copy of the translation. This copy of the text is then covered with observations, corrections and suggestions. Storm does not limit himself to the Norwegian of the new translation, but goes back to a number of other versions of the New Testament, to the Greek original, to the English Authorised (1611) and Revised Standard (1881) Versions, as well as to earlier Danish and Norwegian versions. Each time he finished some work with these notebooks, he gave the date and whether the work has been an initial going-through or a revision. We can assume that this record of how long he spent on the work was required by the committee. One of the early notebooks even contains a note of how long he sat at the Bible work each day, and what else he was occupying himself with. Thus we learn that, on Tuesday 22 January 1889, he worked on the grammar of the Bible translation from 0930 until 1330, and investigated Ibsen's language from 1730 until 2030. It is quite natural that he should have been working on the language of the Bible and the language of Ibsen simultaneously, since for Storm they were both simply examples of the language in its literary register.

As early as September 1888, then, Storm was ready to present 'Kritiske Bemærkninger' on the two books of the New Testament he had been reviewing. His principles outlined here are significant, as he remained true to them all the way to the end of the project nearly 20 years later. He was a highly principled scholar, and it is remarkable the extent to which his views on so many aspects of language remained firm right the way through his long career. His initial comments are then these:

> My impression is [. . .] that *we have gone too far* in altering the style and tone of the older translation. By means of a substantial number of the effected changes, the language has become *less solemn, more everyday*. In order to have Norwegian expressions, the time-honoured expressions, through which the word of the Bible happens to have become familiar and well-loved, have often been altered unnecessarily [. . .] In short: nothing should be changed unless it is *absolutely necessary*. (UBB Ms. 744e)

He fleshes out this view in his 'Bemærkninger' of 1901, written in response to the final draft of the new version. Here he writes that this draft 'bears many signs of a conscious *language reform programme*', and obviously enough this is something that he reacted strongly against. He was highly regarded by the rest of the committee, and his views were valued and on the whole accepted, but it is clear that he felt that revision had been taken further than he felt desirable. He goes on in these 'Bemærkninger' (UBB Ms. 744g) to explain just what sort of reform he did feel to be desirable, and there are no surprises here. He advocates '*moderate language change*':

> but it must take place in a *natural*, unaffected manner, such that the new expressions really are an *improvement*, in that a foreign, unusable or archaic word is exchanged for one which is *usable* and *comprehensible*, not only by country folk but also by town-dwellers.

This is vintage Storm, true to his principles.

These earlier 'Bemærkninger' are precursors to the full commentary on the language of the new translation, namely *Bibelsproget* of 1906, written and published after the new translation had itself appeared. According to Holter (1966: 418 ff.), the reaction to the language of the new translation was largely positive, and the committee's worries on this account appear to have been unfounded. All the same, Storm uses his short book, which was his report on the work and published by the Norwegian Bible Society, to distance himself from some of the more radical, in his view less appropriate, usages adopted; and we will go on now to look at this book.

4.2.3.1.2 Bibelsproget *(1906)*

4.2.3.1.2.1 In their report of 1904, on the publication of the new translation, and quoted by Storm (1906: iii), the translation committee had stated that in linguistic questions it had followed whatever Storm deemed to be appropriate. Storm corrects this statement by pointing out that, while this may have been the case in grammatical questions, it was not true for lexical ones. On the contrary, the choice of lexicon was often a compromise between Storm's more cautious, conservative wishes and the more positively Norwegianising wing of the committee. Consequently, part III of *Bibelsproget* (*Vocabulary*) is twice as long as part II (*Grammar*). Part I on the vocabulary is simply a list of Storm's proposed post-publication corrections to the text. It is divided rather pompously into those accepted by the committee (the majority) and those not. The searcher for truth, the perfectionist, cannot resist finishing this brief first part of his commentary on the language of the new New Testament with a list of spelling mistakes found in the first edition.

4.2.3.1.2.2 At the beginning of part II (on the grammar) Storm sets out his guidelines for reforming the vocabulary of the Norwegian New Testament, what he calls his 'ideal', and they are summarised thus:

> The purpose of the new Bible translation was not simply to achieve a *more correct* version, but also a more homespun Norwegian form, in so far as this was compatible with a *beautiful* and *dignified* style. (1906: 10)

Stylistic dignity is one of the most, if not *the* most, pressing of the guidelines Storm sets. So important is it, in fact, that he repeats this injunction almost verbatim 69 pages later, just before he deals with grammatical modernisation (1906: 79). He is at all times guided by the principle that people expect the language of Holy Scripture to be in a different, 'higher' register than everyday language. To this end it has necessarily to be more archaic than contemporary, colloquial language. By way of comparison, he praises the English Revised Version of 1881, 'where the translation is just *corrected*, but not *modernised*, whereby the ancient august tone from the 1611 Bible is completely preserved' (p. 11). Storm was a great admirer of the 1611 King James Bible (he wrote of 'the language's wonderful power and solemnity' (1896a)), and he is evidently pleased that a recent, more folksy English translation 'has not achieved general acceptance' (p. 11). He was right to be cautious about radical modernisation to the language of the Bible, and he could have found salutary warnings closer to home. Johan Henrik Schrøter's (1771–1851) efforts to introduce a Faroese version of the Gospels met with vigorous opposition from the authorities and from ordinary churchgoers alike.

4.2.3.1.2.3 Apart from the brief introductions to the three parts of the book, *Bibelsproget* is simply a collection of examples. It is Storm at his most uncompromisingly data-oriented. As lists of examples go, however, they are interesting, since, with certain caveats, they represent *Norsk Retskrivning* in practice. Storm put some reform principles into practice in the 1897 *Franske Taleøvelser*, but *Franske Taleøvelser* were consciously popular; he used colloquial Norwegianised forms in order to mirror colloquial French. The language of the Bible was a totally different genre, indeed a more different genre could hardly be imagined. *Franske Taleøvelser*, because of the nature of the book, could never have had any real influence on the development of Norwegian or on users of the language, but with the language of the officially prescribed version of the New Testament to play with, Storm was in a position to make a huge impact. The 1904 New Testament could have been the Stormian equivalent of Aasen's *Prøver af Landsmaalet i Norge*, but it was not pure Storm. It bore the scars of having been conceived by a committee. And in 1906, as we now know, the mood was no longer (if it had ever been) one of conservatism, of adhering to a Norwegian which 'must for the most part preserve the inherited, rightful, noble form of language' (Storm 1906: 79).

4.2.3.2 *Norwegian Literature*

4.2.3.2.1 *Ibsen*

4.2.3.2.1.1 Storm had a lifelong interest in Norwegian literature, not first and foremost as literature per se, but as a source of linguistic data. The writings of authors admitted to Storm's canon provided him with examples of Norwegian usage, usage which had found acceptance, which had been filtered, distilled and purified, and which could be called truly Norwegian by the cautious, moderate, conservative Storm. In pride of place in his canon of Norwegian authors came Ibsen, praised so highly in Storm (1896a) and Storm (1903a). He wrote two pieces specifically dedicated to Ibsen's Norwegian: 'Ibsen og det norske Sprog' in the Establishment's Festschrift to Ibsen (Storm 1898a), and 10 years later the appendix to the official commemorative edition of Ibsen's collected works (Storm 1908a). How interesting that at the end, after decades of strife, the Establishment, Ibsen and Storm should form this trinity.

4.2.3.2.1.2 'Ibsen og det norske Sprog' appears rather self-important. I don't know what the agreement was between Storm and the editor, Gerhard von der Lippe Gran (1856–1925), but Storm's contribution is extravagantly longer than most other items in the book. It is not as though he was the leading contributor. He was in exalted company. King Oscar II of Sweden and Norway wrote the dedication, and other contributors included the author Jonas Lie and the literary historians Georg Morris Cohen Brandes (1842–1927) and Jens Braage Halvorsen (1845–1900). Most of the other items, 'dedicated in admiration' to the great man, are brief recollections or modest personal tributes. Storm, on the other hand, opens up the data banks and, as with much of his later writing, produces something which is really too detailed and quite inappropriate for its context. The first part (pp. 147–171) is neither original nor directly concerned with Ibsen. It is an expanded version of the last part of *Det norske Maalstræv* from 1878, plotting the history of literary Norwegianisms from the hands of Norwegian writers, starting with Peder Claussøn (1545–1614) and ending up with Bjørnson. This section does contextualise what Storm is going to go on to write about Ibsen, namely his exemplary Norwegianisation of the language, but in the context of this book it is just out of place. Storm is a man obsessed. 1898 was the year in which Aars, Hofgaard and Moe's *Om en del retskrivnings- og sprogsspørgsmål* (On a Number of Orthographical and Language Questions) appeared, and reform issues seem to be on Storm's mind. He writes of the ills of 'hybrid languages [*Blandingsmaal*]' (p. 164) and of artificial and inconsistent developments in Bjørnson:

> Amidst all this unrest and fumbling there is one who represents what is *central* to the movement – the calmly and evenly progressive – and that is HENRIK IBSEN. (Storm 1898a: 172)

Storm's study of Ibsen's language is divided up into a section on old-fashioned style in Ibsen, a section on old-fashioned style which has been corrected, and a section on innovations. Storm exhibits an encyclopedic knowledge of Ibsen's language, as always giving strings of examples to demonstrate a particular form or stylistic trait. The whole is overlaid with undiluted admiration for Ibsen's language. This is a Festschrift, of course, and it is usual practice to write warmly of the recipient in such a work. Much of the section on innovations in Ibsen is given over to examples of foreign influence on Ibsen's language, from the other national Scandinavian languages and from German. Storm had made a small study of borrowings from these languages as part of Storm (1881b), and, while he had not resisted foreign loans, he had made it quite clear that they are in many cases unnecessary and should be avoided. He is clearly not happy about some of Ibsen's foreign influences, particularly cases where Ibsen altered Norwegian forms to German ones in later editions. However:

> [. . .] none of these small traces of foreign influence disfigures Ibsen's Norwegianness any more than sunspots disfigure the sun. His Norwegian-

ness nevertheless remains the truest and the heartiest we have yet had. (Storm 1898a: 205)

Despite this unctuousness, Storm's study of Ibsen remains a useful analysis of Ibsen's language and style by someone who really knew and understood that language and style in tiny detail.

4.2.3.2.1.3 At the end of 'Ibsen og det norske Sprog', Storm indicated that he intended to carry out a study of Ibsen's grammar:

> Space and time do not allow the pure grammatical part of this work, the actual 'IBSEN-grammar' to be included here. It will have to be kept for a more detailed investigation, which I hope to publish later. (Storm 1898a: 205, n. 1)

The opportunity arose nine years later, when Storm was accorded possibly an even greater Ibsen-honour than contributing to the Festschrift had been. If being appointed language consultant to the new translation of the New Testament was a mark of the extent to which Storm was part of the Norwegian establishment, then being put in charge of the language of the commemorative edition of the collected works of Ibsen, the ultimate sacred text of modern Norway, was an even clearer mark. As we saw a moment ago, as far back as the 1880s Storm was studying the language of the Bible and Ibsen's Norwegian hand in hand.

Storm's commentary on Ibsen's language (Storm 1908a) was published as the appendix to the fifth volume of the collected works, but it was also published separately under its own cover, with the title *Mindeudgavens Tekst: Retskrivning og Sprogform* (The Text of the Commemorative Edition: Orthography and Linguistic Form). A commentary was not all that was required of Storm. As is clear from his introduction, the job also entailed advising on formulating principles for correcting and modifying the language of the text, in consultation with Henrik Ibsen's family, notably his son, the leading politician Sigurd Ibsen (1859–1930). One of the main issues to deal with concerned the fact that Ibsen never read proofs and left the production of a clean text up to his publishers. Accordingly Danish forms sneaked into the text, and Storm rectifies these, as well as making Ibsen's spelling more consistent, where he found inconsistencies that Ibsen had evidently not intended. Wherever possible, Storm sought 'to proceed with the greatest possible reverence and discretion':

> I have only corrected what I believe the author would himself, on closer investigation, have corrected, if he had lived. (Storm 1908a: 3)

Oh Johan, you loyal servant! All the corrections are listed as the second part of this little monograph.

Part III begins with 'Orthography', and provides a summary of the principles adopted by Ibsen, and in some cases rendered more consistent by Storm himself. Thus he explains Ibsen's practice in respect of the use of upper-case initial letters, the spelling of derived forms, abbreviations, and punctuation, i.e. some of the issues Storm had dealt with in *Norsk Retskrivning*. Just as there were references to *Norsk Sprog: Kraakemaal og Landsmaal* in 'Ibsen og det norske Sprog', so there are copious references to *Norsk Retskrivning* here. It all ties together. This is an ideal opportunity for Storm to show how the language reforms he advocated are in fact exemplified by the most respected and esteemed of modern Norwegian writers. The exercise enables Storm to take the moral high-ground beautifully, following on from the failure of the authorities to accept his reform proposals in 1907. This is not Storm's system, he implies, it is Henrik Ibsen's!

After 'Orthography [*Retskrivning*]' come 'Vokaler' and 'Konsonanter', in which Storm proceeds alphabetically, as was his practice, giving examples of Ibsen's use and non-use of various letters. These sections in particular are little more than strings of examples, and, typically of Storm, there is no attempt to reconstruct Ibsen's system or philosophy. Ibsen's practice varied from one period to another, and he was in fact not desperately interested in the Norwegian language question. He just got on with writing a form of language that was natural for him, which is why he was such a shining example for Storm. All the same, Storm's little study would have been much more interesting and valuable if, for once, he could have behaved out of character and theorised a little. He was, though, over 70 by now, and this was not the time for an old dog to learn new tricks.

Part IV of *Mindeudgavens Tekst: Retskrivning og Sprogform* is 'the actual "Ibsen-grammar"' promised in 1898. Again, true to form, we have a list of examples taken from Ibsen's writings, organised by part of speech. This is very much the Storm of *Større fransk Syntax*. All in all, Storm (1908a) is a worthy study, characteristically careful and detailed, but all the passion of *Norsk Retskrivning* has dissipated. It is as though he threw everything, all his reserves of energies, into *Norsk Retskrivning*, and those energies were then gone forever. Now he is just an elderly man making lists. Of course Ibsen was the national hero just now, immediately after his death, but a Storm who proceeds 'with the greatest possible reverence and discretion' is not the Storm, the storming Storm (the pun had to happen some time!), we have got to know in the course of this chapter.

4.2.3.2.2 *Asbjørnsen and Moe*

4.2.3.2.2.1 Ibsen was not the only author whose writing Storm admired and analysed in his publications. We have already seen the stylistic analyses he made of Aasen, Garborg and others in the Landsmål tradition, and of Bjørnson on the other side of the language gulf. Storm's major publication on the style of Norwegian literature would have been his grandly entitled

'De store Forfatteres Sprog og Retskrivning' (The language and orthography of the great authors), which started to appear in serialised form in
September 1900. Characteristically enough, the level of detail was such that
the parade of *store Forfattere* (great authors) got no further than Asbjørnsen
and Moe, although Storm had intended to produce a second instalment on
Bjørnson and a third on Ibsen. Furthermore, he assumed that the articles
would eventually be combined in book form (letter to Thomsen, 20
December 1900). Another reason for Storm's failure to complete what
must surely have been a larger programme, as implied by the title, is that
there soon emerged other matters to deal with in the press, particularly with
regard to Landsmål, and Storm turned his attention to the articles which
would later be published as Storm (1903a) (see section 4.1.3.5).

4.2.3.2.2.2 Storm (1900) is a study of the increasingly Norwegian forms to
be found in Asbjørnsen and Moe's *Norske Folkeeventyr* as it passed from
its first edition of 1852 through to its sixth edition of 1896/1899, edited by
Moltke Moe. Storm presents this gradual process of Norwegianisation as a
microcosm of the process by which the language was naturally becoming
more and more Norwegian. Storm had the greatest of respect for the
language of the first edition, and we have seen the praise he lavished on
Asbjørnsen's language in *Det norske Maalstræv* of 1878. He goes further
here and sets up Asbjørnsen and Moe's work as '*the basis for the whole of
the subsequent and gradually increasing Norwegianisation of our written
language*' (Storm 1900). But things had gone from strength to strength,
barring a few inconsistencies, with each subsequent edition, such that the
sixth edition is

> a model of popular Norwegian language, at once truly Norwegian and at
> the same time harmonious and moderate. The old-fashioned Danish
> which had remained in older editions has gone. The modern Norwegian
> which has come in its stead, emerges in a flexible, rounded and homespun
> way, not raw, acrid or squawking.

Higher praise from Storm cannot be imagined. So what is so good about this
language?
   At all levels of the language there are developments with each subsequent
edition, developments Storm regards as quite in keeping with the stage the
language had reached, and in no way artificial. He takes each level of the
language in turn to demonstrate this. He starts with 'words and expressions'
and moves on to 'sounds and orthography', particularly the use of 'hard'
consonants, coming finally to 'grammar', word class by word class. Like his
lectures, this is little more than a list of examples, but the reader is never in
any doubt that the point has been fully and forcibly made, and the point here
is this:

The new edition of the Folk Tales is typical of the advances our literary language has made in its popular Norwegian tone and style in the course of the last half-century. (Storm 1900)

What a shame, Storm writes, that Moltke Moe, the praiseworthy editor of the sixth edition, could not have taught Moltke Moe, the 'New Speller', a lesson. A key motivation for writing *De store Forfatteres Sprog og Retskrivning* was to indicate the difference between the reform proposed in the 1898 *Om en del retskrivnings- og sprogspørgsmål* by Moe and his committee colleagues and the type of reform Storm himself advocated and found represented in the gradual reform of *Norske Folkeeventyr*. Maybe Storm never intended to go any further than Asbjørnsen & Moe. Maybe this study was enough to illustrate how the language could be reformed gradually and through the literature, rather than suddenly and by reference to the spoken language alone.

4.3 THE DIALECTS

4.3.1 *The Dialectological Work*

4.3.1.1 Storm writes in the 1902 *Forord* to *Norvegia* that he had been aware of the Norwegian dialects from childhood onwards. This is unsurprising given his early interest in language and given his father's rather itinerant employment. Since that time, he states, he has taken every opportunity to hear the dialects, and he 'scarcely knows of any more captivating or linguistically more fruitful study for our philologists' (Storm 1885a: 7). This listening became more systematic when he undertook publicly funded journeys in various parts of the country in the early 1880s. The first major fruit of his labours was the first issue of *Norvegia* in 1884 (see next section), but his publications on Norwegian dialects were not limited to this journal.

In his very first publication (1860) Storm makes reference to dialectal variation in a general way, by noting prosodic contrasts between the dialects of Kristiania and Bergen, but this hardly ranks as dialectology. In *Norvegia* Storm actually spelt out what he understood by dialectology, the scientific and systematic study of the dialects, writing of '*systematic dialect research* (dialectology)' (1884a: 8). Published work on the Norwegian dialects, and on other aspects of the Norwegian language, languished after the brief appearance in 'Tale og Accent i Forhold til Sang' of 1860, as his attentions were directed instead to the Romance languages. A publication formally devoted to Norwegian dialects would have to wait 24 years, but this does not mean that Storm wasn't thinking about them in the interim. On the contrary, we have already established that the Norwegian language formed the backdrop against which all his other language work was carried out, and the dialects were consequently never far from his mind. Thus there are comparative references to Norwegian dialects in the 1875 'Remarques sur les voyelles atones . . .' (see section 3.3.2.2). By 1893 the Norwegian dialects are being used as evidence for phonetic changes in the Romance languages, and Storm cites the dialect of Valle in Setesdal to explain the diphthongisation of certain Romance vowels (see section 3.3.2.4.3).

In his 1877 application to parliament Storm gives the impression that his work on the dialects is in fact quite far advanced. He writes that he intends in the second part of the *Værk over det norske Sprog* to present the sounds and phonetic features of the dialects 'insofar as I have been able to observe them myself, since I cannot rely on the observations of others' (Storm 1877a: 2). Here we witness Storm's highly empirical approach to research, an approach he had in common with Henry Sweet, but an approach which smacked of arrogance and which did not gain him friends in contemporary Norway. If the 'master' – Aasen – had been able to use other people's collections, then why couldn't Storm? The answer of course is that Storm was seeking after "the truth", and such a sacred mission could not proceed if it was based on potentially fallible findings. He was still adhering to this practical, empirical approach to the study of languages in 1908, writing in the *Forord* to the second part of 'Norsk Lydskrift med Omrids af Fonetiken' that 'as a rule I only give the result of my own observations, according to what is now generally recognised as the only correct method for phonetic research' (Storm 1908b: 133). What is more, it was necessary for Storm to have all the material recorded according to a common system of representation – his own. He thought that the conclusion to the proposed second part of *Værk* ('which will perhaps constitute a third part'):

> should consist of a detailed collection of the most important instances of each sound, a sort of Dano-Norwegian repertoire of a similar sort to that which is to be found in Grimm's *Deutsche Grammatik*, but more precise and far more complete. (Storm 1877a: 2)

Preparatory phonetic work he had done for the ill-fated *Værk* meant that Storm was able to proceed with the first part of his *Norvegia* treatise (see section 4.3.2) so quickly.

4.3.1.2 In 1880 Storm published 'De svenske dialekter' in *Nordisk tidskrift*. On the surface this appeared to be a review of the new Swedish journal, under the editorship of Lundell, *Nyare bidrag till kännedom om de svenska landsmålen ock svenskt folkliv*, but, as with all Storm's reviews, there was much more to it than this. It represented the real foundation stone for Storm's work on the Norwegian dialects, the work that would continue through practical fieldwork and project management during the early 1880s and debouch into *Norvegia*.

Storm opens with a burst of enthusiasm for the new journal, which he regards as heralding a new epoch in Scandinavian linguistics. He gives an overview of previous dialect work in the Scandinavian countries, deeming it to be either too fragmentary (in the case of the work of the Swedish *landsmålsföreningar*) or too unifying, such that the detail of dialect variation is obscured (in the case of Aasen's work). The great strength of this new undertaking by Lundell and his colleagues, according to Storm, is its use of a phonetic alphabet capable of capturing the detail of the dialects with scientific precision, but at the same time able to present this detail according to a common system, making comparison possible.[34] Storm prefers Lundell's alphabet to Bell's Visible Speech system on the one hand, which employs too many compound symbols for individual sounds, and to systems developed in Germany on the other, e.g. by Ernst Wilhelm, Ritter von Brücke (1824–1880) and Hermann Berthold Rumpelt (1821–1881), which are too complex thanks to excessive use of diacritics. (The precursor of the IPA system was not yet established.) Storm goes on to give a brief presentation of Lundell's transcription system. His presentation supposedly satisfies the popular need for a summary of Lundell's system:

> The recent science of sounds plays such a significant role that it cannot be regarded as inexpedient to give a wider public some tastes of it in a semi-popular form. (Storm 1880: 340)

I suspect that Storm's motives are not in fact so public-spirited, or at least not so selfless. His overview of Lundell's transcription system for the Swedish dialects is in fact a comparative presentation, comparing some of the features of Swedish dialects with features of Norwegian dialects, and, to a lesser extent, Danish ones too. Admittedly this is a Nordic journal. Its home was Sweden, but its three editors represented Sweden, Norway and Denmark respectively, and it was also published in these three countries, as well as in Finland. So Storm's programme was a pan-Scandinavian one, placing the work of Lundell and his colleagues in Sweden in a wider context. However, Storm's main interest was the Norwegian situation:

> I conclude with the wish that this meritorious undertaking might make good and lasting progress and might be warmly participated in as well as emulated in the other Scandinavian countries. In particular it is my wish that all Norwegians interested in our beautiful dialects might follow the shining example shown by their Swedish brothers, and might unite in that noble goal, a scientific study of the Norwegian dialects. (Storm 1880: 350)

4.3.1.3 Storm was not someone who let the grass grow under his feet. The first issue of *Nyare bidrag . . .* included Lundell's 157-page treatise 'Det svenska landsmålsalfabetet'. The year after Storm wrote this review, the Norwegian *Forening for norske Dialekter og Folketraditioner* was founded

---

[34] For a discussion of Lundell's *landsmålsalfabet* and its subsequent development in Swedish dialectology, see Eriksson (1961).

(see next section), and Storm's 'Norsk Lydskrift med Omrids af Fonetiken' was under way. Storm was by no means the first nineteenth-century linguist to devise a phonetic "alphabet", but his work began at least as early as Lundell's: there is evidence in Storm's letters to Thomsen that he was thrashing out his own system from 1874. It does not take a literary detective, however, to see the bloodline running from Lundell (1878) to Storm (1884a). But 'all Norwegians interested in our beautiful dialects' did not have to wait until 1884 to receive guidance from Storm in 'that noble goal'.

From 1880 until 1886 Storm received financial assistance from the university's Norwegian travel fund to travel round Norway collecting dialect material, and it is in 1880 that serious interest in the dialects is for the first time to be found in his letters to Thomsen. Despite his unwillingness to rely on other people's findings, he knew that it would not be possible to study every dialect form through single-handed fieldwork, so to complement his own travels he set up what would now be called a sociolinguistic project. In February 1882 he sent out a questionnaire to parish priests throughout Norway, with the following request:

> You would do me a great service by telling me what the following words are called in your village. The aim is to get an overview of the distribution of word-forms across the various villages. It is desired that the words be written exactly according to the pronunciation, leaving out all silent letters, but otherwise using the usual spelling.

A copy of this questionnaire, together with the rather impressive number of responses (including one from his cousin, Lensmann Fr. Storm of Nes in Romerike, north-east of Kristiania), indicating the considerable interest in the dialects around the country, is to be found in the National Library at Ms. 4° 1285 B. Despite his request for 'normal spelling', Storm does give a few tips for the transcription of the more common non-alphabetic sounds, such as [ə] and [ɽ], and, as we have noted before, his guidelines are ideal for non-specialist linguists: encouraging and precise, but not so detailed as to frighten potential informants.

Unfortunately, the search for truth spurred Storm on to seek greater detail, and with each subsequent revision to the original guidelines, the detail became more off-putting (the old story). In 1882 the *Foreningen for norske Dialekter og Folketraditioner* (see next section) published the *Norsk Ordliste til Lydlæren* (Storm 1882a), as a preliminary 'specimen [*Prøvehefte*]' of *Norvegia*. Here Storm wrote:

> The present wordlist is intended for those who intend to study Norwegian dialects. It is therefore more detailed than the little circular sent out earlier, without by any stretch of the imagination being exhaustive. It gives information about the most important instances of the *phonology*, which is what determines the relationship between the dialects, by means

of a collection of the most significant examples of each case. (Storm 1882a: 1)

This word list takes each sound (or rather letter) in turn and, like Storm's own notebooks and in line with his preferred method of cataloguing language data, gives a series of examples of that sound in use in various positions in the word. As Storm explains, 'the words are mainly listed in Aasen's Landsmaal, which in most cases can be regarded as representing the basic form' (p. 1), but some more precise transcription is included too. A new version of the *Ordliste* (Wordlist) appeared in 1884 (Storm 1884b), in conjunction with the long-awaited first part of *Norvegia*:

> The present list contains an excerpt from the larger wordlist for the *phonology*, along with a similar selection of examples for the *morphology*. It is intended for those who, within a short space of time, wish to achieve an overview of one or more dialects, and submit contributions to their description. (Storm 1884b: 1)

Significantly now, the second part of the list is *Norsk Lydskrift med kort Forklaring* – a full list of symbols.

4.3.1.4 The importance of Storm's *Lydskrift*, his phonetic transcription system, cannot be overestimated. Despite the contemporary emergence of what later came to be called the International Phonetic Alphabet, Storm's system predominated in Norwegian dialectology for at least 100 years. Indeed, his system has many advantages over the IPA system as a descriptive device for Norwegian dialects. First of all, it was devised specifically for the sounds of Norwegian, and is not an adaptation of a system of phonemes and secondary features from all the languages of the world. Secondly, its use from the earliest days of 'scientific' Norwegian dialectology onwards meant that Storm's dream of a vast overview of all the Norwegian dialects could be realised in a way that would not have been possible if Norwegian dialectologists had used a variety of different systems for recording the forms. Thirdly – and this has nothing whatever to do with the practicality or otherwise of the system – it has kept Storm's name alive, at least in one area of the linguistics to which he made such extraordinary and far-reaching contributions.

Storm's stranglehold has had certain disadvantages, however. According to Aske (1997: 94), the shadow cast over Norwegian dialectology by Storm and his transcription system has led to a predominance of phonetic and phonological work, to the exclusion of other levels of the language. The gradual institutionalisation of Storm's *Norvegia* transcription system meant that researchers who tried to use other systems tended to be marginalised. Aske cites Nes (1986) when she mentions the case of Christian Bang Vidsteen (1832–1915), who suffered harsh criticism from Storm, above all for failing to use his system, which, via the wordlists and that dialectological bible *Norvegia*, had been officially imposed on the entire community of would-be dialectologists. Vidsteen's work gets listed in *Englische Philologie* (Storm 1892a: 257). Storm is on the whole positive about the usefulness of Vidsteen's studies of western Norwegian dialects, but the phonetics he calls 'rather dilettantish'. Storm had served to divide the community of dialectologists into professionals (those with the correct phonetic background) and amateurs (those without). Aske also mentions Sigurd Kolsrud's (1888–1957) harsh opposition to Hallfrid Christiansen's (1886–1964) dissertation on the dialect of Gimsøy, where, amongst other things, Christiansen failed to follow Storm's transcription system 'to the letter'.

4.3.1.5 Between 1884 and 1901, when Storm returned to the *Norvegia* dissertation, he did not publish anything expressly devoted to Norwegian dialects. As we will see, the events surrounding *Norvegia* were a disappointment to him, and we have already noticed that, whenever Storm was disappointed, he threw himself into other projects. Storm certainly didn't discard the vast amount of knowledge about Norwegian dialects he had amassed in the early 1880s. It served him well in his ongoing polemic concerning language reform, and he plundered data from Norwegian dialects in writing about other languages. The 1892 volume of *Englische Philologie* contains a lengthy excursus on Norwegian dialects, adapted from 'Norsk Lydskrift med Omrids af Fonetiken', and his justification for including such a section, which, despite his apologia (Storm 1892a: 221), is only of the remotest relevance to a book on *Englische Philologie*, is worth quoting:[35]

> Since the appearance of the first edition of my *Englische Philologie* my attention has been more and more directed towards the importance of the study of dialects, as much for linguistics in general as specifically for phonetics. Besides becoming familiar with several Norwegian dialects from my childhood onwards, I undertook study trips each summer between 1880 and 1886, to investigate the dialects on the spot. The yield was more productive than I had dared to hope beforehand. So far I have investigated approximately 150 dialects in more or less phonetic detail. I scarcely know of any more captivating study. A comparative study of the dialects of a language must always be fruitful [. . .] (Storm 1892a: 245–246)

Storm is quite right to boast. This was a fantastic undertaking.

4.3.1.6 His use of data from Norwegian in a comparative context found perhaps its most original outlet in his brief *Om Nabosprog og Grænsedialekter* [On Neighbour Languages and Border Dialects] of 1911. This is a very

---

[35] This entire section is reprinted in Norwegian translation in Jahr & Lorentz (1981: 97–109).

concise list of features evidenced by dialects at linguistic borders, and in its style is a return to the Romance *mélanges* he published right at the beginning of his career. It is also Storm at his most non-theoretical. The data is simply given (an elderly man making lists). First come some examples from the Scandinavian languages, then some data from other Germanic languages and finally some data from Romance languages, with the concluding remark:

> These examples of the influence of neighbouring languages on each other could easily be multiplied, but I have chosen the most significant and most typical cases. (Storm 1911b: 18)

In 1911, Storm had the disappointment of *Norsk Retskrivning* behind him, and only the *Større fransk Syntax* ahead of him. His letters to Thomsen were now sparse and nearly illegible, and he was a man looking back on his life. Why should he have been concerned with 'neighbouring languages and border dialects' at this time? Is it too fanciful to suggest that Storm had come home to where he belonged – on the border? He was a man who had never been fully at home in one place, either literally or metaphorically, a man who had never fully belonged. All that dedication to the Norwegian dialects had, as far as he could see in 1911, not amounted to much, and so his thoughts turn to the unloved dialects, the impure ones, the ones that don't properly belong, the ones that nobody is interested in, and he makes them his own.

We have already dealt with Storm's dialectological methodology in Chapter 1, but before we go on to look properly at *Norvegia*, perhaps the most defining, the most characteristic of all his work, we will take a moment to follow him a little more closely on his summer trips of the early 1880s.

4.3.1.7 Each year from 1880 to 1886 Storm applied for and received a sum of money from the university's fund for research trips within Norway's boundaries. (There was a separate fund for financing trips abroad.) The amount he received varied from 400 to 500 kroner per trip. This appears to have been quite generous. Amund B. Larsen, although not employed by the university, received funding from the same source for the same purpose during this same period, but his grants were substantially smaller, typically half what Storm received. That said, Larsen continued to receive these grants each summer until 1893. Storm wrote a report on what he had achieved each summer, and this report was published in the official journal for school and university affairs, *Norske Universitets- og Skole-Annaler*. Reports appeared regularly from 1881 until 1883 during the year following the receipt and spending of the grant. Reports for 1883 and 1884 appeared together in 1885, and, although Storm would receive two more grants, there were no more reports. This is almost certainly because the nature of *Norske Universitets- og Skole-Annaler* changed. The third series (*3. Række*) reported university activities very fully, but in 1886 a new fourth series began (*Ny række*) which was much more highly focused on the schools, specifically on the school-leaving exam, the *Examen Artium*. Storm did continue to publish in *Universitets- og skole-annaler* (as it came to be known), but his contributions from 1886 onwards concerned schoolteaching matters (Storm 1886b; 1887b; 1888b; 1890a). His notebooks containing dialect data continue through the 1880s and 1890s as late as 1903 (Gudbrandsdalen), although there are considerably fewer of them and they tend to be very brief. They cover the same parts of the country and indicate that, while the funds may have dried up, he was still taking what opportunities he could to renew his acquaintance with the dialects.

In the summer of 1880, Storm set off on his first trip, with 400 kroner in his pocket and good intentions in his mind:

> I wanted to study in particular the phonetics and the grammatical forms, in which the dialects' relationship to each other emerges, as well as was possible in the space of a few weeks. (Storm 1881c: 84)

On this first trip he explains that he traversed Upper Telemark in a zigzag pattern from east to west, and he found people very supportive and helpful. It was Storm's policy to engage the help of informants, and he often sought out places where there would be significant gatherings of potential informants from different parts of the country, places such as barracks and colleges, although he does not seem to have done this on his first trip of 1880. The next year he returned to Telemark, this time with the princely sum of 500 kroner at his disposal. He had to interrupt his research, as he did in several years, to return to Kristiania and carry out his (onerous) duties as English assessor for the *Examen Artium*. While he was in Kristiania he attended the Scandinavian Philologists' meeting, being held there that year (see section 3.3.2.4.2), and after the meeting he travelled back to Telemark in the company of Lundell, who had delivered his polemic on Scandinavian dialectology (Lundell 1881) at the conference. On a number of occasions Storm travelled in the company of other dialectologists. In 1882 he was joined initially by Noreen, and then later by Amund B. Larsen. In 1883 he was joined by Sweet, who also took advantage of the fishing, and stayed with Storm for a while after the trip:

> we went through our joint findings and made observations in particular concerning the characteristic pitches of vowels (those pitches which are produced by whispering; each vowel has its more-or-less fixed pitch, *o* the lowest, *a* in the middle, *i* the highest etc.). (Storm 1885b: 130)[36]

---

[36] According to Sweet (1885a: 587), the two men also took the opportunity to make a study of phrasebooks: 'When I was with Storm in Norway last year, we surveyd nearly the hole field of frazebook literature in the chief European languages, and past a vote of sweeping condemnation on it all, cuming to the concluzion that the only way of mastering idioms was by reading novels and comedies, noting down the necessary ones and lerning them by hart'.

On 21 June 1882 he travelled to Gardermoen, now the site of Oslo's principal airport but then a military station, prior to following an itinerary as follows (Noreen left him after Gardermoen): via Romerike north to Rendalen (where he had lived as a child) and then south again via Østerdalen to Elverum (joined by Larsen), and so across Hedmarken back to Kristiania; north again to Hamar and the same area he had already passed through, but now further north to Tynset, and then Trondheim; south again to Trysil and Hamar, arriving back in the capital on 9 September. In 1883 Sweet accompanied him, and we have discussed Sweet's visits to Norway elsewhere. It is not necessary to say much more about this year's trip than to list the principal places visited from 3 July onwards:

Helgelandsmoen drill ground (north-west of the capital, south of Hønefoss)
Skien
Inner Telemark (Bø, Seljord & Kviteseid, while Sweet went fishing in Dalen!)
Mo and Vinje
Røldal
Odda (Hardanger)
Ulvik and Granvin
Voss (+ a 'little detour to Bergen' (Storm 1885b: 129))
Sogn
Valdres
Hamar
Back to Kristiania on 8 August.

The itinerary for the following year, beginning on 26 July and finishing on 6 September, took Storm via the following places:

Skien across Telemark to
Dalen and Skafså
Valle and Bykle in Setesdal
Sogn and Sogndal
Førde
Hornindal
Volda
Trondheim, and so back to Kristiania

During these summer jaunts Storm managed to traverse much of central Norway, and it does not seem as though the trips of 1885 and 1886 took him any further afield. He did not himself get any further north than Trondheim, and he neglected the south-west corner of the country. The south-east he was already familiar with. In any case, this first-hand experience, coupled with the good responses he had received to his questionnaire, meant that he was able to write in his report for 1884 that he now felt ready to start printing the first part of *Norvegia*.

4.3.2 Norvegia: Tidsskrift for det norske Folks Maal og Minder

4.3.2.1 In February 1881 an open invitation was printed, inviting interested parties to join a new *Forening for norske Dialekter og Folketraditioner* (Society for Norwegian Dialects and Folk Traditions). The gentlemen responsible for this circular were Aasen, Asbjørnsen, Sophus Bugge, Johan Fritzner, Moltke Moe, Ross, Storm and Unger. We have met them all before, with the exception of Johan Fritzner (1812–1893), who worked as a parish priest, from Vadsø in the far north to Farsund in the far south of the country, and amassed a vast linguistic, archaeological and folkloric knowledge, especially concerning the Sami people. His major scientific work was the Old Norse dictionary, whose second and most influential edition (1886–1896) was produced during his retirement.[37] Storm knew from personal experience that around the country there was a great deal of interest in the dialects, and, according to the invitation, the purpose of the society would be:

> on the one hand to effect more vigorous and more comprehensive work in the collection of the material and in its contribution to science, and on the other to constitute a focal point for greater association between the proponents of these subjects.

The Society intended to further this aim:

1. by publishing a pamphlet or, as the occasion arises, also other publications appropriate to their purpose;
2. by recruiting colleagues and collectors in town and country;
3. by holding two-monthly meetings with talks and discussions.

At the first meeting of the new society, on 2 April 1881, officers were elected. Fritzner was appointed president, Moe editor of the proposed journal, and Aasen, Asbjørnsen, Bugge and Jørgen Engebretsen Moe (1813–1882), Moltke Moe's father, Asbjørnsen's collaborator and one of the leading folklorists of the day, were elected as honorary members. The founders' expectations were met, and by the end of the year the society could boast 770 members. At the second meeting of the society, Storm volunteered himself as editor of the linguistic part of the proposed journal, and all seemed set fair for the new undertaking. In April the following year the committee agreed on a name for the society's organ: *Norvegia: Tidsskrift for det norske Folks Maal og Minder* (Norvegia: Journal for the Language and Memorials of the Norwegian People). This wasn't quite the version of the title Storm toys with in his

---

[37] See Olsen (1929).

notebook: 'confer with Moe about the name *Norvegia* Tidskr. f n *Dial.* og *Folketrad.* (Maal og Minder?)' (NBO Ms. 8° 775). Storm's version is more obviously inspired by the title of Lundell's *Nyare bidrag till kännedom om de svenska landsmålen ock svenskt folklif.* As Storm explained in the introduction to the first issue in 1884, the name *Norvegia* was calqued on those of 'distinguished foreign journals like *Anglia* (England), *Germania* (Germany), *Romania* (the Romance world)' (Storm 1884a: 5).

According to the open letter of February 1881, it was intended that the journal should fall into two parts, corresponding to the two parts of its subtitle: a linguistic part under Storm's care, and a part dedicated to folk traditions looked after by Moltke Moe. It was important for the Society that *Norvegia* should not just be an outlet for Storm's studies of dialect phonetics, as this could be offputting for the general public. Consequently it was agreed that the first issue of the new journal would contain first a section by Moe and then a section by Storm, corresponding to their respective specialisms. Storm set about organising his data with characteristic alacrity. In a letter to Thomsen on 19 February 1883 he explains that he is on leave from teaching in order to complete this first issue of *Norvegia*, but there were delays in printing, in part due to the complicated process of ordering the necessary typefaces from Norstedt & Søner, printers of Stockholm: the first part of 'Norsk Lydskrift med Omrids af Fonetiken' (Norwegian transcription system with a sketch of the phonetics) was not ready for publication until 1884. He reports in 1885 that what he did produce 'has involved five years of continuous work' (Storm 1885b: 131). Storm did not actually complete this work in 1884, 'since the board thought that the general public could not tolerate more purely linguistic stuff at once' (Storm 1902), although it is clear from his notebooks that he was already drafting the remainder of the dissertation in 1885.[38] Moe, by contrast, did not produce his promised introduction to folk traditions. Storm's 1902 version of events shows that he was still feeling aggrieved with Moe, unwilling to forgive and forget even 18 years later:

> But a sorry fate hung over this promised continuation. It was constantly promised and never came. New obstacles kept cropping up. We waited and waited until the whole undertaking ground to a standstill. (Storm 1902)

Storm's frustration emerges more forcibly still in several letters to Amund B. Larsen, from which we have quoted earlier. On 5 January 1886, after things had been rumbling on for nearly five years, Storm wrote:

> I do not know what to do with Moe. His work is never going to be ready. My treatise in *Norvegia* came out in Sept. 84. Each time I ask Moe how far

---

[38] See particularly NBO Ms. 4° 1285 F[xxxvii].

he has got, he says that he will *soon* be finished. I am sorely afraid he is one of those unfortunate people who *never* finishes *anything*. (NBO Brevsamling 385)

It is always clear when Storm is really heated about something; the number of emphases (here underlinings) increases. Storm remained unmollified in 1892, describing Moe in another letter to Larsen as 'a *hindrance* to the progress of the cause'.[39] The committee was more conciliatory in its tone in 1901, explaining Moe's inability to finish his contribution by the fact that other commitments had made demands on his time. First of all Moe had to act as executor for Asbjørnsen, following the latter's death in 1885, and then, in the course of the next three years, he had to prepare to take up his professorship. In any case, as Storm told Larsen in 1886, his own contribution was published as the first part of *Norvegia* in 1884, without Moe's contribution as a counterweight.

Storm's contribution consisted of the 13-page programmatic introduction to the journal (Storm 1884a) and the first part of 'Norsk Lydskrift med Omrids af Fonetiken' (Storm 1884/1902/1908). Since *Norvegia* was Storm's first opportunity to write about the phonetics of the Norwegian dialects in a formal way, and since it is precisely his work on Norwegian dialect phonetics and his dialect alphabet of the same name for which he is best remembered in Norwegian linguistic circles today, it is worth dwelling for a moment on his presentation of his programme.

4.3.2.2 The best-known dialect work in 1880s Norway would undoubtedly have been Aasen's, leading to his grammars and dictionaries. Consequently Storm takes great pains to stress the difference between Aasen's work and the work supported and encouraged by the *Forening for norske Dialekter og Folketraditioner*. As always, Aasen is the recipient of fulsome praise. It is here that Storm compares Aasen with Grimm and Diez, as the pioneers of a national philology; he continues:

However, linguistics has not stood still since the appearance of Ivar Aasen. Certain aspects of the language, on which he placed less emphasis, are now the order of the day and require a more detailed and more rigorously systematic treatment in Norway too. This is especially the case with phonetics or the science of sounds, which has become the foundation for the most recent linguistic research. (1884a: 6)

Phonetics lies at the heart of the dialectology being presented here. It is suggested that Aasen represents an outmoded, unscientific methodology, and indeed the approach Storm is advocating – a detailed study of the fine detail of the sounds of the dialects – is in line with the most modern linguistic

---

[39] See Fløtra (1995: 162) for a defence of Moe.

work being carried out elsewhere in Europe. He compares his work and his project with the English Dialect Society which had been founded in 1873, and with comparable work being carried out in the Netherlands, France, Italy and not least Sweden. He expresses the hope that more and more ordinary people will get involved in the task of charting the phonetic detail of the dialects, as had happened in Sweden under Lundell's guiding hand. A phonetic analysis equals a scientific one, in Storm's view, and there is a clever chain of correspondence in Storm's formulation:

> No sounds, no language. No science of sounds, no dialectology, no complete penetration into the characteristics of dialects, their nature and their being, or the often subtle transitions from one to the other. (p. 6)

The dialects were the quintessence of the new Norway. They were language and they were of the people, truly and tangibly different from Danish and from Swedish. Storm's rather neat implication, then, is that phonetics, or rather the new philology based on phonetics, is the national science, that phonetics will uncover what it is to be Norwegian. He admits that Aasen has made a good start, but it is only via detailed phonetic analysis that the full extent of Norwegian sounds will be revealed.

Storm is very eager to stress that the *Norvegia* project has nothing to do with contemporary language politics, that this linguistic enterprise is quite neutral with regard to the language question. He really needed to stress this, given his involvement in the language question, and given his decisive views, which would have been known to potential subscribers:

> The present committee of the Society is made up of men who adopt various positions regarding the language issue, but who unite in their interest in the living popular language and in the whole of popular culture [. . .] *Norvegia* is no party organ. (p. 14)

Storm was seen particularly as an enemy of the Landsmål movement, so his exaggerated praise for Aasen would have helped redress the balance and create an aura of neutrality vis-à-vis language politics. This was no mere smokescreen. Storm was not using *Norvegia* to further his views on the reform of the written language. The rest of the committee would not have allowed this, and anyway he was a multi-faceted linguist, who was as passionate about the phonetics of the dialects as he was about 'moderate-conservative reform'. These were separate issues, unified by the notion of *det levende Sprog*.

Storm's hopes for the new journal went beyond just phonetics, however: 'We must first follow changes in the popular language through space. Next we have to study the history of the language.' Here is his notion of the new philology, the study of a language in all its variety, synchronic and diachronic. Why is such a pursuit desirable? Storm literally had to sell his project to his readers. The society and its journal could only flourish if the society had members and the journal subscribers. As we have seen, the initial membership was encouraging, but the committee was right to worry that too much phonetics might stick in the throats of subscribers. There may have been genuine widespread interest in the dialects throughout the country, but few or none shared Storm's phonetic insight, and his passion for detailed data. Storm's justification of the project was perhaps not the best for making the general public feel as though they were truly involved:

> We are often asked: what is the *use* of this dialect study, this petty search for a load of insignificant variations? Our answer is: our goal is *scientific* profit. Science does not look first and foremost for that which is practically useful, but that which is *instructive*. (p. 10)

So knowledge for knowledge's sake was Storm's goal. This practical undertaking of recording the living language was to have a purely scientific outcome. Once again the practical and the scientific dovetail in a way that indicates the tension, evidenced in the preface to *Engelsk Filologi*, between the practical and the scientific in Storm's thinking. As in that other piece of programmatic writing, we again sense a sort of religious striving for "the Truth" here:

> The task which is upon us is to find scientific truth, to find what *is* and what *has been*, not what *should* be. (p. 14)

As Storm sets out his mission, his search for linguistic truth, his choice of words ('at finde den videnskabelige Sandhed, at finde det som *er* og det som *har været*') strikingly echoes the form of words of the *Gloria Patri* he would have absorbed as a child, growing up in a church household:

> Ære være Faderen og Sønnen og Helligaanden, som det var i Begyndelsen, saa nu og altid og i al Evighed.

4.3.2.3 'Norsk Lydskrift med Omrids af Fonetiken' opens with a brief explanation of what phonetics is, where it has come from and why it is important, as well as a brief explanation of Storm's own transcription system, his *Lydskrift*. A general explanation of fundamental phonetic categories, both segmental and prosodic, leads into the main chapter, chapter III, the (as yet) incomplete presentation of the sounds of Norwegian. Each sound is described in turn with its variants, and plenty of examples from the dialects are provided. The presentation is both synchronic and diachronic, in that the history and variety of each sound is given. Storm begins *Kap. I. Indledning* with the following statement:

> Two sorts of study in particular have caused linguistics to make such strides in recent years:
> 1. Historical language study, what it has been and has become [. . .]

2. The direct observation of the living languages, which emerges especially in phonetics or the science of sounds, the study of the individual elements or components of the languages. (Storm 1884/1902/1908: 19)

Here he is again standing on a boundary, here the boundary between the "old" historical philology and the "new" philology.

4.3.2.4 Others were interested in contributing to the journal. From 1882 Aasen was engaged on a project which would have appealed to Storm, namely recording Norwegian words found in the work of early Norwegian writers, with the intention of producing a 'Bidrag til Folkesprogets Historie' (Contribution to the History of the Folk Language). This was not actually printed until 1954 (see Venås 1996: 297), but Aasen thought that *Norvegia* would be the best place for it to be published. However, after the appearance of the first part of 'Norsk Lydskrift med Omrids af Fonetiken', both society and journal languished. *Morgenbladet* printed a short piece on 7 September 1893, entitled 'What has become of *Norvegia*?', but this scolding didn't help. Moe's contribution to *Norvegia* never materialised, and that was that until 1901, when both society and journal were relaunched. On 23 October 1901 a new invitation was placed in the national newspapers, this time signed by a different committee, consisting of Marius Hægstad, Amund B. Larsen, Gustav Storm and the legal and ecclesiastical historian Absalon Taranger (1858–1930). Given the extent of his involvement and his evident passion for the cause in the early 1880s, we are entitled to wonder why Johan Storm was no longer at the forefront of things. I suspect that he felt he had had his fingers burnt in 1884 over the Moe fiasco, and did not want to risk further disappointment, in the same way that he would not apply for government money a second time. This time the pillar of Johan Storm's 1884 contributions – scientific linguistics – no longer provided the main support for the journal. The journal was now advertised as 'a journal of Norwegian folklore (traditions and language)'; 'the journal's aim', wrote the new committee,

will be, by way of popular and scientific treatises, to advance knowledge of Norway's ancient and more recent folklore, as this is manifested in the popular language, tales, mores and customs.

Language now plays second fiddle to folklore, and scientific now comes second to popular. Storm's uncompromising linguistics in 1884 had not been ideal publicity for this society looking for subscribers and this project looking for participants, so the new committee is maybe trying to be a little more *publikumsvennlig*, a little more 'user-friendly'.

Nevertheless the newspapers were sceptical about the scheme succeeding where it had failed before. Correspondence in *Morgenbladet* raised concern that *Norvegia* was going to be a tacit propaganda organ for the Landsmål movement. Both Gustav Storm and Hægstad responded forcibly to this suggestion, requested that *Norvegia* be left alone and that a language-political issue not be made of it. On 31 March 1903 *Aftenposten* reported the first annual general meeting of the relaunched society, where the main discussion item was the society's failure to attract enough subscribers to be viable. Moe held the view that *Norvegia* was being too scientific, but many other members were of the same opinion as *Morgenbladet*: that subscribers were unwilling to pay good money for something they feared was the unofficial voice of Landsmål. This is odd. The only contributions to have appeared by 1903 were from Storm, who was emphatically not a supporter of the Landsmål movement. But the journal focused on dialects and folk traditions, which smelled rather fishy from a Riksmål point of view. A report in *Aftenposten* on 14 May 1903 probably got the situation about right:

> This 'Journal of Norwegian Language and Lore', which was started a while ago, has not been able to rally as many subscribers as a journal with such an important role for our country and people richly deserves. This is perhaps in part down to the journal's strongly philological character, and maybe particularly to the widespread use of phonetic script, which is difficult for most readers.

By this time Gustav, the *primum mobile* of the new-look *Norvegia*, was dead, and it certainly looked as though a 'sorry fate' hung over the project once again.

4.3.2.5 Although the announcement of the revival of the *Norvegia* project implied that the approach would this time be slightly different, more popular perhaps and less linguistic, the journal kept its name and its dedication to 'det norske Folks Maal og Minder', to language and lore. The first thing to be published after the relaunch was a reprint of the 1884 volume. Storm leapt into action and wrote a new preface to the 1884 material, dated October 1902. He completed the 'Norsk Lydskrift med Omrids af Fonetiken' in 1908, picking up where he had left off in the midst of the consonants, going on now to cover the vowels and diphthongs.

The second volume, edited by Hægstad and Larsen, did not contain any further contributions from Storm, but Moltke Moe was at last represented in *Norvegia*, although not to quite the extent that had originally been envisaged. This second (and last) volume of *Norvegia* is more along the lines originally envisaged by Storm and Moe when they established the journal. The original editors' 'Opraab', their proclamation, was not published at the time, but it is given as part of Gustav Storm's 1908 *Forord*:

> **Norvegia** [. . .] has as its goal to advance knowledge of *Norway's ancient and more recent folklore*, as this is manifested in the popular *language*, *tales* and *conceptual world*. To this end the publication will provide both

longer and shorter collections of beliefs, traditions, and language material, and scientific and popular treatises and descriptions.

And volume II does exactly this. There is some rather serious dialectology from Larsen and Hægstad, but there are also folk tales, some in Storm's *Lydskrift* and some not, some newly transcribed and some reproduced from Aasen, Moltke Moe and others. In short, *Norvegia* appeared to have become in 1908 what it had failed to be in 1884. But the struggle had been too hard for it to survive any longer.

Ironically the ethos of *Norvegia: Tidsskrift for det norske Folks Maal og Minder* did live on in another form, as the journal of Bymålslaget (the urban dialect society), *Maal og Minne*. Bymålslaget was founded in 1902 in memory of Knud Knudsen and in the face of Storm's criticism, and it set up its journal under the editorship of Magnus Bernhard Olsen (1878–1963) in 1909, the year after the final volume of *Norvegia* came out. The aims of *Maal og Minne*, listed inside its front cover, look remarkably familiar:

> *Maal og Minne* has as its goal to provide contributions to the illumination of, e.g., Norwegian language and Norwegian linguistic remains of whatever sort, medieval literature, Norwegian place names and folklore.

Maal og Minne is still going strong. So where did *Norvegia* fail?

It failed in 1884 because of the delays, and because Storm could not moderate "the truth" for his readers. It was the same old problem. For Storm it was all or nothing: the living language had to be captured in all its variety and all its detail, and this was just too indigestible for the ordinary reader. It failed after the turn of the century partly because potential subscribers were sensibly sceptical, partly because of a mistaken sense of the journal and the society having political intentions, and partly because nobody had the energy any more to make it work. It was stillborn. In 1901 when *Norvegia* was relaunched, Gustav Storm was on the wrong side of 55 and doing his brother a favour. In 1909 Magnus Olsen was 31 and his heart was in the task; he remained editor of *Maal og Minne* for 41 years.

Storm and Norwegian certainly shared a 'sorry fate'. Circumstances made the *Værk* project backfire, they caused *Norsk Retskrivning* to fail to have the impact it probably deserved, and they caused the *Norvegia* project to backfire. How different the history of Norwegian might have been!

4.3.3 Norsk Lydskrift med Omrids af Fonetiken *(1884/1902/1908)*

4.3.3.1 So *Nork Lydskrift med Omrids af Fonetiken* (*NLOF*) was the outcome of decades of interest in the sounds of the Norwegian dialects. But it was the summer travels through southern Norway during the opening years of the 1880s which really enabled Storm to focus on the dialects and to assemble enough data to produce this work. One of the little facts about Johan Storm to have seeped into the canon of the history of linguistics is that it was he who encouraged Sweet to write his *Handbook of Phonetics*. We saw in Chapter 2 that Sweet's efforts to get Storm to write a general textbook on prosody were not so successful. But it may be that Sweet encouraged the appearance of *NLOF*. It is true that a variety of opportunities enabled *NLOF*. The summer grants enabled Storm to collect the data, and the establishment of *Foreningen for norske Dialekter og Folketraditioner* gave the work an outlet for publication. However, Norwegian dialects were a hobby for Storm – something to do during the vacations – and I cannot help wondering whether *NLOF* would have remained another of Storm's intended but unrealised projects had it not been for Sweet's encouragement:

> It seems to me that there is a want of practical common sense in L[undell]'s alphabet. He goes back to the antiquated Pitman style, + entirely ignores the later English work, which would have taught him to utilize existing types before making new ones [. . .] Why can't you do something better for Norwegian, instead of ignominiously going back to the Lundell–Sundevall–Pitman standpoint? (Letter of 10 January 1880)

This particular criticism of Lundell is rather unjust, as Lundell did base his system on existing typescripts (see Eriksson 1961). Storm followed Lundell's lead, and, in the event, the method Storm used was actually closely based on Lundell's – with improvements (see below). In any case, Sweet threw down the gauntlet, and Storm picked it up.

Pioneering dialect phonetics and phonology, and particularly the construction of a transcription system, was very challenging work. Storm described it as a 'difficult task' which 'exceeds my powers':

> But I will do what I can; it must be possible to do something. In any case there is nobody in this country who can do it at all well, so I will try, and let future generations do it better. (Letter to Thomsen, 17 December 1882)

Storm laboured in the preparation of *NLOF*. It was far from easy, and it seems from this quotation that he was driven along as much by duty as by inspiration. We follow the birth pains of *NLOF* further in the Thomsen correspondence. On 19 February 1883 he wrote that 'these questions about sounds, and especially the vowel system, are so difficult that I am in doubt at every moment'. Even after publication he admitted that 'there are still many dark points in the Norwegian vowel system as far as I am concerned, particularly that of the west coast' (letter of 22 November 1884). It required the construction and implementation of a system, something that did not come naturally to him. Nevertheless, a system he did construct, and while it may not have resulted from his accustomed linguistic effortlessness, it was a clear and workable system, and one which many other linguists have verified through their own dialectological work, have built on and expanded. Large-scale extension and expansion is a true test of the strength of a building's foundations. There is evidence elsewhere in Storm's work that he was perfectly capable of constructing systems out of his beloved data. It is just that for the most part he chose not to, and so readers of his works and commentators on his methods have tended to view him as an unsystematic linguist. NBO Ms. 4° 1285 F^{xxiv}, for example, is a detailed table of palatalised consonants in the dialects, evidencing clear skill in organising and structuring data. *NLOF* as a whole shows quite a different side to Storm's method and style, compared with the rolling waters of *Englische Philologie* or *Større fransk Syntax*.

4.3.3.2 We noted in Chapter 2 that Storm was not inclined towards the writing of scholarly compendia. For him, knowledge was in perpetual growth, and to write a compendium of his knowledge would be to imply closure. This is why he so disliked writing the article on Romance langues for *Encyclopædia Britannica*, and why subsequent editions of his works simply got fatter rather than taller, so to speak. However, just as *NLOF* shows a systematising Storm, who is not much in evidence elsewhere, so it shows a compendium-writing Storm, who is also out of character. Pages 26–70 of *NLOF* are the 'Omrids af Fonetiken' bit, the 'Sketch of Phonetics'. Storm was very eager that his transcription system should be practical and easy to follow. It was not in intent a scientific undertaking, a scholarly collection of data. *NLOF* belongs with Storm's other popular writings. It was intended for the general public, and it was published in what the journal's editors saw as a journal for the general public. In 1882 Storm had sent out his questionnaire and engaged ordinary people in his great project to achieve an overview of all Norwegian dialects, and *NLOF* is written in this same spirit:

> Although our immediate task is pure science, it is important for us, in addition to this, to include the general public in its results. We have therefore to endeavour to make our presentation as clear and intelligible as possible, in so far as this can be done without being too circumstantial and without diminishing the demands of science. The fact is that we need the support and participation of the public in this matter; without it we can do nothing. (Storm 1884a: 18)

The 1882 questionnaire met with an impressive response, but the responses made little use of the transcription system, and indeed Storm encouraged respondents to use ordinary script for the most part. The *Norvegia* script may have become the "industry norm" for generations of Norwegian dialectologists, but, unsurprisingly, it never realised Storm's popular ambitions to include all the Norwegian people. Had it achieved these ambitions, it would have been the fulfilment of the Anglo-Scandinavian School's dream of taking linguistic science out into the real world, of a seamless carpet running from university to village, from professor to farm labourer. And what linguistic utopia that would have been!

Storm's first act in his attempt to open the science of phonetics up to ordinary Norwegians was to provide a clear, straightforward summary of the current state of the science, its categories and its terminology:

> Before I proceed to the more detailed explanation of the transcription system, I see it as unavoidably necessary to give a sketch of the elements of phonetics or the science of sounds, which is as brief and straightforward as possible. There are now, to be sure, several phonetic textbooks, both of the shorter and of the longer varieties, but they are partly too involved, and partly too difficult for the general public. As this science is still quite new, and it has become clear that many of those who should and could be interested in it have been put off embarking on it due to the inaccessibility of the textbooks, I thought that I should do what I can to solve this difficult problem. For it is in truth not easy to write about these things in a way that can be universally understood. My sketch does not make the detailed accounts redundant, but serves as an introduction to the topic. (Storm 1884/1902/1908: 26)

Another difficult task. Storm was forced to discipline himself, to be concise and to write for a non-specialist audience. It is often the case that imposed discipline of form leads to the most satisfactory results, and Lundell certainly believed that Storm had pulled off a masterstroke. He was of the opinion that 'these pages contain the best introduction to phonetics in any language' (*dessa sidor innehålla den bästa inledning till fonetiken som något språk äger*) (Lundell 1885: 459).

It was certainly clear and concise, and, given its author, utterly up to date. The lengthy section on prosody was particularly valuable. Storm begins his overview of phonetics with a brief description of the speech organs, here and elsewhere in the 'Omrids af Fonetiken' explaining and providing Norwegian translations of the Latinate terminology. He then passes to different voicing states, as in Storm (1860) using plenty of imagery to help a non-specialist audience understand the processes of initiation and phonation. Explanations of vowel articulation and the production of voiceless versus voiced consonants leads to a brief general exposition of the nature of consonant articulation. He then builds up the phonetic edifice as follows:

§ 10. The Relationship between Vowels and Consonants, Syllables, Stress, Intonation, Tone, Length:
1. Vowels and Consonants (p. 33)
2. Syllables (pp. 34–37)
3. Stress [*Eftertryk*] (pp. 37–40)

4. Prosody [*Tone*]
   a. Intonation [*Tonefald*] (pp. 40–42)
   b. Tone [*Tonelag*] (pp. 42–56)
5. Length (pp. 56–67)
§ 11. Glides [*Glidninger*] (pp. 67–70)

The section on tone is by far the longest, and this reflects both Storm's special interest in this area of phonetics and the nature of the Norwegian language. He explains his musical principle for indicating and describing tone variation, as set out in earlier works, and this is a fine distillation of his 'musikalske Princip', and a worthy sequel to 'Tale og Accent i Forhold til Sang'.

4.3.3.3 The rest of *NLOF*, Chapter III, 'Nærmere Forklaring af Lydskriften og Beskrivelse af de enkelte Lyd' (More detailed explanation of the transcription system and description of the individual sounds), is a complete handbook of the phonetic sounds of Norwegian, as far as Storm's research had been able to establish:

> [. . .] a description of every single sound which occurs in the Norwegian language and dialects, together with various others, which are needed to complete the system, and which could possibly later also be found in Norwegian. (Storm 1884/1902/1908: 71)

Storm is quite clear, then, that this is by no means an exhaustive guide to the sounds of Norwegian. Research has only just begun, and these sounds and their associated symbols form a basis from which the study may grow. According to Nes's calculations (Nes 1982: 12), *Norvegia* provides 36 vowel symbols and 61 consonant symbols, so 97 separate sounds. According to Storm's own list (Storm 1884/1902/1908: 175–179), there are actually 54 separate consonant symbols and 38 separate vowel symbols, so 92 individual sounds. This does not include any digraphs, while Nes's figure does. Storm used further symbols elsewhere, giving, again according to Nes's calculations, a total of 133 symbols. Later researchers using the *Norvegia* system found the need for a further 36 symbols, plus 'the many and confusing diacritical signs' (Nes 1982: 13). Precise figures do not really matter. The point is that Storm's set of symbols and associated signs was never intended to be complete. Knowledge is dynamic.

The *Norsk Lydskrift* bit is conventionally arranged by articulatory category. The 1884 part contains bilabial, labio-dental, dental, alveolar, retroflex, postalveolar and prepalatal consonants. The 1908 part picks up with palatal, velar, uvular and glottal consonants, before moving on to unrounded back, front and central vowels, rounded front then back vowels, and finally diphthongs. Examples abound, as is desirable in a presentation of this sort, but so do references to other languages and to the phonetic literature, and so do the inevitable footnotes, which are not so desirable. Storm could not carry through the popular nature of his presentation, and really a popular presentation of the phonetics of Norwegian in this amount of detail could only ever exist in Storm's dreams. Nobody could accuse Storm of not trying to take science out of the Academy, here or through his popular lectures or books. To take an image from the world of Ole rather than Johan Storm, though, the gulf between the "pulpit and the pew" is not always easy to bridge without compromising one of them. In *A Selection of Phrases for Tourists Travelling in Norway* (Bennett 1881) Storm compromised the pulpit, and in *Norvegia* he compromises the pew.

4.3.3.4 The *Norvegia* system was based on clearly stated and rigorously pursued principles. It was intended for use by Norwegians in the study of the Norwegian language, and so it was not desirable simply to adopt either Bell's or Lundell's system. Storm's objections to Lundell's system are explicitly stated in 1884. Lundell's *landsmålsalfabet* is too complicated, too closely based on the Swedish expectations of certain letters, contains Swedish sounds which are not found in Norwegian and vice versa, and does not provide a wholly adequate system for the vowels. All the same, Storm follows Lundell in taking italic Roman letters as his starting point, and he only deviates from the Roman alphabet where its letters are insufficient or ambiguous. The table of the consonants (Storm 1884/1902/1908: 24) shows how the basic stock of italic Roman letters is supplemented. Upper-case letters are introduced ([B] and [D]) for partially voiced bilabial and dental plosives respectively. Retroflex sounds systematically receive a dot underneath the letter, and palatal sounds receive a hook diacritic. As in the modern IPA system, other recognised European letters are introduced (such as [þ] and [ð] and, with Norwegian users in mind, other Old Norwegian letters), but unlike the IPA system, digraphs are quite freely employed. Storm's model variety of Norwegian – his own (*à la* Chomsky) – *det levende, dannede Talesprog*, forms the linguistic core, and sounds of this variety provide the unmarked symbols, the basic lower-case italic Roman letters without modification. Storm of course knew the full range of contemporary phonetic work, and he was therefore able to draw freely on the extra symbols and diacritical practices of a number of other scholars. Nes (1982: 16) attempts to locate the sources of Storm's transcription practices, and finds that, as well as borrowing from Sweet and Lundell, he particularly seems to have followed the practices of Ascoli (his Italian hero – see section 3.2.1.3). Nes also isolates the sources for the principal subsequent additions to Storm's system, and here there is a fairly substantial list of contributors (Nes 1982: 17), with Hallfrid Christiansen (14 signs, eight of them diacritical) and A. B. Larsen (11 new signs, one of them being diacritical) the most prolific.

Storm's grave in Vestre Gravlund

LE TOMBEAU DE JOHAN STORM

Johan Storm died on 26 October 1920. He is not buried in Vår Frelsers (Our Saviour's) graveyard, alongside the other grandees of late-nineteenth-century Norway, but in Vestre (West) graveyard, within walking distance of his home in Kirkeveien. The plot must have been a good one when the Storm family bought it, near the outside of the graveyard, under a tree, and unencumbered by the proximity of too many other souls. But now the main road provides a noisy and dirty backdrop, the underground trains rumble past on their way into Borgen station, and there are other, newer, smarter graves round about.

The grave consists of a solid, unpretentious granite headstone, leaning forward slightly, and adorned only by a standard-issue wreath of plastic heather and plastic pine branches. The patriarch is accompanied in death by his wife, Louise, those sons who survived into old age – Einar, Olaf, Halvard and Aage – and their daughters-in-law. I wondered, when I visited one bleak December day, and left my flowers, who the last person to visit had been.

The site may be anonymous, and it is not easy to find in that vast garden of Oslo's dead, but the tombstone is still impressive, even in its changed surroundings. It still rises above those around it. The top section may be rather grubby and mossy, but the fundament, despite the ravages of the elements, is still bright and clean, and the inscriptions are clearly visible. The star carved at the top has not become tarnished over the decades, but shines out as brightly as it ever did, out over the city, out over the country and the continent, for which Storm gave so much.

REFERENCES

NB 1. The order of the Norwegian alphabet has been followed – æ, ø and å/aa follow z.
   2. Initials have been expanded to full names where possible, but only where such information might be helpful in bibliographical searches.

1 UNPUBLISHED MATERIALS

The National Library of Norway, Oslo [NBO]

Etterlatte papirer [Ms. 8° 2402]
Forelæsninger over fonetik (1883) [Ms. forelesn. 1306]
Forelæsninger over La Chanson de Roland (1883) [Ms. forelesn. 1307]
Sør-østlandske målføre [Ms. 8° 775; Ms. 4° 1285]
Hjælpemidler til Studiet af Indo-europæisk Sprogsammenligning [Ms. 4° 1286]
Fonetiske Samlinger [Ms. 4° 1287]
Kort fonetisk Kursus for Lærere i Engelsk og Fransk [Ms. 4° 1288]
Fonetiske Tegninger [Ms. 4° 1289]
Samlinger til norsk Sproghistorie [Ms. 4° 1290]
Various letters in the Brevsamling [Letter Collection]

Bergen University Library [UBB]

Professor Johan Storms Manuskripter [Ms. 738–744]

The Royal Library, Copenhagen [KB]

Letters from Storm to Vilhelm Thomsen [NKS 4291 – 4°]

Biblioteca Nazionale Centrale di Firenze

Letters from Storm to Count Angelo de Gubernatis [Box 119, folder 5]

2 WORKS BY STORM

1860. Tale og Accent i Forhold til Sang. In: *Illustreret Nyhedsblad* 9, 169–170, 177–178 (30 September & 14 October).
1870. L'influenza dell'osco e umbro sulla lingua italiana. Osservazioni sul libro del professore Demattio: «Origine, Formazione ed Elementi della Lingua Italiana». In: *Rivista Bolognese di Scienze e Lettere* 2:2, 249–276.
1871. *De romanske Sprog og Folk. Skildringer fra en Studiereise med offentligt Stipendium.* Kristiania: Forlagt af Alb. Cammermeyer.
1872a. Trop, troupe, troupeau. In: *Romania* 1, 490–491.
1872b. Review of Petersen, Peter 1872, *Fuldstændigt Kursus i fire Sprog (Norsk, Tydsk, Engelsk, Fransk). Første Hefte.* In: *Morgenbladet*, 29 August 1872, 11 November 1872.
1872c. Review of Krogh, G. C. 1872, *Regler for Udtalen af det franske Sprog.* In: *Morgenbladet*, 22 & 23 August 1872.
1873. 'Musgode'. In: *Romania* 2, 85–86.
1874a. Remarques sur le vocalisme des *Serments de Strasbourg.* In: *Romania* 3, 286–290.
1874b. Bemærkninger i Anledning af Ascoli, *Saggi Ladini.* In: *Nordisk Tidskrift for Filologi og Pædagogik. Ny Række* 1, 158–182.
1875a. Om Tonefaldet (Tonelaget) i de skandinaviske Sprog (Foredraget den 6te Marts 1874).

In: *Forhandlinger i Videnskabs-Selskabet i Christiania Aar 1874*. Christiania: I Commission hos Jacob Dybwad. Trykt i A. W. Brøggers Bogtrykkeri, 286–297. (See also Storm 1983.)

1875b. Remarques sur les voyelles atones du latin, des dialectes italiques et de l'italien. In: *Mémoires de la Société de Linguistique de Paris* 2, 81–144.

1876. Mélanges étymologiques. In: *Romania* 5, 165–188.

1877a. See *Storthingsproposition*.

1877b. Blind Alarm i Maalstrævernes Lejr. In: *Aftenbladet*, 23 & 24 March 1877.

1877c. En ny Art Anmeldelser. In: *Morgenbladet*, 17 November 1877.

1878a. Det norske Maalstræv. In: *Nordisk Tidskrift för Vetenskap, Konst och Industri*, 407–430, 526–550.

1878b. Norsk literaturoversigt for 1877 og nærmest foregaaende Aar: Nordisk filologi. In: *Nordisk Tidskrift för Vetenskap, Konst och Industri*, 381–385.

1879a. *Engelsk Filologi. Anvisning til et videnskabeligt Studium af det engelske Sprog for Studerende, Lærere og Viderekomne. I: Det levende Sprog*. Kristiania: Alb. Cammermeyer (Det mallingske Bogtrykkeri).

1879b. In: Wimmer, Ludvig F. A. 1879. *Beretning om forhandlingerne på det første Nordiske filologmøde i København, den 18.-21. juli 1876*. København: Gyldendal, 157–192.

1880. De svenske dialekter. Review of *Nyare bidrag till kännedom om de svenska landsmålen och svenskt folklif*. In: *Nordisk tidskrift för vetenskap, konst och industri* 3, 333–350.

1881a. *Englische Philologie. Anleitung zum wissenschaftlichen Studium der englischen Sprache. Vom Verfasser für das deutsche Publikum bearbeitet. I: Die lebende Sprache*. Heilbronn: Verlag von Gebr. Henninger.

1881b. Unorsk og Norsk. Review of *Unorsk og Norsk eller fremmede Ords Avløsning*. Av K. Knudsen, Overlærer. Kristiania: Alb. Cammermeyer. 1879–80. In: *Morgenbladet*, 6, 12, & 13 February 1881, 1 & 5 March 1881.

1881c. Beretning om en i Sommeren 1880 foretagen Reise i Thelemarken med Stipendium af de til videnskabelige Reiser i Norge bevilgede Midler. In: *Norske Universitets- og Skole-Annaler*. 3. Række 17, 84–85.

1881d. Review of Sievers (1881). In: *Göttingische gelehrte Anzeigen* 28, 885–896.

1882a. *Norsk Ordliste til Lydlæren*. Kristiania: Foreningen for norske Dialekter og Folketraditioner. (Prøvehefte for *Norvegia*.).

1882b. Lettre de M. Joh. Storm. In: *Revue Critique* 16:49, 449–452.

1883. Engelsk Stil ved Realartium 1882, med nogle Bemærkninger om Realdannelsen. In: *Morgenbladet*, 23, 25, & 26 January 1883.

1884a. Indledning. In: *Norvegia* 1, 1–18.

1884b. *Kortere Ordliste med Forklaring af Lydskriften*. Bilag til *Norvegia* 1.

1884/1902/1908. Norsk Lydskrift med Omrids af Fonetiken. In: *Norvegia* 1, 19–179.

1885a. *Om Maalsagen*. Foredrag bestemt til at indlede en Diskussion i Studentersamfundet, Lørdag den 21de Febr. 1885. Udgivet som Manuskript af Studentersamfundets Bestyrelse.

1885b. Beretning afgiven af Professor Johan Storm om hans dialektologiske Reiser i 1883 og 1884. In: *Norske Universitets- og Skole-Annaler*. 3. Række 21, 129–132.

1886a. Romance languages. In: *Encyclopædia Britannica* 20. 9th edn. Edinburgh: Adam & Charles Black, 661–668.

1886b. Om den latinske udtale i skolerne. In: *Universitets- og skole-annaler*. Ny Række 1, 325–336.

1887a. *Franske Taleøvelser. En systematisk Fremstilling af det franske Talesprog gjennem Samtaler af det daglige Liv, ordnede efter Grammatiken. Mellemtrin*. Kjøbenhavn: Gyldendalske Boghandels Forlag (F. Hegel & Søn). Græbes Bogtrykkeri.

1887b. Om en forbedret undervisning i levende sprog. In: *Universitets- og skole-annaler. Ny række* 2, 161–198, 305–351.

1888a. *Det nynorske Landsmaal: En Undersøgelse*. Kjøbenhavn: Gyldendalske Boghandels Forlag (F. Hegel & Søn). Græbes Bogtrykkeri.

1888b. Nogle punkter af den franske Grammatik nærmere belyste. In: *Universitets- og skole-annaler. Ny række* 3:1, 1–7.

1889. Romanische quantität. Die quantität der romanischen vokale in ihrer geschichtlichen entwickelung. Vortrag, gehalten auf der ersten nordischen philologenversammlung in Kopenhagen, den 21. juli 1876. In: *Phonetische Studien* 2, 139–177.

1890a. Nogle bemærkninger om fransk udtale i anledning af overlærer Schou Bruuns reiseberetning. In: *Universitets- og skole-annaler*. Ny række 5:17, 257–266.

1890b. *Kort fonetisk Kursus for Lærere i Eng. og Fransk*. NBO Ms. 4° 1288.

1892a. *Englische Philologie. Anleitung zum wissenschaftlichen Studium der englischen Sprache. Vom Verfasser für das deutsche Publikum bearbeitet. I: Die lebende Sprache. 1. Abteilung: Phonetik und Aussprache*. Zweite, vollständig umgearbeitete und sehr vermehrte Auflage. Leipzig: O. R. Reisland.

1892b. *French Dialogues: A Systematic Introduction to the Grammar and Idiom of Spoken French by Joh. Storm L.L.D., Professor of Romance and English Philology in the University of Christiania. Intermediate Course*. Authorised English Edition by Geo. Macdonald, M.A., Balliol College, Oxford. London and New York: Macmillan & Co.

1892c. Review of Passy, Paul (1890), *Étude sur les changements phonétiques et leurs caractères généraux*. In: *Phonetische Studien* 5, 199–212.

1893a. Nogle Bemærkninger om Diftongdannelsen i de romanske Sprog. In: C. Jørgensen (ed.), *Forhandlinger paa det fjerde nordiske Filologmøde i Københaven. Den 18–21 juli 1892. Tillæg: Berättelse om Förhandlingarna vid det tredje nordiska filologmötet i Stockholm 10–13 augusti 1886 af Nils Linder*. København: Gyldendalske Boghandels Forlag (F. Hegel & Søn). Trykt hos J. Jørgensen & Co. (M. A. Hannover), xxxiv–xlvii.

1893b. Om musikalsk Tonelag, især i Kinesisk. In: C. Jørgensen (ed.), *Forhandlinger paa det fjerde nordiske Filologmøde i København. Den 18–21 juli 1892. Tillæg: Berättelse om Förhandlingarna vid det tredje nordiska filologmötet i Stockholm 10–13 augusti 1886 af Nils Linder*. København: Gyldendalske Boghandels Forlag (F. Hegel & Søn). Trykt hos J. Jørgensen & Co. (M. A. Hannover), 193–203.

1893c. Review of Vollmüller, Karl & Richard Otto (eds.) 1892, *Kritischer Jahresbericht über die Fortschritte der romanischen Philologie*. In: *Phonetische Studien* 6, 199–212.

1895a. Indfødte Lærere i levende Sprog ved Universitetet. In: *Vor Ungdom* 1895, 18–20.

1895b. *Franske Taleøvelser. En systematisk Fremstilling af det franske Talesprog gjennem Samtaler af det daglige Liv, ordnede efter Grammatiken. Mellemtrin. Tredie rettede og forøgede Oplag*. Kjøbenhavn: Gyldendalske Boghandels Forlag (F. Hegel & Søn). Græbes Bogtrykkeri.

1895c. Review of Ivar Kleiven 1894, *Segner fraa Vaagaa*. In: *Morgenbladet*, 11 August 1895.

1896a. *Englische Philologie. Anleitung zum wissenschaftlichen Studium der englischen Sprache. Vom Verfasser für das deutsche Publikum bearbeitet. I: Die lebende Sprache. 2. Abteilung: Rede und Schrift*. Zweite, vollständig umgearbeitete und sehr vermehrte Auflage. Leipzig: O. R. Reisland.

1896b. Review of Hans Ross 1895, *Norsk Ordbog: Tillæg til* Norsk Ordbog *af Ivar Aasen*. In: *Morgenbladet*, 19 January 1896.

1896c. *Norsk Sprog. Kraakemaal og Landsmaal*. Kjøbenhavn: Gyldendalske Boghandels Forlag (F. Hegel & Søn). Fr. Bagges Bogtrykkeri.

1897a. *Franske Taleøvelser. En Fremstilling af det franske Talesprog gjennem Samtaler af det daglige Liv. Høiere Trin. For Viderekomne*. Kjøbenhavn: Gyldendalske Boghandels Forlag (F. Hegel & Søn). Græbes Bogtrykkeri.

1897b. Norsk og Dansk. In: *Morgenbladet*, 19 September, 24 & 27 October 1897.

1897c. Ofotenbanen – Ofotbanen. In: *Morgenbladet*, 14 November 1897.

1898a. Ibsen og det norske Sprog, In: Gerhard Gran (ed.), *Henrik Ibsen: Festskrift i Anledning af hans 70de Fødselsdag. Udgivet af 'Samtiden'*. Bergen: John Griegs Forlag. Stockholm: C. & E. Gernandts Förlags-Aktiebolag. Kjøbenhavn: Gyldendalske Boghandel (F. Hegel & Søn), 147–205.

1898b. Sproglige Blandinger. In: *Morgenbladet*, 15 & 28 January, 16 February, & 1 March 1898.

1898c. Tysk-Dansk. In: *Morgenbladet*, 3, 10 & 24 April, 8 May 1898.

1900. De store Forfatteres Sprog og Retskrivning. In: *Aftenposten*, 20 September–2 November 1900.

1902. 'Forord' to reprinting of first part of *Norvegia* 1.

1903a. *Landsmaalet som Kultursprog*. Kristiania: Rigsmaalsforeningens Forlag. (Rigsmaalsforeningens Smaaskrifter VIII.)

1903b. Modersmaal. Maallag. In: *Aftenposten*, 28 June 1903.

1904. *Norsk Retskrivning. I: Nystaverne og deres radikale Reform*. Kristiania: Forlagt af Cammermeyers Boghandel.

1904/1906. *Norsk Retskrivning. II: Moderat reformeret Retskrivning*. Kristiania: Forlagt af Cammermeyers Boghandel.
1906. *Bibelsproget. En Fremstilling af Sproget i den nye Oversættelse af Det Nye Testamente (1904)*. Kristiania: Det norske Bibelselskabs Forlag.
1907. Græske Navne paa Nationaltheatret. In: *Morgenbladet*, 19 October 1907.
1908a. Mindeudgavens tekst: Retskrivning og sprogform. In: *Henrik Ibsen. Samlede Værker. Mindeudgave*. Femte bind. Kristiania & København: Gyldendalske Boghandel, Nordisk Forlag. Centraltrykkeriet Kristiania. [Appendix], 1–42.
1908b. 'Forord' to second part of *Norvegia* 1.
1911a. *Større fransk Syntax I: Artiklerne*. Kristiania & Kjøbenhavn: Gyldendalske Boghandel. Nordisk Forlag.
1911b. *Om Nabosprog og Grænsedialekter*. Kristiania: I Kommission hos Jacob Dybwad. (Videnskapsselskapets Skrifter. II. Hist.-Filos. Klasse. 1911, 4.)
1914. *Større fransk Syntax II: Præpositioner*. Kristiania & Kjøbenhavn: Gyldendalske Boghandel. Nordisk Forlag.
1919. *Større fransk Syntax III: Substantiver, Adjektiver og Verber*. Kristiania & Kjøbenhavn: Gyldendalske Boghandel. Nordisk Forlag.
1920. *Ordlister over Lyd- og Formlæren i norske Bygdemaal*. Udgivne ved Olai Skulerud. Utgit for Fridtjof Nansens Fond. Kristiania: I Kommission hos Jacob Dybwad. (Videnskapsselskapets Skrifter. II. Hist.-Filos. Klasse. 1919, 3.)
1983. Om Tonefaldet (Tonelaget) i de skandinaviske Sprog. Reprinted in: Jahr & Lorentz (1983: 30–39).

3 OTHER WORKS CITED

Alford, Henry 1864. *The Queen's English: Stray Notes on Speaking and Spelling*. London: Strahan & Co./Cambridge: Deighton, Bell & Co.
Amundsen Leiv 1957/1960. *Det norske Videnskabs-Akademi i Oslo 1857–1957*. Oslo: I kommisjon hos H. Aschehoug & Co. (W. Nygaard).
Amundsen, Leiv 1961a. Det historisk-filosofiske fakultet: Lærere og forskning. In: *Universitetet i Oslo 1911–1961* 1. Oslo: Universitetsforlaget, 251–476.
Amundsen, Leiv 1961b. Det historisk-filosofiske fakultet. In: *Universitetet i Oslo 1911–1961* 2. Oslo: Universitetsforlaget, 63–88.
Anon. 1882. Review of Storm (1881a). In: *The Spectator*, 17 June 1882, 802–803.
Asher, R. E. & Eugénie J. A. Henderson (eds.) 1981. *Towards a History of Phonetics*. Edinburgh: Edinburgh University Press.
Aske, Jorunn 1997. *Norsk dialektforsking: Historia om ein forskingsdisiplin*. Utrykt hovudfagsoppgåve. Nordisk institutt. Universitetet i Bergen.
Barthes, Roland 1984. *Camera Lucida: Reflections on Photography*. Translated by Richard Howard. London: Flamingo.
Becker-Christensen, Henrik 1981. *Skandinaviske drømmer og politiske realiteter: den politiske skandinavisme i Danmark 1830–1850*. Århus: Arusia.
Bell, Alex[ander] Melville 1867. *Visible Speech: the Science of Universal Alphabetics; or Self-Interpreting Physiological Letters, for the writing of All Languages in One Alphabet. Illustrated by Tables, Diagrams, and Examples*. London: Simpkin, Marshall & Co./London & New York: N. Trübner & Co.
Bell, Alexander Melville 1897. *The Science of Speech*. Washington, DC: Volta Bureau.
Bennett, [Thomas] 1862. *Bennetts Practiske Lærebog i det Engelske Sprog*. Christiania: Paa eget Forlag.
Bennett, T[homas] 1881. *A Selection of Phrases for Tourists Travelling in Norway*. Fourth edn. Enlarged and revised by Johan Storm, Professor of English and the Romance Languages at the University of Christiania. Christiania: H. Tønsberg's Printing Office.
Bielenstein, August Johann Gottfried 1863/1864. *Die lettische Sprache nach ihren Lauten und Formen erklärend und vergleichend dargestellt*. Berlin: F. Dümmler.
Birkeland, Bjarte & Reidar Djupedal 1953. *Norsk folkemål i grunnskrifter og innlegg gjennom hundre år*. Festskrift til Halvdan Koht. Oslo: Det Norske Samlaget.

Bjørndal, Bjarne 1959. *P. Voss og hans samtid: pedagogiske brytningar 1869–1896*. Oslo: Universitetsforlaget.

Bleken, Brynjulv 1956. *Studier i Knud Knudsens grammatiske arbeider*. Oslo: I Kommisjon hos Aschehoug & Co.

Boye, Else M. 1967. *Den gang det het Christiania*. Oslo: Grøndahl & søns forlag/Oslo bymuseum.

Brate, Erik 1891. Ett besök hos d:r Klinghardt. *Quousque Tandem Revy* 10, 73–74.

Bratt, Ingar 1977. *Engelskundervisningens framväxt i Sverige: Tiden före 1850*. Stockholm: Föreningen för svensk undervisningshistoria. (Årsböcker i svensk undervisningshistoria 139.)

Bratt, Ingar 1984. *Engelskundervisningens villkor i Sverige 1850–1905*. Stockholm & Uppsala: Föreningen för svensk undervisningshistoria. (Årsböcker i svensk undervisningshistoria 156.)

Brekke, Knud 1881. *Bidrag til dansk-norskens lydlære*. Kristiania: Fabritius.

Breymann, H[ermann Wilhelm] 1897. *Die phonetische Literatur von 1876–1895: eine bibliographisch-kritische Übersicht*. Leipzig: A. Deichert.

Broch, Olaf 1936. Johan Storm 1836-24. november 1936. In: *Aftenposten*, 24 November 1936, 6.

Bruun, Schou 1890. Indberetning fra overlærer Schou Bruun om en i 1889 foretagen stipendiereise til Frankrig for at studere landets sprog. In: *Universitets- og skole-annaler. Ny række* 5, 197–214.

Bull, Francis 1945. *Tradisjoner og minner*. Oslo: Gyldendal norsk forlag.

Burgun, Achille 1919. *Le développement linguistique en Norvège depuis 1814*. 1ᵉ partie. Kristiania: I Kommission hos Jacob Dybwad. (Videnskapsselskapets Skrifter. II. Hist.-Filos. Klasse. 1917, 1.)

Burgun, Achille 1921. *Le développement linguistique en Norvège depuis 1814*. 2ᵉ partie. Kristiania: En Commission chez Jacob Dybwad. (Videnskapsselskapets Skrifter. II. Hist.-Filos. Klasse. 1921, 5.)

Bødtker, A[dam] Trampe 1922. Mindetale over prof. dr. Johan Storm. In: *Oversigt over Videnskapsselskapets Møter i 1921 med Fortegnelse over Selskapets Medlemmer og over indkomne Skrifter M.M.* Kristiania: I Kommission hos Jacob Dybwad. A. W. Brøggers Boktrykkeri A-S, 50–53. (Supplement to: *Forhandlinger i Videnskapsselskapet i Kristiania* 1921.)

Bødtker, A[dam] Trampe 1938. Oluf Eilert Løseth. In: *Norsk biografisk leksikon* 7. Oslo: H. Aschehoug & Co. (W. Nygaard), 590–591.

Collett, John Peter 1999. *Historien om universitetet i Oslo*. Oslo: Universitetsforlaget.

Collins, Beverley & Inger M. Mees 1999. *The Real Professor Higgins: The Life and Career of Daniel Jones*. Berlin/New York: Mouton de Gruyter.

Curtius, Georg 1866. *Græsk Grammatik til Skolebrug*. Anden omarbeidede norske Udgave, oversat efter Originalens sjette Oplag af Valentin Voss. Christiania: Johan Dahls Forlag.

Dahl, Helge 1962. *Knud Knudsen og latinskolen*. Oslo: Universitetsforlaget.

Danielsen, Rolf, Ståle Dyrvik, Tore Grønlie, Knut Helle & Edgar Hovland (eds.) 1991. *Grunntrekk i norsk historie fra vikingtid til våre dager*. Oslo: Universitetsforlaget.

Derry, T[homas] K[ingston] 1973. *A History of Modern Norway 1814–1972*. Oxford: Oxford University Press.

Derry, T[homas] K[ingston] 1975. *A History of St Edmund's Church Oslo, 1884–1974*. Oslo: Printed in Oslo in 1976 by Merkantile Trykkeri.

Elert, Clæs-Christian 1996. Studiet av ljudläran i Norden fram till 1900. In: Henriksen et al. (1996: 11–30).

Eriksson, Manne 1961. *Svensk ljudskrift 1878–1960: En översikt över det svenska landsmålsalfabetets utveckling och användning huvudsakligen i tidskriften* Svenska landsmål. Stockholm: P. A. Norstedt & Söner. (*Svenska landsmål och svenskt folkliv* B. 62.)

Falk, Hjalmar 1899. *Forhandlinger paa det femte nordiske filologmøde i Kristiania 12te–15de august 1898*. Kristiania: Det norske forlagstrykkeri.

Falk, Hjalmar 1921. Johan Storm. In: *Maal og Minne*, 111–112.

Finkenstaedt, Thomas 1983. *Kleine Geschichte der Anglistik in Deutschland. Eine Einführung*. Darmstadt: Wissenschaftliche Buchgesellschaft. (Anglistik und Amerikanistik.)

Firth, Charles 1929. *Modern Languages at Oxford 1724–1929*. Oxford: Oxford University Press. London: Humphrey Milford.

Fløtra, Jorunn 1995. *Moltke Moe som folklorist*. Oslo: Aschehoug/Norsk Folkeminnelag.

Forhandlinger i Videnskabs-Selskabet i Christiania Aar 1882. 1883. Christiania: I Commission hos Jacob Dybwad. Trykt hos A. W. Brøgger.

Franke, Felix 1900 *Phrases de tous les jours*. 8th edn. Leipzig: O. R. Reisland.

Friis, Jens Andreas 1887. *Lexicon Lapponicum: Ordbog over det lappiske Sprog med latinsk og norsk Forklaring, samt en Oversigt over Sprogets Grammatik*. Christiania: I Kommission hos Jacob Dybwad.

Garborg, Arne 1877. *Den nynorske Sprog- og Nationalitetsbevægelse: Et Forsøg paa en omfattende Redegjørelse, formet som polemiske Sendebreve til Modstræverne*. Kristiania: Cammermeyer. (Facsimile in *Birkeland & Djupedal* (1953: 103–120).)

Gosse, Edmund 1889. Review of *Det nynorske Landsmaal*. In: *The Saturday Review*, 19 January 1889.

Gran, Gerhard (ed.) 1911. *Det kongelige Fredriks Universitet 1811–1911. Festskrift*. Kristiania: Forlagt av H. Aschehoug & Co. (W. Nygaard).

Gundem, Bjørg Brandtzæg 1989. *Engelskfaget i folkeskolen: Påvirkning og gjennomslag fra 1870-årene til først på 1970-tallet*. Oslo: Universitetsforlaget.

Halvorsen, J[ens] B[raage] (ed.) 1901. Johan Frederik Breda Storm. In: *Norsk forfatter-lexikon 1814–1880*. Femte bind S-T. Kristiania: Den norske forlagsforening. I hovedkommission hos H. Aschehoug & Co, 486–493.

Hambro, C[arl] J[oachim] 1937. Johan Storm. In: *Portræter og profiler*. Oslo: H. Aschehoug & Co. (W. Nygaard), 59–75.

Hambro, C[arl] J[oachim] 1950. *De første studenterår: Ungdomserindringer*. Oslo: Gyldendal norsk forlag.

Hammar, Elisabet 1981. *Franskundervisningen i Sverige fram till 1807: Undervisningssituationer och lärare*. Stockholm & Uppsala: Föreningen för svensk undervisningshistoria. (Årsböcker i svensk undervisningshistoria 148.)

Hansen, M[auritz] C[hristopher] 1822. *Forsøg til en Grammatik i Modersmaalet*. Christiania: Trykt i det Wulfsbergske Bogtrykkerie af Rasmus Hviid.

Hansen, M[auritz] C[hristopher] 1828. *Grammatik i det norske og danske Sprog*. Tredie Oplag. Christiania: Trykt i det Wulfsbergske Bogtrykkerie af R. Hviid og paa hans Forlag.

Hansen, M[auritz] C[hristopher] 1846 [1833]. *Norsk Grammatik*. Fjerde Oplag. Tredie Gang aftrykt. Christiania: Trykt i R. Hviids Enkes Bogtrykkeri og paa hendes Forlag af G. Hansen.

Haugen, Einar 1966. *Language Conflict and Language Planning: The Case of Modern Norwegian*. Cambridge, Mass.: Harvard University Press. (Norwegian version = *Riksspråk og folkemål: Norsk språkpolitikk i det 20. århundre*. Trans. by Dag Gundersen. Oslo: Universitetsforlaget, 1968.)

Haugen, Einar 1976. *The Scandinavian Languages: An Introduction to their History*. London: Faber & Faber.

Henriksen, Carol, Even Hovdhaugen, Fred Karlsson & Bengt Sigurd (eds.) 1996. *Studies in the Development of Linguistics in Denmark, Finland, Iceland, Norway and Sweden*. Oslo: Novus forlag.

Hertzberg, Nils 1910. *Minder fra min skolemestertid 1844–1873*. Kristiania: Aschehoug.

Hertzberg, N[ils], Kristoffer Brun & L[udvig] L[udvigsen] Daae 1885. *Om Maalsagen*. Diskussion i Studentersamfundet lørdag den 28de Februar. Udgivet som Manuskript af Studentersamfundets Bestyrelse. Christiania: R. Hviids Enkes Bogtrykkeri.

Heyerdahl, Gerd Høst 1975. Carl Richard Unger. In: *Norsk biografisk leksikon 17*. Oslo: H. Aschehoug & Co. (W. Nygaard), 391–396.

Hirst, Daniel & Albert Di Cristo 1998. *Intonation Systems: A Survey of Twenty Languages*. Cambridge: Cambridge University Press.

Hjelmslev, Louis (ed.) 1941. *Breve fra og til Rasmus Rask*. 2 vols. København: Munksgaard.

Hoel, Oddmund Løkensgard 1996. *Nasjonalisme i norsk målstrid 1848–1865*. Oslo: Noregs forskingsråd. (KULTs skriftserie 51.)

Hoemsnes, Ole N. 1999. *Reiseliv gjennom 150 år: Bennett Reisebureau AS. Bennett BTI Nordic Norge AS. 1850–2000*. Oslo: Europa forlag.

Holter, Helle 1986. *Reform og tradisjon: Johan Storm som språkpolitiker*. Utrykt hovedfagsavhandling. Institutt for nordisk språk og litteratur, Universitetet i Oslo. Våren 1986.

Holter, Åge 1966. *Det Norske Bibelselskap gjennom 150 år 1: 1816–1904*. Oslo: Det Norske Bibelselskap.

324 REFERENCES

Hovdhaugen, Even, Fred Karlsson, Carol Henriksen & Bengt Sigurd 2000. *The History of Linguistics in the Nordic Countries*. Helsinki: Societas Scientiarum Fennica.
Howatt, A. P. R. 1984. *A History of English Language Teaching*. Oxford: Oxford University Press.
Howatt, A. P. R. & Richard C. Smith 2002. *Modern Language Teaching: The Reform Movement*. London & New York: Routledge.
Hurum, Hans Jørgen 1984. Musikklivet. In: Brynjulf Bull (ed.), *Oslo*. Oslo: Gyldendal, 382–404.
Høigård, Einar & Herman Ruge 1963. *Den norske skoles historie. En oversikt*. 2nd edition. Oslo: J. W. Cappelens forlag. (1st edn. 1945.)
Høybye, Poul & Ebbe Spang-Hanssen 1979. Romansk sprog og litteratur. In: Jensen (1979: 231–268).
Høyem, O[lav] J[akobsson] 1881. *Den helige saga og kjørkjesaga: serleg skreve etter 'større Bibelhistorie, en Haandbog o.s.v. ved J. T. A. Tang' i Danmark*. Niðaros: Kosta på prent av O. J. Høyem hjå Johan L. Sundt.
Haakonsen, Daniel 1952. Peter Hjalmar Rokseth. In: *Norsk biografisk leksikon* 11. Oslo: H. Aschehoug & Co. (W. Nygaard), 509–513.
Indrebø, Gustav 1951. *Norsk målsoga*. Ed. Per Hovda & Per Thorson. Bergen: A.S. John Griegs Boktrykkeri.
Jahr, Ernst Håkon 1989. *Utsyn over norsk språkhistorie etter 1814*. Oslo: Novus forlag.
Jahr, Ernst Håkon 1996. Nynorsk språkforskning: en historisk oversikt. In: Henriksen et al. (1996: 84–101).
Jahr, Ernst Håkon & Ove Lorentz (eds.) 1981. *Fonologi/Phonology*. Oslo: Novus forlag.
Jahr, Ernst Håkon & Ove Lorentz (eds.) 1983. *Prosodi/Prosody*. Oslo: Novus forlag.
Jankowsky, Kurt 1972. *The Neogrammarians: A Re-evaluation of their Place in the Development of Linguistic Science*. The Hague/Paris: Mouton. (Janua Linguarum, Series Minor 116.)
Jensen, Povl Johannes (ed.) 1979. *Københavns Universitet 1479–1979 9: Det filosofiske Fakultet II*. København: G. E. C. Gads Forlag.
Jespersen, Otto 1886. Den ny sprogundervisnings program. In: *Vor Ungdom*, 353–381.
Jespersen, Otto 1888. Review of Storm (1887a). In: *Vor Ungdom*, 478–482.
Jespersen, Otto 1901. *Sprogundervisning*. København: Schubothe.
Jespersen, Otto 1904. *How to Teach a Foreign Language*. Translated from the Danish original by Sophia Yhlen-Olsen Bertelsen. London: George Allen & Unwin Ltd.
Jespersen, Otto 1905/1906. Zur geschichte der phonetik. In: *Die neueren Sprachen* 13, 210–224, 402–416, 513–528. (Reprinted in *Jespersen* (1933: 40–80).)
Jespersen, Otto 1909–1949. *A Modern English Grammar on Historical Principles*. København: Munksgaard.
Jespersen, Otto 1920a. Presidential Address. Modern Humanities Research Association. In: Jespersen (1933: 81–97).
Jespersen, Otto 1920b. Obituary of Storm. In: *Berlingske Tidende (aften)*, 28 October 1920.
Jespersen, Otto 1933. *Linguistica: Selected Papers in English, French and German*. Copenhagen: Levin & Munksgaard/London: George Allen & Unwin Ltd.
Jones, Daniel 1918. *An Outline of English Phonetics*. Leipzig: B. G. Teubner Verlag.
Joos, Martin 1958. *Readings in Linguistics: The Development of Linguistics in America since 1925*. 2nd edn. New York: American Council of Learned Societies.
J[oret], C[harles] 1882. Review of Storm (1881a). In: *Revue Critique* 16:41, 284–287.
Juul, Arne 1999. Nordmændenes Professor Higgins. In: *Uddannelseshistorie* 1999, 49–74.
Juul, Arne 2002. *Den levende fonograf: Nordmændenes Professor Higgins*. Odense: Syddansk Universitetsforlag. (University of Southern Denmark Studies in Linguistics 14.)
Juul, Arne, Hans F. Nielsen & Jørgen Erik Nielsen 1995. *A Linguist's Life: An English Translation of Otto Jespersen's Autobiography with Notes, Photos and a Bibliography*. Odense: Odense University Press.
Jørgensen, C[hristian Peter Julius] (ed.) 1893. *Forhandlinger paa det fjerde nordiske Filologmøde i København. Den 18–21 juli 1892. Tillæg: Berättelse om Förhandlingarna vid det tredje nordiska filologmötet i Stockholm 10–13 augusti 1886 af Nils Linder*. København: Gyldendalske Boghandels Forlag (F. Hegel & Søn). Trykt hos J. Jørgensen & Co. (M. A. Hannover).
Kabell, Inge 1996. Et portræt af George Stephens: professor i engelsk ved Københavns Universitet og fremtrædende medlem af den engelske menighed i Danmark i en menneskealder. In: *Magasin fra det kongelige Bibliotek* 11:3, 21–41.

Kabell, Inge 2000. Jespersen and Franke: an academic friendship by correspondence. In: *Bulletin of the Henry Sweet Society* 35, 27–37.

Knudsen, Knud 1856. *Haandbog i dansk–norsk Sproglære*. Kristiania: Trykt og forlagt af J. Chr. Abelsted.

Knudsen, Knud 1867. *Det norske målstræv*. Kristiania: Trykt på forfatterens kostning hos Brøgger & Christie.

Knudsen, Knud 1876. *Den landsgyldige norske uttale*. Kristiania: trykt på forfatterens kostning.

Knudsen, Knud 1881a. *Unorsk og norsk eller fremmedords avløsning*. Kristiania: Forlagt av Alb. Cammermeyer.

Knudsen, Knud 1881b. *Af Maalstriden 1881. Svar til Prof. J. Storm og Litterat A. Larsen m. m.* Kristiania: Trykt paa Forfatterens Kostning hos A. W. Brøgger. Sælges ved Alb. Cammermeyer.

Knudsen, Knud 1895. Prof Joh. Storm, 'Morgenbladet' og målstrævet. In: *Morgenbladet*, 9 June 1895.

Knudsen, Knud 1937. *Knud Knudsens livsminner: barneår og ungdomsår*. Utgitt av bymålslaget. Oslo: Aschehoug.

Knudsen, Knud 2001. *Reiseminner 1847–1892*. Oslo: Bymålslaget.

Knudsen, Trygve 1923. *P. A. Munch og samtidens norske sprogstrev*. Kristiania: Gyldendalske Bokhandel.

Koerner, E. F. K[onrad] 1995. History of linguistics: the field. In: Koerner & Asher (1995: 3–7).

Koerner, E. F. K[onrad] & R[onald] E. Asher (eds.) 1995. *Concise History of the Language Sciences from the Sumerians to the Cognitivists*. Oxford: Pergamon.

Kohler, K. 1981. Three trends in phonetics: the development of phonetics as a discipline in Germany since the nineteenth century. In: Asher & Henderson (1981: 161–178).

Koht, Halvdan 1926. Ludvig Kristensen Daa. In: *Norsk biografisk leksikon* 3. Oslo: H. Aschehoug & Co. (W. Nygaard), 156–167.

Koht, Halvdan 1966. Gustav Storm. In: *Norsk biografisk leksikon* 15. Oslo: H. Aschehoug & Co. (W. Nygaard), 69–77.

Krokvik, Jostein 1993. *Ny Hungrvekja og Jan Prahl*. Bergen: Norsk Bokreidingslag.

Krokvik, Jostein 1996. *Ivar Aasen: Diktar og granskar, sosial frigjerar og nasjonal målreisar*. Bergen: Norsk Bokreidingslag.

Kurschat, Friedrich. 1876. *Grammatik der littauischen Sprache. Mit einer Karte des littauischen Sprachgebiets und einer Abhandlung über littauische Volkspoesie, nebst Musikbeilage von 25 Dainosmelodien*. Halle: Verlag der Buchhandlung des Waisenhauses.

Langholm, Sivert 1999. Hvordan skrive faghistorie. Review of Sandved (1998). In: *HIFO-nytt: Meldingsblad for Den norske historiske forening* 1999:2, 40–45.

Langslet, Lars Roar 1999. *I kamp for norsk kultur: Riksmålsbevegelsens historie gjennom 100 år*. Oslo: Riksmålsforbundet.

Leskien, August 1876. *Die Declination im Slavisch–Litauischen und Germanischen*. Leipzig: Hirzel.

Libæk, Ivar & Øivind Stenersen 1991. *History of Norway from the Ice Age to the Oil Age*. Trans. Joan Fuglesang & Virginia Siger. Oslo: Grøndahl & Søn Forlag.

Liestøl, Knut 1920. Johan Storm. In: *Den 17de Mai*, 27 October 1920.

Linn, Andrew Robert 1996. Rasmus Rask and English. In: Vivien Law and Werner Hüllen (eds.), *Linguists and their Diversions: A Festschrift for R. H. Robins on his 75th Birthday*. Münster: Nodus Publikationen, 307–331.

Linn, Andrew Robert 1997. *Constructing the Grammars of a Language: Ivar Aasen and Nineteenth-Century Norwegian Linguistics*. Münster: Nodus Publikationen.

Linn, Andrew Robert 1999. Charles Bertram's *Royal English–Danish Grammar*: The linguistic work of an eighteenth-century fraud. In: David Cram, Andrew Linn & Elke Nowak (eds.), *History of Linguistics 1996. Vol. 2: From Classical to Contemporary Linguistics*. Amsterdam & Philadelphia: John Benjamins Publishing Company, 183–191. (SiHoLS 95.)

Linn, Andrew Robert 2000. Review of Sandved (1998). In: *English Studies* 81:2, 175–176.

Linn, Andrew Robert 2001. Professor Storm's diary. Historical fact – historiographical fiction. In: *Beiträge zur Geschichte der Sprachwissenschaft* 11:2, 193–219.

Linn, Andrew Robert 2003a. Johan Storm (1836–1920) and the Study of French in Scandinavia. In: Sylvain Auroux (ed.), *History of Linguistics 1999*. Amsterdam & Philadelphia: John Benjamins Publishing Company, 289–301.

Linn, Andrew Robert 2003b. Johan Storm: 'målmennenes og fornorskingsmennenes argeste motstander'. In: Helge Omdal & Rune Røsstad (eds.), *Krefter og motkrefter i språknormeringa: Om språknormer i teori og praksis*. Kristiansand S: Høyskoleforlaget. (Høgskolen i Agder. Forskningsserien 33.)

Linn, Andrew Robert 2003c. 'Fram for eit reint norskt mål!' The høgnorsk movement and language purism in contemporary Norway. Paper delivered at the *Purism in the Germanic Languages* conference, University of Bristol, April 2003.

Linn, Andrew Robert *(forthcoming)*. The Scandinavian languages. In: Peter Schmitter (ed.), *Geschichte der Sprachtheorie* 6:1. Tübingen: Gunter Narr Verlag.

Longum, Leif 1989. *Norsk som forsknings- og studiefag: historiske perspektiver – aktuelle utfordringer*. Oslo: Landslaget for norskundervisning (LNU) og J. W. Cappelens Forlag A.S.

Lundeby, Einar 1983. August Western. In: *Norsk biografisk leksikon* 19. Oslo: H. Aschehoug & Co. (W. Nygaard), 65–70.

Lundeby, Einar 1995. Knud Knudsen: riksmålets fader, bokmålets bestefar. In: *Språknytt* 23:4, 1–5.

Lundell, J[ohan] A[ugust] 1879. Det svenska landsmålsalfabetet. *Nyare bidrag till kännedom om de svenska landsmålen ock svenskt folkliv* 1:2.

Lundell, J[ohan] A[ugust] 1881. Om dialektstudier med särskild hänsyn till de nordiska språken. Föredrag vid andra nordiska filologmötet i Kristiania i allmän sammankomst den 11 augusti 1881. In: *Nyare bidrag till kännedom om de svenska landsmålen ock svenskt folkliv* 3:1, 1–31.

Lundell, Johan August 1885. Review of *Norvegia* 1. In: *Nordisk Revy* 1885, 458–460.

Lundell, J[ohan] A[ugust] 1888. Die phonetik als universitätsfach. In: *Phonetische Studien* 1, 1–17.

Løkke, Jakob [Olaus] 1855. *Modersmaalets Formlære. Udførlig Fremstilling*. Kristiania: Johan Dahl.

Långfors, A[rthur] 1920. Obituary of Storm. In: *Romania* 49, 621.

Mathesius, N. A. 1876. *Engelsk Elementarbok: Första afdelingen, försedd med fullständig ordförteckning och utgörande ett för sig afslutadt helt*. Stockholm: P. A. Norstedt & Söners Förlag.

Matthews, P[eter] H[ugoe] 1993. *Grammatical Theory in the United States from Bloomfield to Chomsky*. Cambridge: Cambridge University Press.

Meyer-Lübke, Wilhelm 1899. *Grammatik der romanischen Sprachen. 3: Syntax*. Leipzig: O. R. Reisland.

Midgaard, John 1989. *A Brief History of Norway*. Revised 10th ed. by Knut Midgaard. Oslo: Aschehoug. (1st edn. 1963.)

Moe, Moltke 1900. *Retskrivning og folkedannelse*. Kristiania: Jacob Dybwad.

Mohn, E[mmanuel Meyer] 1868. *Om Maalsagen og det bergenske Maalstrev*. Bergen: F. Beyers forlag. Trykt hos J. D. Beyer.

Moon, George Washington 1865. *The Dean's English: A Criticism on the Dean of Canterbury's Essays on the Queen's English*. London: George Routledge & Sons Ltd.

Myre, Olav 1943. *En antikvarbokhandler fra nitti-årene. Bertrand Jensen 80 år*. Oslo: N. W. Damm & Søn.

Mørch, Edv[ard] 1904. *Kristianiaminder*. Kristiania: H. Aschehoug & Co. (W. Nygaard).

Nes, Oddvar 1982 (1975). *Storms norske lydskriftsystem (med tillegg) definert ved hjelp av IPA's lydskriftsystem*. 4. utgåve. Bergen: Universitetet i Bergen, Institutt for fonetikk og lingvistikk. (Skriftserie 8, Serie B.)

Nes, Oddvar 1986. Gransking av vestnorske målføre. In: *Nordlyd* 12, 119–137.

Nielsen, Jørgen Erik 1979. Engelsk sprog og litteratur. In: Jensen (1979: 267–296).

Nygaard, Rolf R. 1945. *Fra dansk-norsk til norsk riksmål: Rettskrivningsstrevet i bokmålet inntil 1907*. Oslo: Johan Grundt Tanum.

Olsen, Magnus 1929. Johan Fritzner. In: *Norsk biografisk leksikon* 4. Oslo: H. Aschehoug & Co. (W. Nygaard), 299–300.

Osland, Erna & Arild Midthun 1996. *Ivar Aasen: Ei historie om kjærleik*. Oslo: Det Norske Samlaget.

Palmer, D. J. 1965. *The Rise of English Studies: An Account of the Study of English Language and Literature from its Origins to the Making of the Oxford English School*. Oxford, New York & Toronto: Oxford University Press. (University of Hull Publications.)

Paris, Gaston 1873. Review of *Mémoires de la Société de Linguistique de Paris 2*. In: *Romania 2*, 375.

Passy, Paul 1886. *Dhi Fonètik Tîtcer: Dhi organ ov dhi fonètik tîtcer'z asociécon*, 1886–1887.

Passy, Paul 1887. *Les sons du français, leur formation, leur combinaison, leur représentation*. Paris: Firmin-Didot.

Passy, Paul 1889. Review of *Fedraheimen*. In: *Lə Mɛtr Fɔnetik* 4:2, 21.

Passy, Paul 1902. *Le français parlé: morceaux choisis à l'usage des étrangers avec la prononciation figurée*. 5th edn. Leipzig: O. R. Reisland.

Pedersen, Inge Lise 1996. Dialektforskningen i Danmark med særligt henblik på forholdet til strukturalisme og sociolingvistik. In: Henriksen et al. (1996: 237–273).

Popperwell, Ronald G. 1972. *Norway*. London & Tonbridge: Ernest Benn Limited.

Rask, Rasmus 1817. *Angelsaksisk Sproglære tilligemed en kort Læsebog*. Stockholm: Wiborg.

Rask, Rasmus 1830. *A Grammar of the Anglo-Saxon Tongue, with a Praxis. A New Edition Enlarged and Improved by the Author. Translated from the Danish, by B. Thorpe*. Copenhagen: Møller.

Raudnitzky, Hans 1911. *Die Bell–Sweetsche Schule: Ein Beitrag zur Geschichte der englischen Phonetik*. Marburg: N. G. Elwert'sche Verlagsbuchhandlung. (Marburger Studien zur englischen Philologie 13.)

Regel, Ernst 1882. Review of Storm (1881a). In: *Englische Studien* 5:2, 398–408.

Robert, C.-M. 1887. Review of Storm (1887a). In: *Taalstudie* 8, 140–145.

Robins, R[obert] H[enry] 1974. Theory-orientation versus data-orientation: a recurrent theme in linguistics. In: *Historiographia Linguistica* 1, 11–26.

Sandfeld Jensen, Kr[istian] 1888–1889. Review of Storm (1897a). In: *Nordisk Tidsskrift for Filologi*. 3. Række 7, 35–37.

Sandfeld Jensen, Kr[istian] 1911. Review of Storm (1911a). In: *Nordisk Tidsskrift for Filologi*. 3. Række 20, 167–174.

Sandfeld, Kr[istian] 1983. Vilhelm Thomsen. In: *Dansk biografisk lexikon* 14. Oslo: H. Aschehoug & Co. (W. Nygaard), 504–509.

Sandved, Arthur O. 1998. *Fra 'kremmersprog' til verdensspråk: Engelsk som universitetsfag i Norge 1850–1943*. Universitetet i Oslo: Forum for universitetshistorie.

Sandved, Arthur O. 2002. *Fra 'kremmersprog' til verdensspråk. Bind 2: Engelskfaget ved Universitetet i Oslo 1945–1957*. Universitetet i Oslo: Forum for universitetshistorie.

Sanness, John 1959. *Patrioter, intelligens og skandinaver: Norske reaksjoner på skandinavismen før 1848*. Oslo: Universitetsforlaget.

Saussure, Ferdinand de 1916. *Cours de linguistique générale*. Paris: Payot.

Saussure, Ferdinand de 1983. *Course in General Linguistics*. Translated and annotated by Roy Harris. London: Duckworth.

Schiötz, Eiler H. 1970. *Utlendingers reiser i Norge: En bibliografi/Itineraria Norvegica: A Bibliography on Foreigners' Travels in Norway until 1900*. Oslo, Bergen & Tromsø: Universitetsforlaget. (Norsk bibliografisk bibliotek 44.)

Schiötz, Eiler H. 1986. *Itineraria Norvegica: Utlendingers reiser i Norge inntil år 1900: En bibliografi. Bind II: Supplementer/Itineraria Norvegica: Foreigners' Travels in Norway until 1900: A Bibliography. Vol. 2: Supplements*. Oslo, Bergen, Stavanger & Tromsø: Universitetsforlaget/Norwegian University Press.

Schmitz, Bernhard 1875–1881. *Encyclopädie des philologischen Studiums der neueren Sprachen, hauptsächlich der französischen und englischen*. 2nd edn. Leipzig: C. A. Kochs Verlagsbuchhandlung (I. Sengbusch).

Schmitz, Bernhard 1881. *Encyclopädie des philologischen Studiums der neueren Sprachen, hauptsächlich der französischen und englischen*. 2nd edn. Drittes Supplement: *Nebst einer Abhandlung über die englische Philologie insbesondere*. Herausgegeben von August Kesseler. Leipzig: C. A. Kochs Verlagsbuchhandlung (I. Sengbusch).

Schröer, A. 1887. *Wissenschaft und Schule in ihrem Verhältnis zur praktischen Spracherlernung*. Leipzig.

Seelmann, Emil 1885. *Die Aussprache des Latein nach physiologisch-historischen Grundsätzen*. Heilbronn: Gebr. Henninger.

Seip, Didrik Arup 1936. Knud Knudsen. In: *Norsk biografisk leksikon 7*. Oslo: H. Aschehoug & Co. (W. Nygaard), 476–489.

Seip, Didrik Arup 1952. Hans Ross. In: *Norsk biografisk leksikon* 11. Oslo: H. Aschehoug & Co. (W. Nygaard), 587–599.

Seip, Didrik Arup 1966. Johan Storm. In: *Norsk biografisk leksikon* 15. Oslo: H. Aschehoug & Co. (W. Nygaard), 77–82.

'S.H.' 1897. Review of *Storm* (1897a). In: *Morgenbladet*, 14 September 1897.

Sievers, Eduard 1876. *Grundzüge der Lautphysiologie zur Einführung in das Studium der Lautlehre der indogermanischen Sprachen*. Leipzig: Druck und Verlag von Breitkopf und Härtel.

Sievers, Eduard 1881. *Grundzüge der Phonetik zur Einführung in das Studium der Lautlehre der indogermanischen Sprachen*. Zweite wesentlich umgearbeitete und vermehrte Auflage der *Grundzüge der Lautphysiologie*. Leipzig: Druck und Verlag von Breitkopf & Härtel.

Sievers, Eduard 1885. *Grundzüge der Phonetik zur Einführung in das Studium der Lautlehre der indogermanischen Sprachen*. Dritte verbesserte Auflage. Leipzig: Druck und Verlag von Breitkopf & Härtel.

Sievers, Eduard 1893. Review of Storm (1892a). In: *Literarisches Centralblatt,* 29 April 1893.

Sigmund, Einar 1925. Knud Brekke. In: *Norsk biografisk leksikon* 2. Oslo: H. Aschehoug & Co. (W. Nygaard), 170–171.

Skard, Vemund 1967–1980. *Norsk språkhistorie*. Oslo, Bergen & Tromsø: Universitetsforlaget.

Skirbekk, Gunnar 2001. Mål og meining. Tankar om nynorsken ved eit sekelskifte. In: Elisabeth Bakke & Håvard Teigen (eds.), *Kampen for språket: nynorsken mellom det lokale og det globale*. Oslo: Det Norske Samlaget, 236–249.

Skytte, Gunver 1991. *Kr. Sandfeld. En hovedperson i dansk romanistiks historie*. København: Museum Tusculanums Forlag. (Studier fra Sprog- og Oldtidsforskning 316.)

Spang-Hanssen, Ebbe 1982. Romance studies in Scandinavia. In: Rebecca Posner & John N. Green (eds.), *Trends in Romance Linguistics and Philology. Volume 4: National and Regional Trends in Romance Linguistics and Philology*. The Hague, Paris & New York: Mouton Publishers, 251–271. (Trends in Linguistics. Studies and Monographs 15.)

Steen, Sverre 1923. Thomas Bennett. In: *Norsk biografisk Leksikon* 1. Kristiania: H. Aschehoug & Co. (W. Nygaard), 426–427.

Steffens, K[nut] E[gil] 1991. *Mønstre i oppløsning: Norsk sprogpolitikk og sprognormering frem til annen verdenskrig*. Hønefoss: Statens lærerhøgskole i handels- og kontorfag.

Storm, Oscar 1889. *Slægterne Storm og Breda m. fl.* Horten: C. Andersens Bogtrykkeri.

Storthingsproposition 42. 1877. Angaaende Bevilgning af 1,600 Kroner aarlig i to Aar af Statskassen til Udgivelse af et Værk over det norske Sprog. In: *Kongelige Propositioner og Meddelelser fremsatte for sex og tyve ordentlige Storthing i 1877*. Christiania: Trykt i flere Bogtrykkerier.

Sweet, Henry 1877. *Handbook of Phonetics*. Oxford: Clarendon Press.

Sweet, Henry 1879. Storm's English philology. In: *The Academy*, 11 October 1879, 269–270.

Sweet, Henry 1880. Sound notation. In: *Transactions of the Philological Society* 1880–1881, 177–235.

Sweet, Henry 1881. Review of Storm (1881a). In: *Göttingische gelehrte Anzeigen* 44, 1398–1408.

Sweet, Henry 1882. Review of Storm (1881a) and of Sievers (1881). In: *The Academy*, 30 December 1882, 472–473.

Sweet, Henry 1885a. The practical study of language. In: *Transactions of the Philological Society* 1882–1884, 577–599. (Published version of a paper delivered in 1884.)

Sweet, Henry 1885b. *Elementarbuch des gesprochenen Englisch*. Oxford: Clarendon Press.

Sweet, Henry 1886. *An Icelandic Primer with Grammar, Notes and Glossary*. Oxford: Clarendon Press.

Sweet, Henry 1890. *A Primer of Phonetics*. Oxford: Clarendon Press.

Sweet, Henry 1899. *The Practical Study of Languages: A Guide for Teachers and Learners*. London: J. M. Dent & Sons Ltd.

Sweet, Henry 1908. *The Sounds of English: An Introduction to Phonetics*. Oxford: Clarendon Press.

Sweet, Henry 1913. *Collected Papers*. Arranged by H[enry] C[ecil] Wyld. Oxford: Clarendon Press.

Sørensen, Knud 1971. The teaching of English in Denmark: a historical survey. In: *Pædagogica Historica* 11:1, 90–101.

Sørensen, Øystein 1994. The development of a Norwegian national identity during the nineteenth century. In: Øystein Sørensen (ed.), *Nordic Paths to National Identity in the Nineteenth Century*. Oslo: The Research Council of Norway, 17–35. (KULTs skriftserie 22.)

Sørensen, Øystein (ed.) 1998. *Jakten på det norske: Perspektiver på utviklingen av en norsk nasjonal identitet på 1800-tallet*. Oslo: Ad Notam Gyldendal.

'T.D.' 1911. Review of *Større fransk Syntax I: Artiklerne*. In: *Aftenposten*, 2 July 1911.

Thomsen, Vil[helm] 1902. *Sprogvidenskabens Historie: en kortfattet Fremstilling*. København : G. E. C. Gad.

Thordarson, Fridrik 1977. Hans Vogt. In: *Norsk biografisk leksikon* 18. Oslo: H. Aschehoug & Co. (W. Nygaard), 134–140.

Thorkildsen, Dag 1994. Skandinavismen: en historisk oversikt. In: Øystein Sørensen (ed.), *Nasjonal identitet – et kunstprodukt?* Oslo: The Research Council of Norway, 191–209. (KULTs skriftserie 30.)

Torp, Arne 1996. Knud Knudsen og Ivar Aasen: jamlikar og motpolar. In: *Språknytt* 24:1, 8–10.

Trautmann, Moritz 1894. Review of Storm (1892a). In: *Anglia* 4:10, 289–293.

Venås, Kjell 1992. *I Aasens fotefar: Marius Hægstad*. Oslo: Novus forlag.

Venås, Kjell 1996a. *Då tida var fullkomen. Ivar Aasen*. Oslo: Novus forlag.

Venås, Kjell 1996b. Om Ivar Aasen i eit minneår. In: *Språknytt* 24:1, 1–7.

Venås, Kjell 1997. Om utviklingslære og junggrammatikk i Noreg. In: Andreas Bjørkum, Botolv Helleland, Eric Papazian & Lars S. Vikør (eds.), *Kjell Venås–Målvitskap og målrøkt. Festskrift på 70-årsdagen 30. November 1997*. Oslo: Novus forlag, 262–269.

Venås, Kjell 2000a. *Ivar Aasen og universitetet*. Oslo: Universitetet i Oslo.

Venås, Kjell 2000b. Norsk riksmål gjennom hundre år. Review of Langslet (1999). In: *Nordisk tidskrift för vetenskap, konst och industri* 2000:3, 329–337.

Viëtor, Wilhelm 1882. *Der Sprachunterricht muss umkehren! Ein Beitrag zur Überbürdungsfrage*. Heilbronn: Gebr. Henninger. (English trans. = 'Appendix' to *Howatt* (1984).)

Viëtor, Wilhelm 1903. *Kleine Phonetik des Deutschen, Englischen und Französischen*. Dritte Auflage der 5. Auflage der Originalausgabe entsprechend. Leipzig: O. R. Reisland.

Vinje, Finn-Erik 1978. *Et språk i utvikling*. Oslo: Aschehoug.

Vinje, Finn-Erik 2001. Fra hjemmedansk synspunkt. In: *Skolefokus* 7, 38.

Vistdal, Oskar 2000. *Georg Sauerwein – europear og døl: Ein dokumentasjon*. Bergen: Norsk Bokreidingslag.

Wagner, J. N. 1881. Review of Storm (1881a). In: *Polybiblion* 31, 515–517.

Walton, Stephen J. 1996. *Ivar Aasens kropp*. Oslo: Det Norske Samlaget.

Werlauff, Erich Christian. 1873/1874. Danske, især kjøbenhavnske, Tilstande og Stemninger ved og efter Overgangen til det nittende aarhundrede. In: *Historisk Tidsskrift* 4, 245–412.

Western, August 1882. *Engelsk Lydlære for Studerende og Lærere*. Kristiania: P. T. Mallings forlag.

Western, August 1885. *Englische Lautlehre für Studierende und Lehrer*. Heilbronn: Gebr. Henninger.

Western, August 1888. Mere om den nye sprogundervisning. In: *Vor Ungdom*, 40–70.

Western, August 1889a. Review of Storm (1888a). In: *Lə Mɛtr Fɔnetik* 4:2, 19–20.

Western, August 1889b. Response to Passy (1889). In: *Lə Mɛtr Fɔnetik* 4:3, 38.

Western, August 1889c. Kurze Darstellung des norwegischen Lautsystems. In: *Phonetische Studien* 2, 259–282.

Western, August 1894. Lidt om vor filologiske uddannelse. In: *Meddelelser fra bestyrelsen af 'Filologernes og realisternes landsforening'* 5.

Western, August 1902. *Englische Lautlehre für Studierende und Lehrer*. Zweite, gänzlich umgearbeitete Auflage. Leipzig: O. R. Reisland.

Western, August 1907. *Er vort riksmaal et fremmed sprog? Et indlæg i maalstriden*. Kristiania: J. W. Cappelens forlag.

Western, August 1920. Johan Storm. 24. novbr. 1836–26. okt. 1920. In: *Nordisk Tidsskrift for Filologi*. 4. Række 9, 147–154.

Western, August 1921. *Norsk Riksmåls-Grammatikk for Studerende og Lærere*. Kristiania: Aschehoug.

Wimmer, Ludvig F[rands] A[dalbert] 1879. *Beretning om forhandlingerne på det første Nordiske filologmøde i København, den 18.-21. juli 1876*. København: Gyldendal.

Worren, Dagfinn 1996. *Ivar Aasen-almanakken 1996*. Oslo: Dag og Tid.

Zettersten, Arne 1983. The pre-history of English studies at Swedish universities. In: Thomas

REFERENCES

Finkenstaedt & Gertrud Scholtes (eds.), *Towards a History of English Studies in Europe: Proceedings of the Wildsteig-Symposium, April 30–May 3, 1982*. Augsburg: Universität Augsburg. (Augsburger I- & I- Schriften 21.)

Aars, J[acob] 1876. Review of *A Selection of Phrases for Tourists Travelling in Norway*. 3rd edn. In: *Aftenbladet*, 26 January 1876.

Aarsleff, Hans 1983. *The Study of Language in England 1780–1860*. Minneapolis: University of Minnesota Press/London: The Athlone Press.

Aasen, I[var] 1853. *Prøver af Landsmaalet i Norge*. Christiania: Trykt hos Carl C. Werner & Comp.

Aasen, Ivar 1957. *Brev 1828–1861*. Reidar Djupedal (ed.), *Ivar Aasen: Brev og dagbøker*, vol. 1. Oslo: Det Norske Samlaget.

Aasen, Ivar 1958. *Brev 1862–1896*. Reidar Djupedal (ed.), *Ivar Aasen: Brev og dagbøker*, vol. 2. Oslo: Det Norske Samlaget.

Aasen, Ivar 1960. *Dagbøker 1830–1896*. Reidar Djupedal (ed.), *Ivar Aasen: Brev og dagbøker*, vol. 3. Oslo: Det Norske Samlaget.

GENERAL INDEX